The Soviet Impact
in Africa

The Soviet Impact in Africa

Edited by
R. Craig Nation
University of Southern California
Mark V. Kauppi
University of Colorado

LexingtonBooks
D.C. Heath and Company
Lexington, Massachusetts
Toronto

Library of Congress Cataloging in Publication Data

Main entry under title:

The Soviet impact in Africa.

Includes index.
1. Africa—Relations—Soviet Union—Addresses, essays, lectures.
2. Soviet Union—Relations—Africa—Addresses, essays, lectures.
3. Africa—Politics and government—1960-   —Addresses, essays, lectures.
4. Africa—Strategic aspects—Addresses, essays, lectures.
I. Nation, R. Craig. II. Kauppi, Mark V.
DT38.9.S65S68   1984   327.4706   84-47535
ISBN 0-669-08353-4 (alk. paper)

Copyright © 1984 by D.C. Heath and Company with the exception of Chapter 8, which is Copyright © Richard B. Remnek

All rights reserved. No part of this publication may be reproduced or transmitted in any form or by any means, electronic or mechanical, including photocopy, recording, or any information storage or retrieval system, without permission in writing from the publisher.

Published simultaneously in Canada

Printed in the United States of America on acid-free paper

International Standard Book Number: 0-669-08353-4

Library of Congress Catalog Card Number: 84-47535

To Kate and Kathleen

Contents

	List of Figures and Tables	ix
	List of Abbreviations	x
Chapter 1	Introduction: The Soviet Impact in Africa *R. Craig Nation*	1
Chapter 2	The Soviet Union's Encounter with Africa *Colin Legum*	9
Chapter 3	Soviet Engagement in Africa: Motives, Means, and Prospects *R. Craig Nation*	27
Chapter 4	The Soviet Union and Eastern Europe: Patterns of Competition and Collaboration in Southern Africa *Christopher Coker*	59
Chapter 5	Revolutionary Change in Africa: Some Implications for East German Policy Behavior *Bernard von Plate*	87
Chapter 6	From Intervention to Consolidation: The Soviet Union and Southern Africa *Seth Singleton*	105
Chapter 7	Soviet Arms Transfers to Sub-Saharan Africa *Joachim Krause*	125
Chapter 8	The Significance of Soviet Strategic Military Interests in Sub-Saharan Africa *Richard B. Remnek*	147
Chapter 9	Superpower Competition and Regional Conflicts in the Horn of Africa *Marina Ottaway*	165
Chapter 10	The Soviet Union and Zimbabwe: The Liberation Struggle and After *Keith Somerville*	195
Chapter 11	The Soviet Union and Africa: The Dynamics and Dilemmas of Involvement *Mark V. Kauppi*	221

Suggested Readings	255
Index	259
About the Contributors	273
About the Editors	275

List of Figures and Tables

Figures

1	Map of Africa	xii
6-1	Southern Africa	107
9-1	The Ogaden Campaign, 1977-1978	179
9-2	Areas of Conflict, 1975-1980	189

Tables

3-1	USSR and Eastern Europe: Economic Aid Extended to African Countries	41
3-2	USSR, Eastern Europe, and Cuba: Economic Technicians in Africa, 1981	42
6-1	Soviet and East European Arms Transfers to Sub-Saharan Africa: 1976-1980	110
7-1	Arms Deliveries to Sub-Saharan African States	132
7-2	Value of Arms Transfers to Africa, 1975-1979 by Major Supplier	134
7-3	Numbers of Weapons Delivered by Major Suppliers to Sub-Saharan Africa, 1975-1982	137
7-4	Soviet Arms Deliveries to Sub-Saharan Africa in Comparison to Western Suppliers	137
7-5	Military Personnel from Black Africa Trained by the Major Powers	138
7-6	Soviet Arms Exports, Civilian Exports, and Development Aid for Black Africa	139
9-1	Survey of Opposition Groups in Ethiopia	186
11-1	Relative Burden of Military Expenditures	230
11-2	Value of Economic Aid and Arms Exports to Developing States, Cumulative 1976-1980	234
11-3	Military Forces and Bases in Africa, 1983	240

List of Abbreviations

AAPSO	Afro-Asian People's Solidarity Organization
ANC	African National Congress
BADEA	Arab Bank for Economic Development in Africa
CIA	Central Intelligence Agency
CMEA	Council for Mutual Economic Assistance
COPWE	Commission for Organizing the Party of the Working People of Ethiopia
COREMO	Mozambique Revolutionary Committee
CPSU	Communist Party of the Soviet Union
EEC	European Economic Community
ELF	Eritrean Liberation Front
EPLF	Eritrean People's Liberation Front
FNLA	National Front for the Liberation of Angola
FNLC	National Front for the Liberation of the Congo
FRELIMO	Mozambique Liberation Front
FROLIZI	Front for the Liberation of Zimbabwe
GDR	German Democratic Republic
MNR	National Movement of Resistance
MOLINACO	Movement for the National Liberation of the Comoro Islands
MPLA	Popular Movement for the Liberation of Angola
NATO	North Atlantic Treaty Organization
NDP	National Democratic Party
NFD	Northern Frontier District
OAU	Organization of African Unity
OECD	Organization for Economic Cooperation and Development
OPEC	Organization of Petroleum Exporting Countries

List of Abbreviations

PAIGC	African Party for the Independence of Guinea and Cape Verde
PDRY	People's Democratic Republic of Yemen
PLAN	People's Liberation Army of Namibia
POLISARIO	Popular Front for the Liberation of Saguia el Hamra and Rio de Oro
RDF	Rapid Deployment Force
SACP	South African Communist Party
SADCC	Southern African Development Coordination Conference
SED	Socialist Unity Party (East Germany)
SR-ANC	Southern Rhodesia African National Congress
SRC	Supreme Revolutionary Council (Somalia)
SWAPO	South West Africa People's Organization
UNESCO	United Nations' Educational, Scientific, and Cultural Organization
UNIP	United National Independence Party (Zambia)
UNITA	National Union for the Total Independence of Angola
WSLF	Western Somali Liberation Front
ZANLA	Zimbabwe African National Liberation Army
ZANU	Zimbabwe African National Union
ZAPU	Zimbabwe African People's Union
ZIMCORD	Zimbabwe Conference on Reconstruction and Development (March 1981)
ZIPA	Zimbabwe People's Army
ZIPRA	Zimbabwe People's Revolutionary Army

Source: inside cover of *Africa Report*. Copyright © 1984 by the African-American Institute. Reprinted with permission of the African-American Institute.

Figure 1 Map of Africa

1

Introduction: The Soviet Impact in Africa

R. Craig Nation

Engagement in the Third World has emerged as a vital dimension of Soviet foreign policy over the past several decades and has occasioned an ever-growing list of scholarly publications in both the USSR and the West. Africa has been one of the focal points of this engagement, but despite the substantial amount of attention that it has attracted, the role of the continent in the overall scope of Soviet Third World policy remains unclear. Western accounts differ significantly in their estimates of Africa's importance in Soviet policy calculations and of Soviet prospects in a region which, though weak and subject to external pressures, is also committed to the ideals of independence and nonalignment. This text seeks to address these problems by reviewing and updating analysis of Soviet African policy as it has evolved into the mid-1980s.

The lack of consensus concerning Soviet intentions in Africa in part reflects Africa's own ambiguous international situation. No world region more vividly demonstrates the dilemmas of decolonization, with its unresolved legacies of dependency, political fragmentation, and underdevelopment. Africa as a whole remains bitterly impoverished, socially chaotic, and a prey to political and economic manipulation by outside forces. It is no wonder—given its own expanding global interests and geopolitical rivalry with the United States—that the Soviet Union has sought to assert itself in an arena which was until recently almost entirely the preserve of Western colonialism.

There is another dimension to African reality, however, that balances vulnerability with an immense, but as yet unrealized, potential. Africa is a young continent, with the majority of its sovereign states just entering their third decade of independence, and with nearly half its population of over 460 million under the age of sixteen. Its vast expanses (four times the area of the United States) encompass tremendous untapped agricultural potential as well as a treasure trove of natural resources, and its fifty-one independent nations represent a potentially powerful voting bloc within the United Nations and other international organizations.[1] If Africa's weakness has facilitated great power meddling, its inherent strength and promise have also served to frustrate external actors in their search for permanent influence.

The Soviet Union and Africa

Soviet engagement in Africa has developed slowly, through alternating periods of expansion and contraction. In 1955, the USSR's first important modern initiative into the Third World took the form of an arms transfer agreement with Egypt, and in the subsequent decade the pan-Arabist regime of Gamal Abd al-Nasir became the Soviets' key ally in the northern African and Middle Eastern regions. During the late 1950s and early 1960s (despite an embarrassing setback in the former Belgian Congo, where the USSR proved incapable of defending its chosen candidate in a postindependence power struggle) Soviet influence continued to expand into a number of newly sovereign "progressive" regimes, including Algeria, Ghana, Guinea, Mali, the Sudan, the Congo, and Somalia.[2] The extent of Soviet influence proved to be much less substantial than originally supposed, however, and the ouster of the pan-African socialist leader Kwame Nkrumah of Ghana by his own armed forces in 1966 initiated a period of disappointment and retrenchment, during which former allies like Ghana, Mali, the Sudan, and ultimately Egypt as well, reoriented themselves toward the West.

An apparently more assertive phase in Soviet African policy was launched in 1975 to 1976, when the USSR supported a massive intervention by more than 15,000 Cuban soldiers on behalf of the MPLA faction in the civil war which accompanied Portugal's withdrawal from its former Angolan colony.[3] A second decisive intervention by Soviet-assisted Cuban forces in support of revolutionary Ethiopia in its conflict with Somalia during 1977 to 1978 underlined the emergence of more ambitious Soviet aspirations in Sub-Saharan Africa, and during the late 1970s the Soviet presence expanded on a number of levels, including the signing of friendship treaties with Mozambique, Angola, and Ethiopia (and subsequently with the Congo), expanded commercial interactions, and particularly, an increased tempo of arms transfers.

By 1980 the Soviet position in Africa appeared quite formidable. In the wake of the occupation of Afghanistan in December 1979 the Carter Administration was chided roundly for its failure to deter Soviet expansionism by adequately responding to initiatives in Africa during the 1970s. Adventurism in Africa became a major element in the bill of indictment drawn up by the right-wing of the U.S. foreign policy establishment in an attempt to assert Soviet responsibility for the collapse of East/West detente. The Soviets, some argued, were now excellently situated to continue to exploit Africa's never-ending succession of political crises to their own advantage.

Since 1980, however, dire predictions concerning Soviet intentions have failed to materialize, and Soviet African policy seems once again to have entered a phase of consolidation.[4] Though the USSR has maintained its commitment to socialist oriented regimes, dramatic new initiatives have not been forthcoming, and in some ways Soviet influence might be said to have declined. The Soviets have not succeeded in stabilizing their progressive allies, most of whom continue to confront significant internal and external opposition, nor, by and large, have they been able to secure adoption of Soviet models for political and economic development. Even the closest Soviet allies remain committed to significant economic interaction with the West, and the limitations of the contributions which the USSR is capable of making to Africa's economic development have become painfully apparent. The negotiation, under U.S. diplomatic sponsorship, of security accords between Angola, Mozambique, and the Republic of South Africa in February 1984 likewise represents a setback for Soviet influence, which *Le Monde* has described as potentially "the first concrete sign of a retreat on the part of the Soviet Union in southern Africa."[5]

Soviet Policy in the 1980s

Several explanations may be adduced to help account for the USSR's nonassertiveness in Africa during the 1980s to date. First, it might be argued that the ongoing leadership succession within the USSR has not provided an appropriate political context for major new foreign policy initiatives. It is clear that at least since 1980 the USSR has lacked a strong leader capable of asserting policy directions: Leonid Brezhnev had become visibly senile in the years prior to his death; the brief tenure of Iurii Andropov (November 1982 to February 1984), dominated by incapacitating and eventually terminal illness, did not permit the restructuring of a policy consensus; nor is Andropov's immediate successor Konstantin Chernenko likely to emerge as a strong leader, given both his advanced age and domestic political limitations. What impact these various shifts may have had upon the continuity of Soviet foreign policy is unclear, but leadership transition has certainly had at least some inhibiting effects.

Second, the Soviet Union's increasingly problematic international and internal situations may be discouraging risky commitments in a region peripheral to more essential security concerns. The USSR at present faces significant challenges on a number of fronts, including NATO's intermediate nuclear force deployments and the breakdown of arms control dialogue with the United States; a protracted war of attrition in Afghanistan; the Polish unrest, symptomatic of a deeper, systemic crisis affecting the entire Soviet bloc; the continuing hostility of the People's Republic of China; and a commitment in the explosive Middle East. These dilemmas, when combined with an increasingly troubled domestic economic outlook, might well tend to make African engagement an issue of lower priority.

Finally, it could be suggested that African regional dynamics have not worked to the Soviets' advantage. Soviet Africanists' evaluations of the prospects for radical change in contemporary Africa have become distinctly less optimistic in recent years, and Soviet policymakers seem to have become more aware of the constraints that they confront in the region. Instability and the violent overthrow of established regimes have not benefitted the Soviets in many cases (Uganda, Liberia, Ghana, Nigeria), and the continent has certainly not offered massive opportunities on the scale of those provided by the wave of decolonization in the 1960s or the collapse of the Portuguese empire in southern Africa and the Ethiopian revolution during the 1970s—a situation not likely to extend itself indefinitely, however.

For whatever combination of reasons, Soviet African policy does seem to have entered a period of retrenchment that provides an appropriate moment for scholarly reevaluations. During the decade that has passed since the Portuguese and Ethiopian revolutions of 1974, the Soviet Union and its allies have succeeded in projecting themselves importantly as a force in African affairs. Their engagement is reflected by the continuing presence of substantial Cuban expeditionary forces in Angola and Ethiopia; by Soviet security guarantees to the Front Line states in southern Africa; by the far-flung activities of East German technical and security advisers; by increased tempos of economic and political interaction, arms transfers, and naval visitations; and by the rise of radical African regimes willing to experiment with Soviet methods as models for partial emulation, including the appearance of a self-styled Marxist-Leninist party state in Ethiopia. These represent real accomplishments and need not be undervalued. At the same time, when viewed cumulatively, Soviet engagement in Africa remains distinctly inferior to that of the Western powers. Soviet achievements have proven fragile or reversible in the past, and with increasing involvement the constraints that Soviet policy confronts have also become more visible. The Soviet impact in Africa has not been negligible, and African affairs can no longer be discussed intelligently without taking the Soviet role into account. But Soviet engagement is also subject to the whims of volatile global and regional environments. It is within this dichotomy of involvement and exposure, opportunity and constraint, that the Soviet impact in Africa and future directions for Soviet policy are to be explored.

Common Themes

This text presents a diversity of perpectives and interpretations that cannot conveniently be summarized by any single point of view. Nonetheless, certain underlying themes and at times a consensus of opinion do emerge. First, although Africa is addressed here in its continental dimensions, the primary focus is placed upon Sub-Saharan Africa. This is not to deny the intimate connection that exists between Africa north and south of the Sahara, but rather to acknowledge that Soviet priorities differ significantly in the two cases. In northern Africa (Egypt, Libya, Tunisia, Algeria, Morocco, Mauritania) Soviet policy is defined by the strategic importance of the Mediterranean and proximity to NATO's southern flank, as well as by the larger implications of the politics of the Muslim world and the Middle East. In the Sub-Saharan region the problems of underdevelopment, strategic rivalry in the Indian Ocean, and the southern African crisis loom larger. It is in Sub-Saharan Africa that Soviet engagement has expanded most dramatically in the past decade and where the greatest opportunities for Soviet African policy seem to lie.

Second, this text focuses upon the African policy of the Soviet Union, and to a lesser extent of its East European allies. It is clear that the role of Cuba, the German Democratic Republic, and other communist states in Africa is coordinated with that of the USSR. Further, given their overall dependence upon Soviet sponsorship, these states are constrained to insure that their policy choices broadly coincide with Soviet priorities. The active role of its communist allies does represent a dimension of the overall Soviet impact in Africa, but this does not negate the fact that these states also possess distinct national goals that should be examined in their own terms. This is particularly the case for Cuba's role in Sub-Saharan Africa, which is based upon a long-standing commitment predating that of the USSR, which has differed importantly from that of the USSR in the past, and which is certain to be misunderstood if addressed exclusively as an adjunct of Soviet policy. In general, Cuba's African policy deserves careful independent evaluation.[6] Our emphasis in the present volume is upon the problems and prospects of the USSR.

Third, the contributors coincide in the effort to move debate concerning the Soviet role in Africa outside the confines of a narrow East/West dichotomy. Although both the United States and the USSR approach Africa in the light of their global rivalry, the most important forces conditioning the role of outside powers in the continent remain those indigenous to the continent itself. Approaches that attempt to interpret Soviet African policy through the prism of East/West rivalry generally distort on a number of levels: They overvalue the ability of the Soviets to control complex events from their national territory; miss the constraints that inhibit Soviet initiatives; exaggerate the degree to which calculated dependency relationships translate into meaningful influence; err in typing proudly nationalistic regimes as subservient Soviet "clients"; and negate the strength of Africa's own aspirations as an independent force. The dynamics of decolonization, modernization, tribal and ethnic identity, nationalism, and black self-assertion remain fundamental forces in Sub-Saharan African affairs, which superpowers and analysts ignore at their own peril. The present volume emphasizes the role of regional dynamics as essential to an understanding of ways in which Soviet policy has evolved.

Fourth, a number of contributors take issue with the oversimplified image of the Soviet role in Africa as that of a dynamic, expansionist superpower engaged in a "zero sum" challenge to Western interests and bent upon the goal of "world domination." Not only does this perspective generally exaggerate Soviet capacity; it also ignores that in individual instances it is usually nearly impossible to arrive at a clear and unambiguous distinction that explains how Western and Soviet interests really differ. Indeed, the interests of the superpowers in Africa may be perceived to overlap as often as they diverge—a fact that makes superpower rivalry potentially manageable. This is true even in the continent's most bitterly polarized regions, such as the Horn or southern Africa, where both the United States and the USSR have a common interest in avoiding an uncontrolled escalation of local conflict.

Finally, there is a substantial consensus to the effect that, however one interprets Soviet prospects in the short-term, over the long haul both Western and African interests will be best served by policies that emphasize the priority of economic development. The most fundamental source of instability in Africa is not Soviet meddling but rather the brutal impoverishment that bears with particular severity upon the Sub-Saharan region. Until this underlying dilemma is effectively addressed, no amount of strategic commitment or diplomatic maneuvering will suffice, and political turmoil, sudden changes in international orientation, and the threat of deepening Soviet involvement will remain on Africa's political agenda.

The Contributors

In chapter 2, Colin Legum traces the history of the Soviet Union's encounter with Africa and concludes that on balance the Soviets have achieved remarkably little in the way of permanent influence. The one current exception is Ethiopia, where a pro-Soviet, Marxist-Leninist party state seems to be consolidating itself. Emphasizing the sources of Soviet engagement in Africa and the motives that define policy choices, R. Craig Nation suggests that, despite occasional setbacks, Soviet African policy is informed by a relatively coherent conception of long-term trends and a guardedly hopeful prognosis for the gradual furthering of Soviet interests. Christopher Coker and Bernard von Plate discuss the interaction in Africa between the USSR and its Warsaw Pact allies: Coker by examining patterns of conflicting and converging economic interests and von Plate by focusing upon the evolving East German ideological image of prospects for revolutionary change. Seth Singleton takes up the critical issue of the Soviet role in southern Africa, arguing that Soviet purposes thrive in a climate of intransigence and polarization, which Western policies should be designed to defuse.

It has become apparent over the past decade that the key lever of Soviet influence in Africa has been arms transfers. The evolution of Soviet arms transfer policy in Sub-Saharan Africa is the subject of Joachim Krause's contribution: Krause interprets lack of Soviet restraint in this domain as a significant source of escalating regional tensions. Africa's place in Soviet strategic-military planning is addressed by Richard B. Remnek, who asserts that in the event of a protracted conventional war in Europe or Asia, the military relevance of Africa for the USSR would be relatively modest. Strategic-military interests do not suffice to explain the intensity and duration of the Soviet commitment on the continent. Marina Ottaway and Keith Somerville provide regionally focused studies: Ottaway emphasizes the constraining role of regional factors in examining superpower involvement in the Horn of Africa, and Somerville surveys Soviet relations with the Zimbabwean national movement prior to and after independence. The case of Zimbabwe provides a clear illustration that there is an indigenous, radical alternative in Africa that does not imply dependency upon the USSR. In a concluding chapter, Mark V. Kauppi critiques various widespread misconceptions concerning the Soviet role in Africa and suggests a more measured approach to interpreting the Soviet challenge.

The present volume seeks to contribute to a deeper understanding of the Soviet impact in Africa and, by implication, in the entire Third World, by critically reevaluating the changing nature of Soviet involvement in what appears to be a transitional period marked by consolidation, lowered aspirations, and challenging new problems.

Notes

1. David Lamb, *The Africans* (New York: Random House, 1982), pp. xii–xiii.

2. For a time, West Africa appeared to be developing into a particularly significant sphere of Soviet influence. See Robert Legvold, *Soviet Policy in West Africa* (Cambridge, Mass: Harvard University Press, 1970).

3. Most analysts have concurred in designating the Angolan intervention as a "major departure in Soviet foreign policy." Jiri Valenta, "Soviet Decision Making on the Intervention in Angola," in David E. Albright, ed., *Communism in Africa* (Bloomington: Indiana University Press, 1980), p. 97. See also Hélèn Carrère d'Encausse, "L'U.R.S.S. et l'Afrique: de la détente à la guerre fraîche," *Politique internationale* 1 (Autumn 1979). This view may, however, be challenged. Christopher Stevens has called the intervention a "major change in Soviet tactics" in Africa occurring within a larger strategic continuity. Christopher Stevens, "The Soviet Role in Southern Africa," in John Seiler, ed., *Southern Africa Since the Portuguese Coup* (Boulder, Colo.: Westview Press, 1980), p. 45.

4. In Angola, for example, despite widely voiced fears as to the consequences of an MPLA victory, more U.S. firms are now active than ever before, and they are permitted to repatriate a larger share of profits than under the Portuguese. The Angolan constitution specifically forbids the granting of military bases to foreign powers—a provision that has been carefully observed despite Soviet pressures. See Gerald J. Bender, "Angola: Left, Right, and Wrong," *Foreign Policy* 43 (Summer 1981):53–69, and Nicos Zafaris, "The People's Republic of Angola: Soviet Type Economy in the Making," in Peter Wiles, ed., *The New Communist Third World* (London: Croom Helm, 1982).

5. "Retournement en Afrique australe," *Le Monde,* 22 February 1984, p. 1; Paul Van Slambrouck, "South Africa-Mozambique Pact: A Diplomatic Plum for Pretoria?" *The Christian Science Monitor,* March 16, 1984, p. 7.

6. For general studies of the Soviet-Cuban relationship, see Robert K. Furtak, *Die cubanische-sowjetische Partnerschaft: Entwicklung, aktueller Stand, Probleme* (Cologne: Bundesinstitut für ostwissenschaftliche und internationale Studien, 1980); Mark N. Katz, "The Soviet-Cuban Connection," *International Security* 8 (Summer 1983):88–112; and Jacques Levesque, *L'U.R.S.S. et la révolution cubaine* (Paris: Presses de la Fondation Nationale des Sciences Politiques, 1976).

Cuba's African policy is excellently surveyed in William M. LeoGrande, *Cuba's Policy in Africa, 1959–1980* (Berkeley: Institute of International Studies, 1980). For diverse perspectives on the Soviet-Cuban relationship in Africa, see also Albright, *Communism in Africa;* Jorge Dominguez, "Cuban Foreign Policy," *Foreign Affairs* 57, no. 1 (Fall 1978):83–108; William J. Durch, *The Cuban Military in Africa and the Middle East: From Algeria to Angola* Professional Paper No. 201 (Arlington: Center for Naval Analyses, 1977); Maurice Halperin, "The Cuban Role in Southern Africa," in Seiler, *Southern Africa Since the Portuguese Coup,* pp. 25–44; Wolf Grabendorff, "Cubas Politik in Afrika," *Europa-Arkhiv* 10 (July 1978):411–420; William E. Griffith, "Soviet Policy in Africa and Latin America: The Cuban Connection," in William E. Griffith, ed., *The Soviet Empire: Expansion and Detente* (Lexington, Mass: D.C. Health, Lexington Books, 1976), pp. 337–344; William M. LeoGrande, "Cuban-Soviet Relations and Cuban Policy in Africa," *Cuban Studies* 10 (January 1980) [Special Volume, "Cuba in Africa"]:1–37; and Jiri Valenta, "The Soviet-Cuban Alliance in Africa and the Caribbean," *The World Today* 37 (February 1981):45–53. A portion of the literature is summarized and reviewed in Kenneth Grundy, "Moscow, Havana, and Africa," *Problems of Communism* 30 (July/August 1981):63–68.

A recent Soviet account of the Soviet-Cuban relationship, perhaps revealingly, makes no mention whatsoever of African policy. A.D. Bekarevich, et al., *Sovetsko-Kubinskie otnosheniia 1917–1977* (Moscow: Nauka, 1980).

2

The Soviet Union's Encounter with Africa

Colin Legum

The outstanding feature of the Soviet Union's encounter with Africa is that after more than a quarter of a century of active diplomacy, political and military involvement, it has made so little impact on the continent and failed to consolidate even the few initial gains it had made to advance its strategic interests as a superpower. This description of the Soviets' present position offers a strong contrast with the optimistic predictions and expectations of Moscow and the Communist International that, with the ending of traditional Western colonialism after World War II, a continent "liberated from imperialist oppression" would prove receptive to Marxist ideas.

Analysts who reflect the Soviet position have advanced three main reasons to explain disappointed expectations in the first three decades of decolonization: neocolonialism, the counter-strategy devised by capitalism to ensure the continuing economic and political dependence of the former colonies; the "bourgeois mentality" of the African political class that came to power after independence; and the West's stranglehold control over the trade and commerce of Third World countries, as well as over sources of capital borrowing. This explanation raises two questions: Why did the Soviet bloc fail to develop a convincing strategy of its own to confront neocolonialism? And why was it unable to offer acceptable alternative economic choices to the newly independent states? More directly, why did Moscow fail to retain the alliance of those governments that had chosen it as a strategic ally?

The essential weakness in the Soviet-Marxist analysis is its failure to provide an adequate explanation for the political course taken by African countries, in common with the rest of the Third World, after their independence. The most significant of these developments were the historic emergence of the nonaligned movement at the Bandung conference in 1955 which reflected the determination by the majority of the former colonial territories to avoid becoming embroiled in East/West conflicts (the Cold War); the decision by the overwhelming majority of the newly independent governments—irrespective of their political stripe—to pursue policies likely to maximize their trade and aid relations with the Western powers, the Soviet bloc, and China; and the rejection of communism as a political system by all but a very few governments, as a result of which there were few opportunities for the Soviet bloc to base their relations on close ideological ties (as in the case, say, of Cuba and Vietnam).

An exploration of the reasons for this unpredicted trend in the Third World lies outside the scope of this chapter, but they can be summed up in a sentence: They reflect the objective situation of postcolonial Africa and of the continent's traditional culture. Therefore, any meaningful study of the Soviet experience in Africa should focus more on African realities, interests, and relations than on Soviet objectives and Western counterstrategies. Kremlinologists usually err in seeing Africa through Russian or Western eyes, rather than through African eyes.

A proper perspective of the Soviet encounter with Africa requires a description both of Moscow's objectives and interests and of African objectives and interests. Such a description will help identify the points of conflicting and coverging interests between the USSR and Africa. The dynamic interplay of these fluctuating conflicts and convergences of interests offers the most satisfactory way of interpreting the Soviet experience in Africa into the 1980s. But it is necessary first to describe briefly the place of Africa in terms of global politics and to establish its regional boundaries in this context.

Africa in the Postimperial Age

World War II marked a watershed between the old and the new balance of power relations; it was the beginning of the end of centuries of Western domination and saw the emergence of the challenging new world power, the Soviet Union. Up to that point, Africa was completely dominated by five European colonial powers—Britain, France, Portugal, Belgium, and Spain. Only three countries in the continent were politically independent—Ethiopia, Liberia, and South Africa. Another fifty independent states were born at the critical period in the disjuncture of the balance of world power when the Western democracies found themselves pushed onto the defensive by the USSR in their effort to maintain as much as possible of their former position. In their new role the Soviets had, for the first time in history, begun to achieve the status of a world naval power. To develop its sea power, the Soviet Navy urgently needed to acquire rights of entry into friendly ports, with adequate facilities, from littoral states spread across the five oceans, similar to those traditionally enjoyed by the old imperial navies. At the same time, because of the close relationships between modern air power and naval power, the Soviet Union required a network of airfields that would be available not only for its civil airline, Aeroflot, but also for its military aircraft.

The struggle to establish a new equilibrium in the balance of world power coincided with the advent of the nuclear age. The menacing threat of nuclear weapons delimited the arena within which the risks of armed conflict between the superpowers could be tolerated. The two regions immediately ruled out as too risky were Europe and, less clearly defined, parts of the Western hemisphere. The rest of the world was thrown wide open for competition and rivalry—with the Western powers fighting defensively to retain their political and economic influence over the territories formerly held in colonial thralldom, and the USSR offensively engaged as the challenger to the former status quo.

Two other historic changes characterized this new post-Western Imperial age: the emergence of the People's Republic of China as a reunified, modernizing and revolutionary state with a newly discovered interest in playing a world role; and the emergence of a Third World comprising over one-hundred countries, the great majority only recently released from colonial bondage. It is this Third World that became the principal arena for rivalry between the superpowers, and in which China sought to pit itself against both but especially after Stalin's death, with particular venom, against Moscow. This triangular rivalry was fought not so much over direct political control of these territories; it was more over gaining influence of a kind that would facilitate obtaining economic and military strategic advantages and in winning political support for the rival causes espoused by the major powers.

It is against this background that Africa gained its special geopolitical importance in the struggle to establish a new balance of world power. The continent's strategic importance in terms of ocean politics derives not just from the fact that its littoral states extend along the entire length of the eastern Atlantic and western Indian Oceans, as well as the southern shores of the Mediterranean but also because the littoral states exercise political (if not military) control over such sensitive and important seaways as the Suez Canal, the Red Sea, the south Atlantic passage around the Cape, and the access routes to the oil-bearing Arab Gulf.

These sea connections constitute one of several factors which extend the regional limits of Africa into the Middle East. Another major factor is the intimate connection between Arabic north Africa and the rest of the Arab world—a connection that extends all the way from Mauritania and Morocco, on the Atlantic side of the Maghrib, through Algeria, Tunisia, and Libya to Egypt, and down the Nile valley into the Sudan. This Afro-Arab connection is institutionalized in a number of ways: through the formal links that exist between the Organization of African Unity (OAU) and the Arab League; the membership of a dozen African countries (including Sub-Saharan countries like Guinea, Senegal, Niger, Upper Volta, Mali, and Somalia) in the Conference of Islamic States; and the Arab Bank for Economic Development in Africa (BADEA).

Two further important links are provided by the Conference of Nonaligned States and the Committee of 77, which is concerned with trade relations between North and South. This intimate network of ethnic, economic, and political interests extends Africa's political boundaries into the Middle East; it is therefore unrealistic to treat them as two different regions. In fact, the conflicts in the Arab world make a direct political impact even on Black Africa, as evidenced by the OAU's decision in 1973 to cut off all diplomatic ties with Israel.

The Soviet Interest in Africa

For purposes of this chapter it suffices to identify the four key objectives of Soviet policy in Africa:

1. First is the Soviet plan to expand its political and economic influence in fulfilling the interests and requirements of a world power; this it seeks to do by establishing close ties with governments and political movements (often those in opposition to established regimes); by seeking to influence the policies of regional organizations; and by attempting to influence the course of political developments in strategic areas such as, the Horn of Africa and southern Africa, as well as in inter-Arab conflicts as between Libya, on the one side, and Egypt and the Sudan, on the other. One of its methods in pursuing this particular objective is to give general support to the liberation movements engaged in armed struggle and selective support to those it specifically favors.
2. Closely related to this first objective is its determined effort to diminish Western influence in the continent, taking advantage of the fact that the Western powers are, for historical reasons, generally closely involved with protecting status quo positions and established governments.
3. Its military strategic objectives include the need to extend the global reach of its military delivery capacity; to defend itself against the West's nuclear delivery systems, especially in the Indian Ocean; and to oppose Western strategic military forces (e.g., the Rapid Deployment Force (RDF) and the buildup of a military base on Diego Garcia). For these purposes, it seeks, *inter alia*, to obtain military facilities (not necessarily bases) for its navy and air force and to encourage and support local forces opposed to Western military initiatives (e.g., the Tripartite Alliance of Libya, Ethiopia, and the People's Democratic Republic of Yemen (PDRY) pledged to resist the RDF and to secure the elimination of American bases in the Gulf and Red Sea areas).
4. A high-priority objective is to counteract the influence of the People's Republic of China in Africa as in the rest of the Third World.

It makes more sense to describe the way Moscow pursues these four objectives as tactical rather than as reflecting any grand strategy. The Soviets' tactics often appear to be contradictory and opportunistic. They are decidedly contradictory when judged purely in terms of communist ideology with its commitment to strengthening the progressive forces in the antiimperialist struggle of the international working class. Examples of such contradictions abound: for example, the support given to tyrants like Equatorial Guinea's Nguema Maçias and Uganda's Idi Amin; the support given to a typically bourgeois national leader like Joshua Nkomo in his rivalry during Zimbabwe's liberation struggle with an avowed Marxist like Robert Mugabe; support for Libya's revolutionary Islamic leader Colonel Mu'ammar al-Qadhdhafi, who denounces both communism and capitalism; and support for the late Gamal Abd al-Nasir at a time when he kept hundreds of Egyptian communists in prison.

As for the term *opportunism*: It is generally used in a derogatory sense when applied to those of whose policies one disapproves; of one's friendly allies it is more customary to speak of their pragmatism or flexibility. Moscow is certainly opportunistic, but usually in the sense of grasping opportunities to promote its aims whenever they present themselves. The Soviets have often displayed a flair for opportunely deciding to throw their support behind a particular leader or movement as they did, for example, in backing the military group that dethroned Emperor Haile Selassie at a time when the United States refused Ethiopia's request for greater arms supplies.

In pursuing its world power role, the Soviet Union is often compelled to adapt its policies to take account of African realities and of the particular interests of African governments and leaders. For example, in the conflict over the western Sahara, Moscow found it necessary to consider the effects on their considerable economic investment in Morocco's phosphate industry if it took the side of Algeria. In making the decision to back the Ethiopian military regime, the Kremlin was forced to choose between forfeiting its existing alliance with Somalia and losing its rights to use the naval facility in Berbera and possibly profiting from the Ethiopian revolution. Once Moscow had made the decision to back the Ethiopian military regime, it was left to consider the implications of abandoning its support for the Eritrean liberation struggle, many of whose leaders had become committed to Marxism, thanks in part to the Soviet and Cuban support they had received in the days of Haile Selassie.

Clearly, the practice of Soviet policy in Africa cannot be explained or understood simply in terms of its professed commitment to international proletarian revolution; in fulfilling its new role as a superpower, Soviet behavior is no different from that of any other major power whose priority concern is to pursue its own state interests. This is well understood in Africa, where the USSR is seen and treated not as the world leader of revolutionary internationalism, but as a power contesting for supremacy with the United States.

There is, however, also another important side to Moscow's African policies: Whenever opportunities present themselves to pursue its state interests by emphasizing its commitment to Marxism-Leninism, the Kremlin is naturally keen to respond. One outstanding example of this aspect of Soviet policy has been the remarkably determined manner in which it has insisted on the transformation of military rule in Ethiopia into a classical communist political system.

The most plausible explanation for the direction taken by Soviet policy in Ethiopia is that it sees in the creation of a communist party the best hope for establishing a regime whose close alliance with the USSR will not depend on the whims, or survival, of a particular leader or small group. The new direction taken by Moscow's policy in Ethiopia is the outcome of years of failure in its attempts to establish reliable strategic allies in the Third World, and particularly in Africa. The emphasis here is upon reliable, both in the sense of dependable and continuing. The Kremlin's experience since the beginning of its active involvement in Africa is that (with but a single exception) Soviet ties have not survived the change of the regime with which it had originally established close contacts or where such a regime's own interests and priorities had changed. Such changes have come about either because more profitable alternatives had become available or because their cooperation with the Soviet bloc had failed to satisfy their needs and interests. A common experience of African leaders and governments who took up the Soviet option has been the frustration felt over Moscow's failure to produce adequate economic, technical, and military assistance. These frustrations have usually been accentuated by troubled personal relations between Soviet advisers and Africans, as well as by resentment felt by leaders against what they describe as the insensitive domineering attitudes and pressurizing methods of Soviet diplomats, which, at times, they complain has amounted to bullying. Nor is this description of what has gone wrong in the past in Soviet-African relations just a Western view reflecting an anticommunist prejudice; it is well documented in statements made by African leaders who have broken their close ties with the USSR, (e.g., the late President Anwar Sadat of Egypt, Ja'far al-Numayri of the Sudan, Sékou Touré of Guinea, Siad Barre of Somalia, or Idi Amin).

So far, we have discussed mainly the inability of Soviet policy to exploit the advantages opened up by the ending of colonialism and the failures experienced in those instances where opportunities have occurred for establishing close ties. A fuller consideration of the Soviet experience in Africa will show that its few successes to date have been due less to the appeal the USSR makes as the "vanguard" of socialism and more to the failures and mistaken policies of the Western democracies that have presented openings for Moscow. Overall, Soviet successes have been registered in situations where Moscow's interests have coincided with particular African interests—either the interests of a ruling group, or a wider shared interest in defeating the remnants of colonialism in the continent. What follows is a brief description of Soviet-African relations that will illuminate these two aspects: the failure of Moscow's policies to satisfy particular African aspirations, and the coincidence of Soviet and African interests in particular situations. These two elements are crucial to explaining the recent experience of the USSR in the continent and are pointers to the future. But before continuing this line of exploration it is necessary to describe briefly "the African interest."

The African Interest in the Soviet Union

One overriding African interest determining the continent's relations with the USSR has already been mentioned: the desire by the majority of governments and leaders not to be drawn into East-West conflicts. Some African governments (notably Ivory Coast, Morocco, Senegal, Gabon, and Cameroon) have consistently preferred to adopt a generally pro-Western orientation while at the same time subscribing to the aspirations of the nonaligned movement. On the other side of the coin, a few (notably Ethiopia) have openly identified themselves with the Soviet camp. However, the majority of the fifty-one member-states of the OAU seek the friendship of the West, the Soviet Union, and China, even though individually they may lean more to the West or to China than to the USSR. Angola and Mozambique are exceptions. Though depending heavily on the Soviet bloc for military support for their Marxist regimes, both look mainly to the West for their trade and economic aid. Mozambique is also keen to maintain close ties with China. South Africa is *sui generis;* its regime, for obvious reasons, adopts a fiercely hostile attitude toward all communists.

All the OAU members share the strong sense of resentment felt against any attempt by any of the major powers to force them to take sides over issues which they identify as belonging to the realm of cold war politics. On issues such as the Soviet invasion of Afghanistan and its policy in Kampuchea, the African group at the United Nations has overwhelmingly voted in condemnation of Moscow's position; the majority took a stand critical of Washington over American military intervention in Grenada. Almost without exception, they supported the British military campaign against Argentina over the Falklands.

Thus, the African interest is not to stay neutral on issues that divide the USSR and the United States, but they insist on judging each issue on its merits. What inspires their antagonism is any attempt to compel them to give their automatic support to one side or the other over any particular issue. In the same vein, the overwhelming majority of OAU members strenuously resist any attempt by Moscow to rally them against Beijing.

Although there is no consistency in the foreign policy of the African states, there can be no questioning their unanimity over their right to determine their own foreign relations and their exclusive right to choose their own friends and enemies. One prime example of this is the solid support given to Angola in its insistence that its policy of enlisting the support of Cuban combat troops is its own affair, just as there is no questioning of the military ties between countries like Senegal and Gabon with France, or Kenya with Britain and the United States. Nor is there any questioning of the decision of African members to belong to the Commonwealth of Nations or to the Francophone Community. None, as yet, is a member of the CMEA (Council for Mutual Economic Assistance).

A second major African interest shared by all is to seek for radical changes in the present international economic order. They also share a general interest in keeping open their options to solicit aid from any foreign power willing to offer it on acceptable terms. They see no incompatibility between their nonaligned stance and the treaty relationship which all, except Angola but including Ethiopia, have with the European Economic Community. Their interest is to take advantage of all available opportunities to expand their trading partners; to use the facilities offered by the International Monetary Fund and the International Development Agency (both of which are opposed by Moscow); and to increase the volume of overseas economic aid and technical assistance which, for historic reasons, they find it easier to absorb from the West than from the Soviet bloc. Their experience in working with China, especially in rural development and transport projects, has on the whole been more satisfactory than working with Soviet bloc experts except, possibly, for the East Germans. In the field of military procurement and assistance their choice of foreign suppliers is catholic; but, again, they prefer, wherever possible, not to rely exclusively on any single source for their defense requirements.

Finally, all African governments, whatever their political complexion, share a commitment to ending colonialism and racial domination in the continent. The upsurge of independence in the 1960s had left the continent with what its leaders describe as the "unfinished African revolution": ending Portuguese colonialism; ending white minority rule in Rhodesia and South Africa; and liberating Namibia. The depth of African feelings over apartheid and white supremacy cannot easily be overstated. This African interest in defeating the "remnants of colonialism" is an aspiration with which the Soviets can identify themselves without compromise or ambiguity since their own interest is to liquidate what they identify as "outposts of Western colonialism." Despite the Western democracies' declared abhorrence of apartheid, it has proven more difficult for them to establish their credentials as allies of this African cause because of their historic connections with, and substantial economic interests in, South Africa and, previously, because of Portugal's membership in NATO (North Atlantic Treaty Organization).

For these reasons it has proved easier for the Soviet bloc countries to establish a shared interest with Africans and to give their military and political support to liberation movements in the former Portuguese territories, Rhodesia (now Zimbabwe), South Africa, and Namibia.

Similarly, the conflict between the Arabs and Israel found the Western democracies at a political disadvantage vis-à-vis the Soviets because of their strong support for Israel. This circumstance made the Soviet bloc a natural ally of the Arabs and their African supporters, especially on the issue of an independent Palestinian state. So long as the Arab confrontation states relied on military force as one method of pursuing this struggle, they had little alternative other than to rely on Soviet military and diplomatic support.

The Course of Soviet–African Relations from 1955 to 1984

Having established the principal objectives and interests of the USSR and of Africans, it is now possible to analyze how the convergence and divergence of these interests have had an impact on the continent.

The USSR achieved its first breakthrough in the African-Middle Eastern region in 1955 when President Nasir's military regime, disillusioned with Western policy over Israel, began to develop a close military and economic alliance with Moscow. Having opted for a military confrontation with Israel, Nasir needed a credible strategic ally capable of supplying the Arab cause with substantial military and economic aid. The ambitious Soviet project to build the High Dam at Aswan became the symbol of this new era of Soviet/Egyptian relations. While the Soviet military contribution enabled Nasir to build a modern Egyptian army capable of confronting Israel, it fell short of having a capability to defeat it.

The immediate advantages gained by the USSR from the relationship with Nasir were of three kinds: First, it served Moscow's objective of undercutting Western influence, both in Egypt and in the Arab world; second, it provided the Soviets with a political entry point into the Middle East, where previously it had no effective presence; and third, it secured for the Soviet Navy a base in the Mediterranean at Alexandria.

The decline in the relationship with Egypt, which began in the latter period of Nasir's rule, is attributable to three principal causes. First, the failure of the Egyptians in the Six Day War in 1967 bred disillusionment; this became externalized by blaming the Egyptian defeat on Moscow's refusal to provide the latest, sophisticated military delivery systems regarded as being necessary to enhance Egypt's offensive capacity. There was an element of truth in this Egyptian accusation since Moscow was reluctant to entrust its latest military equipment to the Egyptians for fear of its falling into Israeli, and thus Western, hands; but, no less important, the reluctance can be traced to constraints on Soviet policy in not wishing to push its confrontation with Israel's Western allies, notably the United States, to the point of upsetting the policy of detente in which Khrushchev was engaged. A second reason was that Soviet economic aid had proved hopelessly inadequate for developing Egypt's economy. The third reason was that the combination of the Egyptians' frustrating experiences on the battlefield and the growing economic crisis on the home front had strengthened the forces of the Egypt First movement which reflected nationalist, as opposed to Pan-Arab, priorities. It led to President Sadat's decision to expel the Soviets in 1972 and the opening up of a new bridge to the West.

Moscow's experience in Egypt had as one of its outcomes the reevaluation of Soviet tactics in allying themselves with a regime essentially committed to promoting its own perceived interests. It raised questions about the long-term benefits of relying too heavily on a bourgeois nationalist establishment and on military regimes always liable to being overthrown.

These Soviet concerns were increased by its experience in the Sudan where in 1969 a military coup led by Ja'far al-Numayri overthrew a Western-oriented government and sought Soviet assistance to help consolidate its power. Once again, Moscow was ready to take advantage of this new opportunity to diminish Western influence in a particularly important strategic area. The ties with the Sudan lasted only two years. The reason for the sudden break in 1971 was Numayri's suspicion that the Soviet bloc was closely involved in a communist and Ba'thist coup attempt to overthrow him. A contributory reason was the Sudan's disappointment over the quality of Soviet economic aid.

Earlier, in 1960, Moscow had sought to take advantage of the chaotic conditions produced in the Belgian Congo (now Zaire) as a result of the abrupt ending of Belgian colonial rule. The new prime minister, Patrice Lumumba, found himself engaged in a power struggle with rivals who were supported by various Western agencies; he therefore sought military support in Moscow. But this initiative resulted in strengthening Belgian and American support for his rival, Colonel Joseph Mobutu, who destroyed Lumumba and drove out the Soviets.

The USSR experience in Ghana was similarly frustrated when President Kwame Nkrumah was overthrown in a military coup in 1966. Only two years earlier Nkrumah had sought Soviet military aid to provide him with a palace guard when he began to feel himself under threat from discontented domestic forces who, he believed, were being encouraged by the CIA. However, he had never broken his ties with the West and had resisted pressures from inside his own party to enter into a close alliance with Moscow because of his commitment to nonalignment, his personal rejection of communism as a doctrine alien to Africa, and his strong interest in developing his own new philosopy of African Consciencism as a model for African socialism.

Moscow, though, was rather more successful for almost twenty years in establishing a close relationship with two of Nkrumah's close allies, the late President Sékou Touré of Guinea and President Modeiba Keita of Mali. The entry point for the Soviets in Guinea was provided by the rough manner in which Charles de Gaulle had severed France's relations with Guinea at its independence in 1958. Cut off completely from its traditional source of economic aid and isolated within the Western community, Guinea's leaders had the choice of either capitulating to Paris or invoking an anti-Western factor. Soviet aid made it possible for Sékou Touré's regime to weather the economic difficulties following its independence. But by the late 1970s, when French and other Western attitudes toward Guinea had undergone considerable change and the country's economy was in a state of near-collapse, Sékou Touré's ties with Moscow began to lessen until they reached the point where he cancelled the Soviet Navy's right to free access to the port of Conakry as well as the facilities allowed to Soviet military aircraft which assisted their Atlantic crossing to Cuba. Three other developments also contributed to the decline of the Soviet position in Guinea. First, Sékou Touré had become increasingly isolated from his staunchly pro-French west African neighbors, especially Ivory Coast and Senegal, which allowed his opposition in exile to plot against him. Second, the ending of Portuguese colonialism in Guinea-Bissau in 1973 had removed a major security threat to his regime. And third, the country's experiment with wholesale state ownership of commerce and industry, planned with the help of Soviet experts, was a failure. In fact, the only healthy part of the country's economy was a small but important private sector of mineral and hydroelectric development in an area developed by French, British, and North American multinationals.

Guinea's neighbor Mali was exceptional in that a military regime that had overthrown the leader who had introduced the Soviets in the first place continued the policy of maintaining close ties with Moscow, partly because the alternative was to crawl back to Paris. Whereas Guinea's chief attraction for Soviet military planners was the advantage of having a port for its naval vessels on the west African run, Mali offered the complementary facilities that enabled the Soviet Air Force, as well as Aeroflot, to maintain an efficient air corridor across the huge expanse of the Sahara and a staging-post for the Atlantic crossing. This trans-African, trans-Atlantic staging post was linked, at different times, with airfields in Egypt, the Sudan, and Somalia. The loss of the right to use those airfields reduced the value of the facilities previously available in Mali and Guinea. Despite the Soviet bloc's long association with Mali, it significantly failed to fulfill the economic promise held out by the original agreement with Modeiba Keita. As a result, Mali, which had broken its neocolonial ties with Paris and had withdrawn from the franc zone and other francophone institutions in West

Africa, has begun to resume these relations. It still depends heavily on French economic aid and trade.

As in the case of both Guinea and Mali, the francophone republics of Benin and the Congo established Marxist regimes oriented toward Moscow because of resentment at what they felt to be French interference in their internal affairs and the failure of their domestic economies. The creation of two Marxist regimes in the Francophone Community would appear to have provided fruitful opportunities for developing intimate ties with other communist countries; however, the reality is quite different. Marxism in both Benin and the Congo remains largely rhetorical, and both countries continue to rely heavily on French economic aid, even to help balance their national budgets. There is remarkably little evidence of a Soviet or Cuban presence, or of their influence, in nationalistic Benin. The Congo's economy has recently revived, thanks almost entirely to the exploitation of new oil discoveries made by Western companies. Although the Congo provided all the facilities needed for the Soviet and Cuban military intervention in neighboring Angola in 1974 and 1975, it is arguable that the principal reason for its decision relied less on its wish to help advance Soviet and Cuban interests and more on its own commitment, in line with some other radical African governments, to aid the cause of the MPLA (Popular Movement for the Liberation of Angola). However, the fact remains that it was only because of Soviet and Cuban ties with the Congo that they were able rapidly to develop the bridgehead at Pont Noire from which to fly in their military supplies to the MPLA.

The Soviet bloc's contribution to the liberation struggles in the former Portuguese colonies enabled it to play a divisive and decisive role in the preindependence power struggle in Angola, where the MPLA was opposed by two rivals: the FNLA (National Front for the Liberation of Angola) led by Holden Roberto, and UNITA (National Union for the Total Independence of Angola) led by Dr. Jonas Savimbi. The FNLA had the support of Zaire as well as of China, North Korea, and at different times, of the United States. UNITA had no foreign support during the liberation struggle itself; its backing from South Africa and elsewhere came only in the period of civil war which broke out after the Portuguese decision to quit. Soviet relations with the MPLA's leader, Dr. Agostinho Neto, were troubled during the period of armed struggle. Neto enjoyed closer relations with Cuba. Immediately before Angola's independence an OAU mission had reported that the strongest of the three movements was UNITA; it was thanks only to the effective military intervention by the Soviets and the Cubans that the MPLA finally won the day. A determining factor in the Soviet decision to intervene militarily on the side of the MPLA seems to have been Moscow's concern over the role of China in helping to train the FNLA and its growing involvement with UNITA.

The Chinese, not the Soviets, were principally responsible for helping to arm and train Mozambique's FRELIMO (Front for the Liberation of Mozambique). Because of the close links between FRELIMO and Beijing, the Soviets showed a strong reluctance to support the movement led by Samora Machel. After Mozambique's independence, the FRELIMO government ruffled their Chinese relations by signing a Treaty of Friendship and Cooperation with the USSR. The reason for their decision was that, faced with South Africa's threat to their security, they felt the Soviet Union rather than China had the military logistical capacity required of a strategic ally and was more likely to deter the Pretoria regime from engaging in trans-border attacks. This expectation was not fulfilled either in the case of Mozambique or Angola, Angola also possessing a Treaty of Friendship and Cooperation with the USSR as well as with East Germany.

The fact that the Mozambicans have sought additional sources of military support to that provided by the Soviet Union (including an agreement to engage a Portuguese military training team) suggests some disappointment in the Soviet performance. The Angolans, though, have continued to rely on the USSR, East Germany, and Cuba for all their defense needs. The failure to prevent "punishing" military incursions by the South African Defense Force in both Angola and Mozambique and the growth of armed opposition movements supported by the Pretoria regime (UNITA and the MNR) have compelled both FRELIMO and the MPLA to engage in diplomatic negotiations with the Pretoria regime to reach agreements to lessen the military confrontation along their borders. One lesson of this experience is that there are severe limits to the Soviet's role as a strategic ally in southern Africa—at least for the present.

However, it is not just the case that the Soviet bloc has been unable, or unwilling, to commit the necessary resources (such as those committed to Cuba and Syria) likely to deter the South Africans. Another important reason is that the MPLA and FRELIMO are strongly adverse to introducing cold war politics into southern Africa because of the risks of producing superpower confrontation such as that witnessed in the Middle East. More immediately, both regimes are anxious not to upset their moves toward detente with the Western democracies to whom they look for the kind of economic and technical aid which both badly need. Here is another instance where the USSR, though able to provide substantial military aid, lacks the capability or the readiness, to come to the rescue of the crippled economies of its treaty allies. Already, the three other former Portuguese colonies—Guinea Bissau, Cape Verde, and São Tomé e Príncipe, all of which have Marxist-oriented regimes—have come to rely almost exclusively on economic aid from Western sources. The former has gone so far as to join the Francophone Community.

In the armed struggle for Zimbabwe's independence, the victorious wing of the nationalist Patriotic Front—ZANU (Zimbabwe African National Union), led by Robert Mugabe—received the bulk of its extracontinental aid from the Chinese and owed nothing at all to the Soviets, for reasons similar to those of FRELIMO. Both FRELIMO and ZANU had their liberation bases in Tanzania where there is a small Chinese military presence that facilitated their taking over training of guerrillas. Moscow refused to assist ZANU unless Mugabe disavowed his ideological ties with Maoism; this he proudly refused to do. Because of ZANU's links with China, the Soviets elected to give their support to its rival ZAPU (Zimbabwe African People's Union), led by Joshua Nkomo. This decision—taken purely for reasons concerned with Sino-Soviet rivalry—was made despite the fact that, as mentioned earlier, Nkomo typifies the bourgeois nationalist outlook so frequently denounced by Moscow, and despite the well-established fact that he was receiving financial backing from an important capitalist source in the City of London. In the preindependence electoral contest which was decided in Zimbabwe by the ballot box (unlike what happened in Angola), the USSR was unable to play any role in preventing their flag-bearer from losing disastrously. This left them with the difficult task of having to mend their political fences with Mugabe's government.

The USSR was also faced with the need to make a choice among the rival liberation movements of South Africa; but, in this case, their choice was eased since the leading nationalist force, the ANC (African National Congress), has established a working alliance with the South African Communist Party, which is strongly Moscow-oriented. However, the ANC's effective leader, Oliver Tambo, demonstrated his movement's interest in not being drawn into Sino-Soviet rivalries by visiting Beijing and establishing relations with the People's Republic. What the future holds for this nationalist-communist alliance in the developing struggle in South Africa is still entirely unpredictable, especially since the crucial phase of that struggle will almost certainly be decided by the diverse forces of resistance and opposition within the country rather than by the armed struggle itself.

In Namibia, SWAPO (South West Africa People's Organization), led by Sam Nujomo, made its own choice of strategic allies. Throughout its armed struggle for independence, going back to the 1960s, it has sought to preserve its nonaligned stance, both in relation to the East-West rivalry and in the Sino-Soviet conflict. However, since its external base is in Angola, it has had no option, or hesitation, in accepting the military support which the Soviet bloc and Cuban presence in that country makes possible. Nevertheless, SWAPO still insists on maintaining good relations with China and the West.

The USSR appears to take a long-term view about developments in southern Africa, a position made possible by the predictably long period of struggle that lies ahead before the inevitable crumbling of the apartheid system and of the white-dominated status quo. From a Soviet perspective, the prospect of a lengthy and violent struggle in a modern industrial country like South Africa offers the best hope of producing the kind of revolutionary situation that would increase its opportunities for influencing the final outcome. The fulfillment of these expectations depends largely on whether or not the Western democracies continue to appear, in African eyes, to identify their own interests with those of the Pretoria regime.

Nowhere does one find clearer evidence of the opportunism (i.e., pragmatism and flexibility) of Soviet tactics than in the Horn of Africa. At the time of Somalia's independence in 1960, the Somalis openly proclaimed their new state's national interest by incorporating a five-pointed star in their flag, one point for each of the Somali homelands: two of these were unified in the Somali Republic at the time of independence; Djibouti, the Ogaden region of Ethiopia, and the North-Western Province of Kenya remained to be "rescued." All three missing parts lay in countries heavily backed by the West; therefore, to pursue their national interests, the Somalis perforce had to seek aid for their pitifully poor and weak country from anti-Western sources. They looked first to China but, once this overture became known, the USSR hurried forward with an offer to meet Somalia's requirements: the creation of a modern army of 10,000 men and a substantial program of economic and technical aid. The Soviet interest was to acquire port facilities in the Red Sea at Berbera and Mogadiscio. Thus, both sides' interests were met. In gratitude, the Somalis (a Muslim people) adopted scientific socialism as the basis for their political system. Despite frictions at a social level between Somalis and the large community of Soviet men and women, which had grown up rapidly, all went swimmingly well until the overthrow of Somalia's greatest enemy, Haile Selassie of Ethiopia, an event for which they had long prepared themselves. Then, at the point at which the Somalis were readying themselves to mobilize their secretly organized insurgency movement in the Ogaden, reinforced by elements and supplies from their Soviet-trained army, Moscow changed course. Having first strenuously, but unsuccessfully, tried to persuade Siad Barre to enter into some kind of confederal arrangement with Ethiopia, which would involve the Ogaden, Moscow accepted the Ethiopian military regime's invitation to supply them with arms, following the refusal by the U.S. Administration to do so. Outraged by what they regarded as an act of "uncomradely treason," Barre expelled the Soviets.

The advantages to Moscow of switching from Somalia to Ethiopia are plain. First, it knew perfectly well that the Somali army it had helped to build up was about to be used in an effort to wrest away the Ogaden from Ethiopia—an operation that was bound to be strongly opposed by the OAU. Therefore, if the Soviets remained in Mogadiscio, they would, willy-nilly, be drawn into a conflict with the OAU and could expect to be on the losing side in an Ethiopian–Somali conflict. Second, Ethiopia is a large and potentially rich country, whereas Somalia is small, poor, and politically unimportant in terms of being able to carry much influence in Africa. Third, the prospect of acquiring naval facilities at Ethiopia's two important Red Sea ports, Assab and Massawa, is infinitely more attractive than Berbera and Mogadiscio. However, Moscow took great risks by venturing into Ethiopia at a time when the country was engulfed by violence triggered off both by a power struggle to fill the vacuum left by the Emperor and by regional forces determined to obtain more favored positions in a new Ethiopia. The Eritrean liberation struggle (to which the Soviets had earlier given their support) was being fought with an indomitable spirit that was soon to be matched by the opposition in Tigre and other parts of the old empire. Predictably, too, the Somali army had crossed the border into the Ogaden. Thus, the first challenge to the Soviets was to mobilize massive support to ensure the survival of the embattled military regime of Colonel Mengistu Haile Mariam. They launched a large-scale and highly efficient airlift which demonstrated—as first glimpsed in the earlier operation in Angola—the growing range of the Soviets' military delivery capacity. Simultaneously, and again repeating the Angolan model, they arranged the transport of 14,000 Cuban combat troops, using South Yemen as a staging-point. (This use of Aden provides further evidence of the direct link between the Middle East and African regions.) Once having secured the military regime's position, the Kremlin showed that, profiting from its earlier experiences, it was no longer willing just to rely on a military regime for the maintenance of an alliance into which it had invested considerable resources and prestige. Showing great patience and determination, Moscow skillfully but forcefully persuaded a reluctant Mengistu to establish the structures of a classical communist state and to create a communist party closely tied in with the Soviet system. The success of this new Soviet initiative came to fruition early in 1984 when Mengistu forecast the launching of the Ethiopian Workers' Party in "fulfillment of Marxism–Leninism principles." He announced that the party would become the "sole instrument" to effect the realization of communism, performing the role of the vanguard leadership of a class party, and emphasized Ethiopia's spirit of proletarian internationalism and the need to strengthen the party's unity within the "world socialist system." In an earlier speech to COPWE (Commission for Organizing the Party of the Working People of Ethiopia) Mengistu had compared Ethiopia's revolutionary role in Africa to that of Vietnam in Asia. Reflecting Soviet priorities, Mengistu denounced the United States for its policies of aggression and pledged active support for the peace efforts of the USSR.

It still remains to be seen whether this new communist orientation for Ethiopia will be accomplished and, then, whether it will survive. If it does, it would constitute Moscow's most positive achievement toward fulfilling its key objectives in Africa. Apart from gaining an active ally, the Soviet Navy would be assured of a strong position in the Red Sea.

Moscow's relations with Libya illustrate a different facet of Soviet tactics. It is a relationship between two essentially incompatible partners: Qadhdhafi is committed to activating Muslim fundamentalism in support of his own revolutionary aspirations in the Third World based on the ideology of his *Green Book*, which rejects both capitalism and communism. While these Libyan interests conflict sharply with Moscow's, both share a common interest in their determined opposition to the Egyptian leadership since Nasir. Qadhdhafi has always seen himself as the natural heir to Nasir; to him, both Sadat and Hosni Mubarak were usurpers who betrayed Nasirism and the pan-Arab cause; the Soviets never forgave Sadat and Mubarak for Moscow's expulsion from Egypt. So long as Qadhdhafi's strong commitment is to work for the overthrow of the present Egyptian leadership, it suits Moscow's book to provide the necessary support to achieve that objective, irrespective of their other differences. Soviet critics describe such a policy as rank cynicism; those less unsympathetic to the Soviets would judge it in terms of *Realpolitik*. Moscow stands to gain in the short term by strengthening Libya's capacity to work for the overthrow of the Cairo regime; moreover, its substantial arms deals with Libya (the initial agreement was for $2 billion) are paid for in hard currency, unlike so many of the Soviets' other deals in the Third World where they must rely for payment either upon barter deals or on the never-never system of loan repayments.

Summing Up

From 1955 to 1984, the Soviet encounter with Africa was characterized by erratic and relatively short-lived relationships. In every instance where this relationship took the form of the USSR acting as a strategic ally, it turned out badly; today, the most outspokenly hostile anti-Soviet states in the continent (Egypt, the Sudan, and Somalia) are those with which Moscow had formerly enjoyed the most intimate links. Overall, the Soviets have not succeeded in making much impact either on the political systems in Africa or in expanding their influence in ways helpful to their objectives as a superpower. Although Western influence has declined since the end of the colonial period, it still remains considerably greater than that of the USSR.

Moscow's relations with African states remain largely at a formal and diplomatic level. The Soviet Union's position as a challenging superpower has suffered because of its demonstrated inability to compete with the Western powers, both in terms of its ability to offer conditions for trade and substantial sources of investment capital and its failure to produce large-scale and relevant technical aid programs. Its effectiveness as a strategic ally disappointed the Egyptians and is now being questioned by the Mozambicans and Angolans. However, it has lived up to the expectations of the Ethiopians. Moscow has convincingly demonstrated its growing military delivery systems on two occasions: in assisting the MPLA to win power in Angola and in rescuing the military regime in Ethiopia. Except in the case of Ethiopia, it has failed to undercut the generally friendly feelings exhibited in Africa for China; even the Angolans have reestablished their diplomatic ties with Beijing.

The promising success of a new Soviet strategy in Ethiopia suggests that Moscow is capable of learning from its experience and that its future capacity to promote its objectives in the continent should not be underestimated. Both its greatest test and opportunity for the future would appear to lie in the developing situation in southern Africa. To date, every temporary advantage gained by the Soviet bloc in Africa can be shown to have resulted either directly from misjudged Western policies or because of some temporary coincidence of interest between a particular African government and the USSR. Mistaken Western policies toward South Africa could yet provide the USSR with its most important gain in the continent; but that belongs to the future. In the short term, the most significant development in the Afro/Soviet relationship is the likely gain of a committed ally in Ethiopia.

3 Soviet Engagement in Africa: Motives, Means, and Prospects

R. Craig Nation

Western concern with Soviet involvement in Africa has moved through action/reaction cycles. During the first great wave of African decolonization in the early 1960s, Soviet sponsorship of "African socialist" regimes and a brief and abortive engagement on behalf of the Patrice Lumumba faction in the former Belgian Congo (Zaire) gave rise to a flurry of speculation about an emerging Soviet "threat" on the continent.[1] The reaction proved short-lived, however, as the defeat of Lumumba and the evolution of African socialist leaders in directions more sympathetic to the West undermined its credibility.

The collapse of Marcello Caetano's dictatorship in Portugal and the Ethiopian empire of Haile Selassie in 1974, followed by the gradual emergence of Soviet supported, Marxist-oriented liberation movements in Ethiopia and the former Portuguese colonies of southern Africa altered perceptions once again. The Soviet threat seemed to have reappeared, and a new round of alarmist literature sprang up to document the supposed gravity of the situation.[2] Now, more than a decade later, it has become apparent that here too original concerns were exaggerated. Expanded Soviet engagement in Africa has not led to a dramatic accumulation of influence, and as a result yet another reevaluation is in progress, emphasizing the limitations which Soviet policy confronts, particularly due to the Soviets' inability to supply levels of economic assistance considered adequate for African needs.[3]

These variations in perspective reflect the changing climate of East–West relations, but they also bear witness to the somewhat neglected status of Western studies of Soviet African policy, which remains one of the least intensively explored of all dimensions of Soviet foreign relations.[4] In view of the rather dramatic Soviet initiatives in Africa during the past decade and the degree to which the USSR has made itself a part of the continent's affairs, this relative neglect is rather ironic. The Soviet Union has demonstrated a commitment in Africa of considerable depth, which merits more careful and sustained attention.

This chapter will attempt to explore the motives that stand behind the Soviet Union's expanded engagement in Africa and to assess the degree to which Soviet policy initiatives have succeeded. It argues that the Soviet Union has developed a relatively coherent Africa policy marked by tactical flexibility in the short term, but also by a careful evaluation of long-term structural tendencies and of ways in which the USSR can relate to them positively. In many ways the narrowly focused character of much Western analysis has failed to do justice to the sophistication of this long-term commitment. Patterns of Soviet commentary and political behavior indicate at least the broad outline of an Africa policy which is guardedly optimistic, nondogmatic, and possessed of considerably more substance and coherency than it has often been given credit for.

The Soviet Image of Africa

According to most objective indicators, Africa's economic situation and prospects are bleak. Twenty-six of the world's thirty-six poorest nations are already located in Africa,[5] and at present economic trends are often negative. Sub-Saharan Africa is the world's least developed region, and it is not surprising that the continent has been the source for many of the initiatives seeking to define a "New International Economic Order" (such as the IVth conference of nonaligned nations in Algiers in 1973, or the Arusha [Tanzania] Declaration of the "Group of 77"). Despite significant regional variations, Africa as a whole presents a terrifying spectacle of absolute poverty, malnutrition, sociological imbalance, and attendant political instability.

There is an abundant and generally high-quality Soviet literature which addresses Africa's dilemmas and the role of the USSR in relation to them. Though the harshness of African realities is clearly acknowledged, Soviet commentary attempts to maintain a positive outlook, both by assigning responsibility for the current state of affairs and by rigorously defining alternatives.[6] Soviet African studies remain largely unexplored in the West, but the image of Africa that they present is well-integrated and challenging. They also serve as an important foundation for Soviety policy conceptualization and thus deserve some formal elaboration. *Neocolonialism* and the *Noncapitalist Path of Development*, as the central concepts in Soviet analysis of Africa and the Third World, provide a convenient focus for a summary of its distinctive features.

Neocolonialism

Although neocolonialism is carefully developed as an analytical category in Soviet commentary, in general its usage corresponds to the colloquial sense of the term in everyday political discourse. Thus, according to one formal definition, neocolonialism is described as "the imperialist policy of exploitation and plunder of the independent, liberated nations, pursued with the help of new methods and devices."[7] These "new methods" refer above all to various forms of economic manipulation.

The sources of the neocolonial relationship as outlined by Soviet commentators lie in the legacy of colonialism itself, including "the economic weakness of the young, politically independent governments . . . an orientation toward supplying the needs of the metropoles, and dependence upon the importation of means of production."[8] Despite the formal, political independence achieved by most former colonies after World War II, various forms of dependency are said to have continued to determine the relationship between the industrialized metropole and the developing world periphery. The result is the effective subjugation of the former colonies to continuing imperialist domination.

The attributes of neocolonialism include a familiar catalogue of inequities. Capital investment patterns in the developing world, it is asserted, tend to favor selected areas considered both economically promising and politically secure and thereby aggravate regional inequalities and class stratification. Unbalanced and worsening terms of trade lead to the relative devaluation of Africa's primary commodities on world markets, and borrowing as a source of revenue creates huge burdens of debt servicing and repayment, leaving debtor nations at the mercy of imperialist-controlled international financial institutions. Lack of access to technology and expertise, the inequitable structure of world trade, and the weakness of domestic markets either limit or exclude most developmental options. These exploitative economic relations are reinforced by ideological dependency, due to the West's control over the means of mass communications,[9] by cultural dependency, symbolized by the aping of Western consumerism on the part of Third World elites, and by authority structures that concentrate power in the hands of isolated and corrupt minorities.

The ultimate instrumentality of the neocolonial relationship is identified as the transnational corporation, the "modern conquistador" of imperialism in the colorful image of one Soviet commentator.[10] Exploiting local labor and resources at costs considerably lower than those prevailing on domestic markets within the metropole (though perhaps modestly higher than local norms),[11] transnationals cumulatively extract superprofits that vastly surpass capital outlays, creating a net flow of wealth from periphery to metropole and a process of impoverishment.[12] Beyond their purely economic impact, transnationals are further described as "an important independent force in the world political arena, where they participate actively in furthering the foreign policy of the countries in which they are based, casting aside the principle of the sovereignty of national governments."[13] With extraterritorial privileges, bureaucratic structures that are often more developed and stable than those available to local authorities, and direct links to the metropolitan centers of world capitalism, transnationals are said to represent a political fifth-column for the forces of imperialism.[14]

The result of the neocolonial relationship is the relegation of the majority of African states to the role of producers of undervalued primary commodities on the periphery of the capitalist world economy. "Development" under these circumstances means the growth of export-oriented commodity production, a deformed structure of consumer demand, and a widening gap between elite groups and the mass of producers, with aggravated social tensions and crisis an inevitable by-product.[15] Balanced and independent growth and an effective realization of national potential are, under the circumstances, virtually unobtainable. In the blunt words of Anatolii Gromyko, "The responsibility for the poverty of Africa is borne by imperialism and neocolonialism."[16]

A key political conclusion that emerges from this analysis is that whatever the exigencies of the moment, in the long term the prospects for revolutionary transformations and socialist development in the Third World remain positive. Capitalist oriented development under the aegis of neocolonialism:

> is not only incapable of resolving the sharp socio-economic problems which confront it, but in fact deepens them, and adds to social tensions. Capitalism, as a socio-economic form which has outlived itself, does not have extensive prospects as a mode of development on the [African] continent.[17]

The Soviet concept of neocolonialism thus leads directly to consideration of alternative modes of Third World development, emphasizing prospects for revolutionary change which transcend the context of capitalist imperialism.

The Noncapitalist Path of Development

Though its sources lie in the early years of the Soviet revolutionary experience, the concept of a noncapitalist path of Third World development has evolved in its present form since the early 1960s. The concept posits a two-phase transition for underdeveloped nations toward socialism; a *national-democratic* phase which brings a diverse coalition of progressive forces to power pursuing anti-imperialist policies, and a *revolutionary-democratic* or *popular-democratic* phase marked by the emergence of a vanguard party guided by Marxist-Leninist theory and by a more rapid tempo of socio-economic transformation. Under propitious circumstances, it is argued, the process can enable developing nations to "skip" the stage of capitalism and move directly from colonial dependence to the construction of socialism.[18] The key to the process is the initiatory role of the state sector, which is in effect equated with the vanguard party. In developing the concept of a noncapitalist path the Soviet Union has thus taken sides in regard to a fundamental issue in Marxist political theory, emphasizing the primary role of the state sector in forwarding social change, and the relative autonomy of the superstructure vis-à-vis the socioeconomic base.[19]

The concept of the noncapitalist path also coincided nicely with the USSR's interests, newly manifest in the 1960s, in cultivating relationships with key Third World leaders. Unfortunately, banking on revolutionary democrats such as Modeiba Keita in Mali, Gamal Abd al-Nasir in Egypt, Kwame Nkrumah in Ghana, Ja'far al-Numayri in the Sudan, or Mohammed Siad Barre in Somalia proved to be a risky business, and Soviet efforts to develop such relationships often ended in embarrassing and costly failures. By the mid-1970s a new concept had appeared in Soviet analysis which—while on one hand summarizing and streamlining the noncapitalist development scenario—also introduced an important new note of caution concerning immediate prospects for revolutionary transformation. Beginning in 1975 to 1976, the *state of socialist orientation* became the centerpiece of Soviet theorizing concerning political change in the Third World.[20]

In its most general formulation, socialist orientation refers to the entire process of national democratic and revolutionary democratic development, which is thereby set apart from capitalist oriented development under the conditions established by neocolonialism. As a concept socialist orientation may nonetheless be distinguished from earlier descriptions of the noncapitalist path in at least four areas of emphasis.

1. Socialist orientation presents a more sober estimation of the prospects for revolutionary change given the circumstances prevailing in the Third World, with more emphasis upon the difficulties inherent in the process. It is repeatedly asserted that socialist orientation represents a *subjective choice* on the part of a national democratic leadership. States that adopt the path of socialist orientation enter an experiment for which general guidelines but no fixed rules exist. The transition is fragile and, in certain cases, reversible. In the words of Evgenii Primakov:

> the noncapitalist transition of nations to socialism is accompanied by both objective and subjective contradictions, which in many cases derive from the specifics of a given transformation, where they remain immanent. In some circumstances this leads to a situation where-in a given transition will be interrupted, and the nation will return to the path of capitalist development.[21]

Socialist orientation, it is emphasized, is less an objectively grounded tendency than a possibility, which can be more or less successfully pursued, depending upon the individual circumstances.

2. The attributes of the state of socialist orientation have been more precisely specified and the circumstances under which a harmonious transition to the construction of socialism is achievable more carefully defined. A

recent definition of socialist orientation in Africa which notes the attributes of the process is provided by Anatolii Gromyko:

> The concrete historical conditions for the origins and development of socialist orientation in Africa are determined in large measure by peculiarities specific to each country. But general criteria do exist: the creation and strengthening of revolutionary-democratic parties and vanguard parties animated by the theory of scientific socialism; the liquidation of the exploitation of man by man; the formation and subsequently the consolidation and broadening of the state sector; the carrying out of a far-reaching agrarian reform; the realization of a cultural revolution effecting broad segments of society.[22]

These general tendencies are elaborated upon by Primakov, who specifies four criteria for the pursuit of socialist orientation: (1) *economic criteria* emphasizing the strengthening of the state sector via nationalization, industrialization, and land reform; (2) *social criteria* pointing to a broadening of the class base of the revolutionary regime via the "cultural revolution" with its emphasis upon literacy and politicization, and the development of a "leading" proletarian stratum; (3) *political criteria* calling for the construction of a vanguard party internally, and in external relations the conviction that "alliance with the countries of victorious socialist revolution is the fundament without which a noncapitalist transition of underdeveloped nations to socialism is impossible"[23]; and (4) *ideological criteria* demanding a gradual shift from the "revolutionary petty bourgeois ideology" characteristic of the national-democratic phase to a more orthodox variant of scientific socialism.

Cumulatively these criteria encompass a statist developmental model emphasizing nationalization, planned industrial development, land reform, and cooperative agriculture. They propose alliance with the Soviet bloc to balance, but not necessarily eliminate, dependence upon the West.

3. A more fundamental distinction is made between the national-democratic and revolutionary-democratic phases. Only those states that have made significant progress toward revolutionary-democratic (or popular-democratic) development are now considered serious candidates for a successful pursuit of socialist orientation. In the words of G. Mirskii:

> In fact, life reveals the inappropriateness of identifying within the confines of a single concept (whether this be the noncapitalist path or socialist orientation) two dissimilar processes, two revolutionary "models." What is occurring today in countries such as South Yemen, Angola, and Ethiopia, where vanguard parties either hold or are consolidating power, demonstrates the more radical (from the point of view of the proletariat) character of the socioeconomic systems in formation there, compared with nations of the "first generation" of socialist orientation. In the first case [one is] speaking of a popular democratic revolution, observing correctly that this

is a form of socialist revolution, in the second—merely of a national-democratic revolution.[24]

In effect, much greater emphasis is placed upon selected states where socialist orientation seems to be leading to the consolidation of revolutionary regimes committed to positive relations with the USSR. Angola, Benin, the Congo, Ethiopia, and Mozambique seem to represent the leading candidates for such a "popular democratic" model in Africa.

4. The mechanisms of effective Third World development are defined much more liberally than in the past. In general, the possibility of a "sudden and absolute abandonment of capitalist development" is downplayed, the limitations of fraternal socialist assistance noted, and the objective need for a gradualist, mixed economy approach underlined.[25]

In sum, the redefinitions occasioned by the introduction of the concept socialist orientation point toward less hopeful prospects for rapid revolutionary transformations in the Third World, the need for greater selectivity in identifying regimes with which the USSR can hope to build relationships upon the principle of "proletarian internationalism," and a greater tolerance for mixed developmental models allowing substantial interaction with the West. At the same time, long-range prospects for revolutionary change and the inadequacies of neocolonialism as a context for stable growth continue to be asserted. This becomes particularly clear in examining Soviet reactions to another hotly debated aspect of African developmental politics, the demand for a New International Economic Order.

Soviet responses to calls for a structural reform of the international economic system might best be described as ambiguous. The USSR has formally endorsed the principle in its most general formulations,[26] but Soviet commentators have also been critical of most of the concrete proposals developed in the course of the North–South debate.[27] Thus the Tinbergen *Report to the Club of Rome*[28] is described as reflective of liberal bourgeois priorities seeking to preserve a structure of injustice by ameliorating its more destabilizing dimensions, substituting the mystified notion of interdependence in place of class analysis. The social reformist orientation of the Brandt commission report[29] is also rejected; its suggestions, it is claimed, would only strengthen the structural dependency which is at the root of the Third World's dilemmas. More radical approaches which emphasize the impossibility of overcoming underdevelopment within the confines of the capitalist world economy are also criticized for a tendency to abstract from concrete circumstances. Proposals initiated within the developing world itself (such as the Monrovia Declaration of the OAU of June 1979 and the Lagos Action Plan of April 1980), with their emphasis upon self-reliance, collective action, development of local and regional markets, and politically enforced limitations upon the role of external capital (often characterized as South-

South relations) are discussed more sympathetically[30] but also judged inadequate. A strong implication that underlies Soviet commentary is that ultimately only the creation of a global economic order built upon a socialist federation of states can resolve the problems of uneven and underdevelopment.[31] This is a very distant goal, but it is a protracted process of struggle and confrontation, and not piecemeal reformism, that will lead toward it. The long-term potential for revolutionary transformation remains in place despite occasional setbacks and limited immediate prospects.

Some scholars in the West, noting the difficulty that the noncapitalist path scenario has presented the Soviets as a basis for relations with Third World states, and the degree to which the concept has been hedged in recent formulations, have questioned its continued relevance as an analytical category.[32] In some ways the concept of socialist orientation does conveniently legitimize past Soviet policy choices and might be said to bear traces of opportunism. It might just as well be said, however, to demonstrate the increasingly flexible and nondogmatic character of Soviet foreign policy analysis. In many ways socialist orientation represents a successful attempt to conceptualize the dynamics of revolutionary change in the Third World within a general theoretical framework. Statist, one-party regimes committed to extending national control over indigenous resources and to the ideal of socialism—at least as a source of legitimization—have become widespread in the Third World and embody a trend with certain objective determinants.[33] In the case of Africa, David and Marina Ottaway have described the emergence of "afrocommunist" models as a realistic reaction to the failure of alternative development strategies.[34] So long as much of Africa remains radically impoverished, the search for revolutionary modes of development will maintain its relevance. "It is not accidental," as Soviet analysts would have it, "that it is precisely in Africa where the majority of young governments having chosen socialist orientation are to be found."[35]

Many aspects of the Soviet developmental perspective can be criticized. The party-state model, with its bureaucratic and nondemocratic tendencies, has already demonstrated its inadequacies in the USSR and elsewhere.[36] It is debatable whether Soviet prescriptions in regard to the vital issue of agrarian reform, which continue to emphasize orthodox state farm and cooperative models, are entirely relevant to Africa's distinctive patterns of land tenure. Reliance upon a leading proletarian element is suspect in a continent where up to 80 percent of the population are rural laborers, proletarian internationalism as a basis for international cooperation is not widely accepted, and where the legacy of colonialism has led to the predominance of a more rigid conception of nonalignment.

Nonetheless, Soviet perspectives have the advantages of coherence, flexibility, and sensitivity to key issues. The concepts of neocolonialism and the noncapitalist path represent serious efforts to come to terms with the dynamic of revolutionary change in the Third World, in the context of Marxist-Leninist analysis as it is structured in the USSR. They offer a general strategic perspective around which Soviet policy options may be organized, provide policy choices with an ideological rationale, and allow for considerable tactical maneuvering. There are many indications that the criteria that they establish are considered useful and are taken seriously in the formation of Soviet African policy.

Sources of Soviet Involvement

Ideological formulas such as neocolonialism and socialist orientation help to clarify the context within which Soviet policy in Africa is structured. They emphasize long-term trends, however, and given their abstractness and idealization of Soviet motives, are not necessarily very useful in defining the more pragmatic sources of Soviet initiatives. More immediate Soviet ambitions and concerns may be addressed under the general headings of strategic, economic, and political motivation.

Strategic Motives

Africa is geographically distant from the USSR and does not present imminent security concerns such as those that affect Soviet policy in the Middle East region. Some analysts have described Africa as an area of strategic opportunity and attempted to identify a strategic thrust into the continent inherited by the Soviet regime from its czarist predecessor, but by any fair standard czarist and Soviet initiatives in Africa prior to 1955 were quite limited and peripheral.[37] Recent events have nonetheless demonstrated that African regions do hold some strategic significance in the eyes of Soviet planners. Since the Soviet/Cuban intervention in the Angolan conflict during 1975 to 1976 a worst-case scenario has been developed emphasizing the increasingly central role of Africa in Soviet global strategy. Growing Soviet power projection capacity enabling intervention in regional conflicts, basing and visitation privileges extending the scope of Soviet naval operations, and an armed presence in Africa asserted via proxy forces are said to represent an emerging threat to Western access to African strategic resources, the oil-tanker route transiting the Cape of Good Hope, and the security of pro-Western regimes.[38] This scenario is highly unrealistic, to say the least, since it tends to exaggerate Soviet capacity and to undervalue or ignore Western strengths, but in rejecting grand design arguments one should not neglect the very real strategic concerns that do affect Soviet African engagement.

Soviet strategic motives in Africa differ substantially from region to region, but in every case they are shaped importantly by global rivalry with the United States. In northern Africa, Egypt for years occupied a special position as the keystone of the Soviet presence in the Middle East. The Sadat leadership's engagement in the Camp David process shattered this relationship, and it is unlikely that Sadat's successor Hosni Mubarak will seek to reverse the dynamic of Egypt's developing ties to the West,[39] but the commitment to a role in the Middle East remains, and the Soviets are highly sensitive to U.S. striving for strategic advantage in an area that impacts upon the southern theater of a potential European conflict as well as being contiguous to their own southern flank.[40] This is particularly the case with the emerging infrastructure of the Rapid Deployment Force, which encompasses an important part of northern Africa as well as extending beyond the Arabian peninsula into Southwest Asia.

The Sahelian region and west Africa have substantially less inherent strategic value. Though the attempt has been made to portray Libyan actions in Chad as an aspect of a Soviet sponsored strategic offensive focused on control of the Aouzou strip, the Chadian conflict has clearly regional sources, and direct Soviet involvement has not been an important factor. Similarly in the case of the POLISARIO's struggle for an independent Western Sahara the Soviet Union has striven to maintain stable relations with all parties to the conflict and is clearly not committed to a particular outcome. The tortured, drought-ridden Sahel lacks even the strategic relevance which can occasionally attract superpower attention and aid.

The situation is dramatically different in the Horn of Africa. The Suez-Red Sea-Bab al-Mandab passage is of considerable importance to the Soviet Union as a part of the vital waterway that provides the most direct and economical links between European Russia and the Soviet Far East. The United States has been directly involved in the Horn since the early 1950s, and Soviet commentary emphasizes the strategic importance accorded the region in U.S. planning.[41] The USSR also has a strategic commitment in the Horn dating from a 1963 agreement with Somalia, and the presence of Cuban troops in Ethiopia since 1977 represents an escalation of the strategic stake. Superpower naval competition in the Indian Ocean and the role of Somalia in the Rapid Deployment Force reinforce the region's strategic relevance. Of little inherent importance and economically weak and barren, the Horn is nonetheless perceived to impact importantly upon the military balance in adjacent areas. Both superpowers seem to have accepted it, rightly or wrongly, as a region which their adversary cannot be permitted to dominate.

Southern Africa also possesses a certain objective geostrategic importance. Littoral states in the southeast such as Mozambique or Tanzania could contribute meaningfully to an Indian Ocean presence by donating access to naval facilities. With reliable access to basing facilities in southern Africa and the Horn, the Soviets could importantly reduce the transit time required to project a naval presence in the Indian Ocean from their Pacific Fleet and generally facilitate the maintenance of naval forces in an operational area far from home ports. The USSR has apparently sought naval basing and visitation privileges in the region and is interested in extending air reconnaissance operations, developing communications, and building logistical support systems. Furthermore, the presence of a contingent of Cuban forces in Angola and an implicit Soviet security guarantee to Angola and Mozambique among the Front Line states has developed into a considerable strategic commitment in its own right, particularly given the massive South African armed incursions of recent years.[42] By providing air defense systems (SAM-3s and SAM-6s) to both Angola and Mozambique during 1981 to 1982, the Soviet Union has escalated its own strategic involvement and exposure in a region that promises to generate an escalating tempo of conflict in the years to come.

In the cases of Angola and Ethiopia, the Soviet Union and its allies demonstrated the logistical capacity and political will to project power sufficient to overwhelm relatively underdeveloped local forces under propitious political circumstances. These successes should not be exaggerated and should not obscure the substantial difficulties that continue to affect Soviet military engagement on the African continent. The Soviet Union lacks the ability to decisively project the forces required to defeat more developed regional powers, to engage in a protracted conflict without a secure local base, or to directly confront determined Western resistance. Soviet airlift capacity is limited absolutely, technologically (lack of inflight refueling capacity), and geostrategically (denial of overflight by Turkey and Iran). A massive transfer of Soviet forces and equipment to Africa would require sea transport, which given the naval balance in the Indian Ocean and the clear superiority of Western tactical air power, would be highly risky, if not suicidal.[43]

The much-vaunted Soviet threat to shipping off the Cape of Good Hope is no more credible when examined closely. First, the Cape Route encompasses a number of exposed choke points (the Strait of Hormuz, the Mozambique Channel, the Cape itself) some of which have been exposed for years, especially in light of the cumbersome nature of oil-tanker traffic. Its security does not equate to the security of South Africa. Second, the security of the Cape Route is clearly regarded as a vital interest by the Western powers. Though the Soviets could initiate interdiction, it is doubtful that they could maintain it for very long in the face of determined resistance, and the entire operation appears most unappetizing. Chester Crocker, the Reagan Administration's Assistant Secretary of State for African Affairs, made the point unambiguously during a 1978 Senate hearing: "It is important to distinguish between the extent of U.S. interests and the extent of the threat to it. Direct Soviet interdiction of Western shipping in Southern African waters is not credible under peacetime conditions."[44]

Finally, in the case of southern Africa, the Soviet Union must take into account the overwhelming regional superiority of South African forces.[45] The long-term nonviability of the apartheid-based regime certainly presents the USSR with opportunities, but these must be balanced against the great strategic limitations that South African power poses both for the Soviets, their allies among the Front Line states, and liberation forces within South Africa and Namibia.

When the West's military presence in Africa and adjacent areas is calculated cumulatively, it is clear that a substantial strategic advantage remains in place. At present, U.S. policy seems determined to expand and exploit this advantage in order to frustrate and destabilize leftist regimes. The Soviet Union is to some degree confronted with an African threat of its own, in the form of a U.S.-sponsored effort to recoup losses and discourage socialist oriented development. The Paris-based journal *Jeune Afrique* has stated that "the present chief of the White House [President Reagan], in trying above all to limit the influence of the socialist countries in Africa, is attempting to strengthen, if not create, future pro-American strong points over the entire African continent."[46] The journal goes on to note that a system of defense is to be created and directed against Libya, Ethiopia, and Angola. This system relies on Morocco, Egypt, Sudan, Somalia, Kenya, Zaire, and most importantly, South Africa.

Soviet accounts echo this judgment and underline the existence of an integrated Western security strategy for Africa aimed at eliminating progressive regimes and Soviet influence. "As far as the National Security Council and the Pentagon are concerned," writes E. Tarabrin,

> they view the African continent as one of the basic components of a system of "forward lines" along which "possibilities" for defending the "zones of vital interests of the U.S.A." must be created and extended. Leaning on this imperial conception, Washington has begun to build up its "military presence" in Africa. Emphasis is placed upon nations occupying a geographical position which is convenient from a military-strategic point of view, possessing viable ports, airfields, and other components of a military infrastructure, and also disposing of significant natural resources.[47]

Tarabrin's evaluation echoes a familiar Western indictment of Soviet motives and clarifies the extent to which Soviet engagement in Africa is conditioned by the strategic imperatives of East–West rivalry.

Economic Motives

Soviet economic cooperation with the nations of the Third World remains quite limited in absolute terms, despite the fact that its relative weight as a component of Soviet economic activity is increasing. Though according to Soviet calculations the value of economic interactions with all developing nations more than tripled during the 1970s, at present the USSR accounts for less than 5 percent of total world trade with the Third World.[48] These relationships are even more pronounced in the case of Africa.

The attempt to develop commercial interactions with Africa presents the USSR with a number of special problems. The most intractable of these is the absence of complementarity between the structure of Soviet foreign trade and that of most potential African trading partners. Like many developing nations, the USSR remains predominantly an exporter of fuels and raw materials and an importer of manufactured goods and foodstuffs. The structural foundation for a dynamic commercial relationship with Africa is thus often lacking. In addition, Africa's sheer poverty and lack of hard currency reserves continues to represent a barrier to mutually beneficial economic exchange. Though a distinction should be drawn between the relatively more prosperous states of northern Africa and the impoverished Sub-Saharan region, comparable constraints exist in both cases. Finally, a number of potentially important regional markets (Egypt, Gabon, Liberia, Nigeria, South Africa, Zaire) are dominated by Western capital and effectively closed to significant Soviet penetration.[49] Partially as a result of such problems, even within the restricted context of Soviet economic interaction with the developing world, Africa remains underrepresented. Africa accounted for only 2.3 percent of Soviet trade with developing nations in 1981, and this figure represented a significant decline over the prior decade.[50] Traditionally, Soviet economic programs in the Third World have been concentrated in the nations adjacent to Soviet territory, and Latin America (particularly Mexico) represents the most promising growth region for the future. Africa remains of marginal importance in the overall scope of Soviet economic activity.

Soviet economic engagement in Africa takes numerous forms, including arms sales, nonmilitary commercial transactions, economic aid, and cooperative ventures. Clearly, arms sales, which constitute between two-thirds and three-fourths of Soviet economic commitment in the Third World since 1955, represent a special category of central importance.[51] Africa is the USSR's second largest regional customer for arms (after the Middle East) and the absolute quantity of arms sales has increased dramatically despite the fact that Africa's relative share of total Soviet arms transfers has declined.[52] Given the chaotic interstate relations and domestic instabilities that have prevailed in Africa in the postcolonial era, demand for weaponry is high, and the USSR has been able to develop a profitable export sector, exchanging weapons on very competitive terms for hard currency and raw materials. The revenues thus obtained serve to balance the trade deficit which the USSR carries with developing nations in other sectors, as well as providing a significant hard currency surplus. The bulk of these arms transfers in Africa have involved the northern region, where Libya has replaced Egypt since 1974 as the leading Soviet customer, but the Sub-Saharan region has become increasingly important as well.

In contrast to its significant role as an arms customer, Africa's place in the nonmilitary branches of Soviet foreign trade is modest. Lack of complementarity goes a long way toward explaining this, with the Soviets exporting primarily manufactured goods and importing raw materials, particularly foodstuffs. Fish products, Ethiopian coffee, Moroccan phosphates, and Guinean bauxite represent the most significant Soviet imports, and in no case does an important trade dependency exist.[53]

Soviet foreign aid to Africa has represented less than 20 percent of total Soviet aid to the Third World over the past decade, and again the relative sum devoted to Africa has declined.[54] As in the past, Soviet aid is usually tied, requiring equipment purchases in the USSR, and is granted in the form of long-term loans that must be repaid. Prior to 1970 the bulk of Soviet aid programs in Africa were focused upon Egypt and tended to concentrate upon large "showpiece" projects such as the Aswan Dam. Recently aid and technicians have become more dispersed, a trend toward smaller projects tailored to specific needs has been manifest, and economic criteria have become more important in choosing recipients (tables 3-1 and 3-2). Greater selectivity and the search for reciprocal advantage increasingly characterize Soviet aid programs, which now more often take the form of cooperative arrangements involving other CMEA nations and complex multinational agreements.[55] In 1977 to 1978 the Soviet Union signed such agreements to help develop Moroccan phosphates and Guinean bauxite in exchange for contracted long-term purchases, and in 1982 a multidimensional cooperative arrangement with Angola became the Soviet Union's largest single financial commitment in Africa to date. The limitations of overall Soviet economic capacity will nonetheless continue to restrict the amount of developmental assistance that can feasibly be made available. These limits include shortages of hard currency, the inadequacies of Soviet technology (especially agricultural technology), domestic priorities, and the tautness of Soviet planning with its tendency to create general shortages of transferable resources.

In sum, the Soviet economic commitment in Africa, although not insignificant, is less than in any other comparable world region. The Soviet Union lacks the complex of economic interrelationships possessed by the Western powers, and given its own economic dilemmas and the asymmetry between Soviet and African requirements and potentials, such relations are

Table 3-1
USSR and Eastern Europe: Economic Aid Extended to African Countries
(Million U.S. $)[a]

	1954-1981		1980		1981	
	USSR	Eastern Europe	USSR	Eastern Europe	USSR	Eastern Europe
North Africa[b]	3,250	980	315	—	—	—
Algeria	1,045	525	315	—	—	—
Mauritania	10	10	—	—	—	—
Morocco	2,100	215	—	—	—	—
Tunisia	95	230	—	—	—	—
Sub-Saharan Africa	2,870	1,990	310	280	125	115
Angola	30	100	—	—	—	—
Benin	10	NA	—	—	5	—
Burundi	—	NEGL	—	—	—	—
Cameroon	10	—	—	—	—	—
Cape Verde	5	5	—	—	—	NA
Central African Republic	5	—	—	—	—	—
Chad	5	—	—	—	—	—
Congo	45	60	—	—	—	—
Equatorial Guinea	NEGL	—	—	—	—	—
Ethiopia	400	355	—	—	10	5
Gabon	—	NEGL	—	—	—	—
Gambia	NEGL	—	—	—	—	—
Ghana	95	145	—	—	—	—
Guinea	215	110	5	—	—	—
Guinea-Bissau	10	5	—	—	—	—
Ivory Coast	—	NA	—	—	—	—
Kenya	50	—	—	—	—	—
Liberia	NEGL	—	—	—	—	—
Madagascar	70	35	50	35	—	—
Mali	100	25	—	—	5	—
Mauritius	5	—	—	—	—	—
Mozambique	175	100	—	—	NA	—
Niger	NEGL	—	—	—	—	—
Nigeria	5	220	—	—	—	20
Rwanda	NEGL	—	—	—	—	—
Sao Tome and Principe	NA	NA	—	—	—	—
Senegal	10	35	—	—	—	—
Sierra Leone	30	—	—	—	—	—
Somalia	165	10	—	—	—	—
Sudan	65	270	—	30	—	—
Tanzania	40	75	—	—	—	—
Uganda	25	25	—	—	—	—
Upper Volta	5	—	—	—	—	—
Zambia	20	165	—	30	—	—
Other	1,275	250	255	185	100	90

Source: U.S. Department of State, *Soviet and East European Aid to the Third World, 1981*, February 1983, pp. 17-18.

[a]Because of rounding, components may not add to total shown.

[b]Figures for Egypt: 1954-1981, USSR: 1,440; E.E.: 1,225
                 1980, USSR: 0; E.E.: 300
                 1981, USSR and E.E.: 0.
Specific figures for Libya not cited in original source.

Table 3-2
USSR, Eastern Europe, and Cuba: Economic Technicians in Africa, 1981[a]

	USSR and Eastern Europe	Cuba
Africa	60,600	14,685
North Africa	45,870	5,250
Algeria	11,150	250
Libya	31,700	5,000
Mauritania	50	—
Morocco	2,350	—
Tunisia	600	—
Other	20	—
Sub-Saharan Africa	14,730	9,435
Angola	3,900	6,500
Ethiopia	1,800	1,000
Gabon	10	—
Ghana	80	—
Guinea	660	125
Guinea-Bissau	275	—
Kenya	35	—
Madagascar	100	50
Mali	425	—
Mozambique	1,800	1,000
Niger	15	—
Nigeria	4,400	—
Rwanda	10	—
Sao Tome and Principe	15	—
Senegal	70	—
Sierra Leone	35	—
Somalia	5	—
Sudan	25	—
Tanzania	200	—
Zambia	475	—
Other	395	760

Source: U.S. Department of State, *Soviet and East European Aid to the Third World, 1981*, February 1983, p 20.

[a]Minimum estimates of number present for a period of one month or more. Numbers are rounded to nearest five.

not likely to develop rapidly. The one important exception lies in the area of arms supplies, where the USSR has succeeded in developing a profitable export market.

The marginality of Africa in the USSR's larger economic profile applies likewise to socialist oriented regimes. Despite their Marxist identity, nations like Angola, the Congo, Ethiopia, and Mozambique remain committed to significant economic interaction with the West. In its own commentary concerning the economic policies of the socialist oriented states, the USSR emphasizes the objective need to attract diverse sources of capital investment, the importance of a selective evaluation of individual economic opportunities, and the need for a gradualist developmental perspective.[56] By refusing petitions by Mozambique and Ethiopia for CMEA membership (apparently under pressure from its Eastern European allies), the Soviet Union has in fact encouraged an economic opening to the West, and as a partial result Angola and Mozambique have recently requested to participate in the Lomé III negotiations. In the five-year plan which it launched in 1981 the Congo very purposefully seeks to balance its international linkages and to attract broad-based foreign investment.[57]

Given the amount of attention it has attracted, the issue of Africa's mineral wealth perhaps deserves special mention. Soviet sources carefully document Western dependency upon African resources, particularly strategic minerals such as chromium and platinum derived above all from South Africa.[58] Whether Western dependency is in fact as great as is often claimed is subject to debate, but it is clear that no comparable Soviet dependency exists.[59] Attempts to portray Soviet motives in Africa as an aspect of a policy of resource denial tend to ignore the Soviet Union's own stake in its economic engagements and the fact that ultimately it is the interests of the supplier states that would be most effected by a disruption of markets. An attempt to boycott or redirect vital trade flows would undermine the Soviet Union's political base in Africa and could probably not be successfully imposed at any rate. Resource denial is not a discernible goal of Soviet policy. Secure access to the mineral wealth of Africa is much more likely to be effected by regional instability provoked by the untenable policies of Pretoria than it is by willful Soviet action.

Political Motives

Soviet political and diplomatic behavior in Africa includes a number of relatively stable components that also reveal something about the nature of the motives underlying Soviet African policy. These include: (1) the search for stable state-to-state relations under the general rubric of peaceful coexistence; (2) selective, tactical support for national liberation movements judged sympathetic to Soviet purposes; (3) a wide range of contacts between social, cultural, and political organizations (the Afro-Asian People's Solidarity Organization, the International Union of Students, the World Federation of Trade Union, the World Peace Council) aimed at building a base for improved diplomatic relations; (4) unqualified opposition to the South African Republic, the apartheid system, and the South African presence in Namibia; and (5) the pursuit of cooperative, complementary policies with its Warsaw Pact and Cuban allies.

A foundation for all Soviet initiatives in Africa has been support for the OAU and the mechanisms of inter-African political accommodation which it has established.[60] The Soviet record in this regard is quite good. Both of the large-scale commitments of armed forces in Africa sponsored by the

USSR (Angola and Ethiopia) were undertaken on behalf of recognized governments and with the approval of most OAU members. The USSR has opposed secessionist movements and ethnic separatism even when political advantage might seem to have lain in supporting such tendencies. Despite its own occasionally dubious strategic behavior, the USSR has seconded OAU demands for the liquidation of all foreign military bases on African territory, and there is no evidence of substantial Soviet involvement in the organization of Africa's numerous *coups d'êtat*.[61] Support for national liberation movements is no exception to the rule, as the legitimacy of such movements and of armed struggle as a tactic is widely recognized within both the OAU and the United Nations.

As elsewhere, treaties of friendship and cooperation define special relationships with favored allies, and the Soviet Union has been modestly successful in negotiating such treaties with African states. At present friendship treaties exist with Angola (1976), Mozambique (1977), Ethiopia (1978), and the Congo (1981). The exact nature of the obligations which these treaties carry with them remains eminently vague, however, and the abrogation of former treaties by Egypt and Somalia without notable Soviet reaction indicates that their binding force is relatively small.

On the regional level, Soviet diplomacy has focused on cultivating positive relations with key actors and intensifying ties with socialist oriented states. The Soviets have succeeded in establishing a more important diplomatic presence in Africa over the past decade, but they have also experienced major setbacks. As in the military and economic realms, Soviet diplomatic involvement is very much outweighed by the corresponding Western role.

In northern Africa, since the reorientation of the Sudan and Egypt, in a classic case of diplomatic opportunism Libya has loomed larger as a Soviet regional ally of convenience. There are limits to the Soviet-Libyan influence relationship however; Mu'ammar al-Qadhdhafi's political philosophy and regional ambitions are at odds with Soviet purposes, and the alliance rests upon narrowly instrumental perceptions.[62] Meanwhile, the Soviet relationship with Algeria, a traditional friend in the region, has quietly soured since the death of Houari Boumédienne, as Chadli Bendjedid has sought to disengage from the Western Sahara conflict and to adjust Algeria's international alignments.[63] In west Africa improved relations with Nigeria have been pursued doggedly for years, and despite its pro-Western orientation the Soviets have managed to maintain stable contacts with what is clearly the leading regional power.[64] In the Horn of Africa Soviet willingness to endanger its influence relationship with Somalia by rallying to the support of the Ethiopian revolution seems at least to have been conditioned by Ethiopia's much larger population and potential for regional predominance. Similar calculations emerge from the Soviet approach to other potentially strong regional powers such as Ghana, Cameroon, Zaire, or Kenya. Cautions color the Soviet relationship with socialist oriented regimes as well. The dynamics of nationalism, anticolonialism, and nonalignment translate into a jealous guarding of diplomatic independence, and for its part the USSR has maintained a formal distance from even its closest African allies. In no case has the degree of commitment that characterizes Soviet ties with a Cuba or Vietnam become evident; Soviet policymakers do not seem to feel that the stakes correspond to the costs and risks involved.

It is in southern Africa that Soviet diplomacy appears most challenging and assertive, but also most problematic. The USSR has made a clear commitment to building a regional policy around opposition to apartheid, and its frequent denunciations of the racist regime in Pretoria usually link South Africa directly to U.S. imperial interests. In the words of one commentary:

> South Africa serves the strategists of imperialism in its capacity as an integral part of the world capitalist system, where the "vital economic, strategic, moral, and political interests of the West" are concentrated. Similar to the case of Israel in the Near East, the racist SAR [South African Republic] presents itself as the main fortress of imperialism on the African continent.[65]

The disintegration of Portuguese colonial structures and the creation of radical socialist regimes among the Front Line states has left the USSR well placed to exploit the violent confrontations which Pretoria's intransigence seems bound to create. As a backer of SWAPO and the ANC, and the guarantor of the regimes in Mozambique and Angola, the USSR is a factor in the liberation struggle, even if it is not a central one. The parallel between South Africa and Israel recurs in Soviet analysis, and Soviet strategy seems analogous in both cases: to manipulate the massive unpopularity of the settler states and their close ties with the United States in order to build a foundation for a more dynamic Soviet regional role.[66]

Such a policy contains both opportunities and risks. Repeated South African incursions into the Front Line states and attempts to destabilize their socialist oriented neighbors seem designed to insure that Mozambique, Angola, and perhaps other states as well will be forced to continue to rely upon Soviet and Cuban military assistance. Consistent support for SWAPO and the ANC would seem to bode well for the prospects of enhanced Soviet influence in a South Africa and Namibia finally subject to majority rule. The road to majority rule is beset with dangers however. The Soviet Union is in no position to intervene decisively on behalf of its allies against South Africa and in some ways finds itself overcommitted at present and on the horns of a strategic dilemma. The case of Zimbabwe indicates that a negotiated settlement, even in so explosively divided a region as southern Africa, is not beyond the realm of possibility. Nor is there any reason to believe that black majority regimes in Namibia and South Africa would be any more amenable to Soviet purposes than any other African national government. To argue, as have some analysts, that Soviet influence in southern Africa is based upon a continuation of the present stalemate and that therefore Soviet policy is predicated upon avoiding a negotiated settlement while simultaneously fanning the flames of resistance seems to undervalue the extent to which the USSR too is exposed in the region, with a good deal of prestige and commitment at stake. Like most other external actors, the USSR finds itself riding the tiger's back in southern Africa and is far from being in control of events.

In pursuit of political influence the Soviet Union has functioned cooperatively with its Cuban and Warsaw Pact allies. To describe the role of Cubans and East Germans in Africa as that of puppets or surrogates no doubt tends to undervalue the independent sources of their policies, and one should not exaggerate the extent to which the USSR controls the international behavior of even its closest allies. At the same time, Cuba and the German Democratic Republic (GDR) remain substantially dependent upon the Soviet Union and are certainly constrained not to behave in ways which Moscow considers unacceptable. Cuban and East German policies have independent motives, but they also complement Soviet initiatives and may be considered as an aspect of the overall Soviet impact in Africa. The Cuban military interventions in Angola and Ethiopia turned civil and regional conflicts in directions sympathetic to Soviet interests and allowed resort to a military option without the destabilizing commitment of Soviet troops. The GDR has adopted more specialized functions including the training of security forces and possesses a network of diplomatic relationships with African states that rivals that of the USSR. The role of Cuba, the GDR, and other communist states in Africa must be coordinated with Soviet purposes, and this process of coordination no doubt presents occasional difficulties. But on balance it represents a not negligible extension of Soviet diplomacy that is in many ways comparable to the role of France, Great Britain, and other European powers as an extension of the overall Western presence.[67]

At least brief mention should also be made of the Soviet relationship with one other communist state active in Africa—the People's Republic of China. During the late 1960s and early 1970s China launched a diplomatic offensive in Africa, and the desire to prevent an extension of Chinese influence on the continent was undoubtedly a major source of the Soviet-Cuban intervention in Angola and the broadening of Soviet commitments that followed.[68] The situation at present has altered considerably, however. The policy reorientation that followed the death of Mao Zedong has led to a major reduction of the Chinese role in Africa. China seems more than ever aware of the limits of the resources at its disposal in the search for influence in the Third World and preoccupied with its own development priorities. Sino-Soviet rivalry, once a fundamental source of the Soviet commitment in Africa, has become considerably less intense and does not seem to represent a substantial Soviet concern looking into the 1980s and beyond.

On balance, the Soviet diplomatic approach to Africa bespeaks the caution and constraint that have underlain virtually all Soviet activities on the continent. Regional dynamics, structural weaknesses when compared with Western rivals, and the need to balance and coordinate Soviet interests with those of Cuban and Warsaw Pact allies all place limitations around the scope of Soviet initiatives. These constraints are reflected by Soviet political priorities, where flexibility, careful observance of OAU guidelines, and a readiness to abstract state-to-state relations from their ideological context have characterized an essentially conventional diplomacy built around long-term calculations of advantage. In a continent riven by conflicts on all levels, it is likely that the future will see no lack of opportunity to exploit instability, but the Soviets may be expected to move within a carefully defined margin of costs and risks. Despite occasional setbacks, the Soviet commitment to building a political presence in the long-term seems to have a strong realistic core.

Conclusion

Africa presents Soviet foreign policy planners with a combination of opportunities and dilemmas. An image of Africa that emphasizes the long-term nonviability of the West's dominant position coexists with a sharpened awareness of the limitations which restrict Soviet initiatives in the short term. The inadequacy of military assistance as a means for building influence must be balanced against an inability to provide extensive developmental aid. The possibilities that offer themselves in southern Africa are tempered by the risks of involvement in a region where increasingly violent confrontation seems on the agenda.

Underlying Soviet engagement is the fact that Soviet interests in Africa, though real, are seldom truly vital. Strategic involvement reflects global rivalry with the United States but does not relate to essential security concerns. Economic involvement is modest and does not provide useful policy levers. Political interests are expressed pragmatically and reflect a search for gradual, incremental accumulation of influence.

Two characterizations of Soviet African policy have dominated analysis in the West. The first, which might be designated *geostrategic-expansionism*, views Soviet policy as an integral part of a global strategy aimed at the weakening and subversion of the West.[69] Because of its economic and strategic importance to the Western powers and Japan, Africa is presumed to offer the Soviet Union the opportunity to strike at its global rivals indirectly. It is perceived, in Fidel Castro's charismatic phrase, as the weak link in the chain of imperialism.[70] The steady expansion of Soviet power projection capacity, the coups in Angola and Ethiopia, and the looming issue of apartheid and majority rule in South Africa are said to mark Africa as a major focus of East-West confrontation in the years to come.

The geostrategic argument has no doubt exerted a major influence upon policy formulation in the United States, but it is generally alarmist and overstated.[71] An alternative characterization closer to the mainstream of Western academic evaluations might be termed *defensive opportunism*.[72] This perspective assumes that Soviet African policy is not informed by a grand design and emphasizes that the USSR does not have essential security concerns at stake and is not strong enough to directly challenge the Western powers. The Soviet and Cuban initiatives in Angola and Ethiopia were produced by uniquely favorable conjunctures which are not likely to recur in the near future, nor have Soviet gains as a result of their African involvements been anywhere near as dramatic or permanent as has sometimes been claimed. Overreliance upon arms transfers as a means of penetrating the region and inability to provide allies with adequate economic assistance has emerged as a fundamental contradiction in Soviet policy, which as a result has entered a defensive phase seeking to consolidate the modest gains of the past decade. In general, Africa is presumed to remain very low on the list of Soviet foreign policy priorities.

Both of these characterizations, with their emphasis upon the implications of Soviet initiatives for the West, seem to neglect the historical context within which Soviet penetration of the continent has occurred and to undervalue Africa itself as an independent force. Soviet engagement in Africa might be alternately described as the product of two complementary structural dynamics: the dynamic of superpower rivalry in a bipolar world, with its dialectic of initiative and response, and the dynamic of African decolonization, which has proceeded unevenly and left Africa weak, divided, and a prey to external influence,[73] but which remains a reality underlying all African affairs. These dynamics have drawn the USSR almost inexorably into the maelstrom of African politics, but they also serve to delimit the extent of what the Soviets can hope to achieve.

On one level there is no need for illusions concerning the Soviet role in Africa. The Soviets are engaged for their own hard reasons, relating importantly to their ongoing rivalry with the United States, and African initiatives once again make clear just how compelling the Soviet Union's status as a superpower with global concerns has become. A struggle for influence is being waged by both superpowers in Africa, and as often as not it is the African peoples themselves who are the primary victims. The USSR is neither a principled, adequate, nor reliable source of support for African liberation movements and socialist oriented regimes, and the developmental model that it proposes is at least flawed under African circumstances.

Nonetheless the need for military aid and external sponsorship can make a controlled relationship with the USSR an attractive option for African regimes interested in pursuing radical change and balancing the influence of former colonial powers. The Soviet Union's assertion that neocolonialism represents a primary source of the Third World's contemporary problems is widely shared in Africa itself. Optimistic evaluations of the West's ability to upstage the USSR in Africa by providing a more attractive source for investment and aid should perhaps be more attentive to the context in which development Western-style is presumed to occur and to the kind of developmental model offered. In most cases this is an elite-oriented approach that is bound to intensify class and social tensions.[74] Revolutionary transformations seem on the agenda for Africa's future, and a continuing proliferation of radical regimes driven toward a more positive relationship with the USSR by the imperative of survival is a real possibility.

Soviet motives in Africa can perhaps be best understood in terms of a hierarchy of short- and long-term priorities. Given the Soviet commitment to pursuing a global diplomacy, the centrality of Soviet–American competition, and its own instability in the postcolonial era, Africa has emerged as an important area for strategic, economic, and political competition between East and West. The USSR has been relatively successful in establishing itself as a force in African affairs but is also aware that it lacks the means to directly challenge Western vital interests and has constructed policies around carefully defined tactical initiatives with allowances for reversal or retreat. In the short term there is no Soviet drive for Africa in progress and no imminent Soviet threat.

Tactical flexibility is possible because without essential security concerns at stake, the Soviet Union can afford to build a purposeful long-term strategy around a gradual and incremental extension of influence. The long-term thrust of Soviet policy is less a threat than a challenge, and one that might well be taken seriously. For all their rhetorical and self-serving trappings, the Soviet concepts of neocolonialism and socialist orientation provide a measured evaluation of alternative developmental strategies sensitive to Africa's problems, convinced of the inadequacy of Western models, and focused on the prospects for revolutionary change. Whether the process they describe is more likely to lead to the emergence of an autonomous, indigenous African socialism, or dependent Soviet "clients," is perhaps at present an open question.

In many ways the drama of contemporary Africa has little to do with the USSR. It is the drama of decolonization, of the struggle against apartheid, of the challenges of hunger and underdevelopment. The Soviet Union and its allies have made themselves a part of this unfolding drama and will no doubt have something to say about its eventual resolutions, but their importance should not be overblown. Ultimately the Soviet challenge in Africa is the challenge of Africa itself, and only policies designed to confront African dilemmas in African terms will be in a position to meet it.

Notes

1. See Zbigniew Brzezinski, ed., *Africa and the Communist World* (Stanford: Hoover Institution Press, 1963).
2. For examples see Karl Breyer, *Moskaus Faust in Afrika* (Stuttgart: Seewald Verlag, 1979) and Ian Greig, *The Communist Challenge to Africa: An Analysis of Contemporary Soviet, Chinese, and Cuban Policies* (London: Foreign Affairs Publishing Company, 1977).
3. See Michael T. Kaufman, "Soviet Influence in Africa Seems To Be Fading," *International Herald Tribune*, 24 November 1983, p. 10.
4. A welcome addition to the literature is the recent study by Winrich Kühne, *Die Politik der Sowjetunion in Afrika: Bedingungen und Dynamik ihres ideologischen, ökonomischen und militärischen Engagements* (Baden-Baden: Nomos, 1983). Kühne's work represents a comprehensive study of Soviet Africa policy packed with data and sound judgments.
5. Benin, Botswana, Burundi, Cape Verde, the Central African Republic, Chad, the Comoro Islands, Djibouti, Equatorial Guinea, Ethiopia, Gambia, Guinea, Guinea-Bissau, Lesotho, Malawi, Mali, Niger, Rwanda, São-Tomé e Principe, Sierra-Leone, Somalia, the Sudan, Tanzania, Togo, Uganda, and Upper Volta. See Christophe Butsch, "L'Afrique noire frappée de plein fouet," *Le Monde diplomatique* (November 1982):12.
6. G. Smirnov and A. Triasunov, "Vekhi Sovetskoi Afrikanistiki," *Aziia i afrika segodnia* 12 (1982):18-21, trace the evolution of Soviet Africanology. See also Milena Chelli, "L'évolution historique de l'organisation des recherches sur l'Afrique en URSS," *Revue d'etudes comparatives Est-Ouest* 8, no. 1 (1977):165-178. Anatolii Gromyko, *Afrika: progress, trudnosti, perspektivy* (Moscow: Politizdat, 1981) provides a good recent account. Anatolii Gromyko has been director of the Africa Institute of the Soviet Academy of Sciences since 1977. He is the son of Soviet Foreign Minister Andrei Gromyko.
7. A.A. Rumianstev, ed., *Nauchnyi kommunizm: slovar'*, 3rd ed. (Moscow: Izd. politicheskoi literatury, 1980), pp. 201-202.
8. N. Ermoshkin, "Neokolonializm transnatsional'nykh korporatsii," *Kommunist* 18 (December 1981):97.
9. V. Sivtsev and V. Seidov, 'Informatsionnyi imperializm i bor'ba za novyi mezhdunarodnyi informatsionnyi poriadok," *Mirovaia ekonomika i mezhdunarodnye otnosheniia* [hereafter cited as MEMO] 3 (1983):51-63, and A.A. Ozadovskii, *SShA i Afrika: problemy neokolonializma* (Moscow: Mysl', 1977), pp. 243-293, provide discussions of the problem. The USSR

has sponsored Third World demands for a "New International Information Order" in UNESCO forums over U.S. opposition.

10. I. Ivanov, "Transnatsional'nye korporatsii vo vneshnei politike imperializma," *MEMO* 10 (1981):45.

11. The point is disputed by Soviet scholars. S.I. Kuznetsov, Iu. I. Komar, and V.A. Beilis, *Afrikanskii gorod (kriticheskoi ocherk zarubezhnykh kontseptsii)* (Moscow: Nauka, 1979) attempt to refute the argument that the nascent African proletariat represents a "labor aristocracy."

12. N. Volkhov, "O masshtabakh neokolonial'noi ekspluatatsii osvobodovshikhsia gosudarstv," *MEMO* 9 (1983):47-59 attempts to measure this transfer quantitatively. See also A.A. Gromyko, *Vneshniaia ekspansiia kapitala. Istoriia i sovremennost'* (Moscow: Mysl', 1982), p. 427. One Soviet analyst has estimated that neocolonialism has extracted more real value from the Third World in the past thirty years than in the preceding three-hundred years of outright colonialism. Iu. Alimov, "Dvizhenie neprisoedineniia na vazhnom rubezhe," *Kommunist* 7 (1983):101. See also M. Volkov, "Formy i metody sovremennogo neokolonializma," *Mezhdunarodnaia zhizn'* 2 (1983):20-28.

13. Ivanov, "Transnatsional'nye korporatsii," p. 34.

14. For a definitive current account see S. Iu. Medvedkov, *Transnatsional'nye korporatsii i obostrenie kapitalisticheskikh protivorechii* (Moscow: Mysl', 1982), and for a focus upon Africa, G. Roshchin, "Strategiia transnatsional'nykh korporatsii v Afrike," *Mezhdunarodnaia zhizn'* 4 (1983):70-77.

15. See I. Ivanov, "Kontseptsii 'bednykh' i 'bogatykh' stran: istoki, sushchnost', napravlennost'," *MEMO* 1 (1983):25.

16. Anatolii Gromyko, "Afrika segodnia," *Kommunist* 13 (September 1982):81.

17. Smirnov and Triasunov, "Vekhi Sovetskoi Afrikanistiki," p. 20.

18. The noncapitalist path of development is formally defined as follows: "the process of the gradual accumulation in nations liberated from colonial dependence of the objective and subjective prerequisites for a transition to the construction of socialism . . . one of the paths of transition to socialism for formally backward nations and peoples." *Nauchnyi kommunizm*, p. 198.

19. Vl. F. Li, "Politicheskaia nadstroika v obshchestvakh sotsialisticheskoi orientatsii," *Voprosy filosofii* 9 (1981):3-16.

20. Iu. I. Iudin, *Gosudarstvo sotsialisticheskoi orientatsii* (Moscow: Nauka, 1975) provides important early definitions. See also the insightful account by Sylvia Edgington, "The State of Socialist Orientation: A Soviet Model for Political Development," *Soviet Union/Union Sovietique* 8, no. 2 (1981):223-251.

21. E. Primakov, "Strany sotsialisticheskoi orientatsii: trudnyi no real'nyi perekhod k sotsializmu," *MEMO* 7 (1981):14.

22. Gromyko, "Afrika segodnia," p. 88. Compare with Brezhnev's description in his report to the 26th Party Congress of the CPSU in February 1982: "the development of these nations [states of socialist orientation] along the road of progress does not, of course, proceed smoothly, complicated circumstances arise. But the basic directions are similar *[skhodnye]*. This means the gradual liquidation of the position of imperialist monopolies, the local large bourgeoisie and feudal elements, the limitation of the activity of foreign capital. This means the securing by the people's government of the commanding heights of the economy and a transition to the planned development of productive forces, the encouragement of the cooperative movement in the countryside. This means the enhanced role of the toiling masses in social life, the gradual strengthening of the state apparatus through the activities of national cadre devoted to the people. This means the anti-imperialist character of the foreign policies of these nations. Within them revolutionary parties grow stronger, expressing the interests of the broad masses of laborers." *Pravda*, 24 February 1981.

23. Primakov, "Strany sotsialisticheskoi orientatsii," p. 13.

24. G. Mirskii, "Osobennosti revoliutsionnogo protsessa v Azii i Afrike," *MEMO* 6 (1983):149. Mirskii paraphrases from G.F. Kim, *Ot natsional'nogo osvobozhdeniia k sotsial'nom. Sotsial'no-politicheskie aspekty sovremennykh natsional'no-osvoboditel'nykh revoliutsii* (Moscow: Nauka, 1982), p. 148.

25. Elizabeth Valkenier, *The Soviet Union and the Third World* (New York: Praeger, 1983) develops the point expertly and at length.

26. See *Pravda*, 5 October 1976.

27. See particularly the provocative study by L. Goncharov, "Afrika v bor'be za novyi mezhdunarodnyi ekonomicheskii poriadok," *MEMO* 6 (1981):49-62.

28. Jan Tinbergen (Coordinator), *Reshaping the International Order: A Report to the Club of Rome* (New York: Dutton, 1976).

29. Willy Brandt (Chairman), *North-South: A Programme for Survival* (Cambridge, Mass.: MIT Press, 1980).

30. Soviet commentary emphasizes prospects for regional cooperation. See L. Stoklitskaia, "V poiskakh formuly sotrudnichestva," *Aziia i afrika segodnia* 4 (1982):28-30.

31. Iu. S. Novopashin, "Razvitie mezhdunarodnykh otnoshenii novogo tipa v svete Leninskikh idei," *Voprosy istorii* 8 (1983):5-20, and *Sotsialisticheskii internatsionalizm: teoriia i praktika mezhdunarodnykh otnoshenii novogo tipa* (Moscow: Izd. politicheskoi literatury, 1979).

32. Edgington, "The State of Socialist Orientation," p. 251, argues that despite "its obvious attractions as an ideal form, the model probably faces an uncertain future."

33. See Hartmut Elsenhaus, *Abhängiger Kapitalismus oder bürokratische Entwicklungsgesellschaft—Versuch über den Staat in der Dritten Welt* (Frankfurt am Main: 1981) for elaboration. Elsenhaus contends that the "bürokratische Entwicklungsgesellschaft" (bureaucratized developing society) represents a model that cannot effectively be placed within a socialist–capitalist dichotomy.

34. David and Marina Ottaway, *Afrocommunism* (New York: Africana, 1981).

35. Smirnov and Triasunov, "Vekhi Sovetskoi Afrikanistiki," p. 20. Soviet analysts do not formally list states of socialist orientation in Africa. States that have occasionally been mentioned in association with the category include Algeria, Angola, Benin, Cape Verde, the Congo, Ethiopia, Guinea, Guinea-Bissau, Libya, Mali, Mozambique, São Tomé e Principe, Tanzania, and Zimbabwe.

36. See Fred Halliday and Maxine Molyneux, *The Ethiopian Revolution* (London: Verso, 1981), pp. 268–283 for elaboration.

37. Edward T. Wilson, *Russia and Black Africa before World War II* (New York: Holmes & Meier, 1974) emphasizes historical continuity in Soviet policies.

38. See the comments by U.S. President Ronald Reagan in *Africa Report* 26 (July/August 1980):4.

39. See Mohammed Anis Salem, "The Soviet Union and Egypt after Sadat: Premises, Prospects, and Problems," in Mark V. Kauppi and R. Craig Nation, eds., *The Soviet Union and the Middle East in the 1980s: Opportunities, Constraints, and Dilemmas* (Lexington, Mass.: D.C. Heath, Lexington Books, 1983), pp. 163–180.

40. A. Shvedov and A. Podtserov, "SSSR i strany Severnoi Afriki," *Mezhdunarodnaia zhizn'* 5 (1983):60, note that "As for Northern Africa, the imperialist powers are striving to secure for themselves a military presence in this strategically important region, contiguous to Europe and serving simultaneously as a type of 'bridge' to Africa south of the Sahara."

41. N.N. Tarasov, "Afrikanskii rog v voenno-politicheskikh planakh Vashingtona," *SShA: politika, ekonomika, ideologiia* 4 (1981):30–38. Tarasov asserts that "The place of the Horn of Africa in the global imperialist strategy of the U.S.A. is determined above all by its location at the crossroads of sea lanes between the Indian Ocean and Europe and on the doorstep of the world's most important oil-supplying region (the Persian Gulf, the Near and Middle East, the eastern Mediterranean) which, as is well known, have been declared spheres of 'vital interest' for the U.S.A." (p. 30).

42. In South Africa's "Operation Protea" of August/September 1982 over 10,000 South African troops crossed into southern Angola, and Soviet

military personnel were reported killed and an NCO taken prisoner. See Kühne, *Die Politik der Sowjetunion in Afrika*, p. 226.

43. See the discussion in ibid., pp. 169-174. The author concludes that "The superiority of Western air power in African conflict zones is unequivocal." (p. 173).

44. As cited in ibid., p. 132.

45. South Africa has increased the size of its armed forces in recent years and emphasized conventional combined arms tactics as well as counterinsurgency. See "South Africa: Battle School of Philosophy," *Defense & Foreign Affairs Daily* no. 11, 22 January 1979, p. 2. Its standing forces number over 90,000 and it is capable of mobilizing over 500,000 men. It is quite possible that South Africa is capable of producing nuclear arms of reasonable sophistication. Kenneth L. Adelman and Albion W. Knight, "Can South Africa Go Nuclear?" *Orbis* 23, no. 3 (1978):633-648.

46. Cited from *Jeune Afrique*, 27 October 1982, p. 33 in E. Tarabrin, "Ekspansionistskaia politika SShA v Afrike," *Mezhdunarodnaia zhizn'* 9 (1983):47.

47. Tarabrin, "Ekspansionistskaia politika SShA v Afrike," pp. 46-47.

48. *Postroeno pri ekonomicheskom i tekhnicheskom sodeistvii Sovetskogo Soiuza* (Moscow: Mezhdunarodnye otnosheniia, 1982), p. 16.

49. Note commentary in Roshchin, "Strategiia transnatsional'nykh korporatsii v Afrike," p. 71.

50. Kühne, *Die Politik der Sowjetunion in Afrika*, p. 131.

51. Orah Cooper and Carol Fogarty, "Soviet Military and Economic Aid to the Less Developed Countries, 1954-1978," in Morris Bernstein, ed., *The Soviet Economy: Continuity and Change* (Boulder, Colo.: Westview Press, 1981), p. 254.

52. United States Department of State, *Conventional Arms Transfers in the Third World, 1972-81* Special Report No. 102 (Washington, D.C.: Bureau of Public Affairs, August 1982) provides basic data. See also Stephen T. Hosmer and Thomas W. Wolfe, *Soviet Policy and Practice Toward Third World Conflicts* (Lexington, Mass.: D.C. Heath, Lexington Books, 1983), p. 74, and Bruce Arlinghaus, ed., *Arms for Africa* (Lexington, Mass.: D.C. Heath, Lexington Books, 1982).

53. Mention might also be made of the role that African coastal waters play in the Soviet fishing harvest. The Soviet Union has signed fishing pacts with a number of African littoral states, the terms of which have sometimes proved controversial. See *Jeune Afrique*, 15 November 1978, p. 51.

54. Estimated from Central Intelligence Agency, *Communist Aid Activities in Non-Communist Less Developed Countries, 1954-79* (Washington, D.C.: U.S. Government Printing Office, October 1980). Some Western analysts have contended that in fact Soviet foreign aid totals are consistently exaggerated in Soviet statistics. Richard Bernstein, "Study by British

Challenges Soviet Claims on Foreign Aid," *The New York Times*, 3 January 1984, p. A8.

55. V.D. Popov, *Ekonomicheskoe sotrudnichestvo stran SEV s razvivaiushchimisia gosudarstvami* (Moscow: Ekonomika, 1982), p. 64 cites over 300 such agreements concluded in the Third World by the early 1980s.

56. See particularly L.L. Fituni, *Razvitie ekonomiki nezavisimoi Angoly* (Moscow: Nauka, 1981). Fituni acknowledges the central role played by Western investment in Angola's economy and the need to continue to attract such investment. He emphasizes three factors that help to delimit the impact of Western involvement: (1) the drying up of sources of capital from "traditional" investor nations linked to the former colonial structure (Portugal, South Africa, the Federal Republic of Germany); (2) the growth of the role of new investor nations not significantly present during the colonial period (Italy, Brazil, Sweden); and (3) the fact that all capital investment remains "essentially" under state control and is integrated into a planned, harmonious development perspective (pp. 94–95).

57. Marcel Drach, "Quand la planification se veut au service du développement autocentré," *Le Monde diplomatique* (October 1983):14–15. The Soviet Union ranks a distant fourth (after France, Switzerland, and China) as a source of investment for the Congo.

58. E.N. Kondraskov, "SShA-Afrika: syr'evoi aspekt," *SShA: politika, ekonomika, ideologiia* 7 (1982):67–75, and E. Tarabrin, "Afrika v global'noi strategii imperializma," *MEMO* 2 (1982):26–28. For a Western account emphasizing the same strategic dependency see Walter Schilling, "Südafrika als Problem westlicher Sicherheit," *Aussenpolitik* 4 (1981): 393–402.

59. For an argument downplaying Western dependency see Carl-Wolfgang Sames, "Europe's strategic mineral needs: economic and political aspects," *International Affairs Bulletin* 1 (1981):5–18. Exaggerated reports of impending Soviet shortages have appeared in the Western press (i.e., Herbert Meyer, "Russia's Sudden Rush for Raw Materials," *Fortune* [28 July 1980], but in fact the USSR is well-endowed with most significant strategic minerals. What is at issue is the Soviet ability to economically exploit its own reserves and to supply CMEA allies. See François Geze, "L'U.R.S.S. et les règles du jeu," *Le Monde diplomatique* (March 1981): 10–12.

60. See Z. Takareva, "OAE: balans dvukh desiatiletii," *Aziia i afrika segodnia* 5 (1983):20–23.

61. Kühne, *Die Politik der Sowjetunion in Afrika*, pp. 103–104 notes that there is no convincing proof of important Soviet involvement in any of the forty-odd military coups which have occurred in twenty-two African nations between 1958–1981. The Soviet Union, for its part, accuses the U.S. CIA of repeated complicity in the organization of coups and other forms

of subversive activity in Africa. A. Khazunov, "TsRU protiv Afriki," *Aziia i afrika segodnia* 3 (1983):9-12.

62. Sami G. Hajjar, "The Jamahiriya Experiment in Libya: Qaddafi and Rousseau," *The Journal of Modern African Studies* 18 (February 1980): 181-200, and Oye Ogunbadejo, "Qaddafi's North African Design," *International Security* 8 (January 1983):176-178.

63. Daniel Junqua, " 'Rectification' à Alger, nouvelle donne au Maghreb," *Le Monde diplomatique* (November 1983):1-11.

64. See the special report by L. Geveling and L. Pribytkovskii, "Nigeriia '83: uroki 'vtorei respubliki'," *Aziia i afrika segodnia* 4 (1983):24-31. The coup of 31 December 1983, which overthrew the elected government of Shehu Shagari and brought the Nigerian military back to power under a council headed by Major General Mohammed Buhari, only serves to underline the need for flexibility in the volatile African political environment.

65. A. Urnov, "Al'ians Vashington-Pretoriia i Afrika," *MEMO* 3 (1983):47.

66. The Namibian problem is the most pressing regional concern of the moment. See V. Iu. Vasil'kov, "Problema Namibii i pozitsiia SShA," *SShA: politika, ekonomika, ideologiia* 4 (1983):49-52 for a Soviet critique of the U.S. position.

67. On Cuba's Africa policy see William M. LeoGrande, *Cuba's Policy in Africa, 1959-1980* (Berkeley: Institute of International Studies, 1980). On the GDR see Melvin Croan, "A New Afrika Korps?," *The Washington Quarterly* 3 (Winter 1980):21-37; Winrich Kühne and Bernard von Plate, "Two Germanies in Africa," *Africa Report* 25 (April 1980):11-18; and Bernard von Plate, "DDR—Aussenpolitik Richtung Afrika und Araber," *Aussenpolitik* 1 (1978):73-83. For an East German evaluation see Klaus Willerding, "Zur Afrika-Politik der DDR," *Deutsche Aussenpolitik* 8 (1979):5-19.

68. See Arthur Jay Klinghoffer, *The Angolan War: A Study in Soviet Policy in the Third World* (Boulder, Colo.: Westview Press, 1980), pp. 101-108.

69. See Walter F. Hahn and Alvin J. Cottrell, *Soviet Shadow over Africa* (Coral Gables: University of Miami Center for Advanced International Studies, 1976).

70. *Afrique-Asie*, May 16, 1977, p. 17.

71. See Chester Crocker, Roger Fontaine, Dmitri Simes, and Robert E. Henderson, *Implications of Soviet and Cuban Activities in Africa for U.S. Policy* (Washington, D.C.: Georgetown University Center for Strategic and International Studies, 1979), and the summary and critical commentary in *Africa Report* (January-February 1980):44-53.

72. For examples see David E. Albright, "Moscow's African Policy of the 1970s," in David E. Albright, ed., *Communism in Africa* (Bloomington:

Indiana University Press, 1980), pp. 35-66; Henry Bienen, "Soviet Political Relations with Africa," *International Security* 6 (Spring 1982):153-173; and Kühne, *Die Politik der Sowjetunion in Afrika*.

73. Gérard Chaliand, *L'Enjeu africain* (Paris: Editions du Seuil, 1980) provides an argument to this effect.

74. Nigeria provides a case in point. In this, the largest and potentially most prosperous of Black African nations, the collapse of oil revenues (which declined by more than 50 percent between 1980 and 1983) has helped to create a deeply rooted economic crisis. Confronting the need for stern austerity measures and a devaluation of the naira, it is as yet unclear how Nigeria's new military government will fare. See Laurent Zecchini, "Le Nigéria aux arrêts de rigueur," *Le Monde* (16, 17, and 18 February 1984).

4 The Soviet Union and Eastern Europe: Patterns of Competition and Collaboration in Southern Africa

Christopher Coker

It is perhaps surprising that Eastern Europe's contacts with the African continent have attracted so little attention. In many respects the East European states acting either together or alone have been in the vanguard of Soviet bloc activities. The Czech arms shipments to Egypt in 1955 and three years later to Guinea (the first country in Sub-Saharan Africa to purchase arms from the Communist world) have become a point of departure for any understanding of Soviet-African relations in the early 1960s.

In the sphere of trade as well Eastern Europe led the way; the Soviet Union merely followed. In 1956 its trade with Sub-Saharan Africa was four times greater than that of the Soviet Union.[1] Only the most recent developments have disguised the scope and scale of these initial commitments, understandably perhaps, when one considers that in 1978 the Soviet Union sold Ethiopia 25 percent of the arms it had sold to Africa since 1955 and extended to Morocco a loan that pushed its economic assistance to the continent within reach of America's for the first time in twenty-five years. Nevertheless, it would be unwise to ignore the fact—the massive Soviet arms and aid commitments in the period 1974 to 1978 notwithstanding—that Eastern Europe has played an increasingly significant role in Africa since 1972, a role central to any understanding of the mainsprings of Soviet policy.

The Mineral Factor

Early in 1956 a research group funded by the Soviet Academy of Scientists proposed that Eastern Europe should begin to import commodities directly from Africa. Ever since that time the East Europeans have not felt able to rely exclusively on supplies from their main ally. Not only are their own resources clearly inadequate; falling production within the Soviet Union has

---

I am grateful to Kurt Campbell of the International Institute for Strategic Studies and Alan Smith of the School of Slavonic Studies for bringing to my attention some of the sources cited in the text.

continued to set back the development of its own natural resources at the very time that economic growth has continued to fuel domestic demand.

Generally speaking, the interest of the East Europeans centered on the possibility of deriving the two benefits discussed by the Polish economist, Ignacy Sachs, in 1961:

1. Economic relations with the African countries hold out the long-term prospect of obtaining scarce materials cheaply in exchange for capital and consumer goods.
2. Economic relations with the socialist countries will strengthen the bargaining position of the less developed countries with the imperialist powers.[2]

Once Eastern Europe found itself facing the prospect of competition with the West for access to finite resources, its policy in Africa began to take on a very different dimension and to present challenges of a very different order from those which have been traditionally discussed. To reinforce Sach's arguments one can draw on a number of observations made by both Soviet and East European writers in this period. One Czech economist contended that economic cooperation with the recently independent states of Africa had "great significance for an industrially developed country with an insufficient energy base," such as his own.[3] Ever anxious that the Western multinational corporations (MNCs) might exploit their control of the continent's resources to deny Eastern Europe access to them, the Soviet Union accused the Western powers of deliberately underdeveloping new resources as part of a neocolonial conspiracy to perpetuate Africa's underdevelopment.[4]

It was the extent of Western control over minerals during this period that concerned the Council for Mutual Economic Assistance (CMEA). Since 1945 a very considerable part of world production in raw materials had been concentrated in a handful of large companies. In oil seven leading international corporations controlled 88 percent of the traded product. In aluminum, six firms controlled about 85 percent of the world's smelting capacity. In other areas they managed to maintain control over foreign sources of supply by using vertical integration, long-term contracts, and monopsony arrangements.[5] Even when the Soviet Union was involved in the export of commodities in which the MNCS dominated such as petroleum and aluminum, it was rarely if ever prepared to challenge Western control of the market. In tin and aluminum it coordinated its sales with that of the Western leaders, while in oil it carefully shaved its prices, reducing them only enough to secure the necessary market penetration.[6]

It was no wonder then that Eastern Europe spent the period up to 1973 urging the Third World to take greater control of its own resources. At the

Twenty-first Session of the United Nations General Assembly (1966), the Polish delegation played a crucial role in drafting the resolution on "Permanent sovereignty over natural resources" which enshrined the right of all developing countries to increase control over companies fully or partly operated by foreign capital. Six years later the resolution was revived in a motion adopted at the fourth meeting of the nonaligned countries in Algiers that provided the ultimate rationale for the OPEC embargo of 1973:

> The efforts undertaken or intensified by the Third World are evidence of a deep movement . . . which indisputably contains the seeds of a complete overthrow of the marketing system for the natural resources of the poor countries.[7]

By 1973 the first of Sach's concerns—access to Africa's metals—had become an even more pressing concern. In an article in *International Affairs* some time ago I argued that the measures introduced by the CMEA to increase mineral production in the Soviet Union spurred many East European countries to search for alternative (and cheaper) sources of supply outside the bloc, particularly after 1974 when the emergence of Marxist-Leninist states in Africa itself appeared to offer an opportunity to expand operations in a politically stable environment.[8]

I have no wish to repeat these arguments, only to underline the thesis that the East Europeans were prompted to look to Africa in earnest under pressure from changes within the CMEA with which, in many instances, they were unhappy as well as from changes within Africa after 1974 (most notably the appearance of Marxist-Leninist regimes in Angola, Guinea-Bissau, and Mozambique). Confronted by the Plan for Multilateral Integration which obliged every CMEA member to invest heavily in mining operations in the Soviet Union, obliged after 1975 to pay for Soviet resources at the prevailing market price every year instead of every five, and required to increase their contribution to the CMEA's Investment Fund of which the Soviet Union and Cuba were the only net recipients, it is not altogether surprising that the East Europeans turned to Africa as a much cheaper, if less reliable, option.

At the same time, the prospect of centrally planned economies in Southern Africa prompted the CMEA Secretariat to discuss the possibility of bringing Angola and Mozambique into its own Long Term Joint Cooperation Program for the fuel and raw material industries after its adoption in 1978. Seven years earlier the secretariat had insisted that the coordination of planning between socialist states was likely to provide the main momentum for "extending the international socialist division of labour."[9]

No one in Eastern Europe thought that such a course would ever take place in the absence of substantial political change in the developing world.

Yet this is precisely what transpired in Southern Africa in the wake of Portuguese decolonization. This was most clearly evident in Mozambique where the nationalization of the country's largest coal fields was agreed upon during a visit by the East German Minister of Coal and Energy and supervised by a team from East Germany's Ministry of Mines and Minerals. The GDR's interest in Mozambique's mineral potential extended beyond coal to many other sectors, all of which were provisionally mapped out within the first six months of 1978 by the East German-Mozambique Mixed Commission which toured the provinces of Manica and Zambesia in the summer. Outside Southern Africa the second smallest of the new Marxist-Leninist states, Benin, signed economic cooperation agreements with Czechoslovakia, East Germany, Hungary, Bulgaria, and Poland in the space of a single year (1979). This was also a year that saw the visit to Cotonou of trade delegations from Budapest and Prague.

In view of its earlier contacts with Africa, the scope of these ventures between 1972 and 1979 was quite unprecedented, putting Eastern Europe in the forefront of commercial links between the Soviet bloc and Sub-Saharan Africa. By 1979 there were 185 CMEA companies in the developing world of which just under half (75) were in Africa. Of the latter, 92 percent of their fixed assets were in resource development such as mining.[10] In the same period Romania had established thirty joint ventures in Africa which accounted for 85 percent of its total contracts in the countries concerned. Two-thirds of them were in Sub-Saharan Africa, primarily in metal extraction. Clearly international competition was no longer confined to the superpowers nor to political conflict. The arena in which they competed had been broadened to include commercial conflict. Consequential changes appeared likely to manifest themselves at several different points, but particularly in relations between Eastern Europe and the Soviet Union, and between the Soviet Union and the West.

CMEA and Raw Material Supply

Whether Eastern Europe will continue to rely on Southern Africa's resources, or whether its reliance is likely to increase, is debatable. Colin Lawson has raised two objections to my own interpretation of recent events: arguing that Eastern Europe now regrets its investment in Africa in the 1970s and is actively pressing the Soviet Union to increase its output of minerals and that the latter will be able to meet its allies' demands for the rest of the 1980s and beyond.[11] Neither of these arguments, I fear, bear up to much analysis.

While it is true, for example, that Romania's present Five Year Plan (1981–1985) calls for a greater expansion of trade within the CMEA as a way of avoiding market instability outside it, this objective is intended to be reached at the expense of trade with the West, not with the developing world. Trade with the Third World will probably remain for the foreseeable future at 20 to 30 percent.[12] Second, the Romanians have discovered that concessionary prices for fuels and raw materials upon which it did not rely in the past are considerably more difficult to negotiate with the Soviet Union than its partners. In 1980 it was forced to import 1.5m tons of Soviet oil at OPEC prices rather than the much lower CMEA rates. Trade subsidies from the Soviet Union have been "negligible" relative to other East European countries since 1974.[13] Indeed, low interest rates on Soviet credits fixed under present arrangements at 2 percent per annum have made the price of Soviet raw materials correspondingly high.

Romania is not the only country to have suffered in recent years. Even the existing supply of minerals to the CMEA is proving, if not prohibitively expensive, more expensive than ever. The Soviet Union continues to sell its partners in the CMEA natural resources at a significantly higher price than it does manufactured goods: the export prices of raw materials between 1975-1977 rose at a faster rate than the export prices of machinery and consumer goods.[14] Indeed, the rise in the price of fuels imported by Eastern Europe relative to the price of East European manufactured goods exported to the Soviet Union will probably continue to rise until the mid-1980s as the intra-CMEA price setting formula begins to reflect the near trebling of world energy prices between 1979-1981.[15]

Lawson is certainly right to argue that the expansion of trade with Africa since 1972 has not proved quite the solution to its energy and raw material problems that Eastern Europe originally hoped. In the absence of any significant attempts at central planning, contacts with any African state are bound to be limited. Although Romania's trade with the developing world amounts to no less than 28 percent of its foreign trade—the highest percentage of all CMEA countries and second only to that of the Soviet Union in value—its economic penetration has already run into serious difficulties. A few years ago, Ceausescu disclosed that he had been urged by several advisers to reduce contacts with the Third World since there was no real prospect of coordinating planning between Bucharest and its African trading partners, whatever regimes were in power.[16]

It is one matter, however, to explain why the Romanians have begun to despair of ever improving the planning of their trading partners, but quite another to postulate that they will be able to rely more than they do at present on interexchange mechanisms within the CMEA. For better or worse, they will have no alternative but to exploit the contacts that have been established since 1972 and accept that the appearance of Marxist-Leninist regimes in Southern Africa has provided none of the East European states with any greater advantage than did the advent of socialism in West Africa in the early 1960s.

What of Lawson's second point: that the Soviet Union can supply its partners with what they need, even if the cost may be higher? The most recent CIA studies paint a gloomy picture of deficits of certain basic raw materials over the next ten to twenty years, particularly in the lead and zinc industries.[17] The Soviet Union itself has been forced to enter into several long term agreements with African countries doubling its imports of bauxite and alumina in 1977 with the result that it now depends on foreign alumina for half its requirements.[18] It is in the nonferrous metals field, however, that the Soviet Union's own deficiencies may well prove most telling. These industries have performed lamentably in recent years because of delays in plant modernization, increasing labor shortages and critical transportation problems. The slow development of advanced methods of mining, smelting, and metal rolling have added to the problem.[19] There is certainly no guarantee that any of these factors will have been resolved by the end of the present Five Year Plan (1985).

It is true that import dependence so far exists only for bauxite and aluminum, tin, antimony, tungsten, barium, and molybdenum,[20] but there is already evidence that this situation, far from remaining static, is considerably worsening. Imports of titanium and vanadium are increasing; the costs of mining ore have in some cases overtaken the costs of importing it.[21] Also of significance may be the relatively low levels of Soviet manganese reserves and the progressive exhaustion of higher grade ores, as well as an apparent decline in exports of chromite (from 1.20m tons in 1970 to 0.74m in 1978). The fact that exports to the CMEA increased from 0.22 to 0.39m tons in the same period should not detract from the seriousness of the situation: that only by reducing and in some instances, *terminating* the supply of minerals to its CMEA partners will the Soviet Union be able to remain self-sufficient in certain raw materials into the 1990s and beyond.[22] And there can be no doubt that self-sufficiency will remain for the foreseeable future a major objective of Soviet policy, irrespective of other considerations such as the needs of its trading partners.

But what of those minerals that are not likely to run short, especially asbestos, where demand within the CMEA will probably grow faster than in the free market?[23] Joint investment in projects such as the iron ore mines in Dneprovsk, Mikhailovsk, and Stoilensk, the Kingiesepp phosphorus mining plant, and seven ferro-alloy plants dispersed throughout the Soviet Union offer a chance for Eastern Europe to ensure itself a continued source of basic raw materials while offsetting the infrastructure costs of extraction and transportation. Joint ventures involving deliveries of machinery and equipment in return for repayment of products at a later date, together with the transfer of capital through the Common Production Fund, help offset the increased prices which the Soviet Union has charged since the mid-1970s. As Alan Smith has written of fuel costs:

World oil price changes accelerated this process by giving the East European countries a greater interest in co-operation in joint investment projects but simultaneously gave the USSR the wherewithal to alter prices to effect resource transfers without destroying East Europe's economic interest in the projects.[24]

Unfortunately, neither Eastern Europe nor the Soviet Union has the resources to develop the minerals both of them need. Investment in the Soviet Union is not being generated fast enough,[25] which explains Moscow's continuing interest in Western finance even though relations with the West are at an all-time low. Joint investment schemes are also extremely unpopular with a great many East European planners:

1. All but a few are located in the Soviet Union. Many East Europeans have no wish to see Soviet control over their own economies extended with a corresponding reduction in any future leverage in trade negotiations with Moscow. Czechoslovakia would rather invest capital in modernizing its own industry, partly because it has not been able to meet its *existing* planning targets as a result of too little capital investment in new plant and equipment. Accordingly, it has been forced to reduce energy imports from within the CMEA. It may not be a vicious circle but it is a situation that has severely limited Czechoslovakia's economic options.
2. When many joint ventures were originally set up, very little attention was paid to the respective cost benefits for each partner. Quite often the East Europeans were not told the prices that were to be used to calculate either the costs of each project, or the value of output which would repay the credits that financed them.[26] It is hardly surprising, therefore, that the number of new projects adopted in the present Five Year Plan (1981–1985) is considerably smaller than those launched in the period 1976–1980. In the main, the focus of CMEA cooperation has shifted from direct and joint participation in production to product specialization agreements.

The country that invested most in these joint ventures has been the most critical of CMEA cooperation.[27] The direct dollar content of joint investment projects granted by Hungary to its CMEA partners in the 1970s amounted to no less than 54 percent of the total, an astonishingly high proportion for a country of its size.[28] Even at the time several Hungarian economists complained that the production of uneconomical but local (and therefore "secure") raw material sources such as lignite had limited real growth possibilities. Laszlo Csaba, a senior member of the Research Institute for World Economy at Budapest, contended that although there was no absolute shortage of raw materials within the CMEA, the feasibility of their extraction depended on not taking into account "the efficiency of extracting mineral wealth, the need to advance huge capital transfers, the lack of specialized technology required by conditions in Siberia."[29] Csaba went on to argue that turning the possibilities of increased cooperation into a reality would require the adoption of the same economic reforms which had been broached in the mid-1960s but which had never been carried out. He did not believe that the CMEA could justify massive expenditure on the development of local resources in the absence of more efficient central planning. No wonder, then, that many of his colleagues have begun to talk of "reverse import substitution" to enable the members of the CMEA to obtain from outside the community commodities previously obtained from within it.[30]

But if the East Europeans will have to look to Africa even more than they have already, I would certainly agree with Lawson that they will face severe difficulties not least because in assisting Mozambique and Angola to draw up their own Five Year Plans they have created a more stable environment in which Western capital has flourished. The appearance of East European planners led to a significant shift in both countries away from militant Marxism to more Leninist principles of sound economic management. In Mozambique the *ad hoc grupos dinamizadores* (dynamising groups) lost control of management in the interest of "democratic centralism." Control of the tea plantations was removed from the hands of workers committees and invested in a state tea corporation. When the East Germans were called in by the dos Santos Ministry of Planning (later to be reorganized into the National Planning Commission), political indoctrination classes in the country's factories were held on the workers' time, not the factory's. Not long afterwards production quotas began to appear. Soon after that the workers began to complain that they were being asked to conform to "bourgeois working methods."[31]

The introduction of greater economic discipline after the revolutionary upheaval of 1975–1978 had two results which the East European planners should have foreseen from the outset. First, it restored international confidence in the new states, especially among foreign investors who in some cases returned and who in others expanded their operations, backed in the main by more favorable government insurance guarantees. This was true not only of Mozambique, but also of Angola after the reforms introduced by the new Institute of Planning and Administration which was set up by lecturers seconded from the Humbold University in East Berlin.

Second, and more disastrously, the expansion of Western business highlighted the inefficiency of many East European managers. Within a few years of turning over the management of the Moatize coalfields to the East Germans, Mozambique decided to dispense with the services of sixty East German technicians.[32] Romanian experts in charge of cotton plantations also came up with advice that fell on very skeptical ears. Their introduction of labor intensive machinery took almost no account of why the old Portuguese companies had earlier been dispossessed: their insistence on maintaining a low wage, low capital investment plantation sector. In this case both sides—East and West—ignored the fact that certain forms of economic organization in one political system are frequently unacceptable (or even irrelevant) in another.

On the whole, however, where the East Europeans were found to be wanting, Western capital skillfully exploited its opportunities. In Angola the failure of successive East European attempts to revive the country's ailing railway system prompted the government to ask the Portuguese back. The same was true of the port of Luanda which under East German management became one of the most congested in the world. When invited back, the Portuguese found only 1 percent of its forklift trucks still in operation; within six months of their return, 40 percent were working.

But for the success with which the East European planners revived the economy between 1976-1979, the present position of the MNCs might have been far less favorable. As it is there are now more MNCs in Angola than there were during the last decade of Portuguese rule. And in Mozambique foreign investment has been accorded a far more important role in the country's future development than it was in Portugal's Third National Plan (1968-1973).

The pessimism with which Eastern Europe tends these days to regard its economic interests in Southern Africa is not the least significant aspect of its relations with the continent. It has served to narrow their range of choice and restrict their freedom of maneuver. In doing so it has thrown into much sharper relief the divergences as well as convergences of East European and Soviet interests. It has not created them; they were always present. It is to two of these that I shall now turn: the failure of the East Europeans to cooperate amongst themselves; and their near-unanimous refusal to admit Angola or Mozambique as a member of the CMEA, despite Vietnam's admission in 1978.

CMEA Strategy toward Southern Africa

In 1981 the CMEA Secretariat, taking up a proposal first raised by Czechoslovakia at the 32nd Council session, decided to press ahead with joint sales of goods as a means of paying for African raw materials. The sale of complete plant and equipment could be seen as "buy back" arrangements in reverse, similar in most respects to the type of contracts upon which the East Europeans normally insisted for deliveries of Western investment goods to Eastern Europe. At the 32nd Council meeting, Angola had also agreed to increase its multilateral cooperation with the organization at the expense of existing bilateral links with its individual members.[33] What is interesting is not that these measures have failed to come to much, but why they were under discussion in the first place.

The secretariat recognized, perhaps rather late in the day, that multilateral cooperation might help to resolve the evident signs of increasing competition between its own members, a problem that had first come to light at a conference that convened in Bucharest in 1976. Czechoslovakia is the country with most to lose. By 1980, as much as 73 percent of its imports were fuels, metals, and raw materials from the developing world. The percentage might well have been higher but for the insistence of many African states on exporting manufactured goods in exchange for poor quality Czech imports and their apparent unwillingness to export raw materials to the Soviet bloc when they could get better prices on the open market. At the 1978 CMEA summit, the Czechs were particularly critical of those members who by selling higher quality goods had gained a much better market position in the competition for mineral resources.[34]

Given the fact that Eastern Europe has to compete for a limited supply of minerals (what the African countries feel able to forego in higher Western prices in exchange for a guaranteed price over a longer period) competition between the East Europeans is almost certain to increase, particularly those countries such as Poland, Hungary, and the GDR whose future economic growth has a particularly high energy content. The energy needs of the CMEA as a whole rose by 30 percent between 1973-1978 exceeding those of Western Europe; in some cases they have grown even faster since 1978. In 1981-1982, Libya was unable to meet Poland's import requirements. For countries that cannot turn to import substitution, competition is likely to be particularly fierce. At the 12th Congress of the Society of Economists in October 1982, the Hungarian Minister of Foreign Trade admitted that his country's own lack of resources made it impossible to limit commodity imports from Africa, whatever might be the needs of its partners. In remarking on the differences of opinion between the Soviet Union and Eastern Europe, one should never lose sight of the competition between the East European states themselves which the CMEA, for all its good intentions, can do very little to resolve.

For multilateral cooperation to be really effective, the centrally planned economies of the Third World would need to work much more closely with the CMEA. Angola and Mozambique have both been admitted as observers at CMEA meetings since 1978. But despite the presence of Mozambique's Minister of Planning at the Council's 30th anniversary celebrations in June 1979 and despite talk at its summit the following year of the need to boost assistance to countries of a "socialist orientation," Mozambique was refused admission as a full member when it eventually applied in the summer of

1980. The Polish crisis made any serious application impossible, while adding a timely reminder, if one were needed, of the burden of supporting existing members without inviting in new ones even less able to support themselves without massive financial aid.

It was Khrushchev who used to speak in the early 1960s of the need to go in for planning at the level of the CMEA and only afterwards at the level of the socialist world system as a whole. That was in the immediate aftermath of decolonization when it seemed possible that Africa might progress rapidly on the path of socialist reconstruction. It was not to be; far from progressing, Africa has in all but a few cases regressed. Seven out of ten countries are getting poorer; many cannot even be described as developing. The continent largely remains what it was fifty years ago: backward, internationally isolated, at war with itself. Following the collapse of the political economy of the West African states who had at one time been feted by the Soviet Union, two Soviet economists (Bogomolov and Shiryaev) predicted that the integration of all socialist national economies in one international economy regulated by a common plan went far "beyond the framework of the foreseeable future."[35] Africa's problems are so extensive that it is quite possible that they will not be resolved within the framework of the nation state bequeathed to them by the colonial powers, or within a development model (which accepts Marx's dictum that the developed world merely shows to the undeveloped a reflection of its own future).

Given the unequal level of economic attainment achieved by Cuba and Vietnam, it is not altogether surprising that its wealthier members, notably Hungary and Czechoslovakia, resented having to pay the bill. Both countries are known to have raised serious objections to Vietnam's admission in 1978. Although Kosygin raised the subject of Mozambique's application at the CMEA's Prague summit in 1980, Gustav Husak, the Czech party leader, left him in no doubt at a meeting three months later that this time his own country was not prepared to yield to political arguments that had no foundation in economic reality.[36]

Mozambique's admission was never a serious issue in the eyes of Eastern Europe. That was not the case, however, in the eyes of Mozambique itself as the Soviet Union recognized full well. Machel, after all, was the most anxious of the new generation of Marxist-Leninist leaders to gain recognition from and admission to the family of socialist nations and the most outspoken by far in stressing Mozambique's ideological affinity with its "natural allies." Nothing speaks more for his genuine intent than Maputo's failure to sign the Second Lomé Convention in 1979 despite being party to the year-long negotiations. It is in the light of its refusal to join Lomé that its application to join the CMEA must be judged.[37]

The reason why Mozambique failed in its bid for membership has already been noted. The enlargement of the organization would inevitably have changed its whole raison d'être. Originally designed as a framework for economic integration, the CMEA would have been charged with another role that would have been quite beyond its own competence: that of assisting less developed countries. In this respect, Mozambique's failure was equally damaging to the Soviet Union in highlighting the extent to which the European Economic Community could assist Africa where the CMEA could not. Indeed it forced Mozambique to apply for admission to the Lomé Convention in 1982, an organizaton that the East Europeans have always condemned as a club consisting of ex-colonies and erstwhile colonists. It has never made any secret of its hostility to the convention.

In other circumstances, Mozambique might have been able to claim with some justification that its present state of development did not allow any escape from the imperialist division of labor. But FRELIMO had spent most of the 1960s pointing out that Portugal's reluctance to divest itself of its colonies as Britain and France had done stemmed precisely from the fact that it did not have the resources to establish a neocolonial system on the French or British models. As Amilcar Cabral reminded an audience in London only three years before independence:

> the reason why Portugal is not decolonising now is because it is not an imperialist country and cannot neo-colonise. The economic infrastructure of Portugal is such that she cannot compete with other capitalist powers.[38]

Mozambique's decision to join Lomé was also diplomatically disastrous for the Soviet Union as far as its implications for Southern Africa's future development and Mozambique's pivotal position in the scheme to set up a Southern African economic order independent of South Africa. The fact that only the European Community could finance the scheme had been clear as early as 1979 when the European Commission agreed to act as an intermediary in discussions about the rehabilitation of the Benguela railway. Even in those early days, Brussels had been able to demonstrate the regional spin-offs from Lomé membership despite the fact that Angola had not yet signed the Lomé Convention.

Mozambique's application amounts almost to an admission that the survival of the regime may eventually depend on the European Community, not the CMEA. The community has not only expressed its willingness to discuss funding the Southern African Development Coordination Conference (SADCC); it has also expressed concern about the actions South Africa has recently taken to preempt the SADCC from taking off.[39] In October 1982, the commission expressed its determination "to become directly involved in the development process right up to the frontiers of apartheid."[40]

These initiatives, random though they are to be sure, seem to suggest that the community is quite prepared to become the major determinant of Southern Africa's future, regardless of South African opposition and regardless of the fact that the two countries most at risk from Pretoria are ostensibly allies of the Soviet Union. So far, this is a challenge that the CMEA has been unable to meet despite Soviet prompting.

Southern Africa: The Looking Glass World

The proposition that the Soviet Union intends to deny the West access to Southern Africa's resources and interdict its shipping at the Cape is not self-evident merely because the case is so persistently argued. The real threat may come from quite a different quarter: genuine commercial competition from Eastern Europe. As long as Southern Africa remained a Western sphere of influence, resource denial was largely a matter of strategy, not economics; now that both sides have begun to rely on the same market for supplies, economic competition has become more direct and potentially more disruptive both in terms of its impact on regional stability and its implications for superpower relations.

Political leaders in the West often exaggerate the Soviet Union's freedom of maneuver or see no reason to emphasize the constraints within which it is often forced to act. Obviously, as the most important member of the Warsaw Pact, the Soviet Union largely articulates its aims and defines its interests. That much is not in dispute. Yet it must be asked whether we place too much emphasis on Soviet strategic interests and too little on the commercial interests of its allies. In their preoccupation with the Soviet threat many Western analysts either overlook the East European dimension entirely, or dismiss it as unimportant, or dismiss the East Europeans themselves as surrogates of the Soviet Union.

The Cape Route

Ever since the Soviet navy appeared in the Indian Ocean in 1968, the West has been preoccupied by the threat to the sea routes around the coast of Africa, particularly the Cape. The Soviet Union appears to be able to interdict shipping without risk to its own. Its own internal lines of communications for the most part lie overland while those of the West extend across thousands of miles of ocean through narrow seas adjacent to areas of endemic instability.

This has always been a distorted picture, one that took almost no account of Soviet or East European trade. In its strategic planning, the Soviet

Union may take much less note of its allies' interests than the United States takes of those of the West Europeans, but it is in no position to ignore them entirely. In a much quoted article in *New Times,* Dmitry Volsky found himself asking whether the strategy of interdiction had a future:

> There is, of course, no denying the importance of these routes to the West. It is by these routes that the capitalist world gets a large part of its oil, . . . but these routes are also vitally important for the developing countries . . . which depend on imports of manufactured goods and equipment from Eastern Europe.[41]

Soviet writers have also pointed out that the Cape route carries a substantial percentage of East European trade which is at constant risk of interdiction from the West. NATO may fear an attack along the Cape route, but the Warsaw Pact faces a threat at the Cape itself; it has no doubt as to whose side South Africa will align itself in the event of war.[42]

Far from promoting offensive designs in the region, the Soviet Union is only too aware of the need to defend its own shipping as well as that of its allies. The Soviet navy, of course, has many missions but it is worth remembering that Admiral Gorschkov lists the protection of "state interests" as the first of its peacetime roles. While it is unlikely that threats to the shipping lanes or shipping lines will in themselves determine Soviet policy, both may well influence it.

Poland's Best line has been so competitive in East Africa that at one point in 1980 it looked as though the East African Shipping Line (EASL) might be forced out of business. There continues to be speculation that it may yet be forced into liquidation by the low freight rates that Poland levies.[43]

Most maritime nations have attempted to regulate freight rates by joining appropriate conferences for the major trade routes. Soviet shipping in east African waters is so lucrative that it is not surprising that the Russians have not been very enthusiastic to join the North Western-East African Conference or to accept conference rate structures unless it is on their own terms. They have made known they would only be prepared to join if they were to be given twenty-four of the originally planned fifty-five sailings from Hamburg. They found themselves in a particularly strong position in the period 1982–1983 having launched no fewer than thirty-one sailings on the East Africa route in eighteen months.[44] Even in 1977 the Soviet merchant fleet (Morflot) carried 10 percent of Europe's East Africa trade.[45] That percentage has continued to rise ever since.

In West Africa where the Soviet Union operates a shipping line jointly with Poland and the German Democratic Republic, its interests are even greater.[46] It is interesting that the Soviet navy has shown special interest in the waters off Cape Verde where up to 18 percent of its merchant fleet is to be found at any one time.[47] It is also important to recognize that West Africa is one of its major fishing grounds and that the Soviet fishing industry supplies no less than 9 percent of all food. The importance of fisheries to the food industry and the large domestic requirements for fishery products require the Soviet Union to have direct access to stocks (64 percent of which happen to be located off the coastal areas of developing countries) including West Africa where the Soviets have negotiated bilateral agreements with a score of African countries including Sierra Leone, Guinea-Bissau, and the Gambia.[48]

But above all, of course, it is the presence of Morflot which is crucial to any understanding of Moscow's own preoccupation with the safety of its shipping and the security of its own trade routes. During the postwar years the merchant marine grew from a modest, mainly coastal enterprise to numerically the world's largest fleet. In terms of tonnage since 1960 it has risen in world rank from fourteenth to sixth, increasing its volume sixfold in the process. Ninety percent of its ships are less than twenty years old. Today Morflot has sixty commercial lines and trades with more than 120 countries. In 1982 the Soviet Union added more tonnage to its merchant fleet than any other of the top ten maritime states except Panama. As of April 1983 it had 107 dry cargo ships on order, nearly twice as many as any other country, and 22 container ships, the fourth highest total.[49]

All in all, Morflot carries 50 percent of Soviet trade, substantially more cargo from freight owners of non-Soviet origin, and earns more foreign currency than any other operation after the export of oil and arms. Given the scope of these operations it would be surprising if the Soviet Union were not anxious about the security of its shipping. Its concerns are no less real than the West's; indeed, in some respects they may be greater. It should always be remembered that its merchant fleet constitutes the third most important element in the international network for the movement of raw materials, complementing its rail and pipeline systems, and that the fleet has helped reduce Soviet hard currency trade deficits with the West. In 1966, for example, Morflot's earnings covered 45 percent of its deficits on commodity earnings.[50] That figure is probably much greater today.

Yet it is in the area of fuels and raw materials that Morflot's future role is likely to prove most intriguing, paralleling as it must Western patterns and preoccupations. At present the Soviets are increasing their tanker fleet to supplement or replace their existing vessels with those of the new *Marshal Vasilievski* class which have a capacity of 65,000 tons. The latter may play an important part in carrying supplies of Middle East oil and African minerals to their East European allies.[51] In this light, it is difficult to evaluate objectively who represents the greater threat to the other: NATO or the Warsaw Pact.

Denial of Minerals

The West's second cause for concern is the competition for strategic minerals. It has become very much an *idee recue* that the Soviet Union poses a threat to Western access to Southern Africa without which its economies would not survive for long. This is not a perspective shared by Eastern Europe, or for that matter the Soviet Union. In recent years, two themes have begun to emerge from the works of Soviet political analysts which were briefly touched upon in the past but never fully developed: (1) that the West has shown every inclination to maintain neocolonialism in Africa, whatever the cost,[52] and that it has done so contrary to what so many writers claimed for years; (2) this has been done not to satisfy the need of the MNCs to offload their surplus profits, but to import raw materials upon which its economic future depends.[53]

The first theme was raised at a conference in Budapest in 1976 which met in the wake of Dr. Kissinger's first shuttle to Southern Africa. The cardinal aim of Western diplomacy, one observer later wrote of Kissinger's diplomacy, was to prevent Africa from escaping Western control. The policy was predicated upon "preserving the positions of neo-colonialism, blocking the roads to non-capitalist development and ensuring Africa's pro-Western orientation in the international arena."[54] To explain the Soviet threat to Western interests as essentially the product of the West's predominant position in the region may seem perverse, but at least this interpretation explains why the Warsaw Pact and not Cuba has been most active of late and why the pact has taken an increasing interest in African affairs at precisely the moment that the continent has begun to appear with increasing frequency on NATO's security agenda.

The second fear—that Western mineral needs will lead inevitably to fiercer competition—is even more real. Many East Europeans genuinely fear that should they ever be denied access to Southern Africa's resources, raw material shortages may prevent industry from meeting its production dates and create a multiplier effect throughout the whole economy by increasing the price of raw materials. The future may hold out an unhappy prospect of reduced growth, rampant inflation, and further delays in planning with possible adverse consequences for consumer spending.

Southern Africa, they believe, is entirely at the mercy of international capital. If we look at it from an East European perspective, the *present* threat from the West looks far more alarming than the *putative* Soviet threat to Western interests. Far from losing their influence, the MNCs appear to have become more assertive than ever. The denationalization of *Union Miniere* in Zaire followed closely by the denationalization of the phosphate companies in Mauritania in 1978 appears to give the lie to the claim that Africa has been independent since the early 1960s. Looked at from an East European perspective, the system is still closed. In the same year as the events I have just mentioned, Hungary's Foreign Minister, Frigyes Puja, returned from a visit to Africa with the impression that the West's demands for minerals would continue to impede Africa's chances of "progressive development" for many years to come.[55]

Eastern Europe, in short, has very real interests in the continent which are in no way served by the present predominance of Western capital. Just as the Soviet Union's intervention in Angola has alarmed the West, so the West's attempts to shore up its position in the aftermath of the events of 1975 have served only to heighten Eastern Europe's own sense of insecurity. For the West, the problem posed in its starkest terms is whether to defend what remains of the old order or to coopt and work with the new. For the East Europeans, the matter is at once more simple, but no less problematic—how to defend the "progressive regimes" which have given them access to Southern Africa's resources from the persistent threat of destabilization.

Warsaw Pact Intervention

It was Richard Löwenthal who argued some years ago that the Soviet Union, in keeping with its growing military strength, had moved from old style antiimperialism to a new concept: that of counterimperialism. He described this as "a strategy of fighting Western imperialism by using the familiar imperialist methods of establishing zones of political and economic influence linked to the Soviet Union by firm ties."[56] One need not necessarily subscribe to Löwenthal's model to accept that the Warsaw Pact, whether intentionally or not, has pursued a policy of counterimperialism with increasing success since 1978. As Erich Honecker told a conference in East Berlin in October 1980, the support given by the Warsaw Pact to national liberation movements has "nothing in common with the export of revolution" but is aimed solely against the export of counterrevolution.[57] East European attempts to discredit the Anglo-American initiatives in Zimbabwe and the Contact Group's discussions on Namibia were intended to prevent what the Soviet Union often describes as a NATO directed "offensive against the national liberation forces in Africa,"[58] a theme which was taken up in earnest by Honecker during a visit to Southern Africa in 1979 when he dismissed "the goodwill and honest assistance of the Western States" and talked instead of the extension of NATO's field of activity into Africa.[59] In a communiqué published at the end of his visit to Mozambique, the two countries pledged themselves to oppose NATO's attempts to transform the region into an "international crisis centre."[60]

It is hardly surprising that the Soviet Union has made out such a strong case for a concerted effort on the part of its allies: In the first instance it wishes to prevent a serious clash of interests from arising within the Warsaw Pact; in the second, it recognizes that intervention by the alliance may provide a continuous point of reference for the East Europeans in their dealings with one another and perhaps, more to the point, in their dealings with the Soviet Union. At least they may all agree that their interests in Southern Africa are under constant threat even though their interests may actually conflict.

The Warsaw Pact's intervention in Southern Africa has been one of the most important developments in recent years. One of the conclusions reached at the Budapest conference of 1976 was that political cooperation within the Soviet bloc was at a much more developed stage than economic cooperation. To some extent this is still the case.

To many this may not seem surprising. One would expect the Soviet writ to run more extensively in the political sphere than the economic. In the political sphere, East European interests are not allowed to conflict with those of the Soviet Union. Nevertheless, national foreign policy goals have begun to influence the framework of Soviet policy for the first time. However much Eastern Europe may defer to the Soviet Union, the latter has been forced to take into account the interests of its allies where they have begun to conflict with its own. Those interests have dictated the content of Soviet policy. Indeed, the presence of the East Germans in Africa has given them importance at the point of execution, if not command; and this in turn has had some influence on the commands that are given.

It is not surprising that, given their economic interests in Southern Africa, the region has been the subject of discussion in the Warsaw Pact. In 1978, a year in which the NATO Council meeting in Washington devoted over half its time to discussing African security, the Warsaw Pact discussed aid to the liberation movements in the context of aid to their sponsors, the Front Line States (FLS). The defense of the FLSs against South African intervention exercised their minds even then. Five years later at the summit meeting at Hradcany Castle the focus of their attention was once again directed at "recent acts of aggression committed by the *apartheid* regime against the progressive peoples of Southern Africa" (a reference to South African military incursions into Angola and Mozambique).

Nevertheless, despite their increasing concern for the future of the "progressive regimes" in the area, their own commitment has been minimal. There are three reasons why this has been the case. First, the confidence with which the Soviet Union intervened in Southern Africa in 1975 has largely, if not entirely, evaporated. Before 1974, the few instances of socialist development in Africa offered Soviet politicians even fewer grounds for hope. By the end of that year, however, they had taken to heart three seminal events, all of which caught the Soviet Union itself by surprise: the collapse of the imperial dynasty in Ethiopia, the collapse of the Portuguese empire, and the transformation of the Congolese Workers Party into the continent's first fully fledged Marxist-Leninist party. As Robert Legvold has persuasively argued, these events appeared to confirm that their policy was running with the grain of history, not against it. The developments of 1974 gave them the self-confidence to act decisively on at least two occasions: in Angola and Ethiopia.[61] This apparent confirmation of Soviet ideology merely highlighted the West's belated and rather vain attempts to defy the tide of history by underwriting deformed political societies rather than dynamic ones: the whig oligarchy in Liberia (which fell a few years later); the dynasty of the Lion of Judah; the fossilized rump of empire in Portuguese Africa.

In the last few years, however, this confidence has evaporated as quickly as it appeared. In Angola and Ethiopia Cuban forces are still battling to preserve the states in whose support they were airlifted seven years ago. In Mozambique, the security situation is now so serious that the government may lose control of the provinces of Zambesia and Manica. Despite their Marxist-Leninist affiliations, political change is not impossible. The East Germans have been the first to recognize that because of their weak social bases political change is not even inconceivable in Angola or Mozambique.[62] They can hardly have been reassured by Luis Cabral's overthrow in Guinea-Bissau—the first Marxist-Leninist ruler to be turned out by a military coup.

Eastern Europe's distrust of the West, and the extent to which it holds the West responsible for regional instability, is nowhere more in evidence than in political writings that have tried to make intelligible the endlessly changing pattern of political alignments in Africa. Seven years after Mengistu's rise to power, he has still not created a party apparatus on Leninist lines despite persistent Soviet pressure; Angola is also faced with the not too distant prospect of coming to terms with UNITA, a prospect which Romania foresaw as long ago as 1976 and which explains its refusal to accept the MPLA as the only representative of the Angolan people.[63] Neither Angola nor Ethiopia appear to have escaped from that permanent cycle of political regression that opened for most African countries almost immediately after independence. Marx once called the Germany of the necessary but impossible bourgeois revolution of the mid-nineteenth century "the comedian of a world order whose real heroes are long since dead."[64] The phrase seems particularly apposite for the new African Marxist-Leninist states who are about to enter their second decade of independence without any hope of developing political institutions which might, at the very least, assure the political stability their friends in Eastern Europe would like to see.

Possibly, this gloomy prognosis presents a picture that may seem far less cogent to the Soviet Union.[65] Yet, there does appear to be evidence of a reevaluation of the options confronting the Warsaw Pact. The GDR, for example, has continued to oppose large military involvement in Southern Africa, despite the presence of 10,000 military personnel deployed throughout the continent. Given the uncertain nature of the revolutionary order they would be expected to defend, its reluctance is probably sensible. Recent intelligence reports indicate that the East German general staff was opposed to the idea of replacing Cuban forces in Angola on the understanding that the change would not offset "the cowardice" of the Angolan army in the field.[66] Instead, the GDR has tried to persuade Moscow to accept the Contact Group's plan for a mutual withdrawal of Cuban and South African forces in the expectation that SWAPO will sweep to power in any internationally supervised Namibian elections. The one development it does not want is to be involved in a military stalemate in difficult terrain with the possibility of a clash with South African forces.

The prospect of a conflict with South Africa explains the second feature of the last few years: their reluctance to honor the treaties signed with Angola and Mozambique in the late 1970s. So far, the bilateral treaties between the GDR and Mozambique have remained precisely that. When the Warsaw Pact's Political Committee delegated responsibility for its interests in Southern Africa to East Germany in 1978, it did so in the hope of limiting NATO activity in the region, not provoking it by adventurist policies of its own.

Of the three separate treaties of friendship which the GDR has concluded with Africa's Marxist-Leninist states, only the one with Mozambique contains an agreement to go to each other's assistance in time of crisis. Yet the East Germans have so far failed to honor their commitments. Their reluctance to provide an adequate air defense system against South African air strikes contrasts rather embarrassingly with the Soviet Union's massive military aid package to Zambia after the first Rhodesian raids on Lusaka. The visit of two Soviet warships in February 1980 in the wake of the South African strike on the suburbs of Maputo only served to reinforce the fact that the deterrent against such raids in the future was very much at the Soviet Union's discretion and was neither fixed nor irrevocable.

Neither the Soviet Union nor the GDR could possibly have foreseen the scale of recent South African raids that have involved the largest military mobilization of South African forces since the Second World War. Nor could they have foreseen the impotence of the West in the face of actions that have so patently conflicted with its true interests and that have contributed more to regional instability than the much-vaunted Cuban presence. Ironically, however, because both probably genuinely believe that in the last resort South Africa is a client of the West, rather than an independent actor, they no doubt believe that a conflict between their forces and South Africa would be seen by NATO as a deliberate provocation, quite different

The Soviet Union and Eastern Europe 79

in character from intervention against a non-Western power such as Afghanistan or Cambodia.[67]

The third feature of recent years is one to which I have already briefly alluded: that conflict within the Warsaw Pact has largely been avoided because of the absence of any *fundamental* disagreement among its members. At the moment Eastern Europe wishes to defend the investment that countries such as Poland and East Germany have made in mining operations in Mozambique and Angola. They have deployed military forces to underwrite political stability which in this curious looking-glass world means the centrally planned economies of the region, not the existing capitalist order.

East European states have no wish, however, to exclude Western capital. Indeed, they are the first to recognize that the MNCs still have a role to play in developing the region. They may well wish to bring foreign capital under state regulation, but few have any illusions that new reserves can be developed without Western assistance. Since the mid-1970s, many East European countries have increasingly subcontracted major parts of development contracts to Western corporations in order to reduce the high overheads of mining operations.[68] More often than not, in selecting partners, they have turned to companies with whom they have already established close links in Eastern Europe itself. In Africa, Dunlop and Pirelli have both benefited from their prior association with the Hungarian state trading organizations Chemolimpex and Taurus. The East German trade organization, Unitechna, engaged Krupp in Ethiopia in 1980.

On the East European side it is the countries with the most flexible and decentralized trading structures that have entered into tripartite ventures in Africa, with Hungary leading the field, followed by the GDR and Poland. This cooperation is not an ad hoc affair but has grown up out of years of cooperation between the partners during which both sides have come to understand what each can offer the other.[69] It could well be put at risk by a crisis between the superpowers occasioned wholly or in part by the pursuit of Soviet strategic interests from which its partners in the Warsaw Pact have little to gain and everything to lose. The East Europeans learned at first hand what the invasion of Afghanistan meant for further joint venture cooperation in Eastern Europe. Any further restriction of these operations could have an immediate bearing on its operations in the developing world.

Conclusion

I have tried to show why at present the Soviet Union and Eastern Europe have cooperated and yet why that cooperation may not survive very real differences of interest. Colin Lawson believes, to the contrary, that Eastern

Europe is not particularly interested in Africa; that with the debatable exception of East Germany none expect a greater degree of involvement; and that in the case of future political instability in the region, almost total economic disengagement by the smaller members of the CMEA would both be prudent and likely.

The evidence hardly supports this interpretation. Nor does it support his final assertion that Eastern Europe's attitude leaves the Soviet Union with greater political freedom of maneuver because it knows its allies are not significantly involved. What I do concede is that differences of opinion are not likely to arise as long as the Soviet Union continues to take note of its allies' interests as opposed to its own, which are somewhat more narrowly defined.

Where does all this leave us? Perhaps with only an understanding of the mainsprings of Soviet policy. We must always remember, of course, that there is no analogy with the differences of perception and interest which have recently arisen between the United States and its West European allies. Ultimately, Eastern Europe will be listened to but heeded only if the Soviet Union finds it convenient to do so. But to the extent that both superpowers find themselves baffled by Africa's problems and uncertain of solutions, and more willing than hitherto to allow their respective European partners to influence the shaping of their own policies, the analogy may prove less misleading than previously supposed.

Notes

1. *Communist Aid Activities in Non-Communist Less Developed Countries, 1978* (Washington, D.C.: U.S. Government Printing Office, 1978), p. 10.
2. *Zycie Gospodarcze*, 12 March 1961.
3. Vaclav Mondous, "The Socialist Countries and Their Relations with the National Liberation Movement of the Colonial Countries," *Pravda* (Plzen) 4 July 1963 as cited by Robert Lamberg, *Prag und die Dritte Welt* (Hannover: Verlag für Literatur und Zeitgeschehen, 1966), p. 27.
4. *Narody Azii i Afriki* (Moscow), No. 20, 1961.
5. See Raymond Vernon and Brian Levy, "State Owned Enterprises in the World Economy: The Case of Iron Ore," in Leroy Jones, ed., *Public Enterprise in Less Developed Countries: Multidisciplinary Perspectives* (Cambridge, Mass.: Harvard University Press, 1981).
6. Zuhayr Mikdashi, *The International Politics of Natural Resources* (Ithaca: Cornell University Press, 1976), p. 121.
7. For Polish economic works on Africa, see Jerzy Prokopczvk, *The Third World in Search of a Road to Development* (Warsaw: 1973); Michael Dobroczynski, *Africa and International Trade* (Warsaw: 1972); Zbigniew

Dobosiewicz, *Economic Integration of Less Developed Countries* (Warsaw: 1971).

8. "Adventurism and Pragmatism: The Soviet Union, COMECON and Relations with African States," *International Affairs* 57, no. 4 (Autumn 1981):618-633.

9. Alan Smith, "Plan Co-operation and Joint Planning Activity in the CMEA," November 1978 (unpublished paper).

10. *Christian Science Monitor*, 10 June 1981.

11. Colin Lawson, "The Soviet Union and Eastern Europe in Southern Africa: Is There a Conflict of Interest?" *International Affairs* 59, no. 1 (Winter 1982/1983):32-40.

12. *Revista Economica* 42 (12 November 1982):54. Between 1975-1980 trade with the West dropped from 36 percent to 30 percent.

13. David Shireff, "Romania Tries Its Bankers Nerves," *Euromoney* (November 1981); Jan Vanous and Michael Marrese, "Implicit Subsidies in Soviet Trade With Eastern Europe," University of British Columbia Economics Department Discussion Paper 80-32, p. 54.

14. R. Dietz, *Price Changes in Soviet Trade With CMEA and the Rest the World Since 1975* (Joint Economic Committee of the US Congress, 1979). See also Steven Rosefielde, "Comparative Advantage and the Evolving Pattern of Soviet Commodity Specialisation," in Steven Rosefielde, ed., *Economic Welfare and the Economics of Soviet Socialism* (Cambridge, Mass. and New York: Cambridge University Press, 1981).

15. The Wharton Business School predicts that world market prices will grow only 4.5 percent between 1983-1987. Nevertheless, even this growth rate may lead to a serious deterioration in the terms of trade for Eastern Europe and may demand greater Soviet financial assistance in default of higher Soviet subsidies and a recycling of petrorubles earned from the export of oil, perhaps in the form of low interest rate trade credits. Jan Vanous, "East European Economic Slowdown," *Problems of Communism* 31, no. 4 (July-August 1982):9.

16. *Scinteia*, 4 August 1978.

17. *The Lead and Zinc Industry in the Soviet Union* (U.S. Central Intelligence Agency, ER 8010072, March 1980), p. 10.

18. CIA figures cited in *Africa Contemporary Record*, edited by Colin Legum (London: Rex Collings, 1981), p. C135.

19. V.V. Strishkov, "The Soviet Union," in *Mining Annual Review* (1980) pp. 579-605.

20. *Non-Fuel Minerals Policy Review: Oversight Hearings Before the Committee on Interior and Insular Affairs, Subcommittee on Mines and Mining* (Washington, D.C.: U.S. Congress, 96th Congress, 2nd Session, 1980), pp. 32-46.

21. See *Soviet Economy in Time of Change* (Washington, D.C.: U.S. Congress, Joint Economic Committee, 1979).

22. Walter Labys, "Role of the Soviet Union in Metals Markets: Case Study of Copper, Manganese and Chromite." Paper prepared for the Conference on the Soviet Union in Commodity Markets, Center for International Business Studies, University of Montreal, October 8-9, 1981. The measure of self-sufficiency in copper and lead deteriorated steadily throughout the life of the Tenth Five Year Plan. See Daniel Papp, "Soviet Non-Fuel Mineral Resources: Surplus or Scarcity?" *Resources Policy* 8, no. 3 (September 1982); and *Non-Fuel Mineral Outlook for the USSR Through 1990* (Washington, D.C.: U.S. Bureau of Mines, 1981).

23. Pater Hanel, "The Soviet Impact on the International Trade in Asbestos." Paper prepared for the Conference on the Soviet Union in Commodity Markets, Center for International Business Studies, University of Montreal, October 8-9, 1981, p. 30.

24. Alan Smith, "Economic Factors Affecting Relations in the 1980's," in Karen Dawisha and Philip Hanson, eds., *Soviet-East European Dilemmas: Coercion, Competition and Consent* (London: Heinemann, 1981), p. 120.

25. Harriet Matejka, "Soviet Coal Exports." Paper prepared for the Conference on the USSR and the Markets of Secondary and Primary Materials, Montreal, October 8-9, 1981, p. 13.

26. See Kalman Pecsi, *The Future of Socialist Economic Integration* (Armonk, N.Y.: Sharpe, 1981); and Petro Pavlov, "Problems of the Development and Improvement of the Mineral-Raw Material Complex of CMEA Member Countries, *Mezhdunarodnye Otnosheniia* 6 (1980):53-64.

27. For criticisms by Hungarian economists, see Andras Koves, "East-West Trade and the Foreign Economic Strategy of CMEA Countries," *Kulgazdasag* 5 (1982):3-15; Laszlo Csaba, "World Economic Adjustment and Economic Development in Eastern Europe," *Kulgazdasag* 4 (1982):12-29.

28. Laszlo Csaba, "Some Problems of the International Socialist Monetary System," *Acta Oeconomica* 23, no. 1, 2 (1979):17-37.

29. Laszlo Csaba, "The Place of the CMEA in the World Economy of the 1980's," *Valosag* (July 1982):5.

30. In the fuel industry this has already happened. In 1975 the CMEA produced 70 percent of the oil consumed by its members. By 1980 it was only 60 percent, a figure which is expected to fall below 50 percent by the end of this decade.

31. *African Development* (December 1976).

32. *The Guardian* (London) 11 January 1981.

33. *New African* (January 1978).

34. It should be noted that this has been known for some time. Czechoslovakia was particularly badly hit by the increase in raw material prices after 1973 because of its relatively high consumption of materials (40-50 percent

higher than most industrially advanced countries and higher than most other CMEA members). In an address to the Central Committee of the Czech Communist Party in November 1974, Gustav Husak declared "Generally it must be stated that the period in which it was possible to obtain fuels, energy and raw materials as well as foodstuffs relatively easily and at low prices has ended. This is a new important fact from which we must draw long term conclusions in our economic and political activity." Cited in Vsatislav Pechota, "Czechoslovakia and the Third World," in Michael Radu, ed., *Eastern Europe and the Third World: East vs. South* (New York: Praeger, 1981), p. 100.

35. Cited in Peter Wiles, ed., *The New Communist Third World: An Essay in Political Economy* (London: Croom Helm, 1982), pp. 23–24.

36. See Cam Hudson, "The 34th CMEA Council Session: No Major Initiatives on the Horizon," RAD Background Report, 147 (Eastern Europe), Radio Free Europe Research, 16 June 1980.

37. The Soviet Union by itself is hardly in a position to extend further assistance to its friends in the developing world. According to a NATO report, in 1983 the relations with its friends in East Asia would come under increasing pressure if the postwar reconstruction in Southern Africa continued to demand greater assistance than already given. *The Times* (London), 21 January 1983.

38. Cited in Gary Wasserman, "The Politics of Consensual Decolonisation," *African Review* 5, no. 1 (1975):355.

39. See Christopher Coker, "South Africa: A New Military Role in Southern Africa, 1968–82," *Survival,* 25, no. 2 (March-April 1983):59–67.

40. Ibid.

41. Dmitry Volsky, "A Strategy Without a Future," *New Times,* no. 33 (August 1978):4–5.

42. Vasily Efremov, "The NATO Shadow Over Africa," *New Times,* no. 42 (October 1981):10–11.

43. Peter Janke, "The Soviet Strategy of Mineral Denial," *Soviet Analyst* 7, no. 22 (November 1978):5.

44. *The Challenge of Soviet Shipping* (London: Aims of Industry, 1983), p. 9.

45. James Ellis, "Expansion of the Soviet Merchant Fleet—Implications for the West," *NATO Review* 3 (1979):22, ref. 4.

46. S. Lukyanchenko, *Foreign Trade,* no. 1 (1977):23.

47. Michael Davidchik and Robert Mahoney, "Soviet Civil Fleets in the Third World," in Bradford Dismukes and James McConnell, eds., *Soviet Naval Diplomacy* (New York: Pergamon, 1979).

48. William Black," Soviet Fishery Agreements With Developing Countries," *Marine Policy* 7, no. 3 (July 1983):169.

49. *Wall Street Journal* (Europe), 26 July 1983.

50. Robert Athay, "Perspectives on Soviet Merchant Shipping," in Michael MccGwire, ed., *Soviet Naval Developments* (New York: Praeger, 1973), p. 101.

51. David Scrivener, "Merchant Marine in Soviet Naval Strategy," *Marine Policy* 7, no. 2 (April 1983):119.

52. Anatoly Gromyko, "Western Diplomacy Versus Southern Africa," *International Affairs* (Moscow), March 1979, p. 20.

53. Anatoly Gromyko, "Africa in the Strategy of Western Imperialism," *International Affairs* (Moscow), February 1978.

54. *USSR and the Third World* (1976), p. 155.

55. *Europolitika,* 2 February 1978.

56. Richard Löwenthal, *Model or Ally: The Communist Powers and the Developing Countries* (New York: Oxford University Press, 1977), pp. 359–376.

57. Opening address at the International Conference of Third World Groups, East Berlin, October 1980, "Joint Struggle of the Working Class Movement and the National Liberation Movement Against Imperialism and for Social Progress," (Dresden: Verlag Zeit im Bild, 1981), p. 19.

58. *USSR and the Third World* (1978), p. 98.

59. Pouswarev and Selivanov, "The South Atlantic in NATO's Plans," *Krasnaia Zvezda,* 8 August 1976.

60. *Africa Contemporary Record, 1979–80,* edited by Colin Legum (London: Rex Collins, 1980), p. A167.

61. Robert Legvold, "The Soviet Union's Strategic Stake in Africa," in Jennifer Seymour Whitaker, ed., *Africa and the United States: Vital Interests* (New York: New York University Press, 1978), pp. 154–187.

62. Friedel Trappen and Ulbricht Weishauft, "Aktuelle Fragen des Kampfes und Nationale und Soziale Befreiung in Sub-Saharischen Afrika," *Deutsche Aussenpolitik* 24, no. 2 (February 1979).

63. Liviu Radu, "Romanian Involvement in Colonial Angola," *South African Journal of African Affairs,* 9, no. 3, 4 (1979):150–154.

64. Cited in *Karl Marx: Early Texts* (Oxford: Blackwells, 1971), p. 117.

65. See for example, R. Ulyanovsky, "On Countries of a Socialist Orientation," *Kommunist,* no. 11 (1979):30, for the optimistic (official) line: "On the whole the course of events has confirmed that the tendency towards a socialist orientation arises from amidst the liberation struggle of the peoples of Africa and is reproduced again and again—despite a great many difficulties and sometimes even temporary defeats."

66. *The Washington Post,* 20 October 1982.

67. For Soviet impressions of South Africa as a Western ally, see A. Kislov and V. Vasilkov, "The Current Stage of US Policy in Africa," *Asiia i afrika segodnia,* 9 September 1978, pp. 4–5.

68. For a Polish view of tripartite cooperation, see Leon Zurawicki, "The Prospects of Tripartite Co-operation," *Intereconomics* (Hamburg) 7/8 (1978):184–187.

69. *Business Europe,* 27 June 1980, p. 206.

5

Revolutionary Change in Africa: Some Implications for East German Policy Behavior

Bernard von Plate

It is clearly no coincidence that the German Democratic Republic (GDR) is often mentioned in the same breath with the Soviet Union and Cuba when the African policies of the socialist states are discussed. Why is this the case? One answer certainly emerges from the ongoing involvement of the GDR in a series of highly visible transformations on the African continent. The GDR supported the anticolonial liberation struggles of the MPLA in Angola and of FRELIMO in Mozambique both materially and through propaganda and has remained among both states' closest allies since independence. Ethiopia's antifeudal revolution has benefited from similar GDR engagement. Among the very few journeys that Socialist Unity Party (Sozialistische Einheitspartei Deutschlands [SED]) General Secretary and GDR Chief of State Erich Honecker has undertaken outside of the socialist bloc, two have brought him to Africa. In February 1979 Honecker visited Angola, Libya, Mozambique, and Zambia, and in autumn of the same year he went to Ethiopia and the People's Democratic Republic of Yemen (PDRY). Each of the honored heads of state had either already paid his respects in East Berlin or reciprocated Honecker's visit in the following months. Additionally, it should be counted among the most salient aspects of East German Africa policy that the GDR concluded its first treaties of friendship and cooperation involving nonsocialist bloc states with partners in Africa: Angola, 1979; Mozambique, 1979; and Ethiopia, 1979.

This list of important manifestations of the GDR's Africa policy could easily be extended and brought to include not only the 1970s and early 1980s, but also the two prior decades. A longer list of dates and events, however, would only serve to underline the basic point that the African continent represents a closely monitored area of interest for East German foreign policy.[1] In this regard (and the present chapter assumes this as its foundation) a major emphasis in East German activities is placed upon measures designed to support the claim to power by revolutionary regimes and to facilitate the conditions for such socioeconomic upheavals as seem to correspond to a Marxist-Leninist theory of development.[2] This is illustrated

---

Translated from German by R. Craig Nation

by the strong political interest that the GDR exhibits toward states like Angola, the Congo, Ethiopia, and Mozambique, which both in their own self-estimation and in the judgment of the GDR find themselves on the road toward socialism. These states serve as confirmation for an ideology that asserts that after independence, with historical inevitability, former colonies must begin a process of socioeconomic transformation.

It follows for the GDR that, although the independence of the African states is indeed important, it represents only the first step in a continuing process. Since the West's influence is used to resist this process, the GDR itself can hope to gain lasting allies by providing support and encouragement. In practice, this means that East Berlin attempts, more intensively than in the 1950s and 1960s when the goal of diplomatic recognition dominated its foreign relations, to influence the socioeconomic development of particularly those states designated as "progressive."

Drawing upon the experiences of the 1960s, during which Kwame Nkrumah was overthrown in Ghana and Mali underwent a reversal in political orientation, primary interest is accorded to a stabilization of the revolutionary regime and to its consolidation upon as broad a mass base as possible. The large number of party-to-party agreements which were concluded during the 1970s, and which have since continued in force, confirm these goals, as do reports that the GDR has at least temporarily assumed responsibility for the creation and training of internal state security organs and for the personal protection of revolutionary leaders in Angola, Ethiopia, and Mozambique. In the words of Erich Honecker, these goals of East German Africa policy are summarized as follows: "We attribute special significance to the states of socialist orientation, the development and growth of revolutionary-democratic and vanguard parties in Africa and Asia. For they embody social progress and represent a further great victory for scientific socialism."[3]

Utilizing such a definition of East German interests as background, one can partially measure the degree of success (or lack of success) of East German Africa policy according to how far it has succeeded in furthering revolutionary transformations that increase prospects for a social order with Marxist-Leninist characteristics to emerge. This chapter will utilize scientific-theoretical discussions conducted within the GDR as a means for evaluating the problem. More specifically, in what follows we will not attempt to contrast the *theoretical program* of the socialist oriented states with their transposition *into practice* of the ideological postulates of Marxism-Leninism. Rather, we are concerned primarily with the East German *image* of socioeconomic change in the Third World, and specifically in Africa. This may serve, where interrelationships can be established, as a foundation for some more general assertions concerning the Africa policy of the GDR. The primary question is, how does this policy evaluate the developmental process in Africa, which as Erich Honecker stated at the IXth Party Congress of the SED in 1976, has moved onto the road of social progress? Several conceptual illustrations are advanced in order to contribute to an understanding of the discussions surrounding these themes in the GDR.

Revolutionary Change in Africa: Positive Assessments

The debate over the prospects for socialist revolution and communist seizures of power in the young nation-states of the Third World is as old as the socialist system itself. It began in the course of the Bolshevik Revolution in Russia and has never subsided since. Examining the present state of the discussion in the Soviet Union and the rest of Eastern Europe, it is possible to distinguish between two broadly classified stages in revolutionary transformation. Thus, the beginning of socioeconomic upheaval leads to a *national-democratic revolution,* which in turn opens the possibility for an anticapitalist course of development. National-democratic revolutions are based upon a broad front of all those social groups within a state that find themselves rallied around an anti-Western posture. As a rule this includes the nationalist-oriented middle class, progressive representatives of the intelligentsia, petty bourgeois strata, industrial workers, and the mobilized segment of the rural population. Because of the economic backwardness of nearly all developing countries, their low educational levels, tribal divisions, and the inadequate organizational cohesion of socially and politically conscious forces, among which the working class remains in any case numerically very small, it is, according to the perspective being represented, not yet clear whether in the national-democratic phase of development the working class can force itself forward into a position of leadership. It follows from this evaluation of a heterogenous constellation of forces that the deepening of a national-democratic revolution is often essentially determined by a few leading individuals. So long as they work as an integrating factor in the revolutionary process and contribute to a mobilization of the masses, revolutionary democrats (as they are usually described) function as the irreplaceable leading personalities of a national revolutionary developmental stage.

It is worthwhile to keep this theoretical background in mind, though of course it only encompasses a number of key points and leaves aside the nuances of the discussion as it has unfolded over the past twenty-five years, in particular when one examines recent comments from the GDR concerning the Ethiopian revolution, which is still considered to be in a national-democratic phase.

The dynamic transition from a national-democratic to a *revolutionary-democratic* or *people's democratic* phase of development takes place when the revolutionary forces in a *state of socialist orientation* (a designation that is as a rule applied to the entire process) prove themselves strong enough to dispose of their bourgeois coalition partners and to construct a revolutionary dictatorship. Related to this is the construction of a vanguard party that adopts at least the pretense of adherence to the ideological and organizational principles of Marxism-Leninism.

Measured according to these criteria, in the literature of the GDR both Angola and Mozambique are considered as African states that have reached a revolutionary-democratic phase of development. After his participation in the Third FRELIMO Congress in spring 1977, Werner Lamberz, himself entrusted with particular responsibility for GDR Africa policy, described the transformation of FRELIMO into a vanguard party in the following words: "In this instance the growth of a national-democratic into a people's-democratic revolution became visible for the entire world, the turning point in an historical process was, so to speak, bathed for an instant in bright light."[4] In the same interview Lamberz not only declared that he had witnessed "the birth of a Marxist-Leninist party," but also bestowed upon it the honorable title of a "brother party," a reference which has since then not been repeated officially in reference to FRELIMO nor applied to any other party among the socialist oriented states of the Third World.

The former colonies of Lisbon which became independent in the wake of the Portuguese revolution serve above all as evidence for the GDR that the revolutionary process on the African continent has received a new impetus. The developments in Angola and Mozambique particularly strengthen confidence in East Berlin that on the basis of the changes already introduced, and even if "accompanied by complicated internal and external disputes,"[5] Marxist-Leninist ruling orders will eventually emerge. Correspondingly emphatic were the comments with which the GDR greeted the earlier developments in southern Africa during the mid-1970s.

In representing the Africa policy of the GDR and in judging its successes the Western press seems to orient itself above all around these apparently unclouded and optimistic evaluations. Thus states like Angola, Mozambique, and Ethiopia, given the revolutionary changes that they have accomplished, are often counted as loyal vassals of the Soviet Union and its partners in the Warsaw Pact. This evaluation is applied to the foreign policies of the aforementioned states as well as to their social and political goals. The conclusion drawn from these judgments asserts, as a rule, that it should be a primary task for the West to work against socialist influence in Africa, particularly through support for those states with market oriented economies. The socialist oriented states should in contrast be deemphasized as objects of foreign policy attention on the part of the West.

The question that presents itself in this context is the degree to which propagandistic commentary from the GDR may lead to an *incorrect* estimation of sociopolitical change in the socialist oriented states of Africa if, at the same time, one fails to take into consideration the larger debate within the GDR which often evaluates revolutionary successes in Africa with considerably greater modesty. In other words, it is necessary to look beyond the curtain of official propaganda in order to achieve a more differentiated image of the course of events in Africa and the problems associated with it for the GDR. In such an undertaking one must unavoidably come to terms with several apparently purely semantic distinctions.

Revolutionary Change in Africa:
Critical Alternatives

The scientific-technical discussion concerning the process of revolutionary transformation, particularly as regards Africa, is certainly not new, but it has noticeably increased in intensity in recent years. It provides—and this is its most conspicuous characteristic—an increasingly differentiated treatment of the developing nations and their problems, though without thereby making clear the degree to which insights achieved actually have an impact upon foreign policy practice. Nonetheless one should understand the discussion and its definitional concerns to be more than mere academic word play.

A comparison of relevant passages from Honecker's reports to the IXth and Xth Congresses of the SED in 1976 and 1981 provides a clue to the GDR's perception of social-revolutionary transformation in the states of Africa. In the mid-1970s Honecker introduced his remarks concerning the Third World with the observation: "In accordance with the laws of development of our epoch ever more peoples are effecting the transition from capitalism to socialism." Several sentences later he continues: "The movement of the peoples of Asia, Africa, and Latin America for national and social liberation is a powerful current in the struggle against imperialism. In the period covered by our report [1971-1976] Guinea-Bissau, the Cape Verde Islands, Mozambique, and Angola have completed the transition to progressive development. In Ethiopia the feudal-capitalistic monarchy was overthrown. In Madagascar, with the achievement of national independence, the journey toward social progress has begun." Honecker ends the portion of his report devoted to the Third World with the prophetic words: "The future belongs to socialism and communism."[6] The "anti-imperialistic optimism" in these remarks is unmistakable. In clear contrast, however, both in prioritization and in the tenor of commentary, are the comparable excerpts from the report delivered at the Xth Party Congress in 1981. Honecker begins with general praise for the international activity of the young nation-states, including a few references to support provided by the GDR. Any prognosis concerning future socioeconomic development in the states of socialist orientation is completely absent. Honecker limits himself instead to mentioning the far-reaching political changes in progress and concludes that the socialist alternative as a path of development is winning ever-more power of attraction and influence.[7]

A summary of these two comparable Party Congress reports indicates that in place of the untroubled optimism of the mid-1970s, in 1981 a clearly more modest attitude was dominant. A comparison of the Party Congress reports from the CPSU for these same years indicates that the change in mood was not limited to the GDR. The data underlines, in case there was ever any doubt, the ideological conformity between the GDR and the USSR, also with regard to social change in the Third World.

The change in mood discernible in official party documents finds its equivalent in a critical discussion of the situation of the developing nations, which was begun in the Soviet Union and has been in progress in the GDR for several years. A point of emphasis in the discussion is an evaluation of the progress of the revolutionary transformation process and of its prospects for the future in those developing nations designated as "progressive." Particular attention is directed toward those states which up to now have been subsumed under the general category of states of socialist orientation.

A first result of the scientific-theoretical debate is revealed by the fact that the time-frame within which a fundamental transformation of social relations in the developing nations in question can be expected is, on the basis of experience, presently presumed to be much more extended than was the case during the euphoric atmosphere of the prior decade. This critical appraisal has not become less pronounced despite years of attempts to build influence, particularly in those states that have supposedly taken the "road to socialism," but is rather more emphatically than ever defended by proponents of a critical analysis of the developing nations. The danger of the "reversability" of the revolutionary process has lost none of its significance. It encompasses (with some exceptions) not only the national-democratic states, but also those nations in which the transition to a revolutionary-democratic stage of development has already been completed. Thus Angola, Ethiopia, and Mozambique are indeed counted as states in an advanced phase of revolutionary change, but the issue of the process may in no way be considered as secure.

Particularly in recent years, at least several East German specialists have broadened the designation "socialist orientation" for the national-democratic and revolutionary-democratic states, in order to include the term *real* (real socialist orientation).[8] Assuming that this supplement is not without significance, the following interpretation seems plausible. The qualifier *real* was introduced by the GDR and the other People's Democracies of Eastern Europe to designate a more advanced stage of revolutionary development as the view gained acceptance that the road to a communistic social order would be much longer than initially assumed. The application of the term to the socialist oriented states of the Third World may be understood as both a summons to a more realistic estimation of the levels of development achieved in the revolutionary partner states, as well as the expression of more long-term policy calculations. This interpretation is supported by the fact that in the final instance existing social contradictions are as before perceived as "antagonistic"—a fact that distinguishes real socialism in Eastern Europe from real socialist oriented development in individual developing nations.

It is this more modest estimation of the quality of revolutionary transformation achieved to date in the Third World that stands out when a scholar such as professor Christian Mährdel of the Karl Marx University in Leipzig expresses uncertainty as to whether the road of socialist orientation is in fact leading toward a socialist order with Marxist-Leninist characteristics. Making clear reference to Marxist developmental theory, Mährdel poses the question whether the designation "transition to socialism" that is as a rule applied to the states of socialist orientation in fact appropriately renders the essence of the processes at work in these states in the sense of a "transitional period to socialism," as would correspond to a more orthodox use of terminology.[9]

In view of this distinction it is worth mentioning that Honecker, in his report to the Xth Party Congress of the SED, declined to provide a theoretically based ranking of the states of socialist orientation according to their level of development. That may well have served as a first indication that the results of scientific analysis of revolutionary transformation in the Third World will not remain locked in an academic ivory tower but rather have begun to find their reflection in official pronouncements. To this extent we may consider the theoretical discussion in the GDR—and the various shades of emphasis represented during its course—as an important indicator of both continuity and change in the external relations of the GDR with its revolutionary partners in the Third World.

The designation *socialist orientation,* according to some development research in the GDR, refers above all to a subjective choice. It merely acknowledges the possibility of a socialist future. Mährdel writes in this regard: "that socialist oriented development does not yet constitute the transition to socialism (even though some individual elements are present *in isolation,* which are comparable during this early phase with an authentic, *uniform* revolutionary process of transition to socialism), but rather a form of drawing closer to the socialist revolution, derives first of all from the *objective* fundamentals of this form of revolutionary process" [emphasis in original].[10] It follows as a logical consequence of this statement that Mährdel rejects any equivalence between "the processes really at work today, and what is possible for socialist orientation *in the future*" [emphasis in original].[11]

The critical reconsideration of revolutionary transformations in several African states (and in the entire Third World) currently in progress in the GDR includes the question of to what extent revolutions in Africa may be compared with the assumption of power by socialist regimes in Eastern Europe during the postwar years. In this regard interest is focused upon the role of the working class in the revolutionary transformation process of the socialist oriented partner states. The point of departure for these considerations to date is the assertion that in Eastern Europe the proletariat was able to achieve hegemony from the very outset of the process through "organs of people's power." This state of affairs, however, does not exist in any of the states of socialist orientation. The conclusion drawn is that it would amount to a falsification of the concept of people's democracy in Marxist-Leninist revolutionary theory if this fundamental premise was "modified" in such a way as would lead to the rejection of an irreplaceable feature of a people's democratic revolution. "Democratic 'people's revolution' (as a scientific category) and people's democratic revolutions are not merely interchangeable concepts. Socialist orientation, in the form which it has achieved up to the present, can be compared to a certain extent with 'people's revolution', but its development into a people's democratic form of the transition to socialism remains only a *possibility* and, when also achievable, a *perspective* for the particular (revolutionary or evolutionary) *qualitative transformation* of the hitherto existing developmental forms" [emphasis in original].[12]

The intent of this statement is unambiguous. The People's Republics in Eastern Europe and the People's Republics in Africa (Angola, Benin, the Congo, Guinea, Mozambique) have the label, but certainly not the substance, of power relationships in common. Any attempt to call this decisive difference into question would result in an idealization of the African states that have taken the road of anticapitalist development.

As a further indication of the relevance of specialized, scientific discussions in the shaping of official party pronouncements, it is worthwhile mentioning in the present regard that Honecker, in his report to the Xth Party Congress of the SED with an eye toward Mozambique and other states in the Third World, also speaks of "people's revolutions." He thereby adopts the relevant distinction drawn from revolutionary theory.

The work of Horst Lehfeld of the Karl Marx Higher Party School (Parteihochschule) of the SED Central Committee likewise presents a critical reappraisal of revolutionary transformation processes, which concerning its potential consequences goes well beyond the appraisals already cited.¹³ He is also primarily concerned with achieving an accurate perception and logical grasp of the revolutionary changes occurring in the Third World. Lehfeld asserts that differences of interpretation over a number of concepts have come to light not only within the GDR, but also among the partner states in Africa. As substantiation the author refers to the debating briefs of Mozambique's FRELIMO, Zambia's UNIP, Angola's MPLA, and "many others" at the International Scientific Conference in Berlin during October 1980. His enumeration is particularly worthy of attention because it directs notice to the complete conference protocol, which may be considered as a semiofficial reflection of the conceptions of socialism dominant in the states mentioned.¹⁴ The listing of particularly those parties with which the GDR feels itself to be most closely related may, at the same time, serve as evidence that substantial differences remain hidden beneath superficial, rhetorical accord.

Lehfeld in particular stimulates reconsideration of potential political consequences with the critical remarks that he directs at the concept of socialist orientation—up to now a designation broadly applied to all those Third World states regarded as "progressive" in their social policies. As concerns the relationship between the national-democratic revolution and socialist orientation, Lehfeld provides the following logical observations: as national-democratic revolutions pass through stages in which "real socialism" is not (or not yet) the goal of development, is it in fact correct to apply the term "socialist orientation" to them "in distinction to those nations in which the leading revolutionary forces have decided for a socialist *development* in the sense of scientific socialism?"¹⁵ Lehfeld continues, "the only guarantee for the completion of the national-democratic revolution and the creation of the necessary conditions for its growth into a socialist revolution is the transition to the hegemony of the working class . . . . This process has begun to occur precisely in nations undergoing socialist development."¹⁶ Listing these states as Angola, Ethiopia, Mozambique, and the PDRY, Lehfeld notes that "alliance with world-socialism has here achieved a competely new and much higher character, and clearly a far greater significance than is the case for states of socialist orientation. These nations are thus developing into *brother nations* of the states of the socialist community" [emphasis in original].¹⁷

If one inquires into the political implications of the distinction made by Lehfeld between "orientation" and "development," which indeed is not shared by all GDR theoreticians working with the developing nations, it seems to contain a certain logic. In the case of states like Angola, Ethiopia, Mozambique, and the PDRY, Lehfeld seems to be excluding a *reversal* of the revolutionary process. They are advancing along the road toward the status of "brother states." In view of this novel designation, which to be sure has not found a place in official terminology, one may inquire whether, at least in the opinion of some GDR theoreticians, the GDR's relationship with the states in question might be placed upon the foundation of "socialist internationalism." Such a conclusion, which Lehfeld leaves unspecified, contains as a consequence the commitment to defend the "revolutionary achievements" of the states undergoing "socialist development" up to and including direct assistance from the GDR. In other words, Lehfeld's explanations imply a readiness to apply the Brezhnev Doctrine beyond the immediately contiguous sphere of socialist domination in Eastern and Central Europe.

In contrast to this hypothetical political option extracted from theoretical discussion, however, stands the fact that all treaties of friendship and cooperation concluded by the GDR with partners outside the socialist state system recognize only "proletarian internationalism" as their underlying principle. It is moreover quite unlikely that the GDR is ready for such an extensive engagement and that in the event it would receive the consent of its treaty partners in Africa. For these reasons any translation into practice of Lehfeld's theoretical position is hardly to be expected.

The specialized discussion and remarks described to this point, and their potential political relevance, relate above all to the status and prospects of socialist development in the Third World. The picture traced would be one-sided, however, if it remained limited to the social-revolutionary states. In order to complete the picture it should be noted that the official evaluation of the process of *capitalistic* development has also undergone modifications. At the outset of the 1970s, any and all developmental perspectives were still being denied to the capitalistic states of the Third World.[18] In place of this sweeping judgment, a new outlook has recently appeared within which the following distinction is emphasized: as before, an attempt to develop based upon "dependency" vis-à-vis the large capitalist powers is accorded few prospects, but in contrast some prospects for success (though in the last instance also limited) are now granted to a "national-capitalist" orientation.[19]

A logical pattern emerges from an evaluation of the political relevance of this distinction. The process of differentiation in progress in the Third World and its reflection in the theoretical literature of the GDR are occurring during a period when the economic demands of the developing nations are being directed with increasing frequency not only against the Western industrial states, but also against the socialist states of Eastern Europe. As a counter to these claims, the argument that the former colonial powers bear sole responsibility for the economic backwardness of the developing nations (accompanied by repeated references to the "perpetrators of neocolonial exploitation") has clearly lost resonance, notably since the World Trade Conference in Nairobi during 1976. Given these trends, an increasing number of voices in the GDR now accent the argument that "the restructuring of international economic relations on a democratic foundation is above all dependent upon the extent to which the developing nations themselves carry on a consistent struggle against neocolonialism and effectively control the imperialist monopolies, upon the extent to which the positive experiences of the socialist nations in the creation of independent national economies are taken advantage of."[20] The GDR is openly striving not only to place the Western industrial states in the pillory but also to call attention to the responsibility of the developing nations themselves for their own underdevelopment. The quite positive valuation of the "independent national economy," within which relations of production are no longer made the decisive measure, creates the impression that the GDR has prepared an additional level of argumentation upon which the economic demands of the developing nations can be parried.

This overview of scientific-theoretical discussions concerning the developing nations carried on within the GDR allows two conclusions to be drawn. The concept of an antiimperialist alliance between the GDR and the totality of developing nations retains its validity on one level. It is, however, more than ever a purely ideological formula, which reveals virtually nothing concerning the operational concepts underlying East German foreign policy. It additionally disguises the fact—and special attention should be called to this point—that in the GDR there exists an increasingly differentiated image of developments in the Third World, a trend which has become noticeably more pronounced during the late 1970s and early 1980s. This observation leads to the assertion (and herein lies the second conclusion to be drawn from an analysis of East German research concerning the developing nations) that in the GDR an attempt is underway to utilize less ambiguous designations than has been the case heretofore, when Third World states were grouped together haphazardly under the general categories "socialist oriented" or "progressive," in order to more precisely describe and distinguish between the developing nations according to relative levels of sociopolitical achievement.

Revolutionary Theory and Foreign Policy Practice

In individual instances it has been demonstrated that some, though certainly not all, conceptual categories recommended by GDR theoreticians have found their way into official party pronouncements. A step beyond this was to interpret the scientific debate in terms of its overall relevance for the operative policies of the GDR toward the developing nations. In making such an attempt, however, one must still ask—though without necessarily seeking to deal in any thoroughgoing manner with the ever-controversial problem of the relationship of ideology to a pragmatic assessment of foreign policy interests—what *kind* of political significance can be accorded to formalized ideological concepts such as those in question.

An examination of the discussion carried on since the 1950s concerning the possibilities for revolutionary change outside the communist power-sphere, and over the correct tactics for socialist foreign policy in relation to the young nation-states of the Third World, leads to the conclusion that at no time was the discussion being conducted purely for its own sake. The refinement of an ideological terminology suitable for the Third World has as a rule served immediate political requirements. For example, the concept of the national-democratic state was invented during the late 1950s and early 1960s just as a large number of new states stepped onto the political stage for the first time. In virtually all of these states a strong proletarian base was lacking. In only a few did a communist party capable of acting exist. Only their anti-Western alignment turned the former colonies into desired partners for the socialist camp. The concept of the national-democratic state, as Sylvia Edgington concludes, was "obviously intended to help justify Khrushchev's policy of extending ties with Third World states."[21]

The overthrow of Nkrumah in Ghana during 1966, and Ja'far al-Numayri's turn toward a Western oriented foreign policy in the Sudan five years later, made the inadequacies of a national-democratic concept of development obvious. Both events gave rise to considerable doubt as to the political reliability of national-democratic leadership. According to the disappointed summary of a GDR specialist, a too "extensive concentration of decision-making authority . . . and personification of power" leads to illusions about the real strength of a regime.[22] The conclusion drawn from this argument, both in Soviet and East German publications, was that individual political leaders, on the basis of their as a rule "non-proletarian" origins, tend to succumb all too easily to the dangers of "over confidence and self-aggrandizement," and often degenerate to "petty bourgeois nationalism," giving their hold on power priority over alliance relations with the socialist states.[23] A team of authors comes to a similar conclusion when they point out "that social development often . . . encompasses a certain contradictory character which results from the class-character of petty-bourgeois, revolutionary-democratic leadership forces . . . Social praxis in the majority of the liberated nations with a progressive internal and foreign policy orientation will be distinguished for a relatively long period" by the contradictory social character of the petty-bourgeoisie, drawn simultaneously toward the position of the working class and of the bourgeoisie.[24]

The experiences of the 1960s also found confirmation during the 1970s. The foreign policy reorientations of Egypt and Somalia along with the clear disinclination of Ahmed Sékou Touré in Guinea to subordinate himself to Soviet military interests underlined the ideological unreliability of centralized, one-man regimes. In the face of these setbacks and difficulties the argument insisting upon the necessity for a vanguard party received new impetus. At the same time the familiar ambivalence of national-revolutionary leaders served as ideological justification for offering them support as individuals only so long as the "subjective factor" seemed to be serving "revolutionary progress" and leading to a growth of socialist influence. The cynical dismissal of Teferi Benti, the former Chairman of the Provisional Military Administrative Council of Ethiopia (the Derg), with whom GDR Foreign Minister Oskar Fischer had experienced a "warm encounter" only several weeks before his overthrow, demonstrated how far national democratic leaders temporarily favored by the GDR can fall from one day to another.[25]

The individual steps via which East Berlin translates the goal of indoctrinating and organizing the populations of its African partner states into practical policy cannot as a rule be inferred from information made publically available in the GDR. Very often one encounters the general remark that "in the relations of the SED with revolutionary-democratic parties significant attention will be paid to interactions with social organizations."[26] Reports concerning contacts on the level of mass organizations, however, scarcely go beyond the announcement that they have taken place. Given such a meager availability of sources, the texture of GDR policy cannot be described in detail.

One is nonetheless quite justified in describing the theoretical literature of the GDR as a reliable reflection of the problems with which it is confronted in relations with the "progressive" states of the Third World. To a degree, it does not seem inadmissable to draw inferences with operational relevance from the multifaceted debate concerning the developing nations in progress in the GDR. In this connection it is of secondary importance whether scientific discussions merely react to the exigencies of practical politics or whether they independently prepare the ground for pivotal political decisions. The question, "Which came first?" must in the end remain unanswered.

**Revolutionary Theory and Foreign
Policy Constraints**

It can be confidently asserted that a more cautious evaluation of the chances for successful revolutionary change in the Third World has taken the place of the former revolutionary euphoria in East German policy conceptualization. The positions achieved during the 1970s—especially in Angola, Ethiopia, Mozambique, and the PDRY—are worth defending and developing; however, as secure allies the aforementioned states remain as before merely a hope for the future. Precisely because the process of socioeconomic transformation in the nations undergoing "socialist development" has revealed itself as more long-term and expensive than was originally supposed, the GDR is being forced to concentrate its energies. The export of Marxist-Leninist principles obviously reaches its limits when it cannot simultaneously be combined with a comprehensive program of economic assistance. The leading position of the former Portuguese colonies in southern Africa and Ethiopia in the GDR's trade with developing nations indicates that East Berlin is determined to undertake this double task. However, the fact that the GDR, together with the other CMEA states, has not been able to keep pace with the financial demands of its African treaty partners emerges as a growing problem. Angola and Mozambique in particular have developed prudent contacts with Western industrial states capable of providing needed financial aid. The GDR thus confronts the difficult task of tolerating these contacts on one hand, while simultaneously doing everything possible in order to prevent economic opening to the West from turning into a process placing revolutionary achievements in question.

From the GDR's intensive and multidimensional concentration upon those few African states whose revolutionary progress can be interpreted as a confirmation of its own social order follows the great reserve with which East Berlin approaches revolutionary experiments elsewhere on the continent. The GDR is clearly determined to avoid the political costs that have been associated with setbacks in Africa in the past. With the distinction between socialist orientation and socialist development East Berlin has created an ideological formula that sanctions a cautious reserve vis-à-vis those states whose sociopolitical goals do not (or not yet) correspond to a Marxist-Leninist model. Thus the declared intention of East Berlin to encourage the progress of the states of socialist orientation has in the past remained without material consequences worthy of note. Certainly this situation will not be changing in the foreseeable future.

It would undoubtedly be one-sided to ascribe the increasingly selective interpretation of the sociopolitical interests of the GDR in Africa and the readiness to provide economic aid associated with them entirely to a more differentiated image of future prospects for revolutionary change. The shift in accent in favor of a more realistic stock-taking of the current situation is part of an integrated policy emanating from East Berlin, which must take account of new constraints in its Africa policy and elsewhere. These new constraints include above all the GDR's own limited economic capacity. The level of East German foreign indebtedness and reduced oil deliveries from the Soviet Union have forced the GDR toward a policy in which its own economic interests are accorded clear priority. This is only achievable, however, when the goal of a revolutionary transformation of the global correlation of forces is either withdrawn or put off indefinitely. In relation to those African states which are well-endowed with raw materials such as Angola and Mozambique, it seems that the economic interests of the GDR can be combined with support for a Leninist conception of social policy, at least in the medium term. In relation to the majority of African states this is not the case. The possibilities for the GDR to commit itself to a relationship with the states of Africa founded upon the concept of "proletarian internationalism," when the prospect for mutual economic advantage is not present, seem virtually exhausted.

Given these economic constraints, it is only to be expected when the number of voices in the GDR positively evaluating a national-capitalist developmental strategy increases. Such a strategy corresponds to the main goal of socialist foreign policy—to reduce the political and economic influence of the West—without thereby allowing direct demands upon the socialist states themselves to arise. This trend toward a more pragmatic image of the route via which economic problems in the Third World can be approached at least potentially broadens the field for intersystem cooperative action between East and West. Triangular industrial cooperation could be one area where the GDR might show itself more open and flexible in the future.

Conclusion

The critical reappraisal of the prospects for socialist development in Africa being conducted in the GDR should encourage the West to avoid the rigidly orthodox approach which has been characteristic of the East bloc in the past. The conception of socialist development dominant in several African states is combined with the hope for an accelerated, catch-up industrialization program. For success in the undertaking, however, they require the support of both East and West. The latter should not make its willingness to provide assistance dependent upon the fact that the sociopolitical order in the progressive states of Africa contains pseudosocialistic aspects or does not correspond to a liberal-democratic ideal model. Socioeconomic change in Africa is an urgent requirement in the interest of hungry and impoverished peoples. The attempt to instrumentalize this occasionally revolutionary process of change on behalf of narrow bloc interests stands in contradiction above all to the interests of the affected states. In the literature of the GDR a critical evaluation of a socialist policy for the developing nations is discernible. The West should not lag behind the GDR (and the Soviet Union) in providing its own realistic estimates of the possibilities for revolutionary development in Africa.

Notes

1. An excellent overview of the GDR's Africa policy is provided by Melvin Croan, "A New Afrika Korps?," *The Washington Quarterly* 3 (Win-

ter 1980):21-37. Croan deals in particular with the dependency relationship between the GDR's Africa policy and the interests of the Soviet Union and analyzes its internal and inter-German policy implications. An overview rich in data is supplied by Hans Siegfried Lamm & Siegfried Kupper, *DDR und Dritte Welt* (Munich/Vienna: Oldenbourg, 1975). See also Bernard von Plate, "Afrika südlich der Sahara," in Eberhard Schulz, et al., eds., *Drei Jahrzehnte Aussenpolitik der DDR: Bestimmungsfaktoren, Instrumente, Aktionsfelder* (Munich/Vienna: Oldenbourg, 1979), pp. 657-671.

2. See Croan, "A New Afrika Korps?," p. 22.

3. Erich Honecker, "Bericht des Politbüros an das 11. ZK der SED," *Neues Deutschland,* 14 December 1979.

4. "An Brennpunkten des revolutionären Prozesses in Afrika," *Horizont* 10, no. 9 (1977):3.

5. *Protokoll der Verhandlungen des IX. Parteitages der Sozialistischen Einheitspartei Deutschlands* (East Berlin: 1976), p. 50.

6. Ibid., p. 48*ff.*

7. *Protokoll der Verhandlungen des X. Parteitages der Sozialistischen Einheitspartei Deutschlands* (East Berlin: 1981), p. 48*ff.*

8. In this regard see particularly Christian Mährdel, "Revolutionstheoretische Bemerkungen zur sozialistischen Orientierung gesellschaftlicher Entwicklungen im heutigen Afrika und Asien," *Asien, Afrika, Lateinamerika* 8, no. 3 (1980):421. See also Christian Mährdel, *Afrika im antiimperialistischen Kampf. Probleme eines Kontinents* (East Berlin: 1978), p. 17.

9. Mährdel, "Revolutionstheoretische Bemerkungen," p. 423.

10. Ibid.

11. Ibid., p. 424.

12. Ibid.

13. Horst Lehfeld, "Fragen der nationalen Befreiungsrevolution in Ländern Afrikas und Asiens mit sozialistischer Entwicklung," *Asien, Afrika, Lateinamerika* 10, no. 2 (1982):207-216.

14. *Internationale Wissenschaftliche Konferenz in Berlin vom 20. bis 24. Oktober 1980. Der gemeinsame Kampf der Arbeiterbewegung und der internationalen Befreiungsbewegung gegen Imperialismus und für sozialen Fortschritt* 2 vols. (Dresden: 1981).

15. Lehfeld, "Fragen der nationalen Befreiungsrevolution," p. 209.

16. Ibid., p. 210.

17. Ibid., p. 211.

18. Gertraud Liebscher, "Imperialismus und Entwicklungsländer," *Einheit* 28, no. 3 (1973):371*ff.*

19. Karen Brutenz, *Die befreiten Länder in der Welt von heute* (East Berlin: 1982), p. 31*ff.*

20. R. Grimm, H.-G. Haupt, and I. Richter, "Zusammenarbeit der Mitgliedsländer des RGW mit Entwicklungsländern," *Deutsche Aussenpolitik* 27, no. 2 (1982):16.

21. Sylvia Edgington, "The State of Socialist Orientation: A Soviet Model for Political Development," *Soviet Union/Union Sovietique* 8, no. 2 (1981):229.

22. Gerhard Brehme, *Der nationaldemokratische Staat in Asien und Afrika* (East Berlin: 1976), p. 147.

23. Christian Mährdel, "Die Volksmassen in den nationalen Befreiungsbewegungen unserer Zeit," *Zeitschrift für Geschichtswissenschaft* 25, no. 10 (1977):1282.

24. Grimm, Haupt, and Richter, "Zusammenarbeit der Mitgliedsländer," p. 27.

25. *Neues Deutschland,* 20 December 1976, p. 5.

26. Jürgen Zenker, "Zusammenarbeit der SED mit revolutionärdemokratischen Parteien in Afrika und Asien," *Deutsche Aussenpolitik* 22, no. 10 (1977):105.

6

From Intervention to Consolidation: The Soviet Union and Southern Africa

Seth Singleton

What are the Soviets up to in southern Africa, and what should be done about it? South Africa justifies its massive military buildup of recent years, as well as its increasingly aggressive police actions throughout the region, on the grounds that the Republic is the target of a Soviet-directed "total onslaught."[1] The reality is that there is a symbiotic interaction between the growth of Soviet, East German, and Cuban presence in southern Africa and South Africa's paranoid behavior toward its neighbors: each feeds on and amplifies the other.

The basic Soviet interest in southern Africa as of 1984 is to encourage (1) the polarization of the region and (2) the genesis of a Soviet-African alliance of "socialist orientation" against the United States in particular and the West in general. To serve these ends, the Soviets know that they must provoke the United States into a closer association with South Africa. Thus the great irony is that the Soviet Union and South Africa, because they share an overwhelming interest in moving the United States into closer association with Pretoria, are tactical allies in the restructuring of southern Africa now under way.

The Soviet Union has invested sixty-seven years of policy and propaganda in the idea that the West is the natural enemy of Third World peoples, wanting only to dominate and exploit them in pursuit of profit. While Soviet assumptions and rhetoric have changed very little over two generations, the world has evolved out from underneath them. Asian and African nations increasingly control their own economies and natural resources, and now compete with—and sometimes make war on—each other. On the Horn of Africa, everyone understands that the Soviets sought to gain advantage by exploiting a quarrel among Africans. Being branded as imperialists—as in Afghanistan, Indochina, and the Horn—undercuts the whole edifice and rationale of Soviet policy. In southern Africa, however, Moscow could become the armorer and protector of a cause considered righteous by all Africans and much of the rest of the world.

Based on an article originally published as "The Shared Tactical Goals of South Africa and the Soviet Union," <u>CSIS Africa Notes,</u> No. 12, April 26, 1983, Washington, D.C.

Southern Africa is not important to Soviet security in any way and thus is not worth much financial commitment or risk. Soviet policy has always put the security of the Motherland and of the contiguous empire first; only when that is assured can resources be spared for expansion, and then only in ways that do not risk gains of socialism already won. Africa has had its share of ill-fated Soviet adventures, notably Khrushchev's gamble in support of Patrice Lumumba in the Congo (Zaire) in 1960–1961, and placement of all bets in Zimbabwe in the 1970s on Joshua Nkomo's ZAPU. And, contrary to the view from Pretoria, the Soviets have thus far spent very little in southern Africa. The cost of the 25,000 or so Cuban military personnel in Angola, of a few hundred Soviet bloc military advisors and technical assistance personnel, of equipping and training a few thousand SWAPO guerrillas and handfuls of African National Congress of South Africa (ANC) commandos has been minimal. Since Angola pays for the Cubans in hard cash earned from oil exports to the United States,[2] the whole political-military operation in southern Africa probably costs Moscow less than 2 of the Soviet army's 180 divisions. As for risk, the Soviets thus far have maneuvered carefully to expose no trip-wires that might force intervention to save their reputation. When the South Africans invade Angola, the Cubans, with rare exceptions not of their choosing, stay well out of sight.

Yet if major risk and financial outlay can be avoided, southern Africa offers a unique opportunity for a skillfully played Soviet policy. Soviet strategists fully appreciate that (1) southern Africa is not important per se to the Soviet Union; (2) it is important to the West; (3) the United States is caught between moral opposition to apartheid and the economic and perceived strategic benefits of the status quo. At a time when the Soviet Union is on the military and economic defensive in Europe, the Middle East, and Asia, it has stepped up its diplomatic and propaganda offensive focused on the United States as "the bulwark of militarism and reaction." With appropriate U.S. cooperation, southern Africa could be a prime area of opportunity.

Soviet Policy: 1975–1979

The period of expansion of Soviet and allied influence in southern Africa lasted from the intervention in Angola in 1975 until the Zimbabwe settlement at Lancaster House in December 1979. During this burst of activity, the Soviets transported Cuban soldiers and weapons to Angola; worked with Cubans to train and equip 10,000 or more guerrillas of the ZAPU wing of the Patriotic Front for the war in Rhodesia; fostered East German and Cuban training of several thousand guerrillas of SWAPO's People's Liberation Army of Namibia (PLAN) to fight in Namibia; and after the Soweto

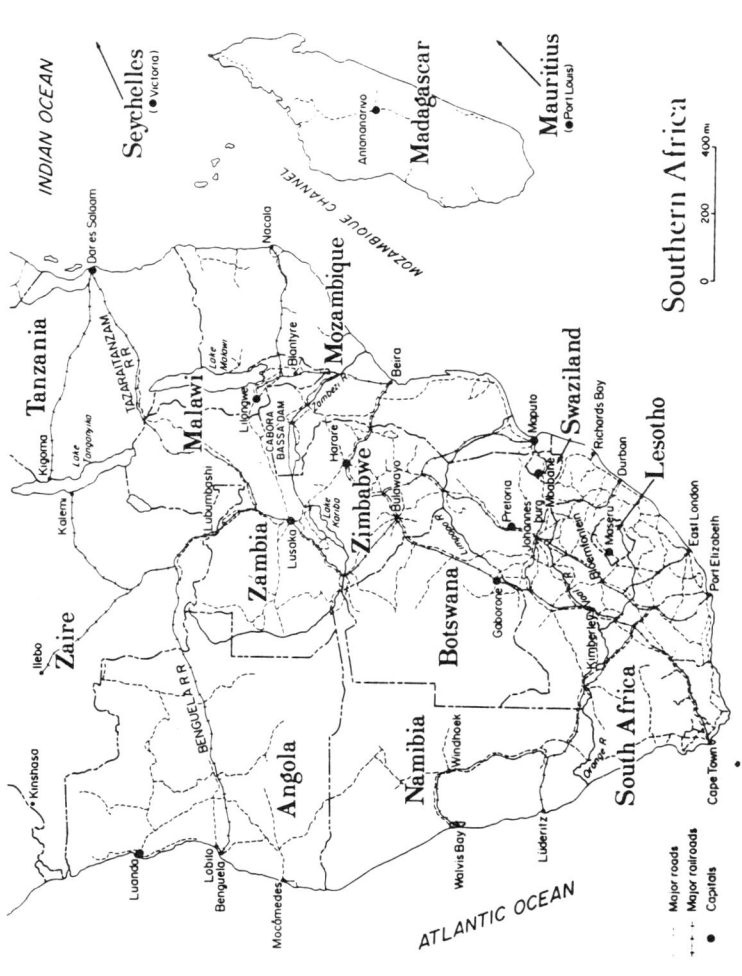

Figure 6-1. Southern Africa

Source: Thomas M. Callaghy, ed., *South Africa in Southern Africa*. Copyright © 1983 Praeger Publishers. Reprinted by permission of Praeger Publishers.

violence of 1976 began training guerrillas of *Umkhonto we Sizwe,* the military arm of the ANC, in Angolan camps.

The offensive military activity was only one side of the policy. The other was the effort to make real communists out of those southern African leaders who accepted Soviet and allied connections. An assessment of earlier failures of their economic, military, and diplomatic support to make permanent allies of countries such as Egypt, Algeria, Ghana, and Guinea led to an extension of the methods used to cement Soviet relations with Cuba. Thus in Angola and Mozambique, the Soviet involvement was not only in (1) technical assistance and military training, but also in (2) party-building, Marxist-Leninist indoctrination, and internal security, and (3) encouragement of reliance on Soviet "might" for protection against the nearby external enemy.[3]

Readjustments since 1979

In 1979 and 1980, Soviet policy received an unexpected blow. Developments in Zimbabwe proved, once again, that Soviet and allied military supplies and training do not create political puppets. In the Lancaster House negotiations leading to Zimbabwean independence, both Joshua Nkomo (whose ZIPRA forces had received the bulk of Soviet support) and ZANU's Robert Mugabe followed their own interests and excluded the Soviets from any effective indirect role. And, whereas the Soviet expectation had been that a Zimbabwe "of socialist orientation" would create an entire Soviet-linked zone across southern Africa, the Mugabe-led government that resulted from the 1980 election held off for almost a year before establishing diplomatic ties with Moscow and has demonstrated a clear preference for Western and Chinese political and economic links.[4] (North Korea, selected to train the Zimbabwean army's Fifth and Sixth Brigades, follows a Third World policy independent of the Soviets and often closer to the Chinese.)

The Zimbabwe setback coincided with the invasion of Afghanistan, increasing turmoil in Poland, Chinese-American collaboration, the deepening crisis of the Soviet economy, and a period of U.S. military expansion. This chain of developments called for a shift from expansion to consolidation of Soviet gains in southern Africa and a lowering of the area in the hierarchy of Soviet concerns. This is unlikely to change in the near future. If Soviet credibility and prestige are challenged in a way that cannot be ignored, the Soviets will act, but they are unlikely to take the initiative.

We must keep in mind that Soviet power projection is not some constant, mindless force. Soviets are Clausewitzians with Leninist objectives. When expansion based on military might reaches its limits, the course is to

From Intervention to Consolidation

defend existing positions, to minimize risks, to build up power, and to concentrate on hearts and minds while waiting for future opportunities. Much less is heard these days about Soviet "might" and "the changing correlation of forces," and much more about U.S. "militarism" and "aggression."[5] In southern Africa the tasks now being accorded most importance are defense of socialism's gains in Angola and Mozambique, cultivation of the other Front Line states, maintenance of Soviet and other allied influence with SWAPO, and establishing that the United States is South Africa's patron and ally and therefore Africa's enemy.[6] These aims are interconnected, and all of them depend on provoking the United States and the West to oppose African interests.

The argument that Soviet involvement in southern Africa is aimed at undermining Western access to the area's strategic minerals isn't wrong, but it puts the cart before the horse. Soviet policy is fundamentally political, not military. Today's strategists are Leninists, not the heirs of Admiral Mahan. If political expansion should provide the opportunities for naval or intelligence facilities, the Soviets would move through the open door. Certainly Moscow would be happy to control the world's supply of chromite and platinum and much of the manganese, gold, and diamonds. But these possibilities are not their basic motivation. In the case of Zimbabwe's chromite, the object was to implant Soviet influence and presence in a liberated Zimbabwe "of socialist orientation." The possible use of that influence at some future time to corner the world chromite market was an intriguing but peripheral consideration.

The Limits of Soviet Influence

In southern Africa, as throughout the continent, the ebb and flow of Soviet power depends on the extent to which this power is needed by Africans. The Soviets, Cubans, and East Germans have varying degrees of influence with the governments of Angola and Mozambique, and within SWAPO and the ANC. In Angola and Mozambique, they train the internal security police and have tried to create a disciplined army politically loyal to the central leadership.[7] Other Front Line states (notably Zambia, Tanzania, and now Botswana) have purchased Soviet arms and/or aircraft, and Zimbabwe has some left over from the liberation war. After Ethiopia and Angola, Tanzania and Zambia were recipients of the greatest value of Soviet arms in 1976–1980. In that period, of a total of $3,995 million in Soviet and East European arms transfers to Sub-Saharan Africa, 34 percent went to the Front Line states. Of the rest, 49 percent went to Ethiopia, leaving a mere 17 percent for the other nations of black Africa.[8] (See table 6–1.)

Table 6-1
Soviet and East European Arms Transfers to Sub-Saharan Africa, 1976-1980
(millions of current dollars)

Ethiopia	$1,950
Front Line States:	
Angola	$620
Tanzania	$320
Zambia	$220
Mozambique	$185
Total	$1,345
Other Sub-Saharan African countries	$700
Total	$3,995

Note the relatively small amount to Mozambique. Also, the Angola figure does not include transfers from Cuba. ACDA figures list $260 million to Angola from "other" sources, probably Cuba, in this period.

Source: U.S. Arms Control and Disarmament Agency, *World Military Expenditures and Arms Transfers, 1971-1980* (Washington, D.C.: U.S. Government Printing Office, 1983), p. 117.

What the Soviets and their allies have been neither able nor inclined to provide, even to Mozambique and Angola, is effective help in rebuilding and developing the region's war-ravaged economies. Angola's budget is heavily dependent on oil exports to the United States, and Mozambique's major source of revenue (from workers' remittances, railroad and port user fees, and payments for electric power) is South Africa. The Soviets import almost nothing from southern Africa and export very little to the region apart from arms. Cubans, East Germans, Soviets, and other East Europeans provide technical assistance, which is cheap (Cuba particularly has many trained and underemployed young people) but nowhere in the Soviet bloc under current conditions of economic stress and retrenchment is there much food, money, oil, or consumer goods to spare for marginal clients. Mozambique, which has never received anything approximating the aid it has sought from the Soviet Union, was apparently turned down in 1981 for membership in CMEA (Comecon). The advantages of CMEA association are implicit in the commitment to "level up" each member to the standards of the richer countries. The overriding factor in Mozambique's failure to gain entry would seem to be that "levelling up" of Cuba and Vietnam is already more than the Soviet economy can afford.[9]

The situation least favorable to growth of Soviet influence in southern Africa is one in which the Front Line states (including Angola, Mozambique, and an independent Namibia under majority rule) enjoy a period of peace and security which allows them to turn toward the tasks of economic development. In those circumstances, what the Soviet Union and its allies have to offer—weapons and military/security training—become largely irrelevant. American, European, and also Brazilian capital and technology become overwhelmingly important. For economic development, the West is the natural ally.[10]

But it is legitimate to ask the question, who can be sure that Western trade and investment would pull Angola and Mozambique away from the Soviet bloc rather than just finance a more comfortable transition into it? The answer depends on how one assesses the internal political and power structure in Angola's MPLA and Mozambique's FRELIMO. Do the Soviets and their allies have power *within* Angola or Mozambique to overthrow and replace any leadership that tries to escape the Soviet connection? How committed are the leaders of the two governing parties to the Soviet bloc (which is not the same as asking if they are committed Marxists, since Tito and Mao were certainly Marxists)?

The Soviets and their allies are engaged in activities that deeply penetrate the political workings of Angola and Mozambique—party organization, ideological training, propaganda coordination, the internal security police. If the leadership can be rendered secure and committed, why not let Gulf Oil pay for Cuban troops and let American taxpayers do for Mozambique what Herbert Hoover's American Relief Administration did for the hungry of Russia in Lenin's day? The catch is that ideological commitment is far less certain in Angola and Mozambique in 1984 than in the Russia of 1921.

Angolan and Mozambican policies are more rather than less pragmatic and self-interested after nearly nine postindependence years of close association with the Soviet Union and its allies. Both countries actively seek European trade and investment, maintain close relations with non-Marxist Front Line states, play key roles in the continental Organization of African Unity and the regional Southern African Development Coordination Conference (SADCC), have been receptive to the efforts of the United States and other members of the five-nation Western "Contact Group" coordinating Namibian independence negotiations, and have indicated that they will soon enter into formal negotiations regarding signature of the Lomé Convention. Angola's recent meetings with South African officials and with the United States, along with Mozambique's April 1982 arms and military training agreement with Portugal and its January 1984 security discussions with South Africa, provide further evidence that the leaders in Luanda and Maputo do not blindly accept the Soviet view that the world is a dialectic struggle.

Have the Soviets, Cubans, and East Germans acquired the leverage to install new leaders in Angola and Mozambique if the current ones were to renege on their government's socialist orientation? Given the fluidities of factional politics in Africa, the Soviets and their allies are among those who do not know the answer to this crucial question, and thus they would have to play such a scenario by ear. In Mozambique, where the FRELIMO leadership under Samora Machel seems united and where only a few Soviet, Cuban, and East German advisers are present, the answer is, probably not. Events of 1981-1983 show little, if any, Soviet reaction against Mozambique's perceptible slide from socialist orientation toward real nonalignment. Angola, with its 30,000 Cuban soldiers and Soviet and East German military advisers, may be another story. Also, in Angola the ruling MPLA is apparently still divided between the dominant, so far pro-Soviet faction which was originally Agostinho Neto's group, and the more "black African" faction who were originally followers of former Interior Minister Nito Alves, who was purged in 1976.[11] The ruling faction may need Cuban-Soviet support against its rivals and may thus be more dependent and more vulnerable. But even in Angola, as in southern Africa generally, the Soviet position rests on voluntary acceptance by Africans. To be seen as subversive manipulators, imperialists of a variety well known in Africa, would defeat Soviet purposes.

Commitments, Credibility, and Intervention in Mozambique and Angola

During Andropov's year as general secretary, the Soviet Union tried to shore up its credibility by taking a firmer position in "defense of the gains of socialism," reversing the drift and muddle of the last Brezhnev years. Andropov and his colleagues—particularly Foreign Minister Andrei Gromyko, who was the real foreign policy chief during Andropov's short tenure—wanted to show that in spite of economic troubles and the crises in Poland and Afghanistan, the Soviet Union would not succumb to a worldwide rollback of Soviet influence engineered by a militantly anti-Soviet administration in Washington. Some positions—for example, in Grenada—might be indefensible. (Grenada was mentioned in both the Soviet-Angolan and Soviet-Mozambican communiques of spring 1983 as a country requiring defense against imperialist aggression, bracketed with Cuba and Nicaragua.) This led, during 1983, to a clear difference in Soviet policy between Mozambique and Angola.

The Soviets have made no claims about the irreversibility of socialism in Angola or Mozambique and have made no binding commitments to save the present governments against internal insurgents or South African attacks. The Cubans could not—and the East Germans would not—send troops to the region without Soviet approval, although the Cubans already in Angola could shift to a more active role. The Soviet Treaties of Friendship and Cooperation with Angola and Mozambique allow intervention if it is invited and if the Soviets agree to it.[12] Angola and Mozambique have similar treaties with Cuba, East Germany, and each other. Moscow uses its friendship treaties—which have almost identical language—as it sees fit. Nothing was done for Syria and the PLO when Israel invaded Lebanon in June 1982, and Iraq has received no help in its war with Iran; on the other hand, the treaty with Afghanistan was cited as a pretext for invasion.

In southern Africa, the Soviets would like to scare off South Africa's hegemonic intrusions into neighboring states and take credit for it, but without making any commitments. In February 1981, following the South African raid on ANC facilities at Matola on the outskirts of Maputo, Soviet ambassador to Mozambique Valentin Vdovin issued a warning, and two Soviet warships made a long-planned visit to Mozambique. These were costless gestures, but they also had no measurable effect on South African policy toward Mozambique. Similarly, in December 1983, following yet another South African incursion northward into Angola, the Soviets issued a strong warning to the South Africans, a warning made more credible by Soviet military supply and the increase of Cuban troop strength during 1983.

Mozambique's socialist orientation is welcome and useful, but the country is not important enough in economic or military terms to risk direct confrontation between Soviet bloc military personnel and the South Africa Defense Force (SADF). Unlike the MPLA in Angola, Mozambique's FRELIMO government does not owe its existence to Soviet or Cuban intervention. During the period of active guerrilla warfare against the Portuguese, most weapons came from China. Upholding FRELIMO is not a test of Soviet credibility. Nor is Mozambique essential to Soviet and allied contacts with SWAPO and the ANC—Angola is. General A.A. Yepishev, head of the Main Political Administration of the Soviet Armed Forces and a Moscow troubleshooter in shaky Third World situations, visited Mozambique in June 1982, just after the military agreement with Portugal. His visit did not result in an expanded Soviet, Cuban, or East German role against the guerrillas of the *Movimento Nacional da Resistencia* (MNR). Nor have the Soviets increased the quite moderate amounts and types of weapons supplied to Mozambique. Whether by Soviet or Mozambican wish, or both, escalation was foregone. Rather, Mozambique has continued to slide out from under "socialist orientation," welcoming the return of Portuguese businessmen, dismantling state farms, and accepting a new American ambassador and increased PL-480 food shipments. Samora Machel did visit Moscow in March 1983, meeting with Yuri Andropov and Foreign Minister Gromyko and Defense Minister Ustinov. The communiqué mentions only a protocol on scientific and technological cooperation as a tangible result of the visit.[13] Whether the Mozambican side asked for, and the Soviets refused to give, economic or military assistance is not known. Samora Machel went to Western Europe (including Portugal) in the fall of 1983, and in January

1984 was negotiating directly with South Africa over the whole range of economic and security issues, including Mozambican sanctuary for the ANC.

No such passivity characterizes Soviet policy toward "defense of the gains of socialism" in Angola. Angola is the key to the entire Soviet bloc position in southern Africa. It provides base and sanctuary for Namibia's SWAPO and the ANC. The MPLA has been pro-Soviet, not pro-Chinese like FRELIMO or ZANU of Zimbabwe, since it came into being in the late 1950s. Soviet credibility with Fidel Castro depends significantly on Soviet aid to Angola, which was more a Cuban than a Soviet interest until the 1975 intervention. In Angola, the Soviets may be justifiably worried that a South African invasion aimed specifically at engaging the Cubans could force their hand.

The Soviet preference has been, and remains, a South African threat to Angola which allows protection and continued influence without much cost or risk. The Warsaw Pact Political Consultative Committee statement of January 1983—Andropov's first (and last)—mentioned southern Africa with the Middle East as a "dangerous situation" and "seat of armed conflict" carrying "the danger of local conflicts erupting on a worldwide scale." By blaming the danger on "the spread of the sphere of activities of blocs to those countries," Andropov seemed to ask the West to avoid escalation.[14]

Through 1983, however, the Soviets sought to show that they would do whatever was necessary to protect the Angolan regime against UNITA and the South African Defense Force. In early 1983 the Cuban expeditionary force had increased to some 25,000 and may have reached 30,000 or more by the end of 1983, as Cuban troops are reduced in Ethiopia and new units are rotated into Angola.[15] When Angolan President Eduardo dos Santos went to Moscow in May, the communiqué reaffirmed MPLA-CPSU party agreements, the 1981-1985 plan for Soviet-Angolan economic cooperation (said to be worth some $2 billion),[16] and insistence on not linking Cuban troop withdrawal to a Namibian settlement.[17] In August and September, as UNITA insurgents gained ground in the central regions, Soviet ships and aircraft offloaded military equipment. Soviet and East German military personnel grew to 2,000 and 5,000, respectively.[18] Finally, as UNITA penetrated to within 100 kilometers of Luanda and the South Africans mounted yet another sweep through southern Angola, this time attacking Angolan army units, Cuban soldiers finally began to fight. Given the sizeable Cuban contingent already in the country, a Soviet troop airlift could create a formidable force in a relatively short time.[19]

The UNITA advance in fall 1983 coincided with the referendum campaign in South Africa in which the National Party persuaded two-thirds of the (white) electorate to allow some Asian and Coloured (but not black) rep-presentation in government. Prime Minister Botha maintained a hard line on the communist "total onslaught" from the north as he pushed this small step toward reform. After the referendum—and as the costs of military operations in Angola mounted—backing off a bit in Angola made sense. As the Soviets and South Africans share an interest in polarizing southern Africa, so do they share an interest in avoiding a costly and unpredictable real fight. Mutual restraint which entrenched Soviet and Cuban influence in a now-destitute Angola—industrial production is now 20 to 30 percent of preindependence levels; 80 percent of export earnings are from oil, and 13 percent from South African-owned diamonds; half or more of the budget goes toward military expenditures[20]—and which left unchallenged South African domination of Namibia, might serve the immediate interests of both Soviets and South Africans.

The presence of Cuban combat troops in Angola is an issue more important in Washington than in Moscow. What the Soviets want is continued contact with the liberation movements and, within Angola, a regime moving ever closer to "the socialist path" and eventual integration into the world communist system, Cuba-style. The Cuban soldiers are there to protect the regime. If the regime is secure without them, and still committed to the Soviet connection, so much the better. That connection is more a matter of party and army cadre training, internal security police and intelligence links, pro-Soviet propaganda, and the merging of Angolan officials into international communist institutions than of the presence of combat troops. Of course, the Soviets have no assurance that Angola will persist in its socialist orientation, with or without the Cubans.

If the South Africans remain in southern Angola, however, and if negotiations for a cease-fire between Pretoria and Luanda, brokered by the United States, fail, the Soviets and Cubans may be tempted to launch a counterattack. Unleashing a Cuban-Soviet force against the South Africans within Angola would be legitimate within international law and the guidelines of the OAU; would be welcomed by many African countries; and, most important, would put the United States on the spot. Cuban troops and Soviet advisers engaged against the Somalis in the Ogaden in 1978 are an African precedent. In fact, one might ask why the Cubans and Soviets have been such half-hearted defenders of Angola's sacred borders until now. The Soviet leadership has been stung by what they perceive as U.S. disdain for their interests and their power. They might be happy to teach the Americans a lesson in Angola—if and only if they were confident of military success.

Zimbabwe and the Front Line States

The Soviets will do what they can to gain influence in Zimbabwe, Zambia, and Botswana, and within SWAPO and the ANC, but not in ways that would place any stress on present friends or alienate Africans of whatever orientation. No evidence exists, for example, that the Soviets considered trying to destabilize Zimbabwe after the 1980 election defeat of Nkomo's Soviet-supported ZAPU. Moscow's strategists judged rightly that destabilization of a liberated Zimbabwe would drastically hurt the image the Soviets seek to project in the region of a disinterested friend of African interests; that a ZAPU coup could provoke a ZANU-led insurgency among the majority Shona of the northeast; and that this new conflict could result in a ZAPU call for Soviet-Cuban-East German aid and protection. The Soviets have no inclination to risk being drawn into another unwinnable counterinsurgency war, particularly in support of a minority government that would be seen as illegitimate by other Africans. In the scenario for Zimbabwe now preferred by the Soviets, (1) the West would fail to provide the anticipated level of economic assistance and investment, and (2) hegemonic meddling by South Africa would destabilize the Mugabe government and further weaken the economy, thus (3) pushing *any* Zimbabwean regime to turn to Moscow and its allies for assistance and political guidance.

In 1983, the first frames of this scenario occurred. Guerrillas in Matabeleland, ZAPU's base, acknowledged that they were trained and armed in South Africa. The press in the United States reported extensively on violence in Zimbabwe (perhaps with South African encouragement), painting a picture of tribalism and lawlessness. Zimbabwe abstained on the UN vote that condemned the Soviet shooting of Korean airliner 007, which angered U.S. Ambassador to the United Nations Jeane Kirkpatrick and other officials. The administration's request for aid to Zimbabwe was then cut from $75 million to $35 million.[21] (The administration was apparently not so angry at China, which also abstained; that Zimbabwe would vote with China should surprise no one.) At the root of all this was Zimbabwean anger that the United States was, as Zimbabweans perceived it, aiding South African destabilization. Such tension fits Soviet, and South African, purposes very well.

Moscow's Namibia Policy

In the case of Namibia, Soviet policy has two objectives. For the present, the focus is on discrediting the U.S. role in the protracted independence negotiations; building the Soviet Union's credentials as the natural ally by association with the cause of liberation and extending communist influence within SWAPO. For the longer term, the preference is for a peaceful transfer of power to a Soviet-linked government of socialist orientation.

Soviet interest in a Namibian settlement is, however, conditional. Stalemate is preferable to a negotiated settlement that leaves the Soviets on the sidelines as in Zimbabwe. Moreover, prolongation of the war has the advantage of reinforcing the role of the East Germans who are training PLAN, SWAPO's military force, and increases the chances that SWAPO's leaders will become comfortable with the Soviet connection. Although a speech by SWAPO President Sam Nujoma was recently included in the CPSU journal *Kommunist,* indicating approval by the mandarins of the Central Committee secretariat's ideological department, SWAPO is still identified as a "national-patriotic" movement rather than a socialist vanguard.[22]

On the other hand, the Soviets and their allies have learned from experience that they lack the power to call the tune at the negotiating table. During the 1979 Lancaster House negotiations on Rhodesia/Zimbabwe, they counseled their friends among the Patriotic Front delegation that true independence could only be won by military victory and warned that the settlement was a British trick to send an occupation force and rig the elections. These arguments had no discernible effect on the Patriotic Front leaders, whose talk-fight strategy needed the Soviets only for the fight part. In Namibia, as in Zimbabwe, the Soviets may be discarded when their role as armorer is no longer relevant. In November 1981, SWAPO Secretary-General Moses Garoeb stated that Namibia under SWAPO would pattern itself on Zimbabwe, following a pragmatic economic policy and prohibiting the mounting of ANC guerrilla activities from its territory.[23] This would be the best possible outcome for the United States, and the least satisfactory for the Soviets. Only South Africa has the ability to block a transfer of power in Namibia by elections, and here, as in other matters, the Soviets count on Pretoria to help their cause.

How Moscow Sees South Africa

Soviet policy regarding the internal situation in South Africa is still taking shape. South Africa is viewed as a developed country, part of the Western economic system, with a real proletariat. The South African Communist Party (SACP) was formed in 1921, joined the Comintern in 1926, and was banned by the Suppression of Communism Act of 1950. When the African National Congress also went underground following the Sharpeville passbook protest and police shootings of 1960, the SACP began to work within the ANC, although it maintains a separate identity and organization. It is traditional communist united front strategy to associate communists with the national cause and endeavor to make them the dominant force, or vanguard, in the front. The communists within the ANC have counselled armed struggle as the only viable strategy and toward that end were instrumental in organizing guerrilla training for young South Africans in Angola after the 1976 Soweto uprisings.[24]

What the Soviets want, and expect, from South Africa is repression of trade unions, of groups in the homelands, of intellectuals, and of other liberal reformist forces. Over time, they reason, all who reject minority rule will realize that the only solution is to join an organized and disciplined revolutionary movement. Since South Africa, unlike other sub-Saharan African states, is perceived as having a proletariat, workers are seen as the primary recruiting ground. Meanwhile, the need for discipline and armed struggle should enable communists gradually to assume leadership within the ANC. Eventually, according to this scenario, an increasingly narrow and repressive white South African state will be confronted by a single consolidated opposing force—a communist-led vanguard party increasingly able to sustain sabotage and guerrilla warfare. This view of the future follows traditional Soviet revolutionary theory.

Writing in the December 1982 *World Marxist Review,* SACP Chairman Yusuf Dadoo confidently asserts that the ANC's military wing, *Umkhonto we Sizwe,* is now well organized, able to operate "in the midst of the masses . . . like fish in water," and increasing its operations against "military-industrial enterprises and strategic installations." He asserts that "anyone who fails to express solidarity with [the ANC] is bound to be treated with suspicion and contempt," and that the goals of the South African Communist Party "go beyond" those of the ANC, although a political revolution establishing majority rule is the "immediate goal." In South Africa, "the material prerequisites for transition to a higher socio-economic formation have already taken shape."[25] In other words, it is the hope of the communist faction within the ANC that the transition to communist leadership may be carried through as a single process when the predicted revolution gets under way.

The real threat to this Soviet strategy is not repression, which serves its purposes. Repression intensifies polarization, creates more hard-line enemies of the regime, and also gets rid of leaders such as Steve Biko, who are useful to Soviet strategy only as martyrs. As Dadoo acknowledges, the real threats are reforms and liberalization that facilitate the growth of a prosperous African middle class and a labor movement with a stake in the economic system. The Soviets and the SACP are counting on the National Party to deepen the polarization required to make their strategy viable.

The China Factor

Before 1975 China, not the Soviet Union, was the major source of arms and outside political inspiration to FRELIMO, ZANU, Tanzania, and Zambia. China was engaged with the FNLA and UNITA in Angola. Part of the Soviet motivation for its southern African gamble of 1975–1979 was to thwart the Chinese. After the successful Cuban-Soviet intervention in

Angola in 1976, China (the Maoists) was castigated as the agent of imperialism (the United States) and of South African fascism in a major propaganda campaign. The Soviet Union replaced China as the largest arms supplier to Tanzania and Zambia. The Soviets armed ZAPU within the Zimbabwe Patriotic Front. FRELIMO, in Mozambique, accepted the entire socialist orientation package, including fealty to the Soviet international line. SWAPO in Angola accepted Soviet arms and East German and Cuban military advisers. While the Soviet effort to convince Africans that the Chinese had sold out was probably less persuasive than Chinese diplomacy and propaganda against the expansionist "hegemonism" of Moscow's "new tsars," southern Africa was a major Soviet success in the Soviet-Chinese cold war lasting from the armed clashes on the Ussuri river in 1969 until the early 1980s. Soviet-Chinese relations reached their nadir in early 1979 when China attacked northern Vietnam and the Soviet Union threatened war. This was the moment also of greatest Soviet success in southern Africa, preceding the Zimbabwe settlement of fall 1979.

Chinese influence and connections never disappeared from southern Africa. ZANU remained pro-Chinese, nor were Zambian and Tanzanian contacts ever broken. In 1982 and 1983 the Soviets pressed for detente with China. Simultaneously, the Chinese upgraded their southern African involvement and credentials, which the Soviets either could not or did not want to prevent. Premier Zhao Ziyang's Africa tour of January 1983 included Zimbabwe, Zambia, and Tanzania. In Lusaka Premier Zhao met with Sam Nujoma of SWAPO and Oliver Tambo of the ANC; both visited Beijing shortly after and were promised arms aid from China. During Zhao's trip Angola and China dramatically announced resumption of relations.

As noted, the Soviets either could not prevent, or did not want to prevent, this restoration of Chinese influence. The long-time Chinese-linked bloc of Zimbabwe, Mozambique, Tanzania, and Zambia may re-form, although not to the exclusion of the Soviets. Anti-Chinese propaganda is now largely absent from the Soviet press. If the Chinese again become involved in liberation in southern Africa, and if this causes strain between China and the United States, so much the better from the Soviet point of view. In a period of retrenchment Soviet policy aims to divide China and the United States rather than attempt new gains at the expense of both.

Implications for U.S. Policy

The United States has three important and legitimate interests in southern Africa: a South Africa in which race does not determine social and political status; continued access to the region's mineral resources and mutually beneficial trade and investment; and limitation or reduction of Soviet influence. The last is a legitimate rather than a knee-jerk interest because the Soviets are indifferent to human rights; because they could conceivably block access to resources; and most of all because they have designed their southern Africa policies to weaken and injure the United States.

Soviet influence is clearly tied to the degree of dissension between Africans and the West. Without polarization and continuing armed conflict in the region, the Soviet Union's political appeal and utility as an arms supplier and protector withers away. Soviet operatives can take advantage of African disenchantment with the West but cannot force the pace. They count on the imperialists to dig their own graves.

Buoyed by the perceived tilt toward South Africa in the Reagan Administration's policy of "constructive engagement," and by the slowed pace of the Western Contact Group's progress toward achievement of a Namibian settlement, Soviet and other communist states are now once again becoming more confident in tone and content. South African occupation of territory in southern Angola has provided new justification for the continued presence in that country of Cuban troops. SWAPO survives and draws recruits to fight another day or year. Nigeria is being cultivated as a potentially important "friend" on the pattern of India, in part by playing on Nigeria's doubts about U.S. policy in southern Africa. Since 1980 the Soviets have engaged in a worldwide campaign to dispel the impression that they are the militarist and imperialist superpower and to pin that onus on the United States. Despite Afghanistan, this campaign has been increasingly successful in Europe and Africa.

The United States could, of course, decide to ignore the larger political implications and encourage South Africa to dominate the entire southern African region by threats, subversion, economic pressures, and selective occupation. This kind of *Realpolitik* would verify Soviet claims about the malign imperialist nature of the United States and would make natural enemies of all Africa and much of the rest of the world besides. Soviet credibility would sharply escalate, and the chances of direct Soviet military intervention would increase. No serious argument can be made for such a risky, immoral, and foolish policy.

The alternative, and proper, course is to become gradually but consistently constructively engaged with the Front Line states; to speak out against South Africa's military buildup and its persistent involvement in the political/security affairs of its neighbors; and to avoid promising to deliver South Africa, which Washington cannot do. The focus should be elsewhere—on economic aid, trade, and investment, in concert with the Europeans, who are far more important to and involved with the economies of southern Africa than is the United States. Angola should be accorded the diplomatic recognition that Washington is almost alone in withholding, and trade with that nation should be increased. Food aid to Mozambique, now resumed, should be increased. The United States should contribute its share and encourage others (including the Soviets, who resist) to contribute theirs to the regional infrastructure of SADCC.[26] Angola and Mozambique should be encouraged in their inclination to become signatories of the next Lomé Convention (which complements their actual European- and Western-oriented patterns of trade and finance) and to join the International Monetary Fund. Above all, the reintegration and development of Zimbabwe should be furthered by both economic and security assistance, most effectively from Britain and perhaps China rather than the United States. In contrast to the Soviet policy of dividing states of socialist orientation from the others, cooperation should be encouraged among all the states of southern Africa. Western and African interests alike will best be served by a shared recognition that what is needed is a period of peace and development that would allow the situation in South Africa to ripen, in whatever direction.

Such a policy does not speak directly to the area's ongoing political and military issues and conflicts, but it does provide a different basis from which they may be approached. The Contact Group should continue its efforts toward internationally supervised elections leading to independence in Namibia, with an understood premise that the new government would not invite a major internal Soviet or East German or Cuban presence, and that Namibia would not become a base for cross-border ANC guerrilla operations into South Africa. The Front Line states—Marxist and non-Marxist—would favor these caveats.

The UNITA insurgency in Angola will not go away either, as long as South Africa supplies it. But the policy framework proposed here, including emphasis on economic development to restore Angola's agriculture and coffee exports, should increase incentives for both UNITA and the MPLA to achieve some reconciliation. The other Front Line states—particularly Zambia, which needs secure transport over the Benguela railway now disrupted by UNITA attacks—would favor such reconciliation. Soviet influence in Namibia is a far more important issue than the Cubans in Angola, who would become largely superfluous.

ANC guerrilla operations and South African reprisals are a destabilization cycle that both South Africans and Soviets promote. Zimbabwe has banned ANC use of its territory, as has Botswana. Mozambique may be more inclined to follow suit if South Africa ends its destabilization via the MNR insurgency.[27]

In sum, the United States and other Western nations should promote by whatever means possible conditions of peace and stability which allow the Front Line states (and an independent Namibia) to turn to their economic development needs. The United States must avoid the trap of being provoked into support for an aggressively hegemonic South African regional policy that furthers the Soviet goal of being perceived as the primary ally and protector of African interests.

Notes

1. For example, see "Southern Africa: Soviet Front Organizations," Information Ministry of South Africa, No. 9/83, August 1983.

2. Pietro Benetazzo, in *The Christian Science Monitor,* 20 January 1984, estimates that Angola pays somewhere between $14,000 to $22,000 a year for each Cuban soldier. This would mean a total payment of perhaps $400 to $500 million per year.

3. For expansion of discussion of Soviet strategy to build "socialist oriented" countries, see Seth Singleton, "Building Vanguard Nations," paper presented at the Institute of International Studies, University of California, April 1982.

4. For background, see David Martin and Phyllis Johnson, *The Struggle for Zimbabwe* (Salisbury: Zimbabwe Publishing House, 1981); also Michael Clough, "From Rhodesia to Zimbabwe," in Clough, ed., *Changing Realities in Southern Africa* (Berkeley: Institute of International Studies, 1982).

5. The leading Soviet foreign language journal *International Affairs* has since 1981 printed a series of articles under the title "Bulwark of Militarism and Reaction" which blame all the world's troubles on the Reagan Administration. In 1983, at the nadir (?) of U.S.-Soviet relations, the United States was compared to the Nazis in its designs on the Middle East. This signals a serious Soviet concern.

6. The English-speaking reader may look at Yuri Tarabrin, "U.S. Expansionist Policy in Africa," *International Affairs* (Moscow) 10 (1983):41-50. Tarabrin, a leading Soviet authority on liberation movements and Africa, writes that "Washington does not conceal its intent to defend the Pretoria regime, including by military means, from the so-called external threat." (p. 42) Tarabrin follows with a list of purported United States' aims which are exactly those of South Africa and repeats throughout the refrain of all Soviet writing that the United States is Africa's enemy because it is South Africa's ally. Tarabrin's article is moderate compared to some Soviet attacks.

7. A brief description of the curriculum and training at the Angolan school to train political officers for the Angolan army, founded with Soviet aid in 1976, appears in Col. Yu. Moshkov, "Zari Angoly" (Dawns of Angola), *Kommunist Vooruzhennikh Sil* (Communist of the Armed Force), no. 20 (October 1982):79. Like other Soviet writers, Moshkov calls the UNITA guerrillas "mercenaries" led by "agent of the CIA Jonas Savimbi" and asserts that South African occupation in Angola has "the direct support of the USA." (p. 78)

8. Arms transfers data in Arms Control and Disarmament Agency, *World Military Expenditures and Arms Transfers, 1971-1980* (Washington, D.C.: U.S. Government Printing Office, 1983), p. 117.

9. For discussion of CMEA and southern Africa by an economic specialist, see Colin Lawson, "The Soviet Union and Eastern Europe in Southern Africa: Is There a Conflict of Interest?" *International Affairs* (London) (Winter 1982-1983):32-40. Also Radio Liberty Research Bulletin 35/84, "Soviet Union said to be forcing allies to aid Cuba," 18 January 1984.

10. Pietro Benetazzo, "Angola Leans on Soviets as War, Economy Go Badly," *Christian Science Monitor,* 19 January 1984; and Benetazzo, "Angola Paradox: Nation Both Loves, Hates Its East-West Patrons," *Christian Science Monitor,* 20 January 1984; Paul van Slambrouck, "Mozambique Tones Down Marxist Rhetoric, Turns 'Practical' on Economy," *CSM*, 28 April 1983; and David Winder, "Why Black Africa Can't Break Hidden Ties With South Africa," *CSM,* 25 March 1983.

11. I am indebted to Carlos Moore for this point.

12. Text of the Soviet-Angolan treaty in Colin Legum, ed., *Africa Contemporary Record, 1976-77,* pp. C151-153; text of the Soviet-Mozambican treaty in ibid., *1977-78,* pp. C17-18.

13. Communiqué in *Pravda,* 6 March 1983.

14. Warsaw Pact communiqué in *Pravda,* 6 January 1983. The partial text in English in *Survival,* March-April 1983 omits the mention of southern Africa. The Warsaw Pact Political Consultative Committee is the authoritative organ for security policies of the entire alliance; communiqués are written by the Soviets.

15. See *New York Times,* 24 January 1984, p. A2.

16. *Africa Research Bulletin,* January 15-February 14, 1982, p. 6324.

17. Comminqué in *Pravda,* 21 May 1983.

18. Numbers of advisers reported in *New York Times,* 25 January 1984, p. A4.

19. On Soviet airlift capabilities, see Dennis M. Gormley, "The Direction and Pace of Soviet Force Projection Capabilities," *Survival* (November/December 1982):266-276. The Soviets could transport at most two airborne divisions, or some 16,000 men, as far as southern Africa in a short time. This would tax capability to the utmost.

20. Benetazzo, *Christian Science Monitor,* 19 January 1984.

21. Other incidents also caused strain. The U.S. Embassy in Harare was denied permission to hold a memorial service for the Marines killed by the terrorist bombing in Beirut. This upset Foreign Service and military officers.

22. Sam Nujoma, "My uvereny v svoiei pobede," (We believe in our victory) *Kommunist* 17 (November 1980):105-106.

23. See Colin Legum, "The Southern African Crisis," in *Africa Contemporary Record, 1981-82* 14 (New York: Africana Publishers, 1982); Garoeb's comment on p. A43.

24. On the relation of the South African Communist Party to the ANC, see Moses Mabhida (the SACP General Secretary), "V bor'be za natsional'noe

i sotsial'noe osvobozhdeniie naroda," (In the struggle for national and social liberation of the people), *Kommunist* 11 (June 1981). See also David Winder, "Waging a War of Sabotage in South Africa," *Christian Science Monitor,* 16 September 1983 and Joseph Lelyveld, "Black Challenge to Pretoria," *New York Times,* 12 October 1983, p. A8. Moses Mabhida says that "the decision on transition to armed struggle and creation of a military wing of the ANC was taken together with the SACP." He also stated that communists are moving up into top positions in the national liberation movement. ANC spokesmen generally deny any leadership on the part of the communists but acknowledge the natural ally role of the Soviet Union.

25. Yusuf Daddo, "Crisis of the Racist System in the South of Africa," *World Marxist Review* (December 1982):19.

26. See "SADCC: A Progress Report," by Bryan Silbermann, *CSIS Africa Notes,* 11 (April 5, 1983).

27. Since the South African Air Force bombing raid of 23 May 1983, Mozambique's stated position has been that ANC members are not permitted to bear arms against South Africa from Mozambican territory (*Africa Research Bulletin,* May 1-31 1983, p. 6829). This issue is the centerpiece of the Mozambican–South African talks in early 1984.

7 Soviet Arms Transfers to Sub-Saharan Africa

Joachim Krause

Since the military support actions carried out by the Soviet Union and Cuba on behalf of Angola and Ethiopia during the 1970s, Western interest in Soviet arms transfer policy in Sub-Saharan Africa has increased considerably. With an eye to the strategic significance of the Cape Route for the Western industrial societies as well as raw material dependencies, concern has been repeatedly expressed that the supply of weapons to Sub-Saharan African states could represent the first step toward a military threat to Africa, and thereby indirectly to the Western world, on the part of the USSR. A complete discussion of the implications of these concerns cannot be provided here, as it would demand a complexly developed exposition of the goals, instruments, and problem areas of Soviet African policy.[1] It is, however, possible to obtain a general picture of the short- and medium-term goals and opportunities of Soviet policy toward Sub-Saharan Africa through an analysis of Moscow's arms export program.

The following discussion seeks to understand the Kremlin's arms exports as a *political* instrument. Although attention will be given to a quantitative representation of arms transfers in Africa, considerably more emphasis is placed upon the regional and global circumstances under which the Soviet Union has employed arms transfers as a means (and as we will see, often as the primary means) to achieve an extension of influence in Africa.

In the first section of the chapter the evolution of Soviet arms policies for Sub-Saharan Africa will be described in historical overview. This will be followed by an analysis of the political motives that have influenced Moscow in shaping its policies. In the third section a structural comparison of Soviet arms transfers with those of the Western states is provided. The two concluding sections are concerned with the questions of what successes the Soviet Union has achieved with its arms policy to date, and what consequences for security policy emerge from them.

Stages of Soviet Involvement

From the end of World War II until the late 1950s the Soviet Union delivered virtually no arms to Black Africa. The first significant phase of arms transfers occurred during the period 1958–1964. Under the post-Stalin

---

Translated from German by R. Craig Nation.

leadership of Nikita Khrushchev the Soviet Union began to engage itself in the affairs of the Third World via grants of economic and military aid, thus challenging the legacy of Western domination inherited from the era of colonialism. The USSR's attempts to leap from the status of a regional power to that of a global power were facilitated by various regional conflicts in progress, the lagging pace of decolonization, and the accession to power in key Third World states of dynamic personalities such as Ahmed Sukarno, Gamal Abd al-Nasir, Kwame Nkrumah, and Ahmed Sékou Touré, whose political ambitions made them amenable to offers of Soviet assistance.

The first arms deal with a Sub-Saharan state was closed at the end of 1958, when Moscow pledged Guinean leader Sékou Touré a small number of anti-aircraft guns, armored personnel carriers, and infantry weapons. At the same time, the Soviet Union and Czechoslovakia began training programs for the Guinean armed forces. In the following two years, the Sudan, Ghana, and Mali likewise became recipients of Soviet military aid.[2]

The first major setback to Moscow's emerging arms transfer policy occurred during the Congo crisis in 1960. Khrushchev's offer to help Prime Minister Patrice Lumumba to regain control of rebellious Katanga province by unilateral military action proved to be disastrous. Soviet aircraft were refused access to Congolese airports by UN authorities on the scene, and Moscow found itself devoid of means to effectively render assistance to Lumumba, lacking military forces appropriate for outright intervention.

There is some reason to believe that after the Congolese adventure Soviet arms transfer policy toward Sub-Saharan Africa became somewhat more cautious. The Soviets nonetheless continued in their general attempt to exploit opportunities in Africa to their own advantage. The extent of Soviet commitment became evident in 1963, when the Kremlin and Somalia negotiated an arms deal estimated at over $35 million (U.S.), the largest single agreement of its kind that had been concluded to date in Sub-Saharan Africa. In closing the deal, the Soviet Union managed to outbid competing Western powers which had offered assistance on a much smaller scale. At the same time, however, the Kremlin found itself embarked upon the support of Somalian irredentism, with its outstanding territorial claims upon Ethiopia and Kenya.[3]

With the replacement of Khrushchev in October 1964 the first phase of Soviet arms transfer policy in Sub-Saharan Africa came to an end. It can be characterized as a phase of "trial and error" in which military assistance was used, in combination with other means, in order to assert a Soviet foothold in Africa. The major emphasis of Soviet policy toward Sub-Saharan Africa was placed upon developing contacts with leading politicians, supporting African concerns within international forums, and providing economic aid. Arms transfers, given the high risks involved, represented only a relatively small dimension of Soviet activities.

The second phase to be discussed ranges from 1965-1971. Khrushchev's successors continued the broad outlines of his policies in the Third World, but they also presided over some important shifts in emphasis. Almost immediately, more demanding criteria were developed for selecting arms clients. While Khrushchev was in power, the Kremlin granted military assistance to virtually any country that requested it. In the process, the Soviet Union won the "friendship" of some rather dubious political leaders, often lacking domestic support and isolated internationally. After 1965 Moscow concentrated its military assistance on those African countries that were of primary strategic interest. In addition, the new leadership attempted to minimize the negative political consequences sometimes associated with arms transfers and took pains to adhere to the established intra-African code of political conduct—especially the 1964 Organization of African Unity (OAU) decision to retain Africa's existing state borders.

The newly established Brezhnev-Kosygin leadership was well aware that they did not have at their disposal a power projection capacity sufficient for intervention in Africa. It is thus not surprising that during the late 1960s the Kremlin began to build up systematically the means that would allow it to operate militarily on a worldwide scale. A first stage in this effort was the growth of the Soviet naval presence in the Mediterranean, and subsequently in the Indian Ocean and South Atlantic, accompanied by improvements in logistical capacity and command and control systems.[4]

Sub-Saharan Africa, however, was not the focal point of Soviet policy toward the Third World in the late 1960s. Quantitatively, Soviet arms transfers to Sub-Saharan Africa grew quite slowly between 1965 and 1971, although Moscow had nonetheless become the fourth-ranking arms supplier in the region (after France, the United States, and Great Britain). The most persistent efforts were directed toward attempts to weaken imperial Ethiopia, which at that time was the United States's closest ally in Africa, and which had granted Washington the use of military facilities on the Red Sea littoral. By strengthening Somalia, the Soviet Union set into motion a regional arms race which placed an additional burden upon the already troubled Ethiopian monarchy.[5] In 1967 Somalia received its first tanks, supersonic aircraft, and other sorts of modern equipment, and nearly 250 Soviet military advisors arrived to supervise their use.

Another Soviet endeavor—of somewhat lower priority than that directed at Ethiopia—was the attempt to support national liberation movements in Angola, Mozambique, Guinea-Bissau, and Cape Verde, thereby indirectly weakening the still-dominant colonial power and NATO member Portugal. Perhaps due to an underestimation of the military potential of the southern African guerrilla movements, or to reluctance to defy Portugal too openly, Soviet support for southern African liberation movements remained limited to a level sufficient to protract the conflict, but not to lead revolutionary forces to victory.⁶

Ironically, it was Nigeria, a close Western ally, that became the second largest recipient of Soviet arms during the phase in question. Due to British and U.S. reluctance to help the federal government in Lagos crush the secessionist movement in Biafra, Nigeria turned to Moscow in search of arms. The Soviet leadership, perhaps surprisingly, agreed to deliver aircraft, artillery, and naval vessels. Soviet aid was a useful, but not decisive, factor, and Nigeria needed nearly three more years in order to subdue Biafra. Nonetheless, Moscow had demonstrated its willingness to accept existing state borders and the integrity of the African state system and probably derived political advantage from the involvement.⁷

Within the scope of Soviet arms transfers those African states which shared a strong commitment to socialism—such as the Congo, Tanzania, Ghana, Mali, and Guinea—played only a minor role, and the net amount of military aid that they received remained comparatively small. Notwithstanding, Soviet relations with Mali, Guinea, and the Congo remained positive, while after Nkrumah's overthrow in 1966 contacts with Ghana disintegrated, and Tanzania drifted toward closer ties with Beijing. By way of compensation, Uganda's Prime Minister Milton Obote requested Soviet arms aid in 1967, and in the following years Uganda became the USSR's third largest arms customer in Sub-Saharan Africa.

The period between 1965 and 1971 can best be characterized as a preparatory phase during which the Kremlin cautiously attempted to maintain and develop its military relationships with selected Sub-Saharan states. Soviet leaders were anxious to avoid unnecessary risks, aware as they were of their own inability to shore up clients in the event of confrontation with the Western powers. In fact, Soviet caution provoked criticism from more militant representatives of the communist world such as China and Cuba.

A subsequent phase in Soviet arms transfer policy may be defined as beginning in 1972. It is marked by a propensity toward greater risk-taking and an enhanced strategic interest in Africa. The years since 1972 have seen an increase in Soviet arms deliveries and military involvement in Sub-Saharan Africa unprecedented in the past.

Several reasons for this increase in arms transfers may be specified: (1) the Soviet capacity both for making available and transporting weapons to Africa had grown significantly; (2) the Soviet military had developed a stronger interest in obtaining support facilities in Africa for naval and aerial operations; (3) new opportunities permitting an extended Soviet involvement in Sub-Saharan Africa had presented themselves; and (4) U.S. foreign policy was mired in a period of hesitancy provoked by the traumas of Vietnam and Watergate. A turning point for Soviet military aid policy was the upgrading of the military relationship with Somalia which occurred in 1972.

With an eye to the potential use of Somalian military facilities, the Soviet Union assisted in a dramatic modernization of Somalia's armed forces. In addition, Moscow aided the ruling, left-wing military council by widening and enhancing military training programs, with a dual emphasis upon military skills and ideological training, and by helping in the suppression of opposition. The Kremlin urged the Somalian leaders to adopt the Soviet model of government and to form a communist vanguard party and related mass organizations. In 1974 the peak of the Soviet-Somalian relationship was achieved with the conclusion of a treaty of friendship and cooperation.[8] The treaty granted the Soviets almost full base rights in the Somalian harbor of Berbera and, by allying Moscow with Somalian irredentism, came close to a mutual aid pact.

While Moscow was forging a closer relationship with Somalia after 1972, it initially displayed a reluctance to over involve itself in Angola, where the approaching end of Portuguese colonial rule had triggered a violent competition for power among three rival liberation movements. Beginning in the spring of 1975 however, Moscow shipped arms to the Popular Movement for the Liberation of Angola (MPLA), which also benefitted from the presence of Cuban advisors. When in October 1975 South Africa intervened in Angola in an attempt to head off an MPLA victory, the Kremlin (in response to Cuban requests) assisted in transferring more than 10,000 Cuban troops and large amounts of weaponry to Angola in support of the MPLA. Strengthened by this critically timed assistance, the MPLA was able to maintain its hold upon the capital of Luanda and to defeat its rivals.[9] The Angolan operation caught many Western observers by surprise, because it seemed to contradict the widespread conviction that Moscow tends to avoid unpredictable risks in making foreign policy decisions. The extent of risk-taking involved in the undertaking remains questionable, however. Local forces were relatively undeveloped, and the victory of communist forces in Vietnam only a few weeks earlier had shown that the U.S. administration was unwilling to react strongly.

By helping the MPLA to defeat its rivals and to repel a military intervention by South Africa, Moscow boosted its prestige in Sub-Saharan Africa considerably. The following years saw a commensurate extension of Soviet military aid. In 1976, socialist Mozambique received Soviet weapons for the first time; Tanzania, Nigeria, and Uganda either revived or extended their military relationships with Moscow; and Madagascar, Benin, Guinea-Bissau, Cape Verde, and Equatorial Guinea also initiated military ties.

A new shock came in 1977 with a reversal of alliances in the Horn of Africa. To this point, Soviet military support for Somalia and the Eritrean liberation movements had helped to shift the regional balance to Ethiopia's disadvantage.[10] The process was confused, however, by the collapse of the Ethiopian monarchy and the rise to power of a Marxist-oriented military council (the *Derg*) under the leadership of Colonel Mengistu Haile Mariam. The Derg broke its ties with the United States and requested Soviet military assistance in 1976. The offer was tempting for Moscow. Ethiopia had served as a bastion of U.S. influence in the Horn of Africa; it was larger and potentially more powerful than its Somalian rival; and it was less problematic in political terms due to the lack of irredentist territorial claims. On the other hand, the Kremlin had invested large sums to construct a military infrastructure in Somalia and had no desire to trade one ally for another. Soviet efforts to arrange a political settlement between the two states failed as Somalia maintained its determination to exploit a perceived military advantage and attempted to impose its territorial claims upon Ethiopia by force. By the autumn of 1977 the Soviet Union had broken military ties with Somalia and dramatically increased its supply of weaponry to Ethiopia.

The big lift of 1977-1978 was the largest single transfer of arms that Sub-Saharan Africa had ever witnessed.[11] (See table 7-1.) Weapons, ammunitions, and supplies valued at over $1 billion (U.S.) were brought into Ethiopia and more than 16,000 Cuban troops were flown in, almost immediately assuming a significant combat role. The Somalian Army and irregular units were overcome rather quickly and forced to adopt guerrilla warfare tactics of resistance. Eritrean secessionist forces were confronted with a similar situation, having suddenly lost Soviet support and now faced with confronting their former ally as a rival.

Though it has undertaken no further massive interventions, since the events of 1977-1978 the Soviet Union has concentrated upon maintaining and extending its presence in Sub-Saharan Africa. Soviet military aid has been focused upon Angola, Ethiopia, and Mozambique, and in addition to delivering arms and educating officers Moscow has also urged these key allies to move closer to the Soviet social and political model. Military ties remain primary, however, and the USSR has emphasized efforts to groom a loyal indigenous officer corp, capable of protecting and furthering a process of revolutionary change.[12] These efforts have been assisted by the fact that within each of Moscow's key African allies, ruling political groups are challenged by armed domestic opposition, dictating continuing dependence upon Soviet support and vulnerability to influence. From Moscow's point of view, the loss of military facilities in Somalia has no doubt been compensated for by new opportunities in Ethiopia, the People's Democratic Republic of Yemen (PDRY), and elsewhere.

In addition to its primary ties with Angola, Ethiopia, and Mozambique, the Soviet Union has continued to sell arms to many other African nations on a smaller scale. These arms clients have included since the mid-1970s states with such varied ideological and geopolitical orientations as Benin, Burundi, Cape Verde, the Congo, Equatorial Guinea, Guinea-Bissau, Madagascar, Mali, Tanzania, and Zambia. Uganda should also be mentioned, as its former dictator, Idi Amin, received large amounts of weaponry from Moscow (table 7-2). In all cases the magnitude of arms transfers in question grew after the events in Angola during 1975-1976.

Political Motivations

What political goals and motives stand behind Soviet arms transfer policy toward Sub-Saharan Africa? The issue is in fact strongly disputed among Western analysts. One school of thought contends that Soviet policy is shaped mainly by ideological priorities. Soviet leaders, it is asserted, have never abandoned their oft-expressed commitment to oppose imperialism and build socialism and communism on a world scale. Soviet African policy is thus interpreted as only one aspect of a global drive for hegemony. In contrast, other analysts argue that in essentials the USSR behaves like any other great power, cautiously manipulating its African connections in search of expanded influence. A third perspective asserts that Soviet arms export policy in the Third World is determined almost exclusively by economic considerations.

Without attempting to resolve this debate in any definitive manner, it seems clear that in the long run Soviet policy toward Africa does contain elements of opportunism, aiming at exploiting favorable conjunctures in order to gain strategic advantage and widen the area of Soviet influence. Although effected importantly by the structure and ideological character of Soviet society, it is in many ways a classical foreign policy orientation. The prioritization of strategic goals within this orientation becomes clear if one analyzes the logic of Soviet support for its key African client states. Angola, Ethiopia, and Mozambique are the leading recipients of Soviet arms primarily because of their favorable locations in military-strategic terms.[13] Ethiopia, like the PDRY, provides an important base for operation in the Indian Ocean and for power projection in Africa and the Arabian peninsula. Mozambique and Angola may serve as cornerstones for extended political involvement in southern Africa. Angola, Ethiopia, and Mozambique are officially acknowledged as states of socialist orientation, but the relative preponderance of strategic over ideological interests becomes clear if one compares the aid granted them with that provided for Benin and the Congo—states which in fact stand much closer to Moscow ideologically but lack major strategic relevance. The friendship treaties concluded between the Soviet Union and Angola, Ethiopia, and Mozambique all contain military cooperation clauses, which the friendship treaty between the USSR and the Congo lacks. Ideology is of course not without some relevance, but it serves mainly to reinforce strategic relationships and does not take priority over them.

Table 7-1
Arms Deliveries to Sub-Saharan African States
(millions of constant 1979 dollars)

	1971	1972	1973	1974	1975	1976	1977	1978	1979	1980
Angola	—	—	—	—	155	283	244	228	130	154
Benin	0	0	0	7	0	0	11	10	10	4
Botswana	0	0	0	0	0	0	11	10	5	0
Cameroon	0	0	0	0	6	12	11	5	0	4
Cape Verde	—	—	—	—	—	0	0	21	30	0
Central African Republic	0	0	0	0	0	0	0	0	10	0
Chad	17	0	0	0	0	12	5	0	0	0
Congo	0	0	0	0	12	6	34	0	20	18
Equatorial Guinea	0	0	0	0	12	0	0	10	0	9
Ethiopia	17	16	15	14	38	61	511	1194	210	435
Gabon	0	0	0	0	0	24	11	10	10	45
Gambia	0	0	0	0	0	6	0	0	0	0
Ghana	0	0	0	14	12	24	23	43	50	0
Guinea	17	16	15	14	25	12	0	21	20	0
Guinea-Bissau	—	—	—	0	6	0	0	10	10	0
Ivory Coast	8	8	7	0	12	12	11	65	70	90
Kenya	17	16	0	42	0	0	11	54	60	54
Lesotho	0	0	0	0	0	0	0	0	0	0
Liberia	0	0	0	0	0	0	5	0	0	4
Madagascar	0	0	0	0	0	12	0	21	20	27
Malawi	0	0	0	0	0	0	0	5	10	9
Mali	0	8	7	0	12	24	34	65	10	9
Mauritania	0	0	0	0	0	24	34	32	10	0
Mauritius	0	0	0	0	0	0	0	0	0	4
Mozambique	—	—	—	—	38	12	34	130	60	63
Niger	0	0	0	0	0	0	5	0	30	4
Nigeria	8	32	31	28	116	61	11	54	110	99
Rwanda	0	0	0	0	0	6	0	10	5	9
Sao Tome and Principe	—	—	—	—	—	0	0	0	0	0
Senegal	0	0	0	0	0	0	11	21	20	9

Country										
Sierra Leone	0	0	0	0	0	0	0	0	0	4
Somalia	0	32	62	127	90	123	93	260	130	172
South Africa	51	213	124	141	168	221	151	130	20	na
Sudan	8	32	15	42	0	61	220	130	100	90
Swaziland	0	0	0	0	0	0	0	0	0	0
Tanzania	51	16	31	7	12	61	69	86	240	36
Togo	0	0	0	0	12	24	11	10	5	4
Uganda	0	8	7	14	90	36	5	21	0	9
Upper Volta	0	0	0	0	6	0	0	0	10	9
Zaire	34	65	31	70	38	147	34	32	30	27
Zambia	8	32	15	14	25	49	23	65	30	172
Zimbabwe	0	8	7	14	6	0	11	5	20	45

Source: U.S. Arms Control and Disarmament Agency, *World Military Expenditures and Arms Transfers, 1971-1980* (Washington, D.C.: U.S. Government Printing Office, 1982).

Note: — = pre-independence; 0 = nil or negligible; na = not available.

Table 7-2
Value of Arms Transfers to Africa, 1975–1979, by Major Supplier
(million current 1981 dollars)

	Total	Soviet Union	United States	France	United Kingdom	West Germany	Czechoslovakia	Italy	Poland	China	Canada	Others
Africa—Total	17,200	9,900	725	1,800	150	925	320	700	270	150	130	2,200
Algeria	1,900	1,500	—	10	—	350	—	10	—	—	—	70
Angola	850	500	—	5	10	10	10	—	20	—	—	290
Benin	30	20	—	5	—	—	—	—	—	—	—	10
Botswana	20	—	—	—	20	—	—	—	—	—	—	—
Burundi	20	10	—	5	—	5	—	—	—	—	—	5
Cameroon	30	—	10	—	—	—	—	—	—	10	5	—
Cape Verde	50	50	—	—	—	—	—	—	—	—	—	—
Central African Republic	5	—	—	—	—	—	—	—	—	—	—	5
Chad	10	10	—	5	—	—	—	—	—	—	—	—
Congo	60	50	—	—	—	—	—	—	—	10	—	—
Equatorial Guinea	10	10	—	—	—	—	—	—	—	—	—	—
Ethiopia	1,800	1,500	90	10	—	5	30	20	10	5	—	160
Gabon	60	—	—	30	—	—	—	10	—	10	—	10
Gambia	5	—	—	—	—	—	—	—	—	5	—	—
Ghana	130	—	—	—	—	50	—	20	—	—	—	60
Guinea	60	60	—	—	5	—	—	—	—	—	—	—
Guinea-Bissau	30	30	—	—	—	—	—	—	—	—	—	—
Ivory Coast	160	—	—	100	—	—	—	—	—	—	—	50
Kenya	120	—	50	10	10	5	—	5	—	—	30	5
Lesotho	—	—	—	—	—	—	—	—	—	—	—	—
Liberia	5	—	5	—	—	—	—	—	—	—	—	—
Libya	6,900	5,000	—	310	10	160	270	450	250	—	—	460
Madagascar	50	30	—	10	—	—	—	—	—	—	—	10
Malawi	20	—	—	10	—	5	—	—	—	5	—	—
Mali	120	110	—	—	—	5	—	—	—	—	—	—
Mauritania	90	—	—	40	5	—	—	—	—	—	—	50
Mauritius	—	—	—	—	—	—	—	—	—	—	—	—
Morocco	1,400	20	310	725	5	50	5	50	—	—	—	250

Soviet Arms Transfers to Sub-Saharan Africa

Country									
Mozambique	240	—	—	—	—	—	—	5	60
Niger	40	170	—	—	—	10	—	—	—
Nigeria	300	150	30	30	50	10	—	—	10
Rwanda	20	—	—	40	—	—	—	—	20
Sao Tome and Principe	—	—	—	—	—	—	—	—	—
Senegal	50	—	—	—	—	—	—	10	30
Sierra Leone	—	—	—	10	—	—	—	—	—
Somalia	440	210	—	20	5	10	30	—	170
South Africa	525	—	20	310	—	—	50	5	150
Sudan	400	10	120	—	—	230	—	20	30
Swaziland	—	—	—	—	—	—	—	—	—
Tanzania	440	300	—	—	5	—	10	20	70
Togo	50	—	—	20	—	5	—	10	20
Tunisia	170	—	50	10	5	10	30	—	50
Uganda	120	110	—	—	5	—	—	—	5
Upper Volta	20	—	—	5	5	10	—	—	5
Zaire	250	—	30	120	—	5	10	30	40
Zambia	150	50	—	—	20	5	10	30	20
Zimbabwe	40	—	—	—	—	—	—	—	40

Source: U.S. Arms Control and Disarmament Agency, *World Military Expenditures and Arms Transfers, 1970–1979* (Washington, D.C.: U.S. Government Printing Office, 1982), p. 127.

As concerns the Soviet Union's purely economic interests in exporting arms, considerable discussion has been stimulated by CIA publications arguing that Soviet arms sales have become more narrowly commercial during the 1970s.[14] There is certainly some merit to the argument, but one should be wary about drawing conclusions too far. Moscow has commonly sold weapons on favorable terms, including competitively lower prices, liberal credit arrangements, low interest rates, and the option to repay in local currency. The terms demanded have recently become more stringent for customers capable of paying in hard currency, in particular, OPEC members. The increased hard currency revenues derived from arms sales have been the result of relatively large transfers to a limited number of newly rich countries. With respect to Sub-Saharan Africa, with the possible exception of Nigeria, the USSR cannot demand the same commercial terms that it does of OPEC members. Moscow has attempted to obtain other economic concessions in exchange for arms, including fishing or mining rights or repayment in U.S. dollars, but if one strikes a balance the cost of Soviet military aid to Sub-Saharan Africa has considerably exceeded the strictly economic benefits obtained.

Arms Transfer Policies in Comparison

The Soviet Union is not the sole arms supplier for Sub-Saharan Africa. France, Great Britain, and the United States continue to provide large quantities of weapons and are actively involved in training and modernizing African armed forces. If one compares Soviet arms transfer policies with their Western counterparts, however, some striking asymmetries appear.[15]

Soviet military aid policy toward Sub-Saharan Africa relies heavily upon deliveries of large quantities of major weapons and weapons systems. During the 1970s the USSR became by far the leading arms supplier for the region, and between 1975 and 1979 Moscow shipped more weaponry to Sub-Saharan Africa than all other suppliers combined, shipments valued at 3.37 billion U.S. dollars. The Soviet Union assumed a large lead as supplier, particularly in the categories of tanks, armored personnel carriers, artillery, fighter aircraft, and anti-aircraft missiles. (See table 7-3.) This represented a dramatic shift since the 1960s, when the USSR ranked fourth in the region as a source of arms, a shift focused on the years 1974-1975. (See table 7-4.) By the late 1970s, approximately 10 percent of all Soviet weapons exports went to Sub-Saharan Africa. Western arms suppliers, in contrast, have always attempted to keep the level of armaments transferred into the region relatively low, emphasizing instead military training and education. Thus, although the USSR leads the West with respect to deliveries of military hardware, it ranks behind France and Great Britain if one adds together the

Table 7-3
Numbers of Weapons Delivered by Major Suppliers to Sub-Saharan Africa, 1975-1982[a]

	USA	USSR	Western Europe[b]
Tanks and Self-Propelled Guns	54	1580	110
Artillery	287	3450	300
APCs and Armored Cars	121	2350	1210
Major Surface Combatants	0	6	16
Minor Surface Combatants	0	63	77
Submarines	0	0	0
Supersonic Combat Aircraft	25	335	55
Subsonic Combat Aircraft	0	130	46
Other Aircraft	40	80	200
Helicopters	4	140	200
Guided Missile Boats	0	10	1
Surface to Air Missiles (SAMs)	0	1830	210

Source: Richard F. Grimmet, *Trends in Conventional Arms Transfers to the Third World by Major Suppliers, 1975-1982* (Washington, D.C.: Congressional Research Service, Library of Congress, 1983), p. 20.

[a]U.S. data are for fiscal years given (and cover the period from 1 July 1974 through 30 September 1982). Foreign data are for calendar years given.

[b]Western European includes France, Italy, the United Kingdom, and West Germany as an aggregate figure.

number of military advisors present in recipient countries or military personnel undergoing training in supplier states. (See table 7-5.)

One further difference between Soviet arms transfer policies and those of other major suppliers lies in the fact that Moscow usually offers more favorable terms for repayment than its Western rivals. Additionally, because

Table 7-4
Soviet Arms Deliveries to Sub-Saharan Africa in Comparison to Western Suppliers
(In millions of current U.S. dollars)

	1961-1971	1976-1980
USSR	182	3995
France	246	880
Great Britain	180	275
USA	196	385
People's Republic of China	39	135[a]
Italy	n.a.	525
West Germany	94	500
Czechoslovakia	14	60

Sources: U.S. Arms Control and Disarmament Agency (ACDA), *The International Arms Trade* (Washington, D.C.: U.S. Government Printing Office, 1974); and ACDA, *World Military Expenditures and Arms Transfers, 1970-1979* and *1971-1980* (Washington, D.C.: U.S. Government Printing Office, 1982 and 1983).

[a]1975-1979.

Table 7-5
Military Personnel from Black Africa Trained by the Major Powers

	Number Trained	Period
USSR[a]	10,840	(1955–1979)
Eastern Europe[a]	1,205	(1955–1979)
France[b]	19,905	(1960–1979)
USA[c]	7,785	(1950–1983)
Great Britain[d]	15,000–20,000	(1950–1982)

Sources:

[a]CIA, *Communist Aid Activity in Non-Communist Less Developed Countries, 1979 and 1954–79* (Washington, D.C.: U.S. Government Printing Office, 1980), p. 16. Figures cited do not include training of guerrilla fighters.

[b]Ministère de la Coopération—Republique Francaise, *Note sur la Coopération Militaire avec les Etats concernés par le Ministère de la Coopération* (Paris: 8 January 1980). See also Jacques Guillemin, *Coopération et Intervention. La Politique Militaire de la France en Afrique Noire Francophone et à Madagascar*. Ph.D. dissertation, University of Nice, January 1979, pp. 73–83.

[c]U.S. Department of Defense, *Foreign Military Sales, Foreign Military Construction Sales and Military Assistance Facts as of September 1982* (Washington, D.C.: U.S. Government Printing Office, 1983), pp. 75–76.

[d]Crude estimate, based on British Department of Defence's official figures on annual training of military personnel from non-NATO countries.

the Soviet Union has no colonial past in Africa, it is to a degree less constrained when contemplating intervention than, for example, France or Great Britain.

While Western military aid policies toward Sub-Saharan Africa are usually uncoordinated, the Soviet Union has been somewhat successful over the past fifteen years in delegating tasks in Africa to its East European allies and to Cuba, thus asserting a multilateral presence in the region. In fact, a rather effective division of labor has developed, with Cuba providing soldiery, the USSR, Czechoslovakia, and Poland supplying weapons, and the German Democratic Republic (GDR) assuming responsibilities in the areas of military training and intelligence.[16] Vietnam, North Korea, Algeria, Syria, the PDRY, and Libya have also proved helpful on repeated occasions by providing military assistance or even supplying troops. Without exaggerating the degree to which Moscow is able to control these dynamics, one may speak of a multilateral system of military cooperation among progressive regimes which consists of an inner and an outer circle. The complexity and flexibility of the network provides the Soviet Union with a considerable number of political and military options that might otherwise not be open to it. In comparison, the coordination of military policies in the Third World among the Western powers is on a much lower level.[17]

Perhaps the most salient aspect of Soviet arms transfer policy in Sub-Saharan Africa is its absolute centrality to the Soviet effort to stabilize its allies and expand influence. This is in sharp contrast to its Western rivals, for whom military aid and arms deliveries represent only subordinate policy instruments. Soviet influence rests almost entirely upon the military aid relationship. The ratio of Soviet military to economic aid to Sub-Saharan Africa during the 1970s was approximately 15:1, and in many years Soviet weapons exports exceeded their entire export of civilian goods. (See table 7-6.)

Various reasons may be cited to account for these imbalances. First, the Soviet Union is by far the world's largest producer of conventional arms and with considerable stocks on hand is able to deliver larger quantities of weapons more rapidly than its chief competitors. Second, the Soviet Union's low profile in military training and education results in part from the persistance of traditional ties between individual African military establishments and their former colonial tutors. Additionally, within many arms-importing states there is a considerable element of mistrust with regard to the intentions of the Soviet leadership. Many Third World leaders, even those with a socialist orientation, are fearful that military education provided by the Soviet Union might make too strong an impact upon officers and soldiers, increasing the potential for communist coups. Long-term military aid relationships with the USSR have often been accompanied by draconic persecution of elements within the armed forces suspected of communist sympathies.

The trend toward a division of labor as regards military responsibilities in Africa among Soviet allies points to Moscow's need for burden-sharing arrangements, both on economic and political grounds. Multilateral coop-

Table 7-6
Soviet Arms Exports, Civilian Exports, and Development Aid for Black Africa
(Millions of U.S. dollars)

Year	Arms Exports[a]	Development Aid[b]	Exports[c]
1975	270	67	197
1976	285	24	184
1977	550	31	281
1978	1400	11	408
1979	615	95	378
Total	3120	228	1448

[a]Deliveries, calculated on estimated Soviet price figures. Source: CIA, *Communist Aid Activities in Non-Communist Less Developed Countries, 1979 and 1954-79* (Washington, D.C.: U.S. Government Printing Office, 1980), p. 14.
[b]Agreements. Source: CIA statistics.
[c]Extracted from *Vneshniaia torgovlia*, official Soviet trade statistics, various volumes.

eration in the field of military aid—especially when members of the non-aligned movement are also actively involved—makes it much easier for the Kremlin to claim that its activities have been undertaken on behalf of the cause of social and political liberation in the Third World.

Soviet Successes and Failures

How successful has Soviet arms export policy in Africa actually been? Beginning with the assumption that Moscow has been motivated primarily by strategic interests, one may assert that the provision of military assistance has been undertaken in pursuit of three interrelated goals: (1) an expansion of Soviet influence over the course of political events in Sub-Saharan Africa; (2) a corresponding reduction of Western influence; and (3) an extension of the USSR's power projection capability and sphere of military operations.[18]

As concerns the first goal, it can be confidently stated that the exports of weapons to the states of Sub-Saharan Africa has been quite successful. Three key factors should be mentioned in this regard: Moscow's readiness to make available modern weapons and munitions in large quantities; the efficiency of Soviet military assistance; and the capacity of the USSR to operate effectively within the extremely sensitive network of inter-African political relations. Nonetheless, the Soviet Union has not enjoyed unbroken successes. As was clearly demonstrated by the experiences of the first ten years of military aid programs, the Soviet leadership has also had to endure a series of setbacks. In this regard, it has proven its ability to learn from mistakes and come to a better understanding of how most effectively to craft arms transfers to the frame of reference of African politics and its reigning sensitivities. The military assistance accorded Nigeria during the Biafran War, support for the MPLA in Angola following the South African invasion, the massive backing provided Ethiopia in its struggle against Somalia and internal secession, and the military help for Front Line states and liberation movements in southern Africa have all occurred according to a pattern which the majority of African states could approve. Only the long-standing Soviet relationship with Somalia contradicted this pattern, and Moscow freed itself from this difficulty during 1977 by associating with Ethiopia at Somalia's expense.

In spite of these advances, however, the USSR has not succeeded in expanding its sphere of political control. Although Angola, Benin, Cape Verde, Ethiopia, Mozambique, and the PDRY may be described as communist states, they are far from being Soviet satellites.[19] The designation "national communist" would perhaps be more appropriate. The ambitious expectations which the Soviet leadership allowed itself in this regard during the mid-1970s have since been provisionally replaced by a more modest evaluation. Certainly though, Moscow's intensive efforts to force the revolutionary process in these countries toward the criteria of real socialism indicate that the hope of attracting internationalist-minded allies in the Third World has not yet been abandoned. The fact that the regimes in Angola, Ethiopia, and Mozambique will remain dependent upon Moscow's support for the foreseeable future—if they are to survive ongoing internal and external challenges—gives the Soviet leadership certain grounds for such hope.

The decisive dilemma in the long run for Soviet arms transfer policy in Sub-Saharan Africa is that the Kremlin is hardly in a position to meet all the related military, political, and economic expectations of its client states. Military assistance for liberation movements and the Front Line states in southern Africa seems to be moving neither toward a collapse of white hegemony in South Africa nor to independence for Namibia. The military superiority of South Africa cannot be seriously challenged by any of its neighboring states in the near future. The military ties between these states and Moscow are in fact repeatedly exploited by Pretoria as a pretext for blocking proposed political solutions or to attract the Western world onto its side. Through air assaults and military commando raids against Angola and Mozambique, South Africa has succeeded in challenging Soviet supplied arms and placing Moscow in an embarrassing situation: The more clearly South Africa demonstrates its military superiority over the Front Line states, the more the Soviet Union is compelled to provide for their defense.

Neither Angola nor Mozambique would be in a position to defend itself alone against a South African assault. Both would require the introduction of Cuban combat forces, and in a short space of time probably Soviet forces as well (for example, air defense units). That Moscow, for its part, would allow itself to be drawn into a major engagement at such a distance from its national territory is scarcely to be expected. It is thus most likely that the Kremlin will pursue flexible arms transfer policies which, on one hand, council a certain restraint on the part of its allies toward South Africa, while simultaneously doing everything possible in order to insure that their dependency upon Soviet help is not reduced due to a diminution of the South African threat.

In political terms Moscow can offer the states of southern Africa very little of substance. The Soviet Union is not acceptable to South Africa as a partner to negotiations, and thus the Soviet leadership cannot serve as a mediator for its arms customers. Because the USSR itself offers no prospects in this regard, Western states are repeatedly pushed back into the diplomatic limelight. As a partial reaction to Soviet arms transfers in southern Africa, in recent years awareness of the urgency of the region's problems has increased in Western capitals and led to both partially successful and unsuccessful mediation efforts (such as the Lancaster House Conference or the five-power initiative concerning Namibia). Under these circumstances a situation could develop whereby the Soviet Union's readiness to provide military help would merely be exploited by southern African leaders in order to increase the weight of their own political demands in a negotiation process from which Moscow would be substantially excluded.

In those regions of Sub-Saharan Africa that are not threatened by the fundamental and explosive conflicts that divide the south, an arms transfer relationship with the Soviet Union can often make good sense politically. First, Moscow has repeatedly demonstrated its reliability and efficiency as a supporter of socialist oriented regimes confronted by internal political resistance or the opposition of tribal and ethnic groups. Second, many African states utilize arms transfers and the provision of military training by the USSR in order to conduct a strategy of political diversification. Convinced as they are that their political, cultural, and economic dependence upon the West cannot be overcome in the short-term, many African states establish military relations with the Soviet Union in order to ensure that, at least in this critical area, their reliance upon the West is not absolute. The Soviet Union continues to offer more favorable financial conditions than the West and is often more readily tolerated as a supplier by African regimes due to the limited nature of its military presence compared to those of France, Great Britain, or the United States. At the same time, however, concern is also growing in Sub-Saharan Africa over Moscow's ability to utilize military relationships on behalf of its own great power interests and to manipulate procommunist officers within national military establishments in order to increase its influence.[20]

Moscow is least of all capable of responding to its allies' requests when they demand economic help. For many African states, a close relationship with the USSR only makes sense when accompanied by increased assistance in the area of economic development. It is precisely here, however, where the balance of Soviet efforts appears most disappointing. Even Angola, Ethiopia, and Mozambique received only minimal economic assistance—between 1976 and 1981 a total that barely exceeds $70 million (U.S.) for all three taken together.[21] Mozambique's request for membership in the Council for Mutual Economic Assistance (CMEA) was turned down in 1981 because Moscow obviously felt incapable of supporting its ailing economy. Similar situations exist in regard to the other nations of southern Africa. The number of Soviet development projects is limited, and their overall value is small. Many projects have collapsed due to the inability of the USSR and its CMEA partners to offer market possibilities for the commodities produced.

Conclusion

The massive influx of Soviet weapons into Sub-Saharan Africa during the 1970s has not been without effect. It has played an essential part in the transformation of Sub-Saharan Africa into an area of increasing militarization. During the past ten years, Sub-Saharan Africa's expenditures for armaments have increased by a considerably greater amount than has national income. The resultant disintegration in what was already a critical economic situation for many countries is painfully obvious. The Soviet Union certainly bears a portion of the responsibility for this state of affairs.

The Soviet Union has of course not been alone as a source of militarization in Sub-Saharan Africa. Portugal (to 1974), South Africa, and the regional ambitions of numerous Black African states have all played a role. Nonetheless, and despite repeated Soviet references to the negative consequences of military expenditures for the developing world, Soviet arms transfer policy has remained aggressive and relatively unrestrained when compared with those of the Western powers.

It may further be noted concerning Soviet military assistance for Sub-Saharan Africa that it has often failed to provide solutions for the problems to which it has been addressed. More often than not, the result has been an increased level of confrontation and reduced prospects for peaceful solutions without any fundamental resolution of underlying problems. In some ways Moscow may be perceived to have an interest in the continuation of conflicts which enable it to function as a relevant actor in regional affairs. On the other hand, however, the Soviet leadership cannot consider its interests to lie in the eruption of an uncontrolled sequence of local wars. Particularly in the event of major hostilities in southern Africa, the weakness of its key allies would very quickly become obvious and make an eventual Soviet interventon, with all its related risks, almost unavoidable.

In many ways it seems that the Soviet attitude toward the problem of southern Africa is similar to their position vis-à-vis the Middle East. In both cases Moscow seeks to prevent political solutions from being concluded without its participation, while simultaneously attempting to manage armed conflicts that threaten to escalate out of control. In both regions the USSR manipulates the dependency of client states relative to its perceived interests of the moment, and in both cases arms transfers represent the key to Soviet influence. It is however, a dangerous and precarious game that is being played. Soviet arms transfer policy in Sub-Saharan Africa represents yet another factor contributing to the destabilization of an already fragile political balance, with unpredictable consequences for both regional and nonregional actors.

Notes

1. See Winrich Kühne, *Die Politik der Sowjetunion in Afrika: Bedingungen und Dynamik ihres ideologischen, ökonomischen und militärischen Engagements* (Baden-Baden: Nomos, 1983).
2. Wynfred Joshua and Stephen P. Gilbert, *Arms for the Third World: Soviet Military Aid Diplomacy* (Baltimore: Johns Hopkins University Press, 1969), pp. 31–52. See also Stockholm International Peace Research Institute, *The Arms Trade With the Third World* (Stockholm: 1981), pp. 620–622.
3. Joshua and Gilbert, *Arms for the Third World*, p. 40.
4. Andrew J. Pierre, *The Global Politics of Arms Sales* (Princeton, N.J.: Princeton University Press, 1982), p. 77.
5. Paul B. Henze, "Communism and Ethiopia," *Problems of Communism* 30, no. 3 (1981):55–74. See also Colin Legum, "Angola and the Horn of Africa," in Stephen S. Kaplan, ed., *Diplomacy of Power: Soviet Armed Forces as a Political Instrument* (Washington, D.C.: Brookings Institution, 1981), pp. 570–637.
6. Thomas H. Henriksen, "Angola, Mozambique, and the Soviet Union: Liberation and the Quest for Influence," in Warren Weinstein and Thomas H. Henriksen, eds., *Soviet and Chinese Aid to African Nations* (New York: Praeger, 1980), p. 61. See also Bettina Decke, *"A terra é nossa": Koloniale Gesellschaft und Befreiungsbewegung in Angola* (Bonn: Informationsstelle südliches Afrika, 1981), p. 249; and Peter Enahoro, "Die Befreiungskriege im Portugiesischen Afrika," in John J. Vianney, eds., *Politische Perspektiven Afrikas* (Bonn: Deutsche Afrika Gesellschaft, 1972), p. 201.
7. Oye Ogunbadejo, "Ideology and Pragmatism: The Soviet Role in Nigeria," *Orbis* 21 (Winter 1978):803–830.
8. J. Bowyer Bell, "Strategic Implications of the Soviet Presence in Somalia," *Orbis* 19 (Summer 1976):402–411. See also Robert E. Harkavy, *Great Power Competition for Overseas Bases* (New York: Pergamon, 1982), pp. 189–191.
9. Arthur J. Klinghoffer, *The Angolan War: A Study in Soviet Policy in the Third World* (Boulder, Colo.: Westview, 1980); John A. Marcum, *The Angolan Revolution*, vol. 2 (Cambridge, Mass.: MIT Press, 1978); and Neil McFarlane, *Soviet Intervention in Third World Conflicts* (Geneva: Graduate Institute of International Studies, 1983), pp. 12–17.
10. Helen Desfosses, "Considerations of Naval and Arab Power in Soviet Policy in the Horn of Africa," in Weinstein and Henriksen, *Soviet and Chinese Aid*, pp. 34–55.
11. Legum, "Angola and the Horn," pp. 615–624. See also Steven David, "Realignment in the Horn," *International Security* 4, no. 2 (Fall 1979):69–90.

12. Winrich Kühne, "Schwarzafrika und die Sowjetunion," *Europa-Archiv* 35, no. 10 (1980):325-334.

13. Joseph P. Smaldone, "Soviet and Chinese Military Aid and Arms Transfers to Africa: A Contextual Analysis," in Weinstein and Henriksen, *Soviet and Chinese Aid*, pp. 76-116; Edward J. Laurance, "Soviet Arms Transfers in the 1980s: Declining Influence in Sub-Saharan Africa," in Bruce E. Arlinghaus, ed., *Arms for Africa* (Lexington, Mass.: D.C. Heath, Lexington Books, 1983), pp. 39-77.

14. See Central Intelligence Agency, *Communist Aid to Less Developed Countries of the Free World, 1977* (Washington, D.C.: U.S. Government Printing Office, 1978); *Communist Aid Activities in Non-Communist Less Developed Countries, 1978* (Washington, D.C.: U.S. Government Printing Office, 1979); and *Communist Aid Activities in Non-Communist Less Developed Countries, 1979 and 1954-79* (Washington, D.C.: U.S. Government Printing Office, 1980).

15. Some of the structural aspects of Soviet arms transfer policy in Sub-Saharan Africa are discussed in George E. Hudson, "Soviet Arms Policy Towards Black Africa: Opportunities and Constraints," in Cindy Cannizzo, ed., *The Gun Merchants* (New York: Pergamon, 1980), pp. 49-67. See also David E. Albright, "Overview of Communist Arms Transfers to Sub-Saharan Africa," in Arlinghaus, *Arms for Africa*, pp. 21-37.

16. Robert M. Bigler, "The Role of the German Democratic Republic in the Communist Penetration of Africa," in Forest L. Grieves, ed., *Transnationalism in World Politics and Business* (New York: Pergamon, 1979), pp. 191-202; Melvin Croan, "A New Afrika Corps?," *The Washington Quarterly* 3, no. 1 (Winter 1980):21-37; and Gavriel Ra'anan, *The Evolution of the Soviet Use of Surrogates in Military Relations with the Third World* Rand Paper p-6420 (Santa Monica: The Rand Corporation, 1979). See also Roger Kanet, "Military Relations Between Eastern Europe and Africa," in Arlinghaus, *Arms for Africa*, pp. 79-99.

17. See Avigdor Haselkorn, *The Evolution of Soviet Security Strategy, 1965-1975* (New York: Crane-Russak, 1978).

18. Roger F. Pajak, "Soviet Arms Transfers as an Instrument of Influence," *Survival* 23, no. 4 (1981):165-173; and Roger Kanet, "Soviet Military Assistance to the Third World," in John F. Copper and Daniel S. Papp, eds., *Communist Nations' Military Assistance* (Boulder, Colo.: Westview, 1983), pp. 39-71.

19. See Marina Ottaway, "The Theory and Practice of Marxism-Leninism in Mozambique and Ethiopia," in David E. Albright, ed., *Communism in Africa* (Bloomington, Ind.: Indiana University Press, 1980), pp. 118-144.

20. A strong warning to this effect was issued by then Nigerian President Obansanjo during his speech before the fifteenth OAU meeting, in Khartoum, during July 1978.

21. Figures are based upon NATO materials, issued by the Permanent Representative of the Federal Republic of Germany on 3 May 1983.

8

The Significance of Soviet Strategic Military Interests in Sub-Saharan Africa

Richard B. Remnek

The marked expansion of Soviet activities in Sub-Saharan Africa over the past decade has been interpreted by some observers as a strategic threat to the West. According to this view, during a major war the Soviets would employ African facilities to attack NATO forces from the flanks, interdict at sea the supplies of Persian Gulf oil that reach Europe and the U.S. from around the coasts of Africa, and deny the West access to African sources of chromium, cobalt, manganese, and platinum—strategic minerals with important military-industrial applications. These ulterior strategic motives, so the argument goes, underlie Soviet policy in Sub-Saharan Africa. They help explain the vast sums the Soviets spent, for example, in constructing military installations in Somalia for their own and Somali use.[1] Is this perception of a Soviet strategic threat in Black Africa accurate or exaggerated? And if exaggerated, to what extent?

The purpose of this chapter is to examine critically this threat assessment by attempting to identify specific Soviet strategic military interests in and around Sub-Saharan Africa and suggesting how they may have affected the thrust of Soviet policy in the area in the past and might affect it in the future. In this chapter, the term *strategic* is used in its narrow, military sense. The focus here is on clarifying what role Sub-Saharan Africa—its resources, territory, and surrounding water—may play in the Soviet peacetime preparation for and prosecution of a major war. Such a war is likely to be fought primarily outside Africa, on a scale either worldwide or limited to a specific military theater (e.g., Europe or Southwest Asia). I shall consider war scenarios around the periphery of Africa (i.e., a NATO/Warsaw Pact war and a superpower conflict in Southwest Asia) and outside the African periphery (e.g., a Sino–Soviet conflict).

For the purpose of this discussion, I have assumed that a major war would be fought by conventional means and over a protracted period, measured in months and perhaps years. This choice is recommended by Soviet doctrinal evidence which suggests that Moscow has recently introduced an independent option for a conventional, protracted war.[2] The Soviets evidently now believe they have sufficient capabilities to fight a coalition war on a global scale and by conventional means, without necessarily escalating to the nuclear level. As part of this shift to a conventional option, the

Soviets have upgraded the antisea lines of communication mission.[3] This shift in Soviet military thinking has important implications for the strategic significance of Africa in Soviet eyes.

Peacetime Access

As noted above, this chapter examines the role of Africa in assisting the Soviets to prepare in peacetime for a major war as well as to fight one. The connection between these peacetime and wartime roles of Africa is complicated by the fact that the Soviet military presence in and around that continent is there largely for reasons of state that have little to do with preparations for a major war. The naval forces deployed off the coasts of Sub-Saharan Africa perform primarily politico-military missions, ranging from the protection of Soviet state interests, such as the hundred or more Soviet civilian vessels that are to be found in the Indian Ocean on any given day,[4] to the implementation of Soviet foreign policy objectives in the Third World. Indeed, the Soviet Navy has become a major instrument in Moscow's diplomacy of force in the Third World.

How Soviet naval forces are employed in peacetime does not tell us much about how they might be utilized in a major war. To an appreciable degree it depends on how we employ our deployed naval forces. For example, should U.S. carrier forces be withdrawn from the Indian Ocean—say, during a crisis leading to a Soviet attack concentrated along the central European front—the Soviets would likely pull their naval forces out of the area too, particularly if they felt no alternative objectives were worth targeting there. The basic point here is that the Soviet forces deployed around Africa in peacetime may not be there in wartime. All that can be safely asserted is that these forces are peacetime instruments of Soviet diplomacy whose wartime roles are highly scenario-dependent.

Because these wartime roles are uncertain, this makes it easier for African states to support the Soviet Navy simply on the grounds that it serves political objectives that are compatible with their own foreign policies. Supporting a local Soviet naval presence usually directly serves the security interests of an access donor. These donors are hence indirect beneficiaries of the naval support they render.

However, in supporting the Soviet Navy they are doing more than this. By facilitating the Soviet Navy's performance of politico-military missions, access donors make it easier for the Soviet Navy to perform other missions, including those of strategic value. Ready access to local port facilities—where repairs that cannot be performed satisfactorily at sea can be made, and crew rest and direct logistic support are available—[5] has enabled the Soviet Navy to support forward-deployed combatants with fewer support vessels and prolong combatant deployments significantly. For example, prior to gaining extensive access to facilities at Berbera in 1972, the average Soviet warship deploying to the Indian Ocean stayed there for roughly five months; in 1973 Soviet combatant deployments to the Indian Ocean lasted around one year.[6]

Lengthening combatant deployments has important operational advantages. First, it reduces the overall proportion of time wasted by Soviet warships in transit from home bases to forward operating areas. In some cases these reductions were substantial. For example, in the 1970s (i.e., before the Soviet Indian Ocean Squadron began to make occasional use of Vietnam's facilities for enroute logistic and maintenance support) it took Soviet naval units approximately three weeks with normal transit speeds of 10–12 knots to reach the Gulf of Aden, their normal Indian Ocean operating area, from their Vladivostok home port (a distance of 6700 nautical miles). Prior to 1973, when Soviet naval deployments in the Indian Ocean averaged five months, to keep one combatant on station continuously in the Gulf of Aden Soviet warships spent roughly four months per year in transit. By more than doubling the length of deployments in 1973, the Soviets were able to cut the amount of transit time by more than half.

Second, lengthening deployments gives the Soviet Navy the ability to meet their force requirements with a smaller inventory of ships, thereby reducing overall operating costs as well as freeing units for other assignments. To be sure, only some of the general purpose forces the Soviets deploy forward—such as submarines and the more modern, missile-capable surface combatants—could be used effectively to perform higher priority missions of strategic significance elsewhere. Other units have very limited combat capabilities and are therefore well suited to the performance of relatively nondemanding state interest missions in the Third World and little else. This applies particularly to the older combatants, such as 900-ton *T-58-class* patrol ships and 1100 ton *Petya-class* frigates that were introduced into service when the Soviets had only a day-sailing navy. Indeed, the Soviets appear to have risked Indian Ocean deployments for the *Petyas*, whose small size and low endurance make them ill-suited for open operations,[7] only after they gained routine access to Berbera.[8] The ready availability of local support facilities appears to have enabled them to prolong the useful service of warships that might otherwise have been scrapped.

Soviet use of African support facilities other than those located in ports is also important. The Soviets have staged routine surveillance flights from airfields in Guinea and Somalia (until 1977), and Angola (since 1977), and Ethiopia (since 1979).[9] Most often the Soviets have used in this role *Il-38 May* ASW planes, whose limited range does not permit them to do much more than aerial surveillance in support of deployed naval forces. However, the Soviets have also staged long-range *Tu-95 Bear-D* maritime reconnaissance aircraft, mostly from west African airfields.[10] This has afforded the USSR surveillance coverage of U.S. naval forces over large expanses of the

Atlantic Ocean remote from Africa. *Bear-Ds* are also capable of providing targeting data for sea-launched cruise missiles—a valuable asset in peacetime naval exercises as well as in wartime (should, of course, the *Bear-Ds* survive long enough to provide the data). The long-range and combat capabilities of the *Bears* suggest that their reconnaissance flights from west Africa can serve strategic as well as politico-military missions.

Though not exhaustive,[11] this list of naval support services rendered by Black African states includes those with clearly identified strategic implications. In general, this support helps the Soviet Navy prepare for a major war indirectly and only to a minor extent.

Wartime Missions: Interdiction

If the strategic military benefits the Soviets derive in peacetime from their activities in and around Africa are indirect and very limited at that, how important might Africa be in the actual Soviet prosecution of major war? Most answers to this question have been based simply on extrapolations of Soviet capabilities that are scenario-independent and pay scant regard to the combat mission priorities and assessments of relative military capabilities that will determine how Soviet combat assets are employed.

The strategic military importance of Africa to the USSR in wartime has been seen generally in two connections: First, warships deployed around Africa would interdict oil tankers from the Persian Gulf; and second, the USSR would stage strike aircraft from African airfields to conduct a flank attack on NATO forces and installations in NATO's southern region and transatlantic convoys of reinforcements and resupplies. Among informed observers only the second thesis has currency.

The reason that the first lacks credibility has nothing to do with the capabilities of Soviet naval forces deployed. Even the most antiquated and least combat-capable of the warships the Soviets deploy off the coasts of Africa can sink a tanker, but so too can a terrorist firing a rocket propelled grenade from an Arab dhow. The point here is that tankers are highly vulnerable to attack. In fact, one wonders whether—if for no other reason than skyrocketing maritime insurance costs—tankers might not put into the nearest port during a crisis leading to war and not return to the sea lanes before the Soviets had been swept from the seas.

This does not mean that Persian Gulf oil supplies would be safe in war—they would not be. Rather, the most efficient and potentially effective way the Soviets could interdict the flow of oil to the West would be through sabotage of oil pumping stations and terminals. The Soviets would be inclined to attempt sabotage were they to believe that the damage would be so extensive that neither repairs nor replacements could be made effectively in wartime conditions. If proxy forces were not available for sabotage missions, the Soviets might employ special operations detachments.

One inobtrusive way the Soviets could infiltrate commando units into place would be to disembark them from deployed warships. While there is no available evidence that special operations units have been attached to the crews of deployed Soviet naval units, the Soviets have the capability to place them aboard those ships by covert means within a few days. For example, they could fly into a local port commandos posing as replacements for civilian crew members aboard Soviet fishing trawlers or other civilian vessels. These commandos could later be transferred from civilian to naval ships at sea. They could even be mixed in with the small Soviet naval infantry forces aboard the amphibious ships which are usually present in waters off the east and west coasts of Africa.

Their targets would probably be oil terminals at Port Harcourt, Nigeria, and Yanbu, on Saudi Arabia's Red Sea coast. Opened in 1981, Yanbu is capable of delivering 1.6 billion barrels per day. Both sites are within a few days transiting time of the principal logistical and maintenance bases of the Soviet West Africa Patrol and Indian Ocean Squadron (Luanda, Angola and Dahlak Island, Ethiopia, respectively). These targets are located in areas where Western naval forces are not normally deployed, and in which activities of such otherwise unimportant naval units as forward-deployed amphibious ships would likely be ignored, particularly in a wartime crisis when attention would be focused elsewhere. Moreover, were Soviet naval forces around Sub-Saharan Africa directed to proceed northward, to the closest home ports (e.g., Odessa for the Indian Ocean Squadron), the Soviets would be better able to achieve deception for their commando operations, since Yanbu and Port Harcourt lie north of Dahlak and Luanda, respectively.

If the Soviets are indeed preparing for a protracted, conventional war, the Nigerian oil terminals in particular might seem to be a worthwhile target. The largest African oil exporter, Nigeria is one of the United States' principal foreign suppliers. In a major protracted war lasting many months, oil supplies from the U.S. strategic petroleum reserve and the Western hemisphere would fall short of demand. The United States would have to turn to the Eastern hemisphere for oil, but we would probably look to Nigeria before the Persian Gulf. That is because Nigeria's sealines of communication to the United States are far shorter than those from the Persian Gulf and are located beyond the probable reach of Soviet military power even in a protracted conflict. I am assuming here that by the time the United States would need Nigerian oil, the south-central Atlantic would be cleared of Soviet naval combatants and the threat posed by Cuba would be neutralized. Hence, the Nigerian oil supply line would appear to be reasonably safe.

Given these considerations, the Soviets might believe the only reasonable chance they would have of interdicting the flow of oil from Nigeria would be by employing naval infantry commandos at the outset of a major war. The naval forces the Soviets deploy around Africa in peacetime could thus play a minor role in wartime interdiction of oil supplies by targeting oil terminals, not tankers.

Wartime Missions: Strike Aircraft Support

Whereas the Soviet sea-based threat to oil tanker traffic seems highly improbable, a better case can be made that the Soviets would attempt to stage bombers from African airfields. Doing so would extend the range and on-station operating time of high performance bombers (such as the *Backfire*) and it would enable the Soviets to employ shorter-range bombers (like *Tu-16 Badgers*) in distant operations.

We also know that in developing an infrastructure in Somalia Moscow built in certain capabilities to support *Soviet* combat operations. The so-called missile-handling and storage facility they built at Berbera was capable of handling a wide variety of air- and sea-launched conventional tactical missiles as well as other ordnance more sophisticated than those the Somalis had or were ever likely to receive.[12] The ordnance storage facility's proximity to both the large airfield then under construction and the port suggests its potential dual use for naval combatants and bomber aircraft alike.

However, it is unclear what contingencies the Soviets had in mind when they built into their support infrastructure at Berbera the capability to support strike aircraft. Before the Shah of Iran's fall, when the Indian Ocean appears in retrospect to have been a relative zone of peace, no conceivable regional scenario would have justified the acquisition of such capabilities. Moreover, with the rudimentary air defense capabilities the Soviets had installed at Berbera (a few SA-2 and -3 SAMs), Soviet aircraft deployed there would have been vulnerable to Western attack. It is improbable that the Soviets would have risked exposing in this manner their *Backfires*—their most formidable combat assets, which moreover would have had high priority missions to perform operating from well-protected air bases on Soviet soil.

It is possible, however, that the Soviets may have intended to use on a contingency basis their older and less valuable bombers, such as the shorter range *Tu-16 Badger Gs* or their longer range *Tu-95 Bear-Bs*, in naval missions in the eastern Mediterranean. Even the shorter-range *Badgers* when fully loaded and refueled in air can easily reach the Mediterranean from Berbera. Any bombers surviving an attack on Western forces might have then been able to return to Warsaw Pact airfields. By staging from Berbera *Badger-Gs*, armed with AS-5 *Kelt* or highly accurate AS-6 *Kingfish* antiship missiles, or *Bear-Bs* with AS-3 *Kangaroo* missiles, the Soviets could have tried to attack

U.S. naval forces in the eastern Mediterranean from a southern azimuth. This could have further complicated the Sixth Fleet's air defense problem in the area. If the reconnaissance assets protecting the Sixth Fleet were concentrated against a threat from the north, it would have left the carriers vulnerable to an air attack from the south.

Although Berbera's rudimentary air defense would have left Soviet bombers exposed, the Soviets may have calculated they could pull off a sneak, back-door attack. When they built these facilities, the Indian Ocean did not have permanently stationed U.S. military forces capable of identifying what planes the Soviets flew into the area. What the Soviet Navy did then in the Indian Ocean was largely unimportant to U.S. military planners. With the West's attention focused elsewhere during a crisis leading up to a NATO/Warsaw Pact war, the Soviets might have thought they could fly bombers unannounced and unnoticed over Afghanistan and western Pakistan (Baluchistan), then refuel and arm the bombers with air-to-surface missiles at Berbera, and take off for the Mediterranean without being detected until the bombers were within combat operational range.

The Soviets may have in fact originally intended such a mission for the *Tu-16 Badger-Gs* that were stationed at Aswan, Egypt, in the early 1970s. To be sure, these units never flew operational missions over the Mediterranean and were stationed at Aswan apparently for exclusive Egyptian use. This does not rule out the possibility that the Soviets would have wanted to use these planes in a wartime contingency against the Sixth Fleet. Perhaps, it is not simple coincidence that the Soviets began to build air combat support capabilities at Berbera about a year after they had been forced to withdraw these *Badger-Gs* from Egypt as part of Sadat's July 1972 repatriation of Egyptian support facilities.

It is important to note that the Soviets have neither deployed bombers to African airfields since their eviction from Egypt nor built ordnance facilities in Africa of comparable capability to the one they lost at Berbera. The reasons for this may be both military and political in nature.

From an operational perspective, the potential wartime value of African airfields for the USSR has probably declined in recent years, largely because it has become much easier for the Soviets to project airpower toward the eastern Mediterranean and the Persian Gulf/Arabian Sea directly from Soviet air bases. This is due primarily to the increased number and improved quality of Soviet bomber assets coupled with the weakening of Iranian defenses. In addition, Soviet use of improved airfields and support facilities in Afghanistan could extend to the shores of the Arabian Sea the range of the fighter protection for *Backfires* operating against U.S. carrier forces.

This is not to deny that there may still be some specific situations in which the USSR could make advantageous use of airfields in Sub-Saharan Africa. In a transitional stage of a war that started in Southwest Asia, for example, airfields in southern Africa could play a prominent role. Should a Southwest Asia conflict escalate horizontally and U.S. carriers be routed around the Cape of Good Hope to the Atlantic, airfields in Mozambique or even Angola could possibly be used for recovery and turn-around of long-range *Backfires*,[13] staging from Soviet home bases against carriers in transit. The unrefueled combat radius of the *Backfire* (2950 nautical miles)[14] would permit it to reach from Soviet airfields targets located about as far south as the Seychelles.

In view of the light air defenses of airfields in Mozambique and Angola, such use would place Soviet strike aircraft in jeopardy. The Soviets might nevertheless take this risk if they calculated they had a reasonable chance of disabling a carrier thereby.

Thus despite obvious hypothetical advantages that wartime use of African airfields would have in extending the reach of Soviet airpower, the actual circumstances in which the Soviets might make effective use of those airfields seem to be few. Due to recent changes in the military environment, such employments appear to be less important now than they may have been only a few years back.

The Problem of Access

The above discussion has been predicated on the assumption that African states would be willing to permit the Soviets to use their airfields (or any other military facilities) in a major war. This assumption would seem to be unwarranted. No Black African leader has ever evidenced a willingness to see his homeland become a battlefield in a NATO/Warsaw Pact war. In fact, even those Sub-Saharan African states that support the Soviet Navy and rely heavily on Soviet arms imports and security assistance continue to depend heavily on Western economic trade, aid, and private investment. With their economies tied to the West, they have much to lose from a NATO/Warsaw Pact conflict, especially if it left the Western economies in ruins. Hence, they would hardly be likely to throw in their lots with the Soviets in a coalition war.

Only in rare instances has a Third World access donor allowed a superpower to develop facilities to be used for purposes that evidently did not directly serve its own security interests. This happened in Somalia in the 1970s. But Mogadiscio's evident willingness to permit the Soviets to build a military support complex capable of being used, perhaps effectively, in support of Soviet strike air combat operations in the eastern Mediterranean does not mean that the Somalis would have permitted these facilities to be used for the apparent purposes they were constructed. We should not assume that a clear understanding regarding the wartime contexts in which these facilities would be utilized by the Soviets preceded their construction. Misrepresentation, wishful thinking, or both, perhaps on the part of each party, may have played a role in the negotiations.[15] Somalia's President Siad Barre apparently believed the Soviets would never need to use them in wartime. He appears to have been sufficiently impressed by U.S.-Soviet progress toward detente in the early 1970s to assume that superpower conflicts were highly unlikely to erupt from a regional crisis. He was, in fact, the only leader of an Indian Ocean littoral nation to state openly in the mid 1970s that the Indian Ocean was already a "zone of peace."[16] He may therefore have thought it safe enough to allow the Soviets to develop elaborate combat support facilities at Berbera.

As matters turned out, Siad Barre was instrumental, perhaps unwittingly so, in arranging matters so that the Soviets apparently never employed the ordnance facility for their own use. In the summer of 1975, soon after the ordnance facility's completion, Siad Barre invited a U.S. congressional delegation led by Senator Dewey F. Bartlett (Republican-Oklahoma) to inspect the Berbera support complex ostensibly in order to disprove photographic evidence about the nature of the complex presented before the Senate Armed Services Committee by Defense Secretary James Schlesinger in early June. The visit of the Bartlett delegation, composed of Department of Defense experts, had the opposite effect. Also the negative publicity garnered by the so-called missile-handling and storage facility in particular did much to erode congressional resistance to the funding of what was then an austere naval support facility on Diego Garcia.[17] In addition, the negative publicity not only seems to have kept the Soviets from using the ordnance facility even for making repairs of the missiles for their naval combatants but also may have dissuaded them from building comparable facilities elsewhere in the Third World.[18]

What this episode suggests is that Soviet interests (in this case, restricting the development of Diego Garcia) have been damaged when they have built support facilities whose employment could not be justified in terms of the host nation's security interests. Today there are no exigencies on the African continent that could rationalize the stationing of Soviet attack aircraft, much less developing facilities for their support. This applies even to southern Africa, for the Soviets have not evinced so far any interest in directly tangling with South Africa's armed forces even in defense of Mozambique or Angola.[19]

My assumption that in a major war Third World access donors would not permit the Soviets to use installations ashore also applies to the use of port facilities. Should, as seems likely, these countries believe their interests would be served best by noninvolvement in a major coalition war, they would undoubtedly withdraw support for the Soviet Navy at the outbreak of hostilities, if not before. However, the support obtained before then would have enhanced the combat readiness and capabilities of Soviet naval forces on the eve of battle. Even if—say, in order to perform higher priority wartime missions elsewhere—Soviet warships were withdrawn from forward areas during a crisis leading to war, the logistical and maintenance services they might have received at local port facilities in peacetime would have better prepared them for the often long voyage home.[20]

In point of fact, whether an access-granting nation would cut off support to Soviet naval forces prior to hostilities matters little. In a major war, Soviet surface combatants and probably submarines as well would not survive long enough to need shore-based logistic and maintenance support after the battle had started. Depending on how successfully these forces maneuvered during the crisis stage, they could be positioned so as to be able to inflict damage to Western naval forces as to make their own sacrifice worthwhile. This is not simply a hypothetical possibility. In the October 1973 Middle East war, Soviet naval forces in the Mediterranean were interspersed with Sixth Fleet units, and our carriers were highly vulnerable to Soviet attack with surface-to-surface missiles.[21] Had a superpower war at sea broken out then, U.S. naval forces would have lost the advantage that the superior range of U.S. sea and land-based airpower normally provides in countering the Soviet surface fleet. This suggests that even if African access donors were to withdraw all Soviet access privileges before the outbreak of a war, the support they had furnished the Soviet Navy in peacetime would have had some wartime value.

Conflict in Asia

In the discussion above, I have examined critically some widely held notions about the potential wartime value of the Soviet use of African facilities. However, since the focus has been on the Soviet employment of their own combat forces in wars involving U.S. forces and fought around the periphery of Africa, this discussion is not complete. The role of Africa in relation to major conflicts fought outside Africa has probably influenced Soviet strategic thinking about Africa significantly.

Africa's role in a possible Sino-Soviet war is an important case in point. The shortest sea lines of communication between the USSR's European and Pacific ports run through the Suez Canal and the Red Sea. (The next fastest Soviet sea lanes to the Far East run around the Cape of Good Hope.)[22] In a Sino-Soviet war, when Soviet rail lines across Siberia would be overloaded or worse severed, the southern sea route would become critically important. Although the stockpiling of war material in the Soviet Far East has reduced the need for rapid reinforcement and resupply of the Far Eastern theater in a Sino-Soviet war, the Soviets would probably still want to secure both

The Significance of Soviet Military Interests 157

unhindered passage for their ships through the Suez Canal and Bab al-Mandab choke points, since this would save roughly two weeks time for vessels traveling at 20 knots (surface only approximation). Moscow would also like to have access to African support facilities available should it be needed by ships in transit to the Far East.

As students of history, the Soviets are mindful of the problems of deploying Russian naval forces to the Far East in the past. In commenting on the voyage around Africa of the tsarist naval squadron that the Japanese sunk at the Tsushima straits in 1905, Admiral Gorshkov wrote in *Sea Power of the State:*

> The history of the Russian fleet and indeed of other fleets still did not know of such a distant and long movement of a huge fleet consisting of a variety of ships, some of which were not fully seaworthy, with no experience of combined long-distance oceanic travel. Over the entire route the squadron did not have a single base for resting the crew, for repair and supply. Most of the shores along which it passed belonged to hostile England.[23]

Certainly the world could not have appeared much different to Soviet military planners in the late 1960s, when the danger of a war with China seemed great. That was before the Soviets started to build the Baikal Amur-Maritime (BAM) rail line along a northern parallel to the Trans-Siberian railroad, before they established a permanent naval presence off the east and west coasts of Sub-Saharan Africa (they did so in 1969 and 1970 respectively); that was also when Chinese influence was strong in Tanzania and South Yemen. One of the factors underlying the Soviets' acute sensitivity toward the Chinese presence in Africa may have been their concern that Chinese influence could be so exercised as to obstruct Soviet sea lines of communication to the Far East during critical crisis situations. (South Yemen's Perim Island abuts the Bab al-Mandab and could be used to block traffic through that choke point.)[24]

By establishing a continuous naval presence around Sub-Saharan Africa the Soviets enhanced their ability to respond to Sino–Soviet crisis contingencies in two ways. First, this naval presence became an important instrument of Moscow's diplomacy of force in the Third World. By demonstrating a capability the Chinese did not possess, the Soviets were able to improve their standing in Africa at China's expense. Second, the ready access to shore-based facilities the Soviets gained to support deployed naval forces would probably also be available if needed by Soviet ships transiting to the Far East during a Sino–Soviet crisis.

Conclusion

To recapitulate briefly, whereas the actual peacetime use of African facilities enhances Soviet preparations for war largely indirectly and to a limited degree, the potential wartime significance of Sub-Saharan Africa to the Soviets is highly uncertain. In a major war involving the United States, it is uncertain whether the Soviets would want to use Black African facilities—certainly they would seem to need African airfields today less than in the past—and even if they wanted to do so, it is unlikely that Sub-Saharan African states would be willing to permit the Soviets such use of their territory. In fact, the Soviet need to use African sea routes, port facilities, and airfields in a war scenario remote from Africa (i.e., the Far East) is much clearer.

It is worth adding that the strategic importance of Africa to the Soviet prosecution of major wars is not limited to African facilities and the Soviet combat forces they support. There are certain targets—economic ones (e.g., oil terminals, cobalt mines, etc.) in a general coalition war, and military installations (e.g., U.S. staging areas) in a major Southwest Asia conflict that the Soviets would probably want to attack with foreign proxy forces, if they were unable to do so with their own. These proxy forces could be recruited for sabotage operations from among the numerous insurgent groups the Soviets and Cubans have trained in Africa over the years or any remaining elements of the 36,000 Cuban troops estimated to be currently stationed in Africa.[25] For example, the Angola-based FNLC (National Front for the Liberation of the Congo), recruited from former members of the Katangan gendarmes, could be mobilized to intervene in Zaire's Shaba province as they did in 1978, but this time with the objective of destroying Zaire's cobalt mines. Indeed, of all the sources of Africa's strategic nonfuel minerals, Zaire's cobalt mines are both the easiest and, as long as the inventory of cobalt in the U.S. strategic stockpile remains significantly behind the goal, the most lucrative target.[26] Thus the Soviets would appear to have ways of attacking targets located beyond the effective range of their own combat forces.

The net impression one may gain from this examination of the strategic wartime importance of Sub-Saharan Africa to the USSR is that the Soviet threat in Africa appears to be less alarming than many have made it out to be and, moreover, that it does not appear to be particularly impressive where U.S. forces employed around the periphery of that continent are involved. The limited strategic military benefits the Soviets derive and may expect to gain from Africa would not seem to go far toward explaining Soviet activism in Africa over the past two decades.

By and large, while the quest for access has given additional impetus to the cultivation of relations with some regimes, it has not altered the fundamental thrust of Soviet foreign policy. For example, concern for the preservation of extensive access privileges in Egypt and Somalia did not prevent the Soviets from taking actions that diverged from the interests of those host nations. When relations with Egypt began to sour, the Soviets simply looked elsewhere for naval access. Although the Soviets "pulled their punches" in dealing with Mogadiscio until they were expelled from Somalia in November 1977,[27] they never acceded to Siad Barre's demand that they not support Ethiopia. In both the Egyptian and Somali cases, they appear to have acted on the assumption that submitting to Third World blackmail over access could establish a dangerous precedent, entailing even greater problems in the long term than losing access.

It is nevertheless clear that the acquisition costs, in both material and political terms, the Soviets paid for the Somali facilities were very great and would never have been borne otherwise. The need for access definitely distorted Soviet policy on the Horn of Africa. In the early 1970s, when the Soviets decided to buy access to Somali facilities with modern weapons, they ignored the warnings of their Africanists about the dangers of dealing with an irredentist regime.[28] Rather, they seem to have taken a calculated risk that a strong U.S.-backed Ethiopia would deter any Somali military adventures. The 1974 Ethiopian revolution, which eventually altered the military balance on the Horn, apparently caught them by surprise. Even in the mid-1970s, when the unstable situation in Ethiopia aroused Somali nationalism, the Soviets did not temper their support for Somalia. Rather, they increased their military aid, in exchange for additional access privileges, while securing Somalia's pledge, written into their 1974 friendship treaty, to use that aid for defensive purposes only. And finally, in opting to become Ethiopia's principal armorer in 1977, the Soviets appear to have miscalculated Somali reactions and wound up as involuntary accomplices to Somalia's aggression. Thus, had the Soviets not been willing to buy access to Somali facilities with roughly $370 million worth of weapons, they would not have had to supply Ethiopia with anywhere near the $1.3 billion worth of weapons they delivered in 1977 and 1978,[29] nor would they have had to bear the probably even-larger direct and indirect costs connected with the intervention of over 13,000 Cuban troops in Ethiopia. Had the Soviets not furnished Somalia with the wherewithal to fight a major war, the Ogaden War would have been about as noteworthy as the POLISARIO conflict in the western Sahara. Without the need for access the Soviets would probably never have aligned themselves so closely with what the rest of Africa regarded as a pariah state. The Soviet-Somali military connection was an expression of the weakness, not strength, of Soviet policy in Sub-Saharan Africa in the early 1970s.

Today, however, the Soviets have more access options than they did over a decade ago when they felt compelled to turn to Somalia for support of their Indian Ocean Squadron. They have succeeded in placing their access "eggs" in two baskets (i.e., Ethiopia and the People's Democratic Republic of Yemen) instead of one. This should improve their bargaining power with each access donor. The Soviets also appear to be trying to use their military assistance to expand their access options. For example, whereas they supplied 50 percent or more of all the arms imported by four Sub-Saharan littoral nations in the decade ending in 1973,[30] the corresponding number of these littoral states for the years 1976 through 1980 has risen to eleven (the Congo, Guinea, Somalia, and the Sudan for the earlier time period and Angola, Benin, Cape Verde, the Congo, Equatorial Guinea, Ethiopia, Guinea-Bissau, Guinea, Madagascar, Mozambique, and Tanzania for the later period).[31] Although usually more is involved in gaining naval access than simply transferring arms, it is nevertheless clear that the Soviets have been able to greatly expand the field of actual and potential access donors. With more African states available to meet the USSR's evidently reduced military support needs, it is unlikely that Moscow will feel compelled in the future to take political gambles for access similar to those it took in Somalia.

Notes

1. The naval support infrastructure the Soviets built at Berbera was one of the most elaborate ones they have built in the Third World (i.e., outside of Cuba and Vietnam). Besides dredging Berbera's harbor and developing port facilities (piers, cranes, warehouses, etc.), the Soviets also expanded Berbera's positioned-on-location storage facilities, built an elaborate ordnance storage and repair installation, and a large airfield with a 13,500-foot runway; they also assembled a long-range communications station. These facilities are described in U.S. Congress, Senate Committee on Armed Services, *Disapprove Construction Projects on the Island of Diego Garcia*, Hearings, 94th Congress, First Session, 10 June 1975; and U.S. Congress, *Soviet Military Capability in Berbera, Somalia*, Report of Senator Bartlett to the Committee on Armed Services (Washington, D.C.: Government Printing Office, 1975). Information on the Soviet use of these facilities is contained in Charles C. Petersen, "Trends in Soviet Naval Operations," in Bradford Dismukes and James M. McConnell, eds., *Soviet Naval Diplomacy* (New York: Pergamon Press, 1979), pp. 37–87. In addition to the Berbera support complex, the Soviets constructed several other airfields and port facilities that were primarily for Somali use. Though an accurate estimate of the total cost of Soviet military construction in Somalia is unavailable, it probably ran into the hundreds of millions of dollars.

2. This evidence is presented in James McConnell, *The Soviet Shift in Emphasis From Nuclear to Conventional* RC490-vol. II (Alexandria, Va.: Center for Naval Analyses, 1983), pp. 23–35.

3. See Ibid., pp. 32–33 and *Statement of Rear Admiral John L. Butts U.S. Navy, Director of Naval Intelligence before the Seapower and Stra-*

tegic and Critical Minerals Subcommittee of the House Armed Services Committee on the Naval Threat, 24 February 1983, p. 16.

4. For an excellent discussion of the economic importance of the Indian Ocean to the USSR, see Lieutenant Commander James T. Westwood, U.S.N., "The Soviet Union and the Southern Sea Route," *Naval War College Review* 35 (January/February 1982):54–67.

5. Indirect logistic support can be provided, though not as efficiently, when auxiliary support or merchant vessels take on consumables for later transfer to naval units in international waters.

6. See U.S. Senate Committee on Foreign Relations, 96th Congress, First Session, *United States Foreign Policy Objectives and Overseas Military Installations* (Washington, D.C.: Government Printing Office, 1979), p. 91.

7. John Jordan, *An Illustrated Guide to the Modern Soviet Navy* (London: Salamander Books, 1982), p. 90.

8. See Lieutenant Commander William F. Hickman, "Soviet Naval Policy in the Indian Ocean," *U.S. Naval Institute Proceedings* 105 (August 1979):50.

9. For further detail see Charles Petersen, "Trends in Soviet Naval Operations," pp. 54–59, and U.S. Department of Defense, *Soviet Military Power,* 2nd ed. (Washington, D.C.: Government Printing Office, March 1983), pp. 93–94.

10. On one occasion, in 1976, the Soviets staged *Tu-95 Bear-Ds* from Somalia's Dafet (Uanle Uen) airfield.

11. The Soviets have also operated a long-range communications station at Berbera until 1977, reportedly to relay messages between the USSR and Soviet naval forces deployed forward. See U.S. Congress, Senate Committee on Armed Services, *Disapprove Construction Projects on the Island of Diego Garcia.*

12. See ibid., p. 7.

13. From Tashkent the air distances are 4500 nautical miles to Maputo, Mozambique, and 4600 nautical miles to Luanda, Angola—well within the 8200 nautical miles maximum range of the *Backfire.* See Bill Gunston, *An Illustrated Guide to the Modern Soviet Air Force* (London: Salamander Books, 1982), p. 130.

14. See *Soviet Military Power,* p. 23.

15. For further elaboration on Soviet-Somali military "cooperation" see Richard B. Remnek, "The Soviet-Somali 'Arms for Access' Relationship," *Soviet Union/Union Sovietique* 10, no. 1 (1983).

16. See Siad Barre's interviews in *Remarques Africaines,* 31 July 1974, pp. 14–15, translated in Joint Publications Research Service, no. 62978, 16 September 1974, *Sub-Saharan Africa Report* no. 1517, p. 103; and *Al-Arabi* (Kuwait) January 1975, pp. 22–23, translated in Joint Publications

Research Service, no. 64245, 5 March 1975, *Sub-Saharan Africa Report* no. 1569, p. 34.

17. A Senate resolution sponsored by Senator Mark Hatfield, which would have suspended funding for Diego Garcia, was defeated soon after the Bartlett delegation visit.

18. According to the Defense Department, Soviet facilities at Dahlak Island, Ethiopia, which is probably the most elaborate base of support for the Soviet Navy in Sub-Saharan Africa, consist of a floating drydock, barracks, helicopter pads, floating piers, and navigational aids. In addition, *Il-38 May* ASW planes stage periodically from the airfield at Asmara. See *Soviet Military Power,* p. 93.

19. This is suggested by a 1980 Soviet article in *Narody azii i afriki* in which the author, having described in detail South Africa's impressive military capabilities, does not even close with the standard pro forma profession of "fraternal" Soviet bloc support for the Front Line African states threatened by South Africa. See T. I. Krasnopevtseva, "Voennopromyshlennyi kompleks IuAR," *Narody azii i afriki* no. 2 (1980): 109-118.

20. As difficult as it is to predict the outcome of various combat scenarios, it is even more difficult to estimate what contribution using facilities in forward areas may make to the effectiveness of the combat forces supported. Such usage may make a significant, perhaps critical, difference; on the other hand, Soviet combatant forces might have been equally effective without their employment. And it is possible, of course, that these combat forces will be ineffective, no matter how much their combat readiness and capabilities are enhanced through using facilities in the forward area.

In most crises, where the outcome—in peace or war—is inherently uncertain, the Soviets would not likely withdraw their deployed naval forces en masse since this would give advance warning of Soviet strategic intentions. Any changes in the composition of those forces would likely be made discretely. The disposition of Soviet naval forces on the eve of the October 1973 Middle East War can serve as a model of how the Soviets might behave in future major crises. The Soviets removed their modern *Kara-class* guided missile cruiser from the Mediterranean on the day before the Egyptian attack, and only a few first generation modern surface combatants (e.g., *Kashin-class* destroyers and *Kynda-class* cruisers) were present when the war started. As Robert G. Weinland of the Center for Naval Analyses has noted, "It is almost as though the Soviets, knowing conflict was imminent and fearing that their naval forces might become directly involved, decided to minimize the potential damage they might suffer through such involvement by withholding their newer, more capable units and deploying their older, less capable units—the loss of which would not be crippling." Robert G.

Weinland, "Superpower Naval Diplomacy in the October 1973 Arab-Israeli War: A Case Study," in Edward N. Luttwak and Robert G. Weinland, *Sea Power in the Mediterranean: Political Utility and Military Constraints* The Washington Papers, No. 61 (Beverly Hills, Calif: Sage Publications, 1979), p. 78.

21. Ibid., p. 74.

22. From Odessa to Vladivostok it is 11,000 miles by sea through the Suez Canal and 17,000 miles around the Cape route. At an average speed of 14 knots it takes thirty-two days by the shorter route and fifty days by the longer one to make this voyage.

23. Admiral Sergei Gorshkov, *Morskaia moshch' gosudarstva* (Moscow: 1976), p. 152.

24. From the June 1967 war until 1975 the Suez Canal was closed. The Soviets may have regarded the closure as a passing phenomenon, for they were acutely sensitive to Chinese influence in Somalia and the Yemens before the reopening of the Canal and have remained so since then. See Remnek, "The Soviet-Somali 'Arms for Access' Relationship," and Lieutenant Commander Charles T. Creekman Jr., U.S.N., "Sino-Soviet Competition in the Yemens," *Naval War College Review* 32 (July/August 1979):73-82.

25. *Soviet Military Power,* p. 92.

26. By contrast, South Africa's production of ferrochromium—another mineral with critical defense applications—is dispersed, its railroad network and port facilities are well-developed and numerous, and its security forces are highly capable. It would therefore be exceedingly difficult for the Soviets to orchestrate interdiction of the flow of South Africa's strategic minerals to the West in wartime.

27. For further elaboration, see Richard B. Remnek, "Soviet Policy in the Horn of Africa: the Decision to Intervene," in Robert H. Donaldson, ed., *The Soviet Union in the Third World: Successes and Failures* (Boulder, Colo.: Westview Press, 1981), pp. 125-149.

28. See Ia. Ia. Etinger, *Mezhdugosudarstvennye otnosheniia v Afrike* (Moscow: 1972), pp. 71-84.

29. See U.S. Arms Control and Disarmament Agency, *World Military Expenditures and Arms Transfers, 1969-78,* (Washington, D.C.: U.S. Government Printing Office, 1980), p. 161.

30. Computed from data in U.S. Arms Control and Disarmament Agency, *World Military Expenditures and Arms Trade 1963-73,* (Washington, D.C.: U.S. Government Printing Office, 1975), pp. 67-68.

31. Computed from data in U.S. Arms Control and Disarmament Agency, *World Military Expenditures and Arms Transfers, 1971-80,* (Washington, D.C.: U.S. Government Printing Office, 1983), p. 117.

# 9

Superpower Competition and Regional Conflicts in the Horn of Africa

Marina Ottaway

The Horn of Africa has been a bone of contention for the major powers ever since the beginning of the scramble for Africa. An area devoid of natural resources, characterized by the presence of deserts along the coast and rugged mountains further inland, the Horn has never provided any wealth for its captors or economic advantage for its allies. Nevertheless, because of the strategic importance of the Red Sea and the Straits of Bab al-Mandab, the Horn has not been overlooked either during the colonial period or thereafter. The competition among Britain, France, and Italy for control of the area was replaced beginning in the 1960s by rivalry between the United States and the Soviet Union.

The strategic interests of the major powers in the Horn led them inevitably to become involved in the regional conflicts endemic to the area. While Britain and Italy to some extent sought involvement in the regional conflicts as a way of furthering their own interests, both the United States and the Soviet Union tried to avoid becoming entangled, but they failed. Despite the enormous imbalance of power between the parties involved, the dynamics of the relations between the superpowers and their regional partners have been determined to a very large extent by the conflicts and interests of the latter rather than the plans of the former.

The complex relationship between superpower competition and regional conflicts in the Horn manifested itself in its most dramatic form in 1977 when Ethiopia and Somalia succeeded in virtually imposing on the United States and the Soviet Union a reversal of alliances. The United States, which since the end of World War II had maintained a military base in Ethiopia, found itself forced out of that country and into a very reluctant relationship with Somalia. The Soviet Union had to abandon its alliance with Mohammed Siad Barre of Somalia to embrace instead the regime of Mengistu Haile Mariam in Ethiopia. While some have argued that the Soviet Union probably benefited from the change (Ethiopia being the biggest and most important country in the Horn), in fact it was forced to make the change after its own policy of forming an alliance with both countries had failed. The Soviets lost a military base in Somalia in the process. How weak, underdeveloped countries like Ethiopia and Somalia could impose their policies on the great powers, and why the regional conflicts influenced events much more than the strategic interests of the Soviet Union and the United States are the issues this chapter will address.

Colonialism and Regional Conflicts

The internal conflicts of the Horn have their roots in a distant past but have been deeply modified during the colonial period. Fighting between the populations of the Ethiopian highlands and of the lowlands has been a recurring theme in the history of the area, as the lowlanders always sought to take over the richer, more fertile land of the plateau, and the Ethiopian emperors fought to broaden their sphere of influence. The conversion of a large part of the lowlands to Islam, while the highlands remained dominantly Christian, added another dimension to the conflict. With the advent of the colonial period and the establishment of fixed, internationally recognized borders, the traditional conflicts eventually took on a new, modern ideological justification as conflicts among nations seeking to win their right to independence and self-determination.

The Ethiopian empire had been historically the most important political entity in the Horn, occupying the central highlands and as much of the surrounding area as the ability and strength of different emperors allowed at different times. The rest of the Horn was occupied by a plethora of small kingdoms and autonomous tribes and clans. This picture changed considerably toward the end of the nineteenth century. The Ethiopian empire, which at the beginning of the nineteenth century was stagnating in a condition of decadence and internal disarray, had progressively revived in the following decades, fending off colonial conquest except in Eritrea. By the turn of the century, under the leadership of Emperor Menelik, it had not only finished the process of consolidation but also started expanding, acquiring new territory, and, most importantly, winning international recognition for its borders. What had been a traditional empire with indefinite and ever-changing boundaries became a modern, defined state with borders established by international treaties.

The rest of the Horn, too, became subdivided into new territorial entities with well-established borders: the Italian colony of Eritrea, to the north and east of Ethiopia; the British protectorate of Somaliland, today's northern Somalia; the Italian colony of Somalia; and finally the tiny French enclave of Djibouti, squeezed between Ethiopia and British Somaliland. It is from this subdivision that the states existing today in the Horn emerged: Ethiopia, made up of Menelik's empire and Eritrea; Somalia, emerging from the union of British Somaliland and Italian Somalia; and the Republic of Djibouti.

During the colonial period, the Horn had been of interest to the European powers not in itself, but in relation to other, more important parts of their empires. Both the French enclave at Djibouti and the British protectorate in Somaliland were established for the sole purpose of protecting the passage through the Red Sea and the Straits of Bab al-Mandab. Only Italy, which had become a colonial power very late and was trying to form an empire from the leftovers of British and French colonization, looked at its possessions in the Horn as an end in themselves.

The result was that the Horn, although conquered, was not deeply penetrated culturally and transformed economically. The major problem for the nomadic population of Somalia remained access to grazing grounds and water; the problem of the Ethiopian rulers remained that of controlling an empire made up of disparate populations and only loosely held together by a weak administrative apparatus. The old problems of the Horn reappeared as soon as colonialism ended: the drive of the lowland population for the control of better grazing grounds, and the attempts of the populations on the periphery of the Ethiopian empire to break away from central control. The ideological justification for these old trends was new, however, because colonialism had brought to the area the language of nationalism and self-determination. In this writer's opinion, this was particularly true in the case of Somalia, which had inherited its hypernationalism from the Italian fascist regime. The new trend was eventually manifested very strongly in Eritrea, which claimed the right to become an independent nation-state and in Somalia, which argued that all territories occupied by a Somali-speaking population belonged rightfully to the Somali state. To what extent Somalia and Eritrea are nations is a controversial and complex issue. It is also irrelevant to understanding the conflicts of the Horn, since what matters is not fact but perception.

The Superpowers

The revival of the regional conflicts was not the only repercussion of the end of the colonial period in the Horn. Another, equally momentous consequence was the reopening of the competition among the major powers for control or at least influence over the area. Initially, Britain tried to step into the vacuum left in the Horn by the collapse of the Italian empire but failed in its bid and was eventually supplanted by the United States and the Soviet Union. The regional conflicts were very important both in defeating British plans and in providing the United States and the Soviet Union with opportunities for penetration in the Horn. Eventually, however, these same regional conflicts also became a major obstacle to the achievement of the superpowers' goals.

The Italian empire in East Africa collapsed in 1941 when the British helped Haile Selassie defeat the Italians, who five years earlier had finally succeeded in conquering Ethiopia. Haile Selassie thus regained his throne and Ethiopia its independence, but the victory was clouded by what in Ethiopian eyes appeared as British interference. Having defeated Italy, Britain took over the administration of its former possessions in Eritrea and Somalia and started devising a new territorial division in the area, which did not please Haile Selassie in the least. Most troublesome to him was the plan to create a Greater Somalia under British protection.[1] This would comprise not only British Somaliland, the former Italian Somalia, and the Somali-inhabited Northern Frontier District (NFD) of Kenya, but also the Ogaden and the Haud, which fell within the internationally recognized Ethiopian borders. When the British in 1944 formally set forth a proposal for the establishment of such a Greater Somalia protectorate, and furthermore suggested that Eritrea should be divided between Ethiopia and the Sudan rather than annexed to Ethiopia as demanded by Haile Selassie, the emperor started casting around for a new ally and found a ready taker in the United States. This was the first of the many episodes in the recent period in which a country of the Horn successfully played one major power against another.

Haile Selassie's immediate interest in the mid-1940s was to reestablish control over the entire area within the legally recognized Ethiopian boundaries as well as to obtain international acceptance for his claim that Eritrea was rightfully part of Ethiopia. He also sought help in building a modern army. What the Americans wanted, on the other hand, had nothing to do with the politics of the area but was related to the role of the United States as a great power in the postwar period. They were interested in Ethiopia for three major reasons: First, the country had the location and the physical characteristics suitable for the establishment of a major communications center; second, it lent itself to serve as a link on air routes toward India and the Far East; and third, as the only independent country in Africa at the time, it afforded the United States an opportunity to establish a presence in the continent, preparing itself to play a greater role in the years to come.

The United States was especially interested in gaining access to a former British communications center near Asmara but could not do anything about it until the United Nations decided the fate of Eritrea.[2] During this period of waiting, Haile Selassie did everything he could to demonstrate his good will toward the United States. In 1945, when Ethiopia decided to set up its national airline, it gave the contract for training to Trans World Airlines. The first concession for oil exploration in the Ogaden was given to an American company, Sinclair, even before Britain had formally returned the area to Ethiopia. In so doing, the emperor wanted to give the United States a vested interest in safeguarding the existing Ethiopian borders. Finally, Ethiopia sent a contingent of troops to fight in Korea. The road had thus been paved, and in 1953, soon after the United Nations implemented its decision to unite Eritrea to Ethiopia in a federation,[3] the U.S. government and Haile Selassie were able to sign a treaty giving Washington a twenty-five year lease on the communications center near Asmara. This was renamed Kagnew Station. In return, the United States agreed to train and equip three Ethiopian military divisions totalling 18,000 men.

The relationship between the United States and Ethiopia established with the 1953 agreement lasted with little change until 1977, when the military government which had succeeded Haile Selassie three years earlier ordered the remaining Americans to evacuate Kagnew Station. The character of the relation remained remarkably stable throughout this period. From the very beginning, it was not based on a mutuality of interests or similarity of aims between the two parties. Rather, they had totally separate but not conflicting goals, and each country used the other to pursue them. The United States's main goal in Ethiopia was to maintain access to the communications station; that of Haile Selassie was to give the United States a vested interest in the survival of his regime, thereby obtaining from the United States aid for modernizing his army and for other purposes of interest to him rather than to the United States. There was never an alliance between the United States and Ethiopia, since an alliance presupposes a joining of forces in pursuit of a common goal.

The possibility of an alliance developing between the two countries arose only after the coup d'etat which brought Mohammed Siad Barre to power in Somalia in 1969 and opened the way for a very close relation between Somalia and the Soviet Union. The containment of Somalia and its Soviet patron was a goal the United States and Ethiopia could share. However, by the time the Americans started worrying about the Soviet presence in Somalia the regime of Haile Selassie was on the wane.

Somalia, which only became independent in 1960, pursued a policy similar to Ethiopia's in relation to the major powers, trying to acquire help in the pursuit of its own goals. However, it had much greater problems in finding a patron because of the fears engendered by its stated intention of liberating all territories inhabited by Somali speakers. This policy promised to create endless conflict in the Horn, without providing benefits to any outside power.

In the immediate postwar period, before the Somali state came into existence, the Somalis had looked with great hope to Great Britain, but their hope was soon dashed. As we have mentioned, the British had raised the idea of creating a Greater Somalia, but this proposal found no favor with the United Nations. Rejecting the British plan, the organization gave the former Italian colony to Italy to administer as a trust territory for a period of ten years, after which it would become independent. Still, the British hung on to other parts of their plan. Thus they did not return the Ogaden and the Haud to Ethiopia immediately, on the ground that they were territories inhabited by Somalis, and continued to hesitate concerning the final disposition of British Somaliland and the Kenyan Northern Frontier District. Eventually, Britain had to give in on the Ogaden and the Haud, returning the former to Ethiopia in 1948 and the latter in 1954. But they continued to hesitate concerning the rest of the Somali-inhabited territories, with disastrous results.

With Italian Somalia scheduled to become independent in 1960, Britain waited until 1958 to start discussing the possibility of granting independence to Somaliland at the same time so that the two territories could join in one state. When a positive decision was reached on this issue, there was not time left to prepare for the unification of Somalia, and in fact some problems developed soon after independence.[4] To make matters worse, Britain continued discussing the possibility of separating the Northern Frontier District from Kenya, giving it to Somalia, till the very eve of Kenyan independence. This fanned the new Somali government's hopes for territorial aggrandisement and angered the Kenyan leadership. In 1962, Britain appointed a commission to determine whether the population of the NFD would prefer to be part of Somalia or of Kenya. The inquiry revealed a preference for Somalia among the Somali-speaking population which predominated the area. The complaints by the new Kenyan leaders, however, convinced Britain to desist from the plan to give the NFD to Somalia, but by this time the damage was done.[5] The Somali government felt more than ever deprived of its right to control all territories populated by a Somali-speaking population, including not only the long-contested NFD, Ogaden, and Haud, but also the French enclave of Djibouti.

The problem of Somali irredentism was not solely of British making. However, British designs concerning the creation of a Greater Somalia, and the clumsy way in which the British government first recommended giving the NFD to Somalia and then withdrew the suggestion, certainly did not help the situation. On the other hand, it should also be remembered that the Somalis had developed their concept of nation and state under the influence of the fascist administration of Italian Somalia, receiving their political education in an intensely chauvinistic climate. Their nationalism developed in circumstances that would have encouraged irredentist ambitions even if the British had pursued a different policy.

The first outburst of hostility in the Ogaden took place almost immediately after Somalia became independent. As early as 1961, skirmishes broke out in the contested area and a brief war was fought there in 1964, leading to an easy Ethiopian victory. There was also fighting in the NFD after the British reversed their decision in 1962, and the problem did not really subside until 1967, when the newly formed Egal government in Somalia initiated a period of detente with its neighbors.[6]

The constant state of war with its neighbors made it very important for Somalia to find a source of military aid. This proved to be a problem.

Britain had abandoned all ambitions to play an important role in the Horn, and Somalia found itself without outside support at a crucial time. It could have probably solved the problem to some extent by abandoning its irredentism, but this was not the inclination of the government and might not even have been politically feasible internally, since the stability of any Somali regime depended at least in part on its determination to pursue the liberation of the so-called missing lands. Somalia thus approached several Western countries with demands for military aid but met with a very guarded response. It was clear to all that Somalia wanted weapons for expansion rather than self-defense and no Western country at this point had an interest in supporting Pan-Somali ambitions. After much debate, in 1963 the United States, Italy, and West Germany jointly offered Somalia a modest military aid package for the training and equipping of a 6,000-man army, adequate for maintaining internal security, but not for fighting a war of expansion. This is not what the Somali government had in mind, and it rejected the offer in favor of a $32 million Soviet military aid package for the setting up of a 10,000-man army. From this time on, the European powers stopped playing a major role in the Horn of Africa, while the United States and the Soviet Union emerged unchallenged as the influential outside powers.

Ethiopia's and Somalia's requirements for military aid maintained stable relations with the great powers for a long period. Ethiopia's need for military aid grew during the 1960s, partly because of the conflict with Somalia and partly because of the problem developing in Eritrea. The emperor had not been satisfied with the U.N. decision because of the large measure of internal autonomy it granted to the region. This meant that the population of Eritrea enjoyed a degree of freedom and self-government very much at odds with Haile Selassie's concept of the monarchy and also created demands for similar rights elsewhere in Ethiopia. After ten years of intense maneuvering, in 1962 Haile Selassie succeeded in disbanding the federation and annexing Eritrea to Ethiopia as a province without special status. It was a costly victory because an Eritrean secessionist movement developed almost immediately. By the time the emperor was deposed in 1974, the Eritrean movements had become a real threat to the central government's control over the province, keeping a substantial part of the army tied down in military operations there.[7]

The problem of Eritrea and the Ogaden repeatedly pushed Haile Selassie to seek additional military aid from the United States. The 1953 agreement was first revised immediately after Somalia's access to independence—and after a timely trip by the emperor to Moscow in 1959. At this time, the United States agreed to help increase the size of the Ethiopian armed forces to 40,000 men, organized into four divisions.[8] By 1970, Ethiopia had received about $159 million worth of military aid.[9] Although economic aid in the same period was considerably larger, amounting to $228 million, it was military aid that constituted the pivot of the Ethiopian–American relation.[10]

Military aid also remained the basis of the Soviet–Somali relation during the 1960s. The two countries had nothing else in common because in all other respects Somalia was a nonaligned country—or more precisely one marching to the beat of its own drum. It received economic aid from anybody willing to provide it: Italy, the Soviet Union, the United States and Communist China were the major aid donors in that period.[11] Domestically, Somalia had a Western-style democratic system, with a plethora of mostly clan-based political parties. Clan relations were much more important than ideology in shaping the country's policies. Externally, Somali interests were purely regional and centered on their pan-Somali ambitions. The Soviet Union was a convenient donor of military aid, but nothing else. Like the United States and Ethiopia, Somalia and the Soviet Union during the 1960s were not allies pursuing a common goal, but partners in a mutually beneficial exchange. Ethiopia and Somalia received their weapons, the United States had its communications station. While the Soviet Union received nothing tangible during the 1960s, it established a presence that paid off after the coup d'etat of 1969.

Internal Change

The role of the great powers in the Horn of Africa became much more prominent during the 1970s. Interestingly, this was due less to a great power's decision to become more involved in the Horn than to the internal changes that both Ethiopia and Somalia experienced in this period. The political events in the Horn provided new opportunities for the Soviet Union and problems for the United States. In the end, however, both countries had to modify their policies and adapt to regional developments they could not control.

The first change—a purely internal affair—came with the coup d'etat carried out in 1969 in Somalia by General Mohammed Siad Barre, the army's commander-in-chief. Although allegations have been made that the Soviet Union was behind the takeover, no evidence to that effect has ever been found. However, the coup did open the door to a much-increased Soviet role in the country. Upon coming to power, in typical military fashion Siad Barre had abrogated the constitution and outlawed the political parties, destroying the formal democracy that had existed until that time. Searching for an ideological justification for this act, Siad Barre inevitably fell on socialism—and scientific socialism at that. In the initial proclamations of the new regime, scientific socialism was a rather vague notion. It was never rigorously defined and it is difficult to detect any clear sign of allegiance to Marxism–Leninism in either the words or deeds of the Somali leadership. However, the military regime turned to the Soviet Union for help in all fields, including the development of political institutions.

The new Soviet–Somali relation had two repercussions of regional rather than purely internal significance—namely, the further growth of the Somali army and the granting of military facilities to the Soviet Union. The years following the coup d'etat saw a massive buildup of the Somali army from about 12,000 men in 1970 to 23,000 in 1975 and 30,000 in 1977.[12] This was accompanied by increased arms deliveries and also by an upgrading of their quality. These changes stemmed from a new agreement negotiated in February 1972, and they were worth anywhere between $300 million and $1 billion.[13] Under the terms of the agreement, the Soviets not only provided arms but also trained some 2,400 Somali military personnel in the USSR, in addition to assigning up to 1,000 military advisers to work with the Somali army.[14] In return for this aid, the Soviets finally obtained a base (at Berbera). The relation between Somalia and the Soviet Union was further cemented in 1974 with the signing of a Treaty of Friendship and Cooperation.

The series of developments triggered by the 1969 coup d'etat in Somalia were all to the benefit of the Soviet Union and greatly changed the relations between the superpowers in the Horn. During the 1960s, the Soviet Union and the United States had maintained only a very low presence in the area. While it is true that they supported rival countries, it would be a gross exaggeration to state that there was anything like a superpower confrontation in the Horn. With the development of the Soviet base at Berbera, the United States started worrying about Soviet penetration and the changing balance of power in the area. By 1975, American intelligence reports revealed a great expansion of the Soviet installations at Berbera, particularly the building of missile-handling facilities. Somali denials that there was a Soviet base in the country were not convincing, particularly after Siad Barre in 1975 invited a U.S. congressional delegation to visit Berbera and see for itself that there was nothing to worry about, only to have the delegation barred by the Soviets from visiting part of the installation.[15]

The only positive aspect of the situation in Somalia, from the American point of view, was that the country had joined the Arab League in 1974. Arab economic aid grew rapidly thereafter.[16] This opened the possibility that a more moderate, pro-Western influence would be exercised on Somalia—particularly by Saudi Arabia, which had sponsored its entry into the league. However, Somalia remained totally dependent on the USSR for military aid.

Ethiopia also underwent major domestic changes in the mid-1970s and these in turn affected the position of the United States and the balance of power in the Horn. Emperor Haile Selassie was deposed in September 1974 by a military committee, the *Derg*, which soon embarked on a program of radical socioeconomic reform. The change was not welcomed by the United States for obvious reasons and created a real dilemma. On the one hand, both the political stance of the new military regime and the technological change taking place in the field of communications suggested that a continuation of the Ethiopian-American relation was neither desirable nor necessary in the long term. A regime that had embarked on a program of socialist reforms was not a promising partner for the United States. Furthermore, Kagnew Station—the original reason for the American presence in Ethiopia—was becoming obsolete. Developments in satellite communications were rapidly decreasing the need for a land station in Ethiopia. The phase-out of Kagnew Station had started even before the overthrow of the emperor, accelerated in part by the lack of security caused by the growth of the Eritrean nationalist movements. As late as 1970, Kagnew Station had been a large establishment with an American population of over 3000 including 1800 military and civilian personnel. By early 1975, the personnel of the station had been reduced to 40.[17]

Before the Soviet buildup in Somalia, it might have been an easy decision for the United States to withdraw from Ethiopia. But in the mid-1970s, this meant leaving the Soviet Union unchallenged in the Horn at a time the United States was increasingly worried about Soviet penetration in Africa. Ethiopia, too, had manifested willingness to continue the relation—not for political reasons, but in order not to interrupt the arms supplies which were particularly needed at the time. The military balance of power between Somalia and Ethiopia had changed. While during the 1960s Somalia had proven no match for the larger, better-equipped Ethiopian army, the buildup of the 1970s had reversed the situation. By 1975, military experts agreed that the Somali army was now better equipped than the Ethiopian one and that the outcome of a new war would not necessarily be a victory for Ethiopia. Adding to the problem, the war in Eritrea had picked up momentum since the overthrow of Haile Selassie. For lack of a better alternative, the Derg was still looking to the United States for military aid; the Americans responded with a cautious increase. In 1974, the United States had provided $12.5 million in grants, $11 million in credits, and $5 million in cash sales. The following year the amount of grants was kept constant, but credits increased to $25 million and cash sales to $20 million.[18] Further cash sales for a value of $100 million were made in 1976.[19] This was much less than Ethiopia had asked for, and no match for the amount of weapons the Soviets were lavishing on Somalia.

The policies of the great powers toward Ethiopia and Somalia in this period were dictated by strategic considerations. The internal changes in the Horn and the regional conflicts created opportunities or raised obstacles but were not determinants of either the Soviet or the American policy. This is particularly true in the case of the United States, which for strategic reasons increased its military aid to a regime it did not approve of and which was becoming increasingly hostile. The Soviet Union did not have to face the same conflict between its strategic interests and the policies of the Somali government. Siad Barre had embraced scientific socialism, and the Somali leadership was very open to Soviet guidance for its economic policy as well as its political organization. Yet there is no doubt that what motivated Soviet policy in Somalia was the determination to have a base on the straits of Bab al-Mandab, rather than the desire to make Somalia into a socialist country. Nor was the Soviet Union particularly concerned about the impact of its aid on the regional conflicts. Paradoxically, it was the effect of this military aid and of the political institutions they had helped Somalia to develop that led to the ultimate undoing of the Soviet position in Somalia.

In order to clarify this point, we need to consider briefly the developments that had taken place in Somalia since Mohammed Siad Barre had seized power. We are concerned here only with the political, not economic, changes. Briefly, Somalia started the decade of the 1970s under the rule of a Supreme Revolutionary Council (SRC), a twenty-five-man body composed of top military officers. In 1976, the SRC had been disbanded and power had been transferred to the Somali Socialist Revolutionary Party, which had been painstakingly built up during the previous five years with a great deal of Soviet help. The creation of the party had significant repercussions on Somali foreign policy. In the initial period after the coup d'etat, the SRC had been very isolated. It had no power base, except within the army, but it did not have to face a significant opposition or a politicized population. This gave the SRC relative freedom from the pressure of clan politics, which had been very important earlier. For all its much-vaunted ethnic homogeneity, the Somali population is deeply divided by clan allegiances, and this has always been a major factor in promoting irredentism. The clans whose territory stretches along the borders—thus giving them members in the neighboring countries—have always been particularly vehement in their nationalism and have forced competing clans to become equally ardent. The isolation of the SRC freed it to some extent from the pressure of the clans concerning the problem of the missing lands. The creation of the party strengthened the position of Siad Barre and his associates by providing a broader base of power and better links to the most affected clans concerning the Ogaden. As a result, whereas at the beginning of the decade Siad Barre had been able to leave the issue of the Ogaden dormant while never renouncing claims to the area, the stronger the political organization became the more the pressure to act mounted. To be sure, internal changes in Ethiopia also influenced Somali nationalism but the creation of a political organization had a great impact as well. The Soviets had helped in the creation of the political organization, but they had not foreseen that their success would have repercussions adverse to their interests.[20]

The internal developments in Ethiopia were even less influenced by the policies of the great powers than those in Somalia yet in the end they had a major impact on those policies. In the space of three short years, beginning in early 1974, Ethiopia was racked in rapid succession by two movements: one spear-headed by the military and directed against the sociopolitical system created by Haile Selassie; and one directed against the Ethiopian state as a territorial and political entity, fought in the name of the "right of the nationalities to self-determination" by a variety of groups and organizations, first in Eritrea and later in many other regions.

The first movement led to the deposition of Haile Selassie in September 1974 and to his replacement by the military committee known as the Derg. This new government embarked on a radical program of economic reform—the land reform it instituted in March 1975 ranks among the most far-reaching and swift in the world. The military failed, however, to find a modus vivendi with the civilian political organizations that had grown up during the course of the revolution and demanded a share of the power. Its own attempts to create a political party in order to break out of its isolation and establish a wider base of power were frustrated repeatedly by the very fact that many strata of the population were already mobilized politically. The task of organizing a political party was much more complicated in Ethiopia than in Somalia where political agitation was nonexistent.

The movement for ethnic self-determination had already been in existence in Eritrea when the revolution broke out. In the general climate of unrest and challenge to the new order—and above all after the military had succeeded in defeating the civilian political organizations at the center—ethnic movements developed very swiftly in all parts of the empire except in the central Amhara areas. By 1977 Ethiopia was plunged into a state of virtual civil war in the capital. Within two years, order had returned at the center, but the government was fighting against a plethora of nationalist movements in the periphery of the country.

The Somali-Ethiopian War and the Reversal of Alliances

The changes taking place within Ethiopia and Somalia affected the relations between them, ending the period of truce initiated by the Egal government in the late 1960s. This truce had been facilitated by the early victories scored by Ethiopia and also by Haile Selassie's success in buying off the leader of the Western Somali Liberation Front (WSLF), a movement that had been supported and armed by the Somali government to operate in the Ogaden and had caused problems for a while.[21]

By 1975, however, relations between the two countries took a decisive turn for the worse. On the one hand, the turmoil in Ethiopia created a good opportunity for Somalia to press its claims. The army was deeply engaged in Eritrea, where the nationalists had emboldened to the point of launching an attack on the provincial capital of Asmara in January 1975. Soon thereafter, the land reform had triggered local rebellions in many areas. While none was a serious threat to the government itself, together they were keeping the army busy trying to reestablish order. As the opposition of several civilian political organizations became more militant—with a state of civil war developing by 1977—the Ethiopian government appeared very weak and Siad decided that the time could not have been better for pushing his territorial claims. As we have seen, following the creation of the political party pressure to act was mounting in Somalia as well. Thus both the situation in Ethiopia and that in Somalia encouraged Siad Barre to pick up the flag of nationalism again.

This development alarmed the Soviets a great deal, although they should have expected it. Since 1972 they had been involved in a massive program of military buildup, and the only logistical outlet for this disproportionately large Somali army—one of the biggest and most costly in Africa relative to the size of the population—was territorial expansion. The Soviet Union had no interest in Greater Somalia; what it wanted from its ally was a military facility on the coast, and the fate of the land-locked Ogaden was of no strategic interest. Furthermore, from the Soviet point of view, the renewal of the Somali claims on the Ogaden was very poorly timed since they were beginning to see new opportunities in Ethiopia. The Soviets' reluctance to support Somali claims only increased after the Derg approached them in 1976 about the possibility of obtaining arms.[22] This request raised for the Soviets the tantalizing hope of gaining a dominant position in the entire area. They already had facilities at Berbera and at Aden, on the other side of the Straits of Bab al-Mandab. If they could establish a comparable presence in Ethiopia, they would have a dominant position on that waterway. But in order to realize such an objective they needed peace between Somalia and Ethiopia, and Somali policy was moving very rapidly toward war.

The situation began to deteriorate for all parties beginning in late 1976. The Derg found itself facing mounting opposition in the capital and an increasing threat in Eritrea where the countryside was in the nationalists' hands. There was, furthermore, disquieting evidence about Somali infiltration in the Ogaden, while the U.S. government had refused to provide arms and ammunitions in the amounts the Ethiopians had requested.[23] Furthermore, in February 1977 a final showdown within the Derg itself led to the triumph of the more radical faction led by Mengistu Haile Mariam. This group embarked immediately on a policy of repression of all types of opposition, plunging the country into a real civil war which increased even further the need for arms.[24] The only positive development from the Ethiopian point of view was that the mission sent to Moscow at the end of 1976 had succeeded in extracting from the Soviet Union a promise of $100 to $200 million in military aid. Only a trickle was arriving, however. Somalia was primed for war; the WSLF, re-launched in 1975, was stronger than ever. It is probable that even if Siad Barre had decided to play along with the Soviet Union and lay aside the claims to the Ogaden he could no longer have controlled the situation. At any rate, we can only speculate on this point because there is no evidence that he tried.

The United States and the Soviet Union were forced into a position where they could no longer wait and see what happened. Still, the United States refused to make any decision. The Soviets made a bold but unsuccessful move through Fidel Castro, who arranged for a meeting between Mengistu and Siad Barre in Aden and proposed to them the creation of a federation of Ethiopia, Somalia, and South Yemen. The proposal was rejected, however, forcing the Soviets to make a difficult choice between the two countries. On the one hand, the Soviets had military facilities in Somalia and were understandably reluctant to lose them; on the other hand, Ethiopia was the most important country in the Horn and a bigger prize provided it maintained control over Eritrea. Without that region, Ethiopia would be a landlocked country of no particular strategic importance, and in 1977 the possibility that Ethiopia would lose Eritrea appeared very real. The Soviets thus hesitated in making a commitment and continued to try and play both sides. When Mengistu visited Moscow in May 1977, the Soviets apparently promised a further $500 million worth of arms and also encouraged Ethiopia to move more troops into Eritrea, assuring Mengistu that they would keep Somalia from attacking in the Ogaden. However, they were not in a position to honor this guarantee because they had lost all leverage over the Somali government. In fact, Somali troops, thinly disguised as WSLF volunteers, were probably already in the Ogaden at the time. By July, regular Somali units started openly crossing the border.

From then on, the policies of Ethiopia and Somalia were unambiguous. Somalia was engaged in an all-out effort to conquer the Ogaden, with total disregard of what effect this would have on its relations with the Soviet Union. From the Somali point of view, there was no point in safeguarding these relations if it did not help Somalia attain its territorial goals. In fact, from the perspective of that overriding interest, the Soviets had become more a hindrance than a help. Ethiopia was not in a position to choose or play subtle games. In the summer of 1977, it was in a desperate situation as one town after another fell to the nationalists in Eritrea and the Somalis penetrated deeply into the Ogaden (figure 9-1). The United States had long been written off as a potential ally. In fact, in April 1977 the Derg had taken the decisive step of closing down Kagnew Station, the American consulate in Asmara, and a military medical research facility, as well as some United

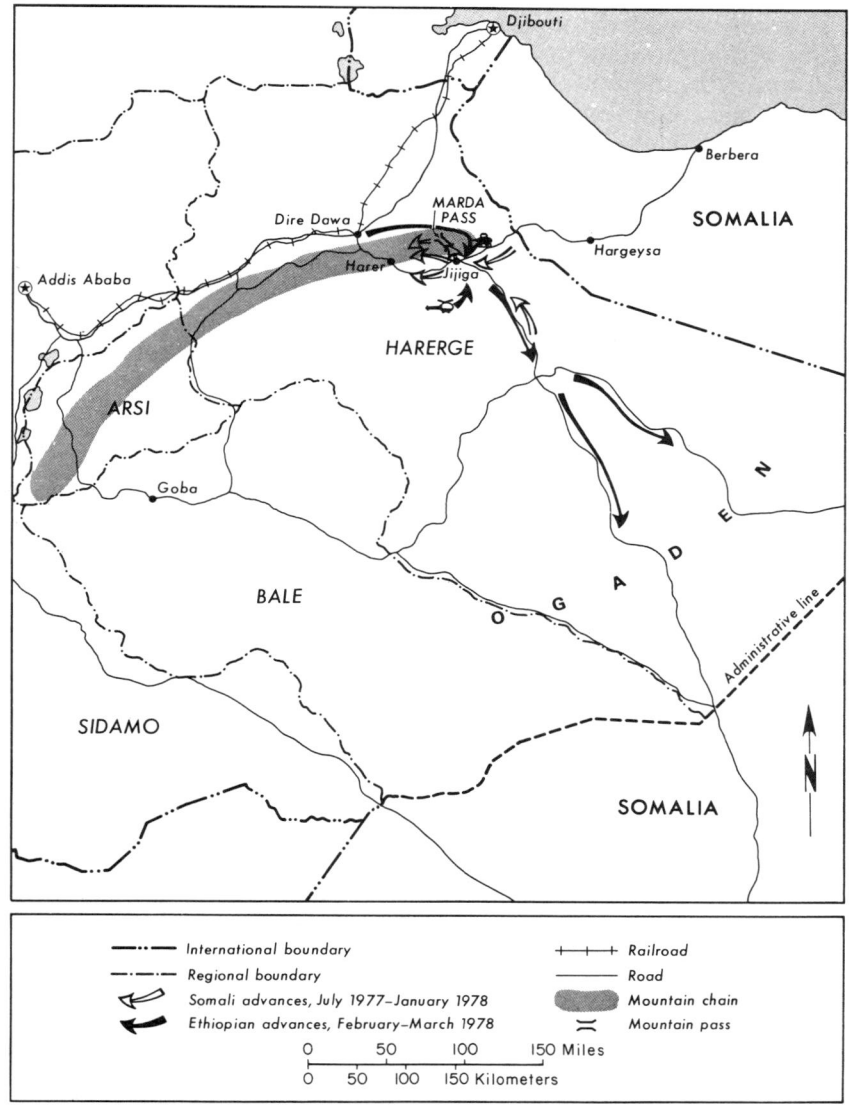

Source: *Ethiopia: A Country Study* (Washington, D.C.: U.S. Government Printing Office, 1981), p. 270.

Figure 9-1. The Ogaden Campaign, 1977-78

States Information Service (USIS) libraries. These steps were largely symbolic—the U.S. government had finally decided to close down Kagnew Station within a few months—and were directed at showing to the Soviet Union that Ethiopia was giving up its long-standing relationship with the U.S. government.

Despite the Ethiopian courtship and the Somalis openly flaunting their wishes, the Soviets hesitated throughout the summer. Only after Siad Barre unilaterally abrogated the Treaty of Friendship and Cooperation in November 1977 did they mount a massive air and sealift of arms to Ethiopia. Cuban troops also started arriving at this time. With this aid—but also thanks to the fact that the Ethiopian army did not disintegrate politically under the impact of repeated defeats—the Derg managed in the following months to push the Somali army back to the border and to recapture most of the towns it had lost in Eritrea.

The new alliance between Ethiopia and the Soviet Union posed a challenge for the United States, but opinions were sharply divided within the Carter Administration on how to respond to it. One line of thought was that the United States had no real interest in the Horn and thus no reason to get involved in a purely local conflict. After disentangling itself from a difficult relationship with Ethiopia, the United States should avoid getting involved with Somalia. First, Somalia was bent on a policy of territorial expansion that did not receive the approval of any African country since it challenged the Organization of African Unity (OAU) principle that colonial borders should be respected. Second, Somalia set forth claims not only on the Ogaden but also on an area of Kenya, a pro-Western country. Those claims were dormant at the time, but Kenya was worried about them and would not welcome any American policy toward Somalia that might imply tolerance, or even approval, of Somalia's expansionist policies. Thus, from a regional perspective, it would be a poor decision for the United States to rush to the aid of Somalia just because the Soviet Union had taken the side of Ethiopia. This viewpoint, however, was opposed by others in the Carter Administration—above all National Security Adviser Zbigniew Brzezinski—on the grounds that if the United States sat on the sidelines it would give a totally free hand to the Soviet Union, allowing it to become the arbiter of the situation in an area of strategic importance.[25]

Because of these conflicting viewpoints, the Carter Administration failed to follow a consistent policy. In May, after Ethiopia had closed Kagnew Station, the United States contacted the Somali government suggesting that it would make available military aid if Somalia terminated its close relationship with the Soviet Union. Siad Barre later claimed that the United States had in fact promised military aid at this time. When Somali troops were openly committed to fighting in the Ogaden, however, the Carter Administration pulled back, making it clear that it would not provide any weapons until Somali troops had been withdrawn from Ethiopia. It also refused to allow Saudi Arabia and Iran to transfer U.S. arms to Somalia. Since France and Great Britain, which had been considering the possibility of giving military aid to Somalia, also decided against it at this time, Somalia was left without sources of military aid during the war. The regionalist perspective had thus prevailed and continued to dominate American thinking about Somalia until late 1979, when the seizure of American hostages in Iran and the Soviet intervention in Afghanistan renewed U.S. interest in Somalia. At this time the United States was developing a rapid deployment force, and Somalia began to be considered as one potential staging ground for the force.

A second round of fighting in the Ogaden in early 1980—Somali troops again crossed the border into Ethiopia at this time—slowed down negotiations between Somalia and the United States and increased American caution in dealing with its new partner in the Horn. In August 1980 an agreement was finally initialed whereby the United States committed itself to provide Somalia with $40 million in military credits and $5 million in budgetary support over a two-year period.[26] This was a fraction of the initial Somali demand for $2 billion in economic and military aid over a ten-year period. In exchange for its aid, the United States gained access to the facilities at Berbera. But Washington remained a very reluctant partner, in part because of the fear that Somalia would use American weapons for war against its neighbors and because of growing doubts about the real strategic value of Berbera in a Middle East conflict. The United States waited until 1983 before it started carrying out some extension work at Berbera—and even then it did not intend to station permanent personnel there. The level of military aid to Somalia, furthermore, increased only marginally when the initial agreement was renewed in 1982.

In the seven years that have passed since the changes of alliances of 1977, the situation in the Horn has remained conflict ridden, but in a very predictable manner. Somalia has continued its attempts to take over the Ogaden through the WSLF and at times via its own troops. The Eritrean movements have continued their attempts to liberate Eritrea, conquering towns, losing them again to the Ethiopian army, and squabbling among themselves. The repeated Ethiopian offensives have not succeeded in dealing a severe blow to the nationalists, but neither have the nationalists, after 1977, come close again to winning a military victory. In other words, the situation in Eritrea is stalemated, although the stalemate is maintained only at the cost of the high levels of fighting. The Soviet Union and Cuba have stood behind Ethiopia throughout this period, although Cuba has tried, somewhat hypocritically, to disassociate itself from the Ethiopian policy in Eritrea. Cuban troops are committed to fight only against Somalia in the Ogaden. The reason for this is that the Eritrean movements were receiving some Cuban aid—and particularly Cuban recognition as progressive movements—when they were fighting against the feudal regime of Haile Selassie. It is a matter of great embarrassment to the Cubans to be siding now against a movement they hailed as heroic and progressive in the past. Nevertheless, with over 16,000 troops stationed in Ethiopia at the peak, Cuba has given Ethiopia considerable help in maintaining control not only over the Ogaden but also over Eritrea since their presence has allowed a greater part of the Ethiopian army to be transferred to the northern front. The Soviet Union provided very large levels of military aid, although the exact figures are difficult to determine. The amount provided between 1977 and 1980 has been estimated at anywhere between $1 and $2 billion; whatever the exact figures may be, there is no doubt that the aid was very sizeable, partly because the Soviets found themselves in the unfortunate position of having to provide Ethiopia with enough weapons to counterbalance the large amounts they had earlier given Somalia. After 1980 Soviet military aid has continued, although at a somewhat lower level.

The Soviet Union has not received much in return for its aid, certainly less than what Somalia had been willing to offer. Above all, the Ethiopian government has refused to give the Soviet Union facilities on the mainland, although it has agreed to permit it to use the Dahlak Island (off Massawa on the Eritrean coast) to anchor a drydock that had once been at Berbera and also to develop other installations. Ethiopia has been much more forthcoming with symbolic gestures: It signed, for example, a Treaty of Friendship and Cooperation with the Soviet Union in 1978; it launched many violent attacks on China in its newspapers; and it refused to condemn Soviet intervention in Afghanistan. It is difficult, however, to attribute to any of these moves a concrete strategic value. This is true, I would argue, even concerning the Treaty of Friendship and Cooperation. The example of how Egypt in 1976 and Somalia in 1977 unilaterally abrogated similar treaties, without the Soviet Union taking any steps in retaliation, raises serious questions about the real value and meaning of such agreements. In fact, the relationship between Ethiopia and the Soviet Union seems to be the opposite of that between Somalia and the United States. In the latter case, Somalia is the forthcoming partner, anxious to offer the United States something concrete so as to cement the relationship and obtain more aid in return. Ethiopia seems to be much more certain of Soviet interest and thus does not feel the need to offer much.

Limits of Great Power Influence

The history of the relations between the great powers and the countries of the Horn presents some unique characteristics as well as some features that can be considered typical of the problems arising in the dealings between countries where a huge imbalance of power and resources exists. The reversal of alliances that took place in the Horn in 1977 is unique: There is no other example of a complete, swift, and symmetrical reversal anywhere else in the Third World, although there are of course many examples of one country changing its foreign orientation. Other aspects of the situation are much more typical. In fact, the history of the Horn in this period illustrates well the extent and limits of influence of the great powers in peripheral areas of the world and the limits that regional problems impose on the strategic, geopolitical maneuvers of the great powers. We will turn to these issues here, considering them first from the point of view of the great powers.

The great powers' interest in the Horn, as pointed out earlier, was purely strategic because the area offered no economic wealth that could be attractive to outsiders. While exploration for oil and gas had been periodically undertaken in the contested Ogaden ever since the 1940s, neither had been discovered in commercially exploitable quantities at this writing. Economic motives can be safely ruled out as determinants of the policies of the great powers. The success or failure of these policies thus can be judged purely in terms of the attainment of strategic objectives.

The United States was quite successful in attaining its goals in Ethiopia from 1953 till the early 1970s, when the war in Eritrea started posing a safety problem and a political dilemma. Kagnew Station was an American base for over twenty years, providing the United States with constant, everyday payoffs. It was not an installation that might have become important in the case of war but one useful under normal circumstances to facilitate communications. In fact, if we consider all relationships between the countries of the Horn and the great powers, the one between Haile Selassie's Ethiopia and the United States was the most successful and the only one that clearly paid off from the point of view of the great powers. A major reason for this success is simply that Kagnew Station was established at a time when the Third World countries were much less sensitive than they are now about allowing foreign bases on their territories.

The second reason for the success of the Ethiopian–American relationship was the narrowness of U.S. interests in the area. The Americans only wanted a communications center and never irritated the Ethiopian government by asking for more. The fact that they had no other interest in Ethiopia also meant that they could pay back the emperor any way he wanted and this again kept problems from arising.

For its part, Ethiopia, too, never tried to change the terms of the relationship until after the coup d'etat. To be sure, the emperor always asked for a larger military aid package than the United States was willing to provide and he even went to Moscow at one point to demonstrate that the United States should not take his allegiance for granted. All this, however, was a normal part of the bargaining process and never constituted a real threat to the relationship. Two factors explain this constancy: One is that Ethiopia enjoyed a period of extraordinary internal political stability at the time; the second is that the situation in the Horn of Africa was also relatively stable. Both these statements need some explanation and qualification. The domestic political stability of Ethiopia was marred in 1960 by an attempted military coup d'etat; in the following years, unrest spread among the students so that the university and even the secondary schools were in a state of constant turmoil. Both the attempted coup d'etat and the student agitation, however, showed the lack of substantial organized opposition in the country. The coup failed because there was no real organization within the army, and the emperor was able to draw on a network of personal ties to reestablish his control. The student unrest was just that—limited to the schools and unable to give rise to a wider political movement.

The exception to this picture of stability and disorganization of the opposition was the situation in Eritrea. This could have affected the relationship between the United States and Ethiopia very directly because Kagnew Station was in Eritrea. However, the Eritrean movements did not become a real threat until the 1970s, so that the problem for the United States remained more potential than real. The expansionist policy of Somalia, for its part, did not mar the U.S.-Ethiopian relationship in the 1960s—not only because Ethiopia had shown it could easily handle the military challenge, but also because the United States had no interest in the Ogaden. The problem of Soviet penetration did not arise until the 1970s. In fact, the major worry of the United States up to the coup d'etat was what would happen after the death of the emperor. Haile Selassie's age was perceived by the United States as the most destabilizing element in the situation.

This complex of conditions which allowed the United States to attain its objectives in Ethiopia was not repeated again either in the relationship between the Soviet Union and the two countries of the Horn or in the relationship between the United States and Somalia. First, the political climate of the Third World was very different in the 1970s, and the granting of military bases to foreign powers had become a much touchier political issue. Second, both Ethiopia and Somalia were quite unstable in this period. Somalia—relatively stable until the 1977 war—was badly shaken by the defeat. Clan politics revived again and the position of Siad Barre was periodically severely threatened. Third, the regional conflicts had become acute. There was no longer any possibility for a great power to be involved in the Horn without being involved in the conflict in the Ogaden and even Eritrea. Fourth, both Ethiopia and Somalia during the 1970s had very specific political goals that were not necessarily compatible with great power interests. Earlier, both countries had wanted modern armies in the same way in which all developing countries want a modern army. True, Somalia never had abandoned its intention to liberate the missing lands, but during the 1960s its army was so weak compared to that of Ethiopia that military conquest could safely be ignored by the great powers. During the 1970s, this was no longer possible. An alliance with Somalia in particular meant consciously arming it for the conquest of the Ogaden.

As a result, neither the United States nor the Soviet Union achieved much through its relationship with the countries of the Horn during the 1970s, before or after the change of alliances. The Soviet Union of course obtained a base at Berbera but had to give it up within a few years; in Ethiopia, it received very little. The situation faced by the United States after 1979 was very similar: The Somali government was extraordinarily forthcoming in offering access to military facilities, but the price for it was the risk of heavy involvement in the Ogaden. The United States avoided the problem by keeping its relations with Somalia at a minimum level, neither giving nor receiving anything very substantial.

It seems possible to conclude, then, that the degree of success or failure of the great powers in the Horn was based not so much on how skilled their policies were as on the compatibility that existed at different times between their goals and those of Ethiopia and Somalia. These were never identical because neither Ethiopia nor Somalia were concerned with strategic issues and the Soviet Union and the United States had no interest in the Horn disputes. The most that ever existed was a compatibility of interests that allowed a trade-off of military aid for access to facilities.

The compatibility of the regional goals of Ethiopia and Somalia and the geopolitical goals of the great powers is thus the key to the success of the great powers' policies in the Horn. An additional conclusion is that for all their might the United States and the Soviet Union have no leverage on the regional conflicts. This was a lesson that the USSR in particular learned the hard way in 1977, when it assumed it could prevent Somalia from attacking the Ogaden and found it could not. This lack of leverage is largely due to the fact that the superpowers do not have a sufficient interest in the area to use drastic measures to enforce their will. As we have argued at the beginning, the Horn is important only as a means to protect or gain access to other areas, and as a result interest in it has always been somewhat lukewarm. Neither superpower has seen it worthwhile to use physical force to defend its position in the area. Furthermore, neither the United States nor the Soviet Union can offer a political solution to the regional problems. Not only would a political solution be extremely difficult to reach both in the Ogaden and in Eritrea, but the great powers have no cards to play. The Soviet Union, for example, tried to convince Ethiopia and Somalia to join in a federation, but such a federation presents an advantage only to the

Table 9-1
Survey of Opposition Groups in Ethiopia

Opposition Group	Sites of Activity	Objective(s)	Political Orientation	Foreign Supporters	Comments
Eritrean People's Liberation Front (EPLF)	Eritrea	Independence for Eritrea	Marxist-oriented	Syria, Sudan, Kuwait, Somalia	Largest and most effective of Eritrean secessionist movements; believed to have 25,000 well-armed troops holding Nakfa front in mid-1980
Eritrean Liberation Front (ELF)	Eritrea	Secession, but would settle for federal union and separate Eritrean Marxist organization	Marxist-oriented, predominantly Muslim	Syria, Sudan, Saudi Arabia, Kuwait	Hard-hit by 1978 Ethiopian offensives; numerous defections to EPLF
Eritrean Liberation Front-Popular Liberation Forces (ELF-PLF)	Eritrea	Independence for Eritrea	Moderate nationalist, anti-Marxist	Sudan, Egypt, Saudi Arabia, and other conservative Arab states	Break-away group from EPLF; small combat force, but more effective at propaganda abroad than fighting in Eritrea
Western Somali Liberation Front (WSLF)	Harerge	Union with Somali	Somali nationalists	Somalia	Reportedly controls roads and much of the countryside in the Ogaden
Somali-Abo Liberation Front (SALF)	Bale, Sidamo, and Arsi	Union with Somalia or creation of separate state	Somali and Oromo nationalists	Somalia	Linked to WSLF. Controls much of countryside in southern Bale, Arsi, Sidamo regions
Ethiopian People's Revolutionary Party (EPRP)	Addis Ababa, western Tigray, Gonder, and southern regions	Overthrow of PMAC• and establishment of civilian Marxist regime	Marxist-Leninist	Somalia	Underground in Addis Ababa and other urban centers; believed to be active in countryside as EPRA
Ethiopian People's Revolutionary Army (EPRA)	Tigray and Gonder	Same as EPRP	Marxist-Leninist	n.a.	Claims to be arm of EPRP; operates against government and rival insurgent forces

Organization	Region	Goals	Ideology	Foreign Support	Status
Ethiopian Democratic Union (EDU)	Gonder, Gojam, and western Tigray	Overthrow of PMAC* and establishment of democratic regime	No clear ideological identity; projects liberal image abroad, supporters include officers of imperial regime and Amhara and Tigray peasants	Sudan	Setbacks in 1978 sharply reduced military effectiveness
Oromo Liberation Front (OLF)	Northern Bale and Sidamo, Arsi, and southern Shewa	Autonomy for Oromo regions or establishment of independent state	Nationalists, several political factions	Somalia, Syria	Small-scale insurgency; cooperates with WSLF and SALF
Tigray People's Liberation Front (TPLF)	Western Tigray	Autonomy for Tigray or union with independent Eritrea	Marxist	Sudan, Syria, Somalia	Badly mauled in 1978 Ethiopian offensive, but continues guerrilla activities with small force in close cooperation with EPLF. Carries on separate wars with EPRA and EDU
Afar Liberation Front (AFL)	Southern Eritrea and eastern Welo	Autonomy in tribal territory	Traditional allegiance to tribal shaykhs, but factionalized	Saudi Arabia, Somalia, Djibouti	Guerrilla activity in tribal territory; cooperates with Eritrean secessionists. Military effectiveness diminished by Ethiopian sweep in early 1980. Fighting among rival factions
Afar National Liberation Movement (ANLM)	Southern Eritrea and eastern Welo	Afar autonomy	Marxist	n.a.	Cooperates with PMAC* against AFL and traditional tribal leadership

Source: *Ethiopia: A Country Study* (Washington, D.C.: U.S. Government Printing Office, 1981), pp. 310–311.

*Provisional Military Administrative Council.

n.a.—not available.

Soviet Union from a geopolitical perspective. Peace, it could be argued, is in the interest of both Ethiopia and Somalia, but if this were enough to convince them to lay down arms, they would have done it already.

In the case of Eritrea, too, the great powers cannot help much to bring about a solution because the Eritrean movements are very independent of either great power, having always received aid from a variety of sources, above all the Arab world; furthermore, they now rely for much of their military equipment on what they capture from the Ethiopian army. The Soviet Union had some contacts with the Eritrean Liberation Front (ELF) before the revolution, above all through the Italian Communist Party, and in 1980 tried to use these contacts to encourage negotiations. The problem was that by this time the ELF had long been superseded by the Eritrean People's Liberation Front as the major fighting force, and contact between the Ethiopian government and the ELF was useless. (See table 9-1 for a list of other opposition groups. See also figure 9-2.)

It could be argued that the United States and the Soviet Union not only could do nothing to help solve the conflicts of the Horn but worsened them by providing large amounts of military equipment to both countries. While there is some truth to the argument, the statement needs qualification. Undoubtedly, very large amounts of arms have been given to the two countries, particularly by the Soviet Union: The figures normally cited are about $1 billion to Somalia and $1 or $2 billion to Ethiopia by the USSR alone. Neither country could have purchased such amounts on its own. At the same time, there is no reason to think that there would not have been war without the Soviet and American weapons. The first war in the Ogaden took place at a time when Somalia hardly had an army. The war in Eritrea started when the Eritrean guerrillas were rag-tag bands of bandits and the Ethiopian military was very modestly armed. In other words, both the Ogaden and Eritrean conflicts long antedated the arms race initiated by the great powers. There is no doubt that the escalation in the quantity and type of arms only made the wars more damaging to all parties, but there is no way of calculating the real cost of U.S. and Soviet policies to the local populations. The great powers, at any rate, did not create or encourage the conflicts, simply because they did not serve their own interests. They provided the arms and thus contributed to the escalation of the fighting in the pursuit of other objectives. But it was the countries of the Horn that deliberately tried to manipulate the great powers in order to obtain aid in their own regional conflicts.

Conclusions

There are several conclusions concerning the relations between the great powers and countries of the Third World that can be reached on the basis

Superpower Competition and Regional Conflicts

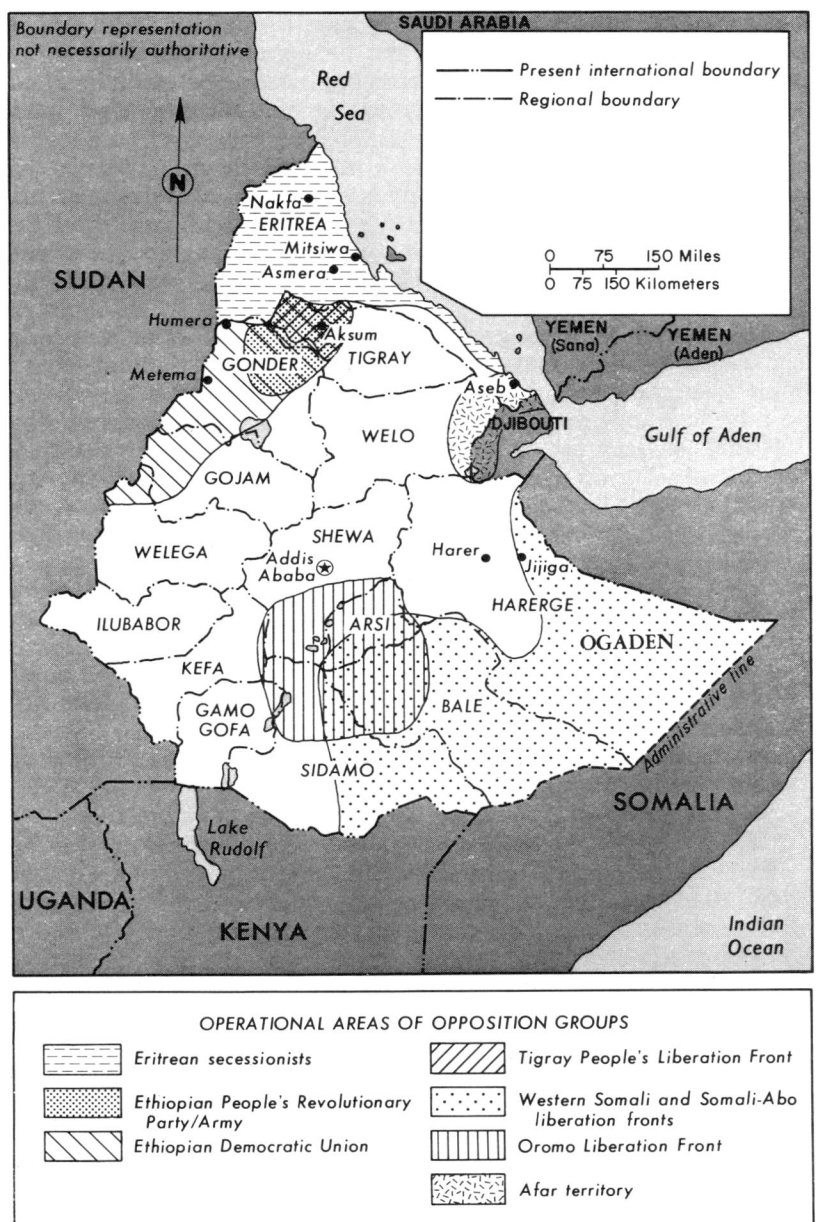

Source: *Ethiopia: A Country Study* (Washington, D.C.: U.S. Government Printing Office, 1981), p. 264.

Figure 9–2. Areas of Conflict, 1975–80

of the events analyzed above. One is that the U.S. and the Soviet powers do not lend themselves at all to being used in situations of marginal importance such as the one under discussion. The stakes in the Horn have not been sufficient for either great power to risk the international repercussions of an open intervention, but they are vital to Ethiopia and Somalia. The result is that the difference in the power of the United States and the Soviet Union on one side and Ethiopia and Somalia on the other is almost cancelled. The United States has been particularly cautious in its policies because it has access to other countries in the area: Egypt, Kenya, and the countries of the Arabian Gulf. The Soviet Union has greater interest in the Horn because it has fewer alternatives around it; but even the Soviets have not brought their might to bear in the regional conflicts.

There is a tendency among the countries of the Third World to see the great powers as both capable of and involved in endless manipulation of the developing countries in order to pursue their own policy objectives. The example of the Horn shows that the capacity of the great powers to manipulate underdeveloped countries is limited and that the stakes are often not high enough for the great powers to make use of their force. For their part, Third World countries are not defenseless either and do their share of manipulating. Since they are not afraid of causing international repercussions and upsetting world peace, they can be extremely ruthless in their policies and surprisingly successful in manipulating the great powers. Thus Somalia succeeded in convincing the Soviet Union to provide it with weapons it could only have wanted to follow an expansionist policy, despite the fact that the Soviet Union did not want such a policy. Ethiopia went one step further, securing active help from the Soviet Union and Cuba in maintaining its territorial integrity. The United States has so far not allowed itself to be manipulated by Somalia, and earlier in Ethiopia it managed to keep on the sidelines of the Eritrean conflict. But its strategic interests suffered as a result.

The final conclusion is that it is impossible for the great powers to be successful in their strategic designs unless their policies are also successful from a regional point of view. Both the United States and the Soviet Union apparently hoped that the regional problems could be ignored; the evidence shows clearly that this was a major fallacy.

Notes

1. John Spencer, a foreign policy adviser to Haile Selassie in this period, argued that the British also intended to impose a virtual protectorate on Ethiopia and that the emperor turned to the United States to safeguard his country's independence. This is not an accurate description of British

plans but probably reflects closely Haile Selassie's perception of the situation. John Spencer, *Ethiopia, The Horn of Africa and U.S. Policy* (Cambridge, Mass.: Institute for Foreign Policy Analysis, 1977).

2. Under the terms of the Italian peace treaty the United States, the Soviet Union, Britain, and France were to decide the fate of the former Italian colonies. The four could not agree with each other, and the decision was transferred to the U.N. General Assembly, which finally voted on the issue in 1950. Marina Ottaway, *Soviet and American Influence in the Horn of Africa* (New York: Praeger, 1982), pp. 152-153.

3. See G.K.N. Trevaskis, *Eritrea: A Colony in Transition* (London: Oxford University Press, 1960), for a detailed discussion of the politics, in Ethiopia and the United Nations, surrounding the decision.

4. See Bernard Braine, "Storm Clouds Over the Horn of Africa," *International Affairs* 34 (1958):435-443, for a discussion of the British policy concerning unification; and Margery Perham, *The Government of Ethiopia*, 2nd ed. (Evanston, Ill.: Northwestern University Press, 1969), p. xxxvi, concerning the problems developing after independence.

5. See A.A. Castagno, "The Somali-Kenyan Controversy: The Future," *Journal of Modern African Studies* 2 (1964):165-188.

6. See Irving Kaplan, et al., *Area Handbook for Somalia* (Washington, D.C.: Government Printing Office, 1969).

7. For details on the history of the Eritrean movements, see Bereket Hapte Selassie, *Conflict and Intervention in the Horn of Africa* (New York: Monthly Review Press, 1980).

8. U.S. Congress, Senate, Committee on Foreign Relations, *United States Security Commitments and Agreements Abroad, Part 8, Ethiopia: Hearings Held by the Subcommittee on U.S. Security Agreements and Commitments Abroad,* 91st Congress, 2nd Session, June 1, 1970.

9. Ibid., p. 1889.

10. Ibid.

11. Total foreign aid to Somalia from independence to 1967 has been estimated at $320 million, including loans and grants. Some $95 million of this total came from Italy, $59 million from the Soviet Union, $47 million from the United States and $23 million from China. See Kaplan, et al., *Area Handbook for Somalia,* p. 353.

12. See London Institute for Strategic Studies, *Military Balance, 1975-76* and *1977-78* (London: Institute for Strategic Studies).

13. The figure of $1 billion in Soviet military aid to Somalia has been used by the press and has most often been cited. It presumably includes the cost of training and the improvement in facilities as well as arms transfers. The U.S. Arms Control and Disarmament Agency estimated more soberly that between 1973 and 1977 the Soviet Union transferred to Somalia $260 million worth of military equipment. See *World Military Expenditures and*

Arms Transfers, 1968-77 (Washington, D.C.: Arms Control and Disarmament Agency, 1979).

14. See U.S., Central Intelligence Agency, *Communist Aid to Less Developed Countries of the Free World, 1977* (Washington, D.C.: Central Intelligence Agency, 1978), p. 4.

15. See U.S. Congress, Senate, "Soviet Military Capability in Berbera, Somalia," *Report of Senator Dewey F. Bartlett to the Committee on Armed Services,* July 1975, p. 19.

16. Estimates of Arab aid to Somalia vary widely. Kaplan put the figure at $140 million by 1977; see Irving Kaplan, et al., *Area Handbook for Somalia,* 2nd ed. (Washington, D.C.: Government Printing Office, 1977), p. 222. A figure of $675 million is given in U.S. Central Intelligence Agency, *Communist Aid to Less Developed Countries of the Free World, 1977*, p. 19.

17. Despite this reduction in size and the scheduled closure, Kagnew Station was still considered an important link in the U.S. military communications system, as argued repeatedly by government witnesses at congressional hearings in this period. See, for example, the statement by Williams Schaufele, Assistant Secretary of State for African Affairs in U.S., Congress, Senate, Committee on Foreign Relations, Subcommittee on African Affairs, *Ethiopia and the Horn of Africa,* 94th Congress, 2nd Session, 4–6 August 1976, p. 113. Schaufele stated that there were no plans for a phase out of Kagnew at this time, but this does not appear to be exactly correct.

18. Ibid.

19. Colin Legum and Bill Lee, *Conflict in the Horn of Africa* (London: Rex Collings, 1977), p. 70.

20. For more detail concerning the formation of the party and its consequences, see Marina Ottaway, *Soviet and American Influence in the Horn of Africa,* p. 82.

21. The movement started around 1964 in the Bale province of Ethiopia, where a rebellion by the local landlords against the rule of Addis Ababa provided the Somali government with an opportunity to launch and arm a pro-Somali movement. In 1970 Wako Gutu—the leader of what had by then become the Western Somali Liberation Front—surrendered, or more precisely, was bought off by Haile Selassie. The WSLF was re-launched after 1975. Selassie, *Conflict and Intervention in the Horn of Africa,* p. 105-111.

22. It is not known for sure when the Derg first approached the Soviet Union concerning military aid. Probably, a first request was made early in 1976 and rejected. In December 1976 an Ethiopian delegation visited Moscow and reportedly obtained the promise of $200 million worth of military aid. This agreement was not made public, however, and arms were not sent immediately. See Marina Ottaway and David Ottaway, *Ethiopia: Empire in Revolution* (New York: Africana Publishers, 1978), p. 103.

23. In January 1976 the Derg circulated discretely in diplomatic circles a report entitled "War Clouds in the Horn of Africa," which provided detailed information about Somali infiltration in the Ogaden. Many of the incidents mentioned in the report were confirmed by independent sources, above all relief organizations working in the area. Ottaway, *Soviet and American Influence in the Horn of Africa,* pp. 163-164.

24. Ottaway and Ottaway, *Ethiopia: Empire in Revolution,* pp. 142-148.

25. See Elizabeth Drew, "Brzezinski," *New Yorker,* 1 May 1978, pp. 90-130; and "Brzezinski Calls Democrats Soft Toward Moscow," *The New York Times,* 30 November 1980.

26. *The Washington Post,* 28 August 1980.

10 The Soviet Union and Zimbabwe: The Liberation Struggle and After

Keith Somerville

Throughout the struggle of the African nationalists in Zimbabwe, the Soviet Union expressed its support for the cause of African liberation from white minority rule and from the early to mid-1960s onward became increasingly involved in the liberation struggle as a supplier of arms, material aid, and training to the nationalist forces led by Joshua Nkomo and his Zimbabwe African People's Union (ZAPU). The Soviet Union gave strong diplomatic support to the cause of African nationalism in Zimbabwe at international forums such as the United Nations and showed itself to be implacably opposed to the white minority regime in Salisbury (Harare after April 1982). It was expected by many observers in the West, and feared by many Western governments, that when majority rule was attained, Moscow would become a close friend of the new government and be in a good position to exert influence over it. These expectations were voiced even after the victory of Robert Mugabe and the Zimbabwe African National Union (ZANU) in Zimbabwe's first postindependence election.[1]

In the three years since independence it has become abundantly clear that, far from benefiting from its support for Nkomo and ZAPU, the Soviet Union has little if any influence in Zimbabwe, and in fact has had to bear the stigma of backing ZAPU, somewhat as the Ancient Mariner had the Albatross hung around his neck. Relations have certainly improved over the three years of independence, but they are still far from close. Although he has indicated his intention to do so, Robert Mugabe has yet to visit Moscow, and no high-ranking Soviet delegations have appeared in Harare.

The situation must have come as a great shock to the Soviet Union. The leadership in Moscow had undoubtedly hoped that because of its staunch support for ZAPU during the liberation war, its reputation as a friend of progressive nations in Africa and the Third World, and its cooperative relations with Mozambique (whose leaders had become firm supporters of ZANU), it would be in on the ground floor when the Mugabe government took office. Despite ZANU's overwhelming election victory, the Soviet Union expected Nkomo and ZAPU to play an important role in the postindependence government, and the message of congratulations sent by the CPSU and Soviet state leaders had been addressed to Nkomo and Mugabe jointly.

Early on, however, the Mugabe government made it clear that it intended to follow a policy of strict nonalignment. Addressing the UN General Assembly in September 1980, Mugabe committed his country to support the nonaligned movement and stressed that Zimbabwe wanted to remain on friendly terms with all states. He gave particular emphasis to the independent nature of Zimbabwe's foreign policy, saying "We believe that our association must never bring us into a situation where we have to submit to the will of others."[2] Mugabe's words must be interpreted in context, of course. The close relations forged between the liberation movements and a number of socialist countries have undoubtedly had some effect on the nature of Zimbabwe's relations with those states. Even though Nkomo is no longer a member of the Zimbabwean government, members of ZAPU still are, and it is not inconceivable that they could have some influence on the course of foreign policy (even if only peripherally) and on the state of relations between the Soviet Union and Zimbabwe as well. Nevertheless, the worst fears of the West suddenly seemed unfounded, and the Soviet Union confronted a major foreign policy setback.

This chapter seeks to examine the development, current state, and prospects of Soviet relations with Zimbabwe. First priority will be given to an account of the relationships built up between the liberation movements and Moscow in the course of the liberation struggle. The nature of these relationships has played a decisive role in determining the attitude of the Mugabe government toward Moscow and vice versa. An examination of Soviet-Zimbabwean relations in the postindependence period will follow, supplemented by analyses of Soviet policy toward the Zimbabwean liberation movements and of the basic attitudes of the nationalists toward the socialist countries. The role of the Front Line states in the USSR-southern Africa relationship will also be examined.

The Soviet Union and the Zimbabwean National Movement

The first contacts between the Zimbabwean nationalists and the Soviet Union, China, and other socialist states were made prior to the split in the nationalist movement in August 1963, probably sometime during the extensive travels undertaken by Joshua Nkomo and his lieutenants in the late 1950s and early 1960s. At that time the main forums for interactions between Third World political and liberation movements and the socialist countries were the meetings of such bodies as the Afro-Asian People's Solidarity Organization (AAPSO) and conferences like the Afro-Asian Conference and the All African People's Conference in Accra. These conferences were attended by representatives of newly independent states, national liberation movements, and socialist countries and socialist and communist parties. It is known, for example, that Nkomo, then head of the Southern Rhodesian African National Congress (SR-ANC), attended the Accra Conference in December 1958.³ The conference was also attended by Soviet and Chinese AAPSO delegates, including a Chinese member of the AAPSO Permanent Secretariat.⁴ In 1960, the second AAPSO Conference was held in Conakry, Guinea. The Soviet Union and China were both represented, and at the meeting Nkomo, then de facto leader of the National Democratic Party (NDP, the successor to the banned SR-ANC), was elected to the AAPSO Executive Committee.⁵

It is inconceivable that neither the nationalists nor the socialist states would not have made use of these conferences to initiate relations, given the desire of the nationalists for international support and the declaratory policy of the Soviet Union and China to support national liberation struggles and extend their relations with the Third World. In addition, in the USSR the Soviet Afro-Asian Solidarity Committee is one of the main bodies for liaison with liberation movements. The Committee's officials serve as the Soviet representatives on bodies like the AAPSO. The offices run by the nationalists, first by the NDP and then by its successor ZAPU, in Cairo, Dar-es-Salaam, and London also served as contact points.⁶ Egypt was a particularly good meeting place because of the Nasir government's close relations with the Soviet Union, and ZAPU representatives in Cairo were invited to visit both the Soviet Union and China.⁷ In early 1961, Nkomo made a number of trips to Cairo, where the AAPSO had its headquarters, and also visited Nairobi, Damascus, and Addis Ababa.

In January 1963, ZAPU's National Chairman and effective deputy to Nkomo, Ndabaningi Sithole, attended the AAPSO Conference in Moshi, Tanzania. This conference, attended by Soviet and Chinese delegates, saw the Sino-Soviet split carried onto the Third World and African stages. Sithole has indicated that it was around the time of these meetings in the early 1960s that the Zimbabwean nationalist movement gave up its basically reformist stance and moved toward planning the overthrow of the white minority regime and, in connection with this objective, became "involved with communist states."⁸ As a result of the early contacts, in mid-1962 a group of Zimbabwean Africans traveled to Ghana, Algeria, China, and Czechoslovakia to receive military training.⁹ For a short period—from late 1961 to late 1962—some of the training in the Ghanaian camps had been carried out by Soviet instructors, though later these were replaced with Chinese and Ghanaian instructors.¹⁰ That some form of cooperation had been established between ZAPU and the Soviet Union and other socialist states in the early 1960s was in fact loudly proclaimed by the Rhodesian authorities. They published details of the discovery of arms caches of Soviet and Chinese made weapons and the capture of Soviet and Chinese trained saboteurs belonging to ZAPU. The Salisbury regime clearly expected these disclosures to be damaging to ZAPU internationally.¹¹

The Zimbabwean nationalist movement split on 8 August 1963, when disgruntled members of the ZAPU executive formed the Zimbabwe African National Union (ZANU). The former ZAPU members involved were Ndabaningi Sithole, who became ZANU's first leader, Robert Mugabe, Leopold Takawira, Moton Malianga, and Nathan Shamuyarira. The break resulted from dissatisfaction with Nkomo's leadership and the tactics followed by ZAPU under his direction. ZANU was immediately perceived as a more militant organization and it made clear from the start that it was determined to take a more active stance in seeking to achieve its objectives. Within a month of ZANU's formation (in September 1963) five members of the party, including the present Minister of State in the Prime Minister's Office, Emmerson Munangagwa, were sent to the People's Republic of China for a six-month training course, which included military science and political education.[12] In 1964, ZANU leader Ndabaningi Sithole visited Beijing at the invitation of Chinese authorities.

A second group of ZANU cadres, including the future Zimbabwe African National Liberation Army (ZANLA) Chief of Operations, William Ndagana, received training in Ghana in 1964,[13] where they were trained by Ghanaian instructors in semiregular warfare and by Chinese instructors in guerrilla warfare and political education. Following the course, Ndangana led the "Crocodile Commando," which was responsible for the first white death in the liberation war in July 1964.[14] The group, including Ndangana, then went on to China in 1965 for advanced training. In China, the ZANU cadres received instruction at a military school near Beijing, where Chinese officers also received advanced training.[15] Ndangana returned from China to take command of the first ZANLA intake at the Itumbi training camp in Tanzania. A third group, led by future ZANLA commander Josiah Tongogara, was trained at Nanking Academy in Beijing during early 1966.[16]

While ZANU was developing its aid relationship with China during the early 1960s, ZAPU's external links were extended considerably wider. Through its close ties with the South African African National Congress (ANC), ZAPU came into contact with representatives of Eastern European states, and Nkomo sought and received Soviet and Eastern European aid. One former ZAPU member trained in Moscow in the late 1960s believes that Nkomo approached the Soviet Union for aid during the early to mid-1960s, following the failure of the West to give any indication of supporting the African cause in Rhodesia. When the approach was made, the USSR was concerned primarily to find out whether ZAPU had significant support from the African population of Rhodesia.[17] Nkomo was obviously able to convince the USSR of ZAPU's credentials, as between March 1964 and October 1965 ZAPU recruits received training at four centers in Moscow.[18]

The relation was not exclusive, however. At the same time, despite the Sino–Soviet split and ZANU's cooperative relationship with China, a ZAPU leader named James Chikerema visited China in January 1964, and ZAPU cadres received training in Nanking.[19] In the early 1960s, in the words of Bruce Larkin, "if there were competing factions in a country, China tried to keep a delicate balance among them, maintaining contacts with all."[20] However, as the Sino–Soviet split became further exacerbated and the liberation struggles in Africa gained pace, the affiliations of the liberation movements became more fixed. In the Zimbabwean case, ZAPU came to monopolize support from the Soviet Union and ZANU became more closely identified with China. The Soviet Union—even before the issue had become so clear cut—had always been less eclectic than the Chinese in supporting the liberation movements. It tended to give support to one movement in each territory and confined its support to that movement alone. ZANU had approached the Soviet Union for aid in the early stages of the liberation struggle—around the time that the first ZANU cadres were being sent to China—but the Soviet Union had refused to provide any assistance.[21]

By 1969, the exact policy of the Soviet Union toward the liberation movements in Zimbabwe had become clearer. The USSR was one of the sponsors of the International Conference in Support of the Liberation Movements in the Portuguese Colonies and Southern Africa, held in Khartoum in January 1969, a conference attended by seven African liberation movements, all of which received Soviet aid.[22] The Soviet Union dubbed these seven movements the authentic liberation movements. The most important liberation movements that had not been invited to the meeting (ZANU, the Pan-Africanist Congress of South Africa, UNITA, and COREMO of Mozambique) issued a critique of the conference, distributed by the Chinese Xinhua news agency, stating that the meeting was "calculated to control the liberation struggles of the Portuguese colonies and southern Africa. . . ."[23] This rather overstated the level of Soviet influence over the movements in question, but the strength of the condemnation indicated the developing dichotomy. For several years prior to the Khartoum conference it had been becoming increasingly clear that Moscow viewed ZAPU as the only legitimate national liberation movement in Zimbabwe. This was evidenced by Soviet commentary on the Rhodesian liberation struggle, which tended to emphasize ZAPU activities and publications while ignoring those of ZANU.[24] Despite the fact that ZANU had commenced an armed struggle against the white minority regime with attacks in 1964 and 1966, Moscow ignored the very existence of the organization.

Following the largely unsuccessful military actions by ZANU between 1966 and the end of the decade, the movement strengthened its links with

China. In January 1969, eight Chinese instructors arrived at the ZANLA training camp at Itumbi, Tanzania. These instructors were to play an important part in the adoption of a new politico-military strategy by ZANU/ZANLA.[25] The Chinese trained ZANLA cadres at Itumbi and Mgagao, and these cadres then trained ZANLA guerrilla fighters at other camps such as Chifombo.[26] Much of the training concentrated on Maoist teaching on the mobilization and politicization of the population and the conduct of a protracted armed struggle. ZANU's Chief Political Commissar, Mayor Urimbo, believes that China's approach had a very great effect on ZANU's ideology and tactics and asserts that ZANU "saw Chinese ideology as the most effective when organizing the people."[27]

Chinese support for ZANU remained constant throughout the remainder of the liberation struggle. In addition to training, China supplied weapons (mainly small arms, explosives, and mines). China was unable to supply heavy weapons of the sort that would have been invaluable to ZANU in the closing years of the struggle: particularly antiaircraft weapons, antitank missiles, and light artillery. ZANU also received material support from North Korea, Romania, and Yugoslavia. The North Koreans supplied some heavy weapons and played an important role in training ZANLA cadres.[28]

During the latter phase of the liberation struggle, however, ZANU's need for heavier and more sophisticated weapons became desperate. In 1978 Mugabe stated his intention of seeking such weapons from the Soviet Union and other socialist states and by 1979 was able to say that ZANU was "expecting aid from socialist countries that have not assisted us in the past."[29] The countries referred to were probably Cuba and Bulgaria. On behalf of ZANU, Presidents Nyerere and Machel of Tanzania and Mozambique had approached both Cuba and the USSR to request aid. Cuba reacted by agreeing to supply some aid and advisers. It is thought that Cuba eventually supplied a few arms to ZANU; it certainly supplied a number of advisers to help train ZANLA cadres at camps in Mozambique. Some sources said at the time that as many as 500 Cuban military instructors were training members of Mugabe's wing of the liberation movement in Mozambique.[30]

Moscow's response was in fact quite different. Machel had dispatched Marcelino dos Santos, one of the most pro-Soviet of FRELIMO leaders, to Moscow to ask the Soviet Union to start supplying heavy weapons to ZANU. The Mozambicans, who had allowed ZANU to infiltrate Rhodesia from their territory since the early 1970s and who had an extensive knowledge of the abilities and position of ZANU in the liberation struggle, were well acquainted with ZANU's need for such weapons. However, Brezhnev refused to receive dos Santos and his appeal for help for ZANU. Nyerere's petition to Moscow had no greater effect and neither did formal requests from him to the Soviet Union not to take sides between the two wings of the liberation movement.

The Soviet Union made it very clear that it was only willing to give support to Mugabe if ZANU stopped siding with the Chinese and if Mugabe stopped describing himself as "a Marxist-Leninist of Maoist Thought."[31] Moscow also wanted to see ZANU dissolve itself and accept the leadership of Nkomo. Because of ZANU's unwillingness to accept this ultimatum and Moscow's unwillingness to budge from support for Nkomo alone, "ZANLA did not get one pistol or one bullet from the Russians."[32] ZANU was rebuffed by the Soviet Union and its allies, particularly the German Democratic Republic (GDR), on a number of occasions when officials or leaders of those states visited southern Africa. Sources close to ZANU have indicated that the rebuffs were conveyed to Zimbabwean representatives, and on at least one occasion to the present Deputy Prime Minister Simon Muzenda, in a most insulting fashion. A Soviet Deputy Foreign Minister, Leonid Ilichev, is said to have very rudely rebuffed ZANU requests for aid during a visit to Mozambique.[33] In the end, the only Soviet arms ZANU received were those supplied by Mozambique and Ethiopia,[34] against the wishes of the USSR.

ZAPU, on the other hand, benefited substantially from its relations with Moscow. Throughout the liberation struggle in Zimbabwe, the Soviet Union highlighted comments by ZAPU leaders that indicated a leaning toward socialism but completely ignored the fact that, as Colin Legum has pointed out, "Despite his Russian patronage, Nkomo is the African leader whom most white Rhodesians and Anglo-American businessmen would like to see win . . . "[35] Moscow also made no public reference to the rifts within ZAPU in the 1970s that led a group of ZAPU defectors (notably James Chikerema) to form FROLIZI together with a number of ZANU defectors. The Soviet Union provided military and other forms of training for ZAPU cadres at centers in the USSR. Rex Nhongo, the eventual head of ZANLA, was trained in Moscow, for example. The USSR also supplied weapons for ZAPU guerrillas. These generally were supplied on a bilateral basis rather than through the African Liberation Committee of the OAU, which was the channel favored by most African states. The GDR and Czechoslovakia are also thought to have supplied weapons to ZAPU.[36] The Soviet Union provided everything from pistols to heavy artillery and antiaircraft missiles (of the type used by ZAPU to shoot down an Air Rhodesia Viscount aircraft in the late 1970s). All the military training provided by the USSR took place in the Soviet Union until the MPLA government took over in Angola, after which some Soviet advisers trained ZAPU cadres on Angolan territory. Cuba also supplied weapons and training.

When ZANU reopened the military struggle in Zimbabwe in 1972, the ZANU successes and operations were more or less ignored by the Soviet media. Only when ZAPU opened its military campaign later in the decade did Moscow react. From the mid-1970s onward, the Soviet media gave fairly wide coverage to the fighting in Zimbabwe, concentrating on the activities of ZAPU. In the late 1970s, ZAPU visitors to the Soviet Union and Eastern Europe became commonplace. Nkomo was a very frequent visitor to Moscow and his comments or interviews were often broadcast by Soviet radio, particularly on broadcasts beamed to Africa. During his visits and in his pronouncements, Nkomo was lavish in his praise of Soviet support.

This all-round support was stepped up in the mid- to late-1970s and ZAPU began to receive large quantities of sophisticated and heavy weaponry. At one stage the Soviet supply of heavy weapons to ZAPU's forces in Zambia was so substantial that Zambia, which had become worried by the presence of large stocks of sophisticated weaponry on its territory,[37] stopped the flow of weapons to ZAPU until agreement had been reached between Zambia, ZAPU, and the USSR over methods of supply. At the conclusion of the Lancaster House Conference in December 1979, the Soviet Union gave ZAPU $60 million worth of arms, including SAM-7 missiles, artillery up to 120mm, armored vehicles, recoilless rifles, light weapons, and ammunition.[38]

Throughout the last years of the liberation war, Moscow kept up a steady stream of pro-ZAPU propaganda on its foreign radio services and in its media. Statements and interviews by senior ZAPU officials were broadcast often. On the other hand, virtually no mention was made of ZANU and no interviews or statements by ZANU leaders were broadcast. Although the USSR welcomed the formation of the Patriotic Front in October 1976—as it had welcomed the attempt to forge unity between ZANU, ZAPU, the ANC, and FROLIZI in 1974—Moscow's comments on Patriotic Front activities concentrated on those of the ZAPU wing, and Joshua Nkomo was frequently referred to as "leader of the Patriotic Front."

In 1979, the two wings of the Patriotic Front reached agreement on the formation of a joint executive committee whose task would be to set up a unified operational command. Although Moscow's declaratory position was one of supporting unity between the liberation movements, its public reaction was little more than lukewarm. *Pravda* referred to the decision as "a constructive response" to the OAU's steps toward "intensifying material, moral, and diplomatic support for the freedom fighters."[39] The Soviet attitude was perhaps due to apprehension about the role ZANU might play in a unified movement and fears that if it supplied arms to a joint ZANU–ZAPU force it would be indirectly aiding an ally of the Chinese. Later in 1979 a contingency plan for setting up a Patriotic Front government in liberated territory intended to counter the formation of the Zimbabwe-Rhodesia government of Abel Muzorewa and Ian Smith was put to the Front Line states and leaders of ZANU and ZAPU by a Cuban envoy, Raul Valdez Vivo. The plan, thought to have Soviet backing or even to have been drawn up by the Soviet Union, was for Cuban troops to help secure a safe zone in guerrilla-held territory in which an independent Zimbabwe would be proclaimed, with Nkomo as its leader and Mugabe as the number-two man in charge of defense. For some reason, however, Nkomo turned the idea down and the whole thing fell through.[40]

In the last two years of the liberation struggle the Soviet Union gave great prominence in its commentary to the successes being achieved in the guerrilla war. It neglected to say that most of the fighting was being carried by the ZANU wing of the Patriotic Front using Chinese and North Korean weapons. At one stage Radio Moscow claimed that the Patriotic Front controlled 40 percent of Rhodesia's territory. *Izvestiia* reported that the Zimbabwean guerrillas had intensified military operations on five fronts and that the liberation war was entering its final phase.[41] This was no exaggeration, as it was the successes of the Patriotic Front operations that eventually drove Smith and Muzorewa to the Lancaster House negotiating table. Moscow, however, sought to give the impression that it was Nkomo's supporters who were behind the intensification of the war. While it is true that ZAPU's military forces were becoming more active, it was nonetheless ZANLA that was bearing the bulk of the fighting.

The Soviet Union had always taken a very critical line toward Western initiatives to bring an end to the Rhodesian conflict. Often it was correct in attacking the initiatives for being attempts to give Rhodesia independence without effectively transferring power to the black majority. However, it was equally critical of the initiative adopted by the Commonwealth at the Lusaka Commonwealth Conference in August 1979. In the months between the Lusaka conference and the Lancaster House negotiations, Moscow presented the British position as a cunning one and quoted comments by Nkomo that the new proposals were "maneuvering" and did not correspond "to the Zimbabwe people's interests."[42] The Soviet Union was undoubtedly taken aback when the Patriotic Front began to take an interest in the proposals. The Soviet media then had to change its tack and praise the "flexible and highly principled stand" of the Patriotic Front.[43] *Pravda* noted that the Front Line states had approved the "constructive position" taken by the Patriotic Front at Lancaster House, though it became evident from the tone of Soviet comments that the Soviet Union was distrustful of the signs of progress being made at the talks and perhaps resented the fact that while they had been the staunch supporters of the armed struggle, the outcome of the war might eventually be decided by a conference from which they were excluded.[44] The level and types of arms supplied to ZAPU lead one to believe that Moscow expected the war in Zimbabwe to reach a conventional stage and perhaps thought that the future of Zimbabwe would be decided on the battlefield alone.

Even when agreement was reached at Lancaster House the Soviet Union was skeptical about the terms and their chances of success. It tried to salvage something from the conference by referring to comments by Nkomo that the agreements reached at Lancaster House were a result of the support "given to the Zimbabwe patriots by the front-line states, the peoples of the socialist countries, and all progressive mankind."[45] It cannot be denied that Soviet aid was vital in enabling the nationalists to fight the liberation war and that it was the war that forced Smith and Muzorewa to the negotiating table, but one cannot help but feel that the Soviet comments were more a result of sour grapes than a sober analysis of the situation. The Patriotic Front also exhibited signs of anxiety during the ceasefire period and the run-up to the election. The Soviet comments and doubts about the agreement were perhaps reasonable ones. They were voiced not only to make people aware of the problems of implementing elections and a transfer of power but also for propaganda purposes to show that the Soviet Union—and not those who had arranged the agreement—was still the true friend of Zimbabwe.

During the elections, the Soviet media was critical of the refusal of the British to allow Soviet reporters into the country to cover the voting. *Izvestiia* commented, "All the indications are that the colonial and local punitive forces are so keen to get preparations for the 'free' elections underway that they are no longer interested in keeping up the attitude of supporters of 'the freedom of information'."[46] The first election dispatch published by *Pravda*, sent by its Luanda correspondent, noted that 93 percent of the electorate had voted but that the elections had been "characterized by an atmosphere of threats and repressions against the Patriotic Front supporters." The dispatch quoted members of Nkomo's wing of the Patriotic Front on the conduct of the elections and warned "that in the event of the election results not being to the liking of Washington and London, there may be a military coup."[47]

Pravda reported the election results on 5 March and said they had been greeted with "great joy" by the African majority. The report said ZANU had won "the major success" but that ZAPU would have a large representation in parliament. The report, and the congratulatory message sent by the Soviet leaders to Mugabe and Nkomo, did not explain that ZANU candidates had opposed those of ZAPU and that the victory was one for Robert Mugabe, with ZAPU and Nkomo reduced to a secondary role for the time being.

**Soviet Relations with Zimbabwe
since Independence**

Once the dust had settled after the elections and Prime Minister-Elect Mugabe had begun choosing his cabinet and preparing to assume power, it became evident that Moscow had backed the wrong horse and that its future relations with the Zimbabwe government would be far from smooth.

Soon after Mugabe's victory, Leonid Brezhnev sent a message to the new prime minister promising that the Soviet Union would continue to stand by the people of Zimbabwe. The message read in part:

> The convincing victory of Zimbabwe's patriots is the natural outcome of the many years of heroic struggle waged by the people of Zimbabwe under the leadership of the Patriotic Front . . . With all my heart I wish you, and through you, the entire people of Zimbabwe, great new successes. You may rest assured that, as during the difficult years of the struggle for independence, the Soviet Union will continue to be on the side of the just cause of the people of Zimbabwe.[48]

The message, of course, seemed to miss the point of Mugabe's election victory—that it had been a victory primarily for ZANU and not for the Patriotic Front as a whole.

That the message and other Soviet overtures to the ZANU leadership had little effect was made clear by the rebuff given to Soviet (and East German) attempts to establish diplomatic relations with Zimbabwe prior to the official independence celebrations. The Soviet Union apparently made a number of attempts to negotiate the establishment of relations in the period between ZANU's election victory and Zimbabwean independence. Soviet diplomats based in Lusaka and Maputo tried to meet Mugabe when he visited these capitals, but he refused to receive them. It seems that President Machel, by then a close friend of both the USSR and Zimbabwe, did little to help the Soviet Union in its effort to improve relations with the new Zimbabwean leaders.[49]

A Soviet delegation was invited to attend the independence celebrations in April 1980. When the delegation arrived, however, it was given no great reception by ZANU, in contrast to the Chinese delegation which was met by Mugabe and Kumbirai Kangai, the future Minister of Labor and Social Services. The Soviet delegation, which was led by one of the lower-ranking Politburo members, Sh. R. Rashidov, included Deputy Foreign Minister Ilichev. This was an exceptionally clumsy move: Ilichev had been instrumental in rebuffing ZANU requests for aid and, along with Soviet Ambassador to Zambia Vasilii Solodovnikov, is thought to have been in the forefront of Soviet policymaking on the Zimbabwean issue. Another clumsy Soviet move was to allow the delegation, in contravention of normal diplomatic practices, to meet with leading members of ZAPU's military wing, including the ZAPU military intelligence chief Dumiso Dabengwa.[50] It is noteworthy that invitations to the independence celebrations were not extended to other members of the Soviet bloc that had supported Nkomo, though Romania, which had aided both movements, was invited.

After the early moves to establish relations had been rebuffed, the Soviet Union adopted a two-pronged approach to Zimbabwe. On the one hand, an effort was made to project a very positive image of the new government and its policies and to combine this with repeated requests to open negotiations on the establishment of diplomatic ties. On the other hand, comments by ZAPU members noting the Soviet Union's contributions to the independence struggle and the inappropriateness of the government's failure to establish full relations were highlighted. Despite these efforts, however, a formal diplomatic relationship with Zimbabwe remained an elusive goal in the postindependence period as well.

China, by way of contrast, had established diplomatic relations with Zimbabwe immediately after independence had been proclaimed, and the Chinese were quick to warn Mugabe against Soviet attempts to stir up opposition within Zimbabwe itself. Mugabe's government obviously suspected that the Soviet Union's links with ZAPU meant that it might consider supporting the "out" faction in opposition to the new leadership. ZANU's fears were undoubtedly increased by the continuation of Soviet arms supplies to ZAPU after the announcement of Mugabe's election victory. This clearly explains the lack of a reaction by the Mugabe government to the Soviet Union's unilateral announcement recognizing independent Zimbabwe on 17 April 1980.

Undeterred, the USSR continued its policy of lading praise upon the policies and objectives of the Mugabe government. Singled out for particular mention were efforts in the areas of land redistribution, the transformation of education and health services, and the dissolution of oppressive structures inherited from the Smith regime.[51] The first Soviet journalist to visit Zimbabwe—Boris Asoian of *New Times*—reported on it very favorably, describing it as the most developed state in Black Africa. Other Soviet commentary noted the country's antiracist and antiimperialist foreign policy and its intention to cooperate closely with progressive neighbors such as Mozambique.[52]

By October 1980, however, with the USSR apparently no closer to establishing relations with Zimbabwe, Radio Moscow began broadcasting comments by ZAPU officials criticizing the Mugabe government more sharply for its failure to formalize ties. A Radio Moscow bulletin in Shona (the majority language in Zimbabwe) carried a statement by a ZAPU spokesman, Mark Nziramasanga, which typified these criticisms. The statement read in part:

> In Zimbabwe . . . after obtaining our independence we are surprised to see that the representatives of other countries such as America, Britain, and Western Germany, who had supplied our enemy with weapons and against whom we fought, were among the first to have been granted diplomatic missions in Zimbabwe. To date, the Soviet Union, as far as we know, has

not yet been granted a diplomatic mission in Zimbabwe. . . . Let us not forget our true friends such as the Soviet Union and other socialist countries, who gave us unquestionably substantial aid.[53]

In November 1980, the Moscow Shona service broadcast what was said to be a letter from an African listener in Bulawayo. The letter accused the enemies of the Zimbabwe liberation movement, including the "Western exploiters," of trying "to sow the seeds of hatred between Zimbabwe and the Soviet Union." At the same time Joshua Nkomo, whose relations with Mugabe and ZANU were rapidly deteriorating, spoke out in favor of relations with the USSR and expressed his sorrow at the failure of the government to open such relations. These Soviet and ZAPU comments cannot have come as sweet music to the ears of the ZANU leadership and are likely to have had the opposite effect to that desired.

Right up to the end of 1980, it seems as though ZANU intended to avoid establishing diplomatic ties with Moscow. During the course of the year three Soviet diplomatic missions had been sent to Harare, but each time Zimbabwean Foreign Minister Simon Muzenda refused to receive them. There was still a strong current of feeling among ZANU members that Moscow's links with ZAPU meant that diplomatic ties were out of the question. Enos Nkala, then Minister of Finance and a leading ZANU hardliner on relations with ZAPU, said in Bulawayo that unless Moscow dropped its support for Nkomo, it would not be allowed to open an embassy in Harare.[54] Although other ZANU spokespersons warned against taking Nkala's statements as official policy, they were given further credence when Simon Muzenda denied that the government was snubbing the Soviet Union and GDR, but cited "certain requirements" that needed to be worked out before relations could be established.[55]

These "requirements" related to the nature of Soviet relations with ZAPU. Given the Mugabe government's suspicions about Nkomo's objectives, it wanted to ensure that in the event of a major conflict with ZAPU (of the sort that seemed to be developing around the time of the Entumbane conflicts in November 1980 and February 1981, and of the arms cache finds and the dismissal of Nkomo from the Cabinet in February 1982), the Soviet Union would not take ZAPU's side and recommence the supply of weapons. That ZANU leaders were concerned about Soviet weapons supplies to ZAPU was made clear when Mugabe refused an offer from Nkomo to bring into Zimbabwe Soviet made aircraft and T-34 tanks held by ZAPU in Zambia, arguing that utilization of the arms would make Zimbabwe dependent on the USSR for replacement parts and advisers.

Nonetheless, by the very end of 1980 Mugabe had indicated his willingness to open relations with Moscow. In an interview with the Soviet weekly *New Times* he said, "As for the Soviet Union, we want to be friends with it, and we have repeatedly declared our readiness to establish diplomatic relations. This would help us gain a better understanding of each other and more fairly assess our stands on various issues."[56] Final agreement on the establishment of relations came in February 1981, ten months after independence. The Zimbabwean government issued a statement on 21 February marking the formal establishment of diplomatic relations, stressing that the guidelines for relations were noninterference in each others' affairs. Zimbabwean Foreign Minister Witness Mangwende said the principles for relations included an agreement that the two governments would not enter into any arrangements or negotiations with any organization without prior consultations and the explicit approval of each government. This was a clear reference to Soviet relations with ZAPU.[57] Mangwende has since remarked to the author that Zimbabwe had a few teething problems with the Soviet Union, but that after a while the USSR "got out of its old shell and recognized reality."[58] This had enabled Zimbabwe to consider the establishment of diplomatic relations.

Since the establishment of diplomatic ties, relations between the two states have gradually improved. Evidence of this has been provided by Zimbabwean messages to Soviet leaders on occasions such as the October Revolution anniversary. No such ties had existed prior to the establishment of relations, but the two countries have grown warmer and now exhibit signs of friendliness and a willingness to increase contacts. In his message to Brezhnev on the 1981 anniversary of the October Revolution, Zimbabwean President Banana said that the October Revolution had ushered in a new era for mankind. He added that Zimbabwe was looking forward to the further deepening and strengthening "of our economic, technical, and cultural cooperation for the mutual benefit of our people."[59] Prime Minister Mugabe had earlier said that "The Zimbabwean people responded with profound satisfaction to the high appreciation of our victory in the liberation struggle that was given by Leonid Brezhnev . . . The government and people of Zimbabwe are profoundly satisfied with the establishment of diplomatic relations with the Soviet Union . . . A qualitatively new stage has begun in the development of Soviet–Zimbabwean contacts. We are striving for their further expansion in the interests of both peoples."[60]

Despite these fine words, however, Soviet–Zimbabwean relations remain at a fairly low level. Trade is insignificant; the Soviet Union did not attend the ZIMCORD donors' conference and has not provided any financial or material aid apart from token educational and technical assistance and an offer of one hundred scholarships for Zimbabweans to study in the USSR. On the other hand, agreements have been reached for cooperation in the media and trade union fields. An agreement on exchanges of information and cooperation was signed in Harare on 17 December 1982 between TASS and the Zimbabwe Inter-African News Agency. At the signing ceremony, the chairman of the Zimbabwe Mass Media Trust, Dr. Sadza, remarked that the agreement would strengthen understanding between the two states and help to end Zimbabwe's dependence on the Western mass media, "inherited from the colonial past."[61] During a visit to the Soviet Union in August 1983, the Acting General Secretary of the Zimbabwe Congress of Trade Unions, Abisha Kupfuma, reached agreement with the Soviet All Union Central Council of Trade Unions on Soviet assistance to Zimbabwe in the form of joint trade union training seminars and exchanges of experience.[62] Zimbabwe has also concluded media and trade union agreements with Yugoslavia, Bulgaria, and the GDR.[63]

Since independence, no high-ranking Soviet delegations have visited Zimbabwe and neither have any Zimbabweans above the rank of Deputy Minister visited the Soviet Union. Mugabe has, however, paid two visits to China, and has visited North Korea, Yugoslavia, Romania, and Bulgaria. In 1983 he paid visits to a number of Eastern European countries, including Czechoslovakia, the GDR, and Hungary. During the visits mention was made of the growth in friendly relations on the state-to-state level, and significantly, between ZANU and the ruling Marxist-Leninist party in each state. Much time was spent discussing economic and trade relations as well as international affairs. The general impression given by the visits and the communiques issued at their conclusion was that the Mugabe government was now willing to enter into closer relations with these states even though they had sided with Nkomo and ZAPU during the war. The Zimbabweans seemed particularly interested in economic and technical cooperation with the GDR, which is generally seen as the most technically advanced of the Soviet bloc states.

Following his visit to Eastern Europe, Mugabe expressed his intention to visit the Soviet Union. He announced that he would be visiting Moscow before the end of 1983 at the invitation of the Soviet authorities.[64] This certainly indicates a great improvement in relations with Moscow, and a number of reasons may be suggested to account for it. The first and most important is that it has become evident that the Soviet Union has assured the Mugabe government that it has cut its links with ZAPU. The tone of Soviet statements on Zimbabwe have indicated that the Soviet leadership accepts Mugabe, at least in public, as the political leader of Zimbabwe. Little if any mention is now made of Nkomo by the Soviet media. Soviet radio broadcasts and newspaper reports have been meticulous in their dealings with the ZAPU-ZANU conflicts of the postindependence period, and no adverse commentary was apparent when Nkomo was sacked from the Zimbabwean Cabinet. Generally, the Soviet Union has blamed the problem of rebel activity in Matabeleland on South Africa. It has certainly not suggested, as Nkomo and ZAPU have, that ZANU is trying to crush ZAPU or that it is acting as an ethnically based party rather than a national one.[65]

It would seem, therefore, that after a poor start, relations are gradually improving between the Soviet Union and Zimbabwe. However, given the time it has taken for the two countries to establish cordial relations and the lingering doubts the Zimbabwean government must have about the Soviet Union's true feelings toward it, it is unlikely that the two states will move toward the kind of relationship that exists between the USSR and Mozambique or Angola. What seems far more likely is that Zimbabwe will adopt a position more akin to that of Zambia and Tanzania. These states have been reasonably keen to develop trade and economic ties with the USSR but have generally been wary of the level of Soviet engagement in southern Africa and have tried to ensure that when the Soviet Union becomes involved in African affairs, it does so on African terms.

Soviet Attitudes toward the Zimbabwean Liberation Movements

Throughout its history, the Soviet Union's leaders and theoreticians have stressed the importance of the relationship between the world revolutionary process and the progress of national liberation struggles in developing countries.[66] It is in the light of a general Soviet support for the cause of national liberation that one must view the Soviet approach to the liberation struggle in Zimbabwe.

From very early on, the Soviet Union viewed the situation in Zimbabwe as a struggle between the forces of national liberation, represented by the African nationalists, and the forces of colonialism and imperialism. It unambiguously accepted Nkomo as the leader of the Zimbabwean liberation struggle and ZAPU as the legitimate liberation movement, labeling ZANU soon after its creation as a "splittist" organization. Soviet commentators on African affairs have consistently noted the problem of unity in African movements, both in the pre- and postindependence situations, and stated their belief that unity was essential for the successful conclusion of the fight for liberation and social change.[67]

In ideological terms, the Soviet Union described ZAPU as a "revolutionary-democratic" party which was "leading the struggle of the masses" against colonialism and racism. A revolutionary-democratic party, in Soviet terminology, was described as one which expresses "the interests of the working masses and of all anti-imperialist strata of the population . . . Usually they are broad-based national organizations, essentially national fronts. . . ." Such parties form during the course of a liberation struggle, and their goal is "the elimination of the colonial regime, the winning of national independence and the creation of a sovereign state. In the course of this liberation struggle, a revolutionary nucleus of progressive forces forms; this is the basis for the creation of revolutionary-democratic parties."[68]

It is undeniable that ZAPU was essentially a national front encompassing a wide range of political and social groups and thus could legitimately be termed a revolutionary-democratic party following Soviet practice. However, the Soviet Union was very rigid in its application of theoretical concepts and, once a movement had been labeled as "revolutionary" or "splittist," seemed unable to reassess the nature of the movement. Thus, despite ZANU's evident successes in Zimbabwe, a fact acknowledged by the Marxist-Leninist government in Mozambique, the Soviet Union adamantly refused to accept its legitimacy. On the other hand, evidence of Nkomo's close links with Western governments and multinationals, and the failure of ZAPU to pursue the liberation war in as militant a fashion as ZANU, did nothing to shake Soviet support for ZAPU.

Another notable aspect of the Soviet approach to the liberation war was its view of the appropriate methods of struggle. While advocating armed struggle and guerrilla methods, the Soviet Union placed great emphasis on the supply of sophisticated weaponry. Although it provided political education of a Marxist character to ZAPU cadres, it placed far greater emphasis on the purely military aspects of the struggle. The Chinese, on the other hand, placed greater stress on the need for the politicization of the population and for the creation of a firm popular base before the launching of a guerrilla struggle. The effects of these varying approaches can be clearly seen in the different strategies adopted by ZAPU and ZANU.

The other consistent aspect of the Soviet approach to the Zimbabwe issue was its condemnation of the role of the Western states—notably Britain and the United States—whose interests were described as being bound up with the white supremacist authorities in Rhodesia and whose attempts to settle the Zimbabwe crisis were dismissed as plots to deprive African nationalists of their rights and perpetuate colonialism in southern Africa. The Soviet Union viewed Anglo-American proposed solutions at best as halfhearted and insincere, at worst as aimed at consolidating their interests and preventing the success of the liberation struggle. In the criticisms of the Western plans for a negotiated settlement were implicit criticisms of the nationalist movements for becoming involved in the imperialists' *maneuvers*, as they were generally termed. The Soviet Union continued to denounce Western policies in Zimbabwe right up to the transfer of power to Mugabe's government. Since independence, any indication that Britain or the United States has been unhappy with Zimbabwean policies has been seized upon by the Soviet Union to demonstrate what it believes to be a fundamental conflict of interests between the Western capitalist powers and developing states with radical leaderships such as Zimbabwe.

The Zimbabwean National Movements and the USSR

The approach of the nationalists to relations with the Soviet Union and other socialist states was, in the first place, guided by necessity. During the early years of political activity against the white minority government, the African nationalists appealed to Britain for help in bringing about majority rule. Nkomo and his lieutenants in the ANC, NDP, and ZAPU frequently petitioned in London and at U.N. headquarters, but to no avail. By the time of the banning of ZAPU in September 1962, it had become clear that little declaratory support and no concrete action would come from Britain, other Western states, or the United Nations. The only alternative left was to turn to those willing to provide material aid and training. Although the liberation movements were by no means opposed to the socialist states, neither were they really politically inclined toward them. They were certainly not creations of the Soviet Union or China and sought and accepted aid for purely utilitarian reasons. As Ndabaningi Sithole, the founder of ZANU and its leader for over a decade, has said, "Ideology did not arise, it was a question of necessity. It was imperative that the white regime was brought to its knees and dismantled. This was realized by the USSR and China, but they hoped that ideological commitments would grow."[69]

It is clear from the early policy statements of both ZAPU and ZANU that the movements were not Marxist, though they did project a clear commitment to socialism. In its first independent policy statement, ZANU promised it would "establish a nationalist, democratic, socialist and Pan-Africanist republic."[70] It called for the liquidation of colonialism, settlerism, neocolonialism, and imperialism and announced that major industries would be nationalized. But the policy did allow for the existence of a private economic sector and said it would encourage foreign investment. ZAPU's positions were very similar. In fact, the split within ZAPU was not primarily ideological but focused on the character of Nkomo's leadership. When ZANU was formed it was almost identical to ZAPU in ideological terms but more militant in its approach to implementing policies.

Both movements did, and to a great extent still do, represent a wide spectrum of political views. Both have their radical socialist wings but also their more capitalist-inclined wings. ZANU has become more radical under Mugabe's leadership and now officially espouses Marxism-Leninism. ZAPU—whose leader, Nkomo, is more oriented toward the capitalist market system despite his effusive statements of admiration and support for the Soviet Union during the liberation war—contains a strong radical left-wing. This group has always been more closely associated with the movement's guerrillas and its younger members rather than with the old leadership centered around Nkomo. The radicals were considered to be closer to Moscow during the war, and one of the leading radicals, Jason Z. Moyo, led the ZAPU military branch until his assassination in 1977. Moyo, along with George Silundika (who died while holding the transport portfolio in the first postindependence government), was seen as the key link to Nkomo within the organization. Within the ZAPU guerrilla movement, Alfred "Nikita" Mangena and Dumiso "the Black Russian" Dabengwa seem to have been Moscow's closest friends, as their nicknames indicate. Mangena died during the liberation war and Dabengwa is now being held in detention on suspicion of plotting against the government (and with sending a letter to request Soviet help against "imperialists" in Zimbabwe). This has meant effectively that the radical wing has been deprived of its leaders. With ZAPU's attention now centered on the domestic situation in Zimbabwe, the question of ideology and links with the USSR seem to have faded into the background.

As the liberation struggle intensified during the 1970s, the liberation movements necessarily moved toward closer cooperation with the socialist states, ZAPU with the USSR and GDR and ZANU with China. Both began to adopt more radical approaches to the armed struggle. ZANU, whose military and political tactics were strongly influenced by the Chinese, followed Maoist-style politicization and mobilization tactics and stressed the importance of protracted guerrilla warfare. While not denying the efficacy of guerrilla tactics, ZAPU was more influenced by the Soviet emphasis on sophisticated weaponry and preparation for more conventional warfare when the guerrilla stage had weakened the Smith regime. One of the effects of this dichotomy was that ZANU seemed to become more imbued with Chinese-style methods of political work and adopted a political ideology tinged with Maoist organizational ideas and Marxist/Maoist terminology. Although sections of the ZAPU leadership and part of the guerrilla forces also adopted more radical approaches to the social aspect of the liberation struggle, the movement as a whole was less affected by relations with the USSR than ZANU was by its links with China.[71]

Following the conclusion of the war and the downgrading of links with Moscow, ZAPU's public commitment to socialism declined and Nkomo took to a more capitalist oriented line opposed to the socialist policies declared by the ZANU leaders. Nkomo's basic adherence to a private enterprise based system was demonstrated by ZAPU's accumulation of considerable amounts of property and several substantial businesses in Bulawayo. Although this may have been intended partly to ensure the party's financial position, it was also used by Nkomo to illustrate an alternative model of development to that posited by Mugabe's government.

Since assuming power in 1980, ZANU has continued to stress its adherence to Marxism-Leninism, though it has followed a necessarily pragmatic course in running the economy and has made it clear that Marxism-Leninism is a long-term rather than an immediate prospect for the country.

ZANU adheres to certain aspects of Marxism-Leninism in organizational matters as well, particularly in the area of party organization.[72] However, it cannot be stressed too strongly that ZANU's commitment to the ideology of socialism and to Marxist concepts has been developed through the experiences of the liberation struggle and of the politicization and mobilization of the Zimbabwean people rather than through the importation of foreign ideas. Certainly ZANU was influenced by Chinese methods during the liberation war, but there is no evidence that the commitment to Marxism-Leninism is anything but an indigenous development. It is very noticeable that the Soviet Union makes no references to Zimbabwean adherence to Marxism and only acknowledges that it follows progressive and socialist-inclined policies. This is yet another indication of the Soviet Union's lack of influence over the course of events in Zimbabwe.

The USSR, Zimbabwe, and the Front Line States

An aspect of the relationship between the liberation movements and the USSR that has so far been dealt with only in passing is the role of the Front Line states. These not only provided support for the liberation movements and bases for their cadres and guerrillas but also served as channels for aid from the Soviet Union and other states.

From the split in the Zimbabwean national movement in August 1963 to the birth of independent Zimbabwe in April 1980, there was an evident split between the Front Line states over which was the more effective and legitimate liberation movement. Zambia, partly because of the friendship between President Kenneth Kaunda and Joshua Nkomo, strongly supported ZAPU and failed to recognize ZANU (though it allowed ZANU to operate from Zambia and maintain offices in Lusaka). Tanzania, on the other hand, was much closer to ZANU, and President Nyerere was consistently wary of Nkomo's motives and intentions. At the time of the split in ZAPU, Nyerere had been strongly critical of Nkomo's policy of running the movement from abroad and of his failure to return to Rhodesia at times of great stress for the party. When ZANU was formed, its more militant approach was appreciated by Nyerere and he allowed ZANU to set up camps and training centers in Tanzania. As the struggle escalated during the 1970s, Tanzania and Zambia, and later Mozambique, played a vital role in supporting the guerrilla movements, providing bases and canvassing for support internationally. Both Nyerere and Machel approached the USSR and Cuba to request support for ZANU.

In the later stages of the war, the border between Mozambique and Rhodesia was the main crossing point for the guerrillas and Mozambique played the major role as the base area for the guerrillas of ZANLA. Even before Mozambique's independence, FRELIMO had allowed ZANLA guerrillas to set up bases in FRELIMO-controlled areas and had helped ZANLA prepare for the opening of a new offensive in 1972. As the ZANU offensive launched from Mozambique progressed, the FRELIMO leadership saw increasingly that it was ZANU that was fighting the war and winning the support of the people and that it had an equal or better claim than ZAPU to be recognized as an effective liberation movement. This helps to explain Machel's decision to approach the USSR and Cuba on ZANU's behalf. It is very possible that Machel risked spoiling his increasingly close relationship with the USSR in the late 1970s when he loaned Soviet weapons to ZANU following the USSR's refusal to help the movement.

That the Soviet Union's support for liberation movements was coordinated from Lusaka shows the importance of Front Line states as links between the Zimbabwean nationalists and countries such as the USSR. Most of the leading nationalist groups in the region had their headquarters or a regional office in Lusaka,[73] and at least until Mozambique's and Angola's independence it was the center for Soviet activities in southern Africa. Of all the Front Line state leaders, with the exception of Seretse Khama of Botswana, Kaunda was the most wary of Soviet and Chinese involvement in southern Africa. But when it became clear that the West would not give the necessary support to the liberation movements or put sufficient pressure on Rhodesia or South Africa, Kaunda stressed the necessity of ending minority rule in Rhodesia through armed struggle, with communist support. In an interview with Colin Legum in 1975, Kaunda set out his position regarding the role of the communist powers in southern Africa and in so doing summed up the whole outlook of the Front Line states on Soviet and Chinese intervention:

> The Western Countries have refused to extend a hand of friendship to us by responding positively in Rhodesia. The worst they have feared all along—the factor of communism—must now inevitably be introduced in Zimbabwe because majority rule must now be decided on the battlefield . . . The Western countries should not blame anybody when the Angolan episode repeats itself in Zimbabwe, as the freedom fighters will turn to the Eastern bloc countries, the only ones willing and prepared to help them achieve their freedom.[74]

Conclusion

In conclusion it should be reemphasized that in Zimbabwe the Soviet Union followed a consistent policy of giving support to the cause of national liberation in general and to a particular liberation movement as its chosen "candidate"; a policy that had been followed in Angola, Mozambique, South

Africa, and South West Africa/Namibia. Once it had chosen the movement to support it stuck to it like glue and came to regard offshoots and rival liberation groups as splittist. The USSR firmly opposed the extension of Chinese influence in southern Africa, and as ZANU was both a movement that had broken away from ZAPU, the USSR's ally in Zimbabwe, and a movement in receipt of Chinese aid, it was doubly damned in Soviet eyes. ZANU was dismissed as neither a legitimate representative of the liberation forces nor a viable fighting force. That the USSR made a mistake in taking this view and was inhibited by its dogmatic approach to the problem from gaining a clearer picture of the relative standing of the movements and their chances of success is very clear.

Since independence, the Soviet Union has had to adjust its assessments of political events in Zimbabwe. For all intents and purposes, the USSR has now dropped its support for ZAPU (at least overtly) and recognized that it must make the best of things and seek to cooperate with the Mugabe government. It now portrays this government and its policies very favorably in its media comments, though it has not made great efforts to do more than establish normal diplomatic relations. Although it has offered a few scholarships, trade and aid are almost nonexistent and do not seem likely to increase dramatically in the future. The Soviet Union is no doubt still wary of Mugabe's friendly relationship with China and is inhibited from taking a more active attitude toward Zimbabwe by the evident coolness of the regime toward closer relations with the USSR.

For their part, Zimbabwe's leaders seem happy with what might be described as "normal diplomatic relations" with the USSR. Although the ZANU leadership denied taking a cool attitude toward the Soviet Union in the immediate postindependence period, it was very clear that this was the case. What the ZANU government wanted from the USSR was an indication that it had ceased to support ZAPU and was prepared to accept the ZANU-dominated government as the only legitimate representative of Zimbabwe. Now that suspicion about Soviet motives has subsided, ZANU appears to view the USSR as just another state—though of course a very powerful and influential one—with which it would be useful to have friendly relations.

The future of Soviet-Zimbabwean relations is thus likely to be an unexciting one for the time being (it could of course change dramatically with a change in government in Zimbabwe or a change of leadership within ZANU) as both sides seem relatively satisfied with the present state of affairs. Whether or not the USSR would like greater influence in Zimbabwe, however, the ultimate success or failures of its policies will be determined significantly by the attitude of the Zimbabweans. The attitude of Zimbabwean nationalist leaders throughout the liberation war, whether Nkomo, Sithole, or Mugabe, was that Soviet or Chinese support was necessary for the conduct of the struggle, a struggle whose final aim was the liberation of Zimbabwe and not the formation of a pro- or anti-Soviet state. The overall Zimbabwean attitude to the USSR—and a political moral of the protracted liberation struggle as a whole—is summed up in the words of Ndabaningi Sithole, written when he was still in the forefront of the nationalist movement:

> A great question is being posed by the great powers. Whither Africa? West or East? This question is often asked as if there was nowhere else Africa can go: Either she goes West and not East, or she goes East and not West. This attitude is much to be regretted in that it seems to disregard altogether that free and independent Africa has a right to her own ways . . . The whole purpose of African nationalism was not to destroy Western imperialism in order to make room for the Eastern bloc, or to deliver free and independent Africa back to the West. The purpose of African nationalism was to create a free and independent Africa with a distinct posture of its own, befriending both the West and the East but bowing down to neither.[75]

Notes

1. One exception was British Foreign Minister Lord Carrington, who had been closely involved in the successful negotiations for an end to the conflict in Zimbabwe, and who strongly denied that Mugabe "was a Marxist puppet of the Soviet Union." See *The Economist*, 16 August 1980, and the account of proceedings in Parliament on 4 March 1980, cited in *Africa Research Bulletin* 17, no. 3 (1980):5622.

2. Colin Legum, ed., *Africa Contemporary Record 1980-81* (London: Rex Collings, 1981), p. B934. (Hereafter cited as ACR).

3. Richard Gibson, *African Liberation Movements* (London: Oxford University Press, 1972), p. 156.

4. Bruce D. Larkin, *China and Africa 1949-70* (Berkeley: University of California Press, 1971), p. 47.

5. Ibid., p. 49.

6. This is suggested by John Day in *International Nationalism: The Extra-Territorial Relations of Southern Rhodesian African Nationalists* (London: Routledge and Kegan Paul, 1967), pp. 96 and 102. It was confirmed by Ndabaningi Sithole (National Chairman of ZAPU until the formation of ZANU in 1963, and then President of ZANU until 1975) in an interview with the author in Harare, 13 April 1982.

7. Day, *International Nationalism*, p. 102. Day's account provides details of visits by ZAPU leaders.

8. Sithole in conversation with the author.

9. Gibson, *African Liberation Movements*, p. 161.

10. William Scott Thompson, *Ghana's Foreign Policy 1957-1966* (Princeton, N.J.: Princeton University Press, 1969), pp. 225-226. This contention is supported by Nathan Shamuyarira, a direct participant in the liberation struggle and now Zimbabwean Minister of Information, in *Crisis in Rhodesia* (London: Andre Deutsch, 1965), pp. 202-203.

11. Southern Rhodesia Ministry of Information, Immigration and Tourism, *No Hide-Out* (Salisbury: Government Printer, 1966).

12. David Martin and Phyllis Johnson, *The Struggle for Zimbabwe* (Salisbury: Zimbabwe Publishing House, 1981), p. 11.

13. Ibid.

14. Martin and Johnson, *The Struggle for Zimbabwe*, pp. 23-24, and interview with William Ndangana, ZANLA Chief of Operations and ZANU Central Committee member, in Harare, 16 April 1982.

15. Interview with Ndangana.

16. Martin and Johnson, *The Struggle for Zimbabwe*, p. 11.

17. Interview with Joshua Mpofu, former member of ZANU, presently a Research Fellow in Political Science at the University of Zimbabwe, in Harare, 7 April 1982.

18. Anthony R. Wilkinson, *Southern Rhodesia: The New Politics of Revolution* (Harmondsworth: Penguin, 1976), p. 230.

19. Gibson, *African Liberation Movements*, p. 164, and Wilkinson, *Southern Rhodesia*, p. 230. According to Nathan Shamuyarira, Chinese aid to ZAPU was suspended in 1965. See Nathan Shamuyarira, *National Liberation Through Self-Reliance in Rhodesia, 1956-1972* (Ph.D. dissertation, Princeton University, 1976).

20. Larkin, *China and Africa*, p. 187.

21. Interview with Mayor Urimbo, ZANU Chief Political Commissar and Central Committee member, in Harare, 16 April 1982.

22. The movements in question were the MPLA (Angola), PAIGC (Cape Verde), FRELIMO (Mozambique), MOLINACO (Comoro Islands), SWAPO (Namibia), ANC (South Africa), and ZAPU.

23. Larkin, *China and Africa*, p. 187.

24. See, for example, V. Ryabtsev, "Rhodesia: Racialist Hide-Out," *International Affairs* (Moscow) 1 (January 1966):99-102. See also the commentary from Radio Moscow, 30 May 1977. (This and all other radio and news agency sources, unless otherwise noted, are taken from the BBC Monitoring Service, Summary of World Broadcasts.)

25. Martin and Johnson, *The Struggle for Zimbabwe*, p. 12. This viewpoint was confirmed in conversation with William Ndangana, Mayor Urimbo, and Mark Dube, former ZANLA Chief of Training and now a Zimbabwean Deputy Minister, in Harare, 16 April 1982.

26. Interview with George Rutanhire, a ZANLA guerrilla and political commissar during the liberation war, and currently Deputy Minister of Youth and Sports, in Harare, 15 April 1982.

27. Interview with Urimbo.
28. Interviews with Urimbo and Dube.
29. *The Daily Telegraph*, 8 February 1979.
30. *ACR 1978-79*, p. A69.
31. Ibid., p. A19.
32. Martin and Johnson, *The Struggle for Zimbabwe*, p. 317. The Zimbabwean Foreign Minister, Witness Mangwende, told the author that "ZANU never got even a single penny from the Soviet Union." Interview in Harare, 16 April 1982.
33. Interview with David Martin, former *Observer* correspondent, presently head of the Zimbabwe Publishing House, in Harare, 14 April 1982.
34. Fred Halliday and Maxine Molyneaux, *The Ethiopian Revolution* (London: Verso, 1981), p. 267.
35. Colin Legum, "Southern Africa: The Year of the Whirlwind," *ACR 1975-76*, p. A19.
36. Interview with Joshua Mpofu.
37. Ibid.
38. *ACR 1981-82*, p. 863.
39. *Pravda*, 30 July 1979.
40. Martin and Johnson, *The Struggle for Zimbabwe*, pp. 305-307, and Colin Legum, "The Continuing Crisis in Southern Africa," *ACR 1978-79*, p. A19.
41. *Izvestiia*, 5 May 1978.
42. Radio Moscow, 6 August 1979.
43. Radio Moscow, 19 October 1979.
44. *Pravda*, 28 October 1979.
45. *Pravda*, 19 December 1979.
46. *Izvestiia*, 22 February 1980.
47. *Pravda*, 2 March 1980.
48. TASS, 5 March 1980, cited in *Africa Research Bulletin* 17, no. 3 (1980):5623.
49. *ACR 1979-80*, p. A28.
50. Interviews with journalists based in Harare.
51. See, for example, Georgii Voitsekhovskii's commentary on Radio Moscow World Service in English, 17 March 1980.
52. Radio Moscow in Zulu, 4 November 1980.
53. Radio Moscow in Shona, 16 October 1980.
54. *ACR 1980-81*, p. B937.
55. Radio Johannesburg, 4 October 1980.
56. *New Times* no. 45 (1980).
57. Radio Salisbury, 21 February 1981.
58. Interview with Witness Mangwende.
59. *The Herald* [Harare], 7 November 1981.

60. TASS in English, 27 April 1981.
61. TASS in Russian, 17 December 1982.
62. Radio Harare, 14 August 1983.
63. Keith Somerville, "Zimbabwe's Economic Relations with the Socialist States," *African Business*, July 1982.
64. Radio Harare, 29 June 1980.
65. See, for example, Aleksey Nikolayev's commentary on the 1980 Bulawayo clashes on Radio Moscow in Shona, 18 November 1980, and Radio Peace and Progress's commentary on Pretoria's attempts to destabilize Zimbabwe, 18 January 1983.
66. See John J. Dziak, *The Soviet Union and the National Liberation Movements: An Examination of the Development of a Revolutionary Strategy* (Ph.D. dissertation, Georgetown University, 1971).
67. Nikolay Gavrilov, "Africa: Classes, Parties and Politics," *International Affairs* (Moscow) 7 (July 1966):39–40.
68. "Communists, Revolutionary Democrats and the Noncapitalist Path of Development in African Countries," *Voprosy istorii KPSS* (October 1975), as cited in *Current Digest of the Soviet Press* 27, no. 51:2–5.
69. Interview with Sithole.
70. ZANU policy statement, Salisbury, 21 August 1963 as cited in Christopher Nyangoni and Gideon Nyandoro, eds., *Zimbabwe Independence Movements* (London: Rex Collings, 1979).
71. Interviews with Sithole, Urimbo, Ndangana, and Rutanhire.
72. See "Ideological and Revolutionary Education," *Zimbabwe News* [ZANU] March/July 1981, pp. 21–22.
73. See Douglas G. Anglin and Timothy M. Shaw, *Zambia's Foreign Policy: Studies in Diplomacy and Dependence* (Boulder, Colo.: Westview, 1979), pp. 238–239.
74. *The Observer*, 15 February 1975.
75. Ndabaningi Sithole, *African Nationalism* (London: Oxford University Press, 1968), p. 182.

11

The Soviet Union and Africa: The Dynamics and Dilemmas of Involvement

Mark V. Kauppi

Explanations abound concerning what has motivated Soviet policy toward Africa since the early 1970s. One does not have to rely on formulations that emphasize some sort of carefully crafted master plan to explain Soviet involvement on the continent.[1] More convincing explanations emphasize, to varying degrees, the congruence in the 1970s of a number of factors:

> The collapse of the Portuguese empire which accompanied the revolution in Portugal
>
> The overthrow of Emperor Haile Selassie in Ethiopia by radical military officers who required support to consolidate control
>
> An improvement in the Soviet Union's power projection capabilities as part of the changing "correlation of forces" that gave the Soviets the ability—if not self-proclaimed right—to intervene in conflicts far from its shores
>
> Soviet perceptions of weak U.S. resolve following the American defeat in Vietnam
>
> Promotion of the Soviet Union's political-security interests (particularly via access to maritime facilities for its expanding navy) as befits a superpower with global interests
>
> The implementation of the technique of cooperative intervention whereby Soviet logistical support is combined with Cuban combat troops and East German security personnel
>
> African leaders requesting outside powers to come to their aid against internal and external enemies.[2]

Underlying all of these factors is a long-term trend that has allowed the Soviets to take advantage of these developments, generally in a reactive manner: the continual political, economic, and social instability that plagues virtually all Third World countries. These indigenous forces cannot be blamed on Moscow. Certainly the Soviets, as well as other outside powers, at times have exacerbated various situations in their search for influence or out of a desire to supplant a rival. But Moscow has not been the primary source of such instability, nor would Soviet disengagement from the continent end such troubles.³ Western powers would do well not to give the Soviets credit for revolutions and coups Moscow does not instigate and which the Soviets have trouble controlling. Otherwise, there is a danger of contributing to African perceptions that overestimate Soviet strength, encouraging the very situation the West would prefer to avoid: African dependency on the USSR.

Although this combination of factors has allowed the Soviets to be opportunistic in the 1970s, these same forces also have been the source of a number of dilemmas, constraints, trade-offs, and unintended consequences for Moscow. If one views events in Africa from only a bipolar, superpower perspective, seeing the continent as a strategic chessboard, there is a danger of underestimating these problems. Conversely, it is also a mistake to ignore the reality of superpower competition in the Third World. It cannot be wished away. This chapter discusses how the complexities and dynamics of contemporary African realities and international politics have restricted the further advance of Soviet influence in Africa in recent years. The conclusion briefly discusses Soviet prospects on the continent. While specifically relating to the Soviet experience, certain points in this chapter will also hopefully be germane to those interested in American involvement in Africa.

Underlying this analysis are two assumptions. The first has already been mentioned: any attempt to understand Soviet involvement in the Third World involves an appreciation of short- and long-term factors and trends operating at the international, regional, and local levels. The challenge is to understand their interrelationships and their relative importance. In a chapter of this length, this is more of a professed desire than an attainable goal. Second, it is a mistake to focus solely on particular Soviet actions (such as in Angola in 1975 and Ethiopia in 1977) if this means slighting the *consequences* of these actions over time. In other words, one must be aware of not only the more spectacular Soviet initiatives in Africa, but how the nature of Moscow's involvement has changed over the years.⁴

Dichotomous Labels Are Misleading

Pro-Moscow versus Pro-West

There is a tendency—particularly pronounced in American news magazines—to label African regimes as either pro-Moscow or pro-West. Very often the text of an article is accompanied by a map of the continent with Soviet client states shaded in various hues of red, the color determined by the perceived level of dependency on Moscow.⁵ Although such dichotomous labels might have some initial utility, they tend to obscure more than they reveal by ignoring the complex and convoluted nature of African politics. As a generalization, the foreign policies of African states and movements are not so much pro-Moscow, pro-Washington, pro-French, or pro any other foreign power, but are rather driven by the natural desire of elites to gain or maintain control over their respective countries. This holds true no matter what a government's or guerrilla organization's ideological orientation happens to be. With the decolonization of Africa completed, it tends to be African leaders themselves who invite in outside advisers and supporters for their own political-military purposes.[6] Expediency is more often than not the raison d'etre for a particular foreign policy alignment, not some desire to be considered pro-Moscow or pro-Washington. Several examples illustrate this point.

Angola. Jonas Savimbi, the charismatic leader of the National Union for the Total Independence of Angola (UNITA) who has continued to fight against the Popular Movement for the Liberation of Angola (MPLA) since the latter seized control of the government in 1975, was an admirer of Mao in the early 1960s (and even met with the Chinese leader in 1964). But he dropped the Marxist rhetoric when the 1974 coup in Portugal promised decolonization; then he turned to Europe for support which he lost in 1975 and struck a deal with South Africa which has allowed Savimbi to continue his war against the MPLA.[7] Furthermore, what is one to make of the rather odd coalitions in which UNITA and the National Front for the Liberation of Angola (FNLA- the third group involved in the 1975-1976 power struggle) were supported by the United States, China, Zaire, North Korea, Romania, and India, while the MPLA was backed by the USSR, Cuba, Sweden, Denmark, Yugoslavia, and Nigeria?[8] Are such labels as "pro-communist" or "pro-West" more instructive in the Angolan case than the fact that the support bases of the FNLA, MPLA, and UNITA tend to be found in three different Angolan tribal groups?

Chad. In July of 1983, the Reagan Administration authorized $10 million for military supplies on the grounds that the government in N'Djamena was threatened by a Libyan-backed insurgency. A similar operation was carried out in November 1981 by the French and the Americans to aid in the formation of an Organization of African Unity (OAU) peacekeeping force. The purpose of the force was to support the president at the time, Goukouni Oueddei, and prevent his possible overthrow by Libya. But in a strange reversal, Goukouni is now the very Libyan-backed rebel leader who is to be defeated by the 1983 U.S. military aid program! This confusing civil war began over twenty years ago, and during that time at least eleven different factions and some six military forces have fought for control of this desolate country, all at one time or another supported by Libya. The current struggle involves two long time rivals from the Moslem northern part of the country. The factions present themselves as pro-Libyan or pro-Western depending on their needs and the political-military circumstances at a particular point in time. Ideology is irrelevant, allegiances to outside powers transient.[9]

The Horn. In the early 1970s, Soviet arms helped to transform Somalia into a regional power. With the military takeover in Addis Ababa in 1974 by radical officers, the United States, Ethiopia's traditional ally, could no longer bring itself to arm a government bent on repressing secessionist movements in the Ogaden and Eritrean regions—not to mention other elements of its own population. The Soviets stepped in to fill the arms gap and, unable to calm the traditional enmity between Somalia and Ethiopia, threw its support behind Ethiopia. Another interesting reversal thus occurred: Marxist Somalia expelled Soviet advisers and now became an ally of the United States, and Ethiopia became the protege of the USSR.[10]

Sudan. Events in Khartoum over the years also illustrate how questionable it is to assume any sort of permanence to the idea of a regime being consistently pro-West or pro-East. In the 1960s, Sudan was considered to be strongly oriented to the West, only to move temporarily to a pro-Soviet position following the 1969 coup whose leaders hoped to establish a socialist system along the lines of Gamal Abd al-Nasir's Egypt. But a communist-supported coup attempt in 1971 and a July 1976 Libyan supported invasion led President Ja'far al-Numayri to move toward the West. Libyan threats, a troubled relationship with Ethiopia, and internal problems provided the background to the expulsion of ninety Soviet military advisers and half the diplomatic mission in May 1977. In April of the following year, the United States granted the government in Khartoum a military aid package which included twelve F-5 fighters. Today Numayri is deemed one of Washington's strongest allies and a bulwark against further Communist and Libyan infiltration and influence in northeast Africa.[11]

It should also be noted that in some cases, a movement or a government becomes pro-Moscow primarily because of actions taken by Western powers. The best example involves the regime of the late President Ahmed Sékou Touré of Guinea in which the key to understanding events in that country is to be found in the French, not Soviet, connection. Granted independence in 1958, Touré's nationalist rhetoric offended Charles DeGaulle, resulting in an order from Paris to strip Guinea bare upon the French pullout. DeGaulle pressured Western allies to shun also Touré's new regime, and predictably the government in Conakry turned toward the Soviet Union for aid. In 1975 Guinea was even used as a staging post for Cuban troops being airlifted to Angola, but since that time—for a number of reasons soon to be discussed—Touré gradually turned to the West.

Another case would be the Congo where there are currently about 250 Soviet military advisers and 2000 Cuban troops. As one Western diplomat has stated, "The Congolese leaders ran into the arms of the Russians soon after independence because of a total lack of interest from the West toward a country in political turmoil and deprived then of strategic raw materials."[12]

Ideological Labels

For some observers of Soviet actions in the Third World, the terms *socialism* and *communism* are literally and figuratively red flags. The danger, of course, is in assuming that ideological systems and concepts developed out of the Western experience maintain their original meaning and connotations in quite different contexts. The African experience shows this to be a highly dubious proposition.

First of all, it is useful to distinguish between socialism as an ideology of liberation and socialism as the guiding doctrine of a state. As an ideology of liberation, socialism is a pragmatic choice and a particularly powerful tool for political mobilization when linked to the even more powerful ideology of nationalism.

Second, even if the leadership of a newly independent country is committed to building a self-proclaimed socialist state, there is a tremendous gap between the rhetoric and the reality of what is actually being achieved. The Soviets themselves realize this and have no illusions. Hence, in the 1970s the term *socialist orientation* was coined to describe such Third World states. A key element involves an actual Soviet and allied presence in a developing country in order to cement ties with Moscow and to help in the eventual attainment of a truly socialist state.[13] Creation of a vanguard party is also necessary in order to institutionalize socialism, although the Soviets have come to recognize that military elites can play a progressive role.[14]

Third, and most important of all, the Soviet Union and African states tend to have very different conceptions of what constitutes socialism in practice. It cannot be too strongly emphasized that all self-proclaimed African socialists or Marxists have uniformly insisted that their brand of socialism develops out of indigenous conditions and particular historical circumstances that do not necessarily parallel those found in the Soviet experience. The adoption of these ideologies is not the result of Moscow's imposition. This holds true for even such self-proclaimed Marxist-Leninist states as Angola, Mozambique, and Ethiopia. As Marina Ottaway has noted, "Socialism in Ethiopia and Mozambique is not simply the transplant of a foreign ideology. It reflects a complex process of social, political, and economic change shaped not only by ideological choices but also by power struggles and hard economic necessity."[15] Consequently, not only is it incorrect to assume that socialism has the same connotations in Moscow and on the African continent, but the term has different meanings within Africa itself. The "ujamaa Socialism" preached by Julius Nyerere of Tanzania and Zambia's "humanism," for example, leave much to be desired from the Soviet perspective, and in form and content differ from the Marxism of Mozambique.[16]

Nor do Marxists, once in power, simply follow the dictates of Moscow due to an ideological affinity. Support of Soviet calls for anti-imperialist policies does not mean African leaders agree with all of Moscow's foreign policies. Similarly, having finally dismantled the old colonial regimes, there is no desire to replace Western hegemony with Soviet hegemony. Nationalism and nonalignment, which have so frustrated Western policymakers, also have bedeviled the Soviet Union. Without recognition of the paramount role played by pragmatism in the policy calculations of even the most radical African leaders, it is extremely difficult to make any sense of the mosaic of African politics. Some African leaders have become quite adept at mouthing the correct ideological phrases, depending on whether they are wooing the East or the West for economic and military assistance.[17] Choosing allies based solely on the criterion of ideological affinity—a Manichean approach to the Third World—can result in failed policies and setbacks for both the West and Moscow.

Marxism and Capitalism

One of the more interesting aspects of the African political scene has been the willingness—if not eagerness—of socialist and Marxist regimes to maintain, strengthen, or re-establish economic ties with the capitalist West. If anything, this trend has accelerated over the past five years. Perhaps the most bizarre juxtaposition is found in Angola where Cuban troops protect the Gulf Oil operation in the Cabinda enclave from rebels supposedly sympathetic to the West. The reasons for recent African interest in attracting Western investment and foreign multinationals stem from a number of factors which have contributed to economic chaos if not virtual economic collapse. In southern Africa, failed socialist policies have led to food and other consumer shortages, guerrilla operations in Mozambique and Angola have aggravated economic conditions, and government leaders also have had to deal with the worst drought in fifty years.[18]

In Angola, after some 350,000 Portuguese left, the country faced an illiteracy rate of 90 percent, a skilled labor shortage, and very few individuals competent enough to run the country once the MPLA came to power. Dissatisfaction with the government has grown over the past two years as poor economic management has contributed to the virtual breakdown of the food distribution system. Not only have the Soviets provided very little economic aid—they have bred resentment by demanding that arms transfers and the cost of supporting over 20,000 Cuban troops be paid for by oil revenues. Nevertheless, as one Angolan academic has stated, his country cannot deal with its problems, "So what do you think would happen if we cut our lifeline to the one country that's been an ally from the start?"[19]

In the People's Republic of the Congo, a self-proclaimed Marxist state, no less than *The Wall Street Journal* gives the regime a better free market rating than neighboring "capitalist" Zaire. Mobutu's regime is described as a "purportedly free capitalist country . . . which is in fact a totalitarian state that seeks to control all economic activity above the subsistence level." This is in comparison to "the purportedly communist country of Congo, which in fact has discovered the benefits of the free market (and appears to be) largely free of the corruption and routine restriction that plague Zaire."[20] Since the 1979 coup by current President Denis Sassou N'Guesso, the Congo has increasingly turned to the West to develop its economy (particularly its oil reserves) and by 1982 the United States was the Congo's largest trading partner.

Mozambique has suffered an economic decline due to natural disasters, border conflicts, guerrilla warfare, a failing socialist agricultural system, and lack of management skills.[21] The economy is worse than at the time of independence, and this country of twelve million persons and twice the size of California has a per capita gross national product of $140. In 1980 the government began to experiment with a carefully controlled mixture of private and state enterprises and expressed a desire to increase ties with the West.[22] Mozambique's leader, Samora Machel, reiterated in 1983 his desire to increase economic contact with the West and began to seek openly U.S. investment in the country's energy resources as well as continue to express interest in the European Economic Community's Lomé Convention and its trade benefits.[23] The year 1983 also witnessed a new emphasis on small farms and private enterprise in an attempt to improve the day-to-day standard of living. As Machel stated, "We must end our hostile attitude to family and private enterprise."[24] Furthermore, Maputo's government leaders as well as those in Luanda have complained about the level and quality of economic assistance from the Soviet Union, although they continue to profess adherence to Moscow and Marxist doctrine. Part of the reason for such loyalty is certainly due to threatening guerrilla activity and South African military incursions which increase Mozambique's dependence on the Soviet Union. The country's foreign policy, therefore, is predicated upon maintaining old friendships and expanding the circle of new ones.[25]

In Guinea, Marxist rhetoric, diplomatic isolation, human rights violations, and disastrous economic policies were the hallmarks of Sékou Touré's reign. An abrupt reorientation of foreign and economic policies began, however, in the late 1970s. Several reasons for these changes have been given. First, Touré reportedly became disenchanted with the amount of

Soviet economic aid, Moscow's invasion of Afghanistan, Soviet overfishing in Guinea's territorial waters, and the amount of income derived from a Soviet-run bauxite mine. As a result, he ended Soviet reconnaissance flights and turned down a request to develop a naval warship base at Conakry. Second, a sense of internal and external security has allowed Touré to improve relations with France, Senegal, and the Ivory Coast and to be less fearful of a Western presence in his country. Third—and most important of all—the socialist experiment of some twenty-five years has been deemed a failure in this mineral-rich country. Touré's desire to receive economic aid from the West resulted in his visit to Washington, D.C. in 1983 where he urged American businessmen to invest in Guinea.[26]

In Ethiopia—a country of 32 million people—the economy is staggering due to oil import bills, diminished returns on coffee exports, and the maintenance of black Africa's largest army (300,000) which has had to deal with secessionist movements in Eritrea, conflicts with Somalia in the Ogaden, and internal dissent. The Soviets have even become a convenient scapegoat for all that has gone wrong with the economy, an experience to which Americans and Europeans can relate. As a result of its seemingly insurmountable problems, Marxist Ethiopia has asked for Western aid, U.S. investment, and food relief to deal with a widening famine.[27]

The former Portuguese colony of Guinea-Bissau is also following these economic trends. After a 1982 internal power struggle, the country has moved away from Soviet-style economic management to one seeking Western aid and investment. In March 1983 it was granted a $13.1 million loan from the World Bank to engage in petroleum exploration and hopefully to interest Western oil companies in production deals.[28]

In Equatorial Guinea in 1979-1980, the Soviets lost the use of a communications and intelligence post as well as fishing rights. The expired fishing agreement had allowed the Soviets to keep 75 percent of their catch and sell the remainder to the host government for hard currency. Similar exploitive fishing agreements had been negotiated with Guinea-Bissau, Mozambique, and Guinea and have resulted in ill feelings toward Moscow.[29]

David Rockefeller—certainly no fan of Marxist economic doctrine—toured a number of African socialist countries in 1982 and concluded that left-wing regimes were disillusioned with Soviet aid and sought closer ties to the West. He commented, "I really am convinced that socialism for most of the African leaders I talked with meant a very specialized thing and has little to do with Marxism."[30] Although a questionable statement, it is a fact that radical and socialist regimes are attempting to benefit from increased economic ties with the West. Besides the countries already discussed, others include Benin, Cape Verde Islands, Mali, São Tomé and Principe, Ghana, Madagascar, Mauritius, and the Seychelles.[31]

It should also be noted that this turn to the West for economic aid is not out of some new-found desire to become politically aligned with capitalist countries. It is born of desperation. Twenty-two of the world's poorest states are found in black Africa, the region has the highest death rate in the world, during the 1970s economic output per person rose slower in sub-Saharan Africa than in any other part of the earth, and in eight states the economies actually shrank. Only nine black African states can feed themselves, and in seven others agricultural output is declining. Prospects for the rest of the 1980s are even worse at a time when spending on weapons continues ever upwards. (See table 11-1.) The Soviets have basically provided arms, military advisers, and a small amount of economic aid in return for increased self-esteem, minerals, fishing rights, and some votes in the United Nations. But the African states need capital, technology, aid, and access to markets, which only the West can provide on the required scale. It is for these pragmatic reasons that socialist and Marxist leaders find it necessary to plead for Western economic assistance.[32]

Reputation for Opportunism

While observers of the Soviet Union may differ as to the fundamental and underlying motivations of Soviet foreign policy, virtually everyone agrees that Moscow has been opportunistic with respect to its actions in the Third World. Wherever there is instability and the potential to exploit anti-Western sentiment, the Soviets can be expected to take at least tentative steps to enhance their own position. Most often, Kremlin leaders are granted grudging admiration for what is generally seen as wily and astute political maneuvering, and it is bemoaned that the United States cannot play the game equally well.

The problem with such a perspective is that it ignores placing a particular Soviet action in a broader African and historical context. The cumulative impact over time of such opportunistic actions is actually to tarnish the image of Moscow as a reliable ally and reduce the credibility of its claims of trustworthiness. This observation concerning Soviet policy applies to movements trying to gain power or governments trying to hold on to it. By way of example, the Egyptian, Algerian, and Sudanese communist parties all have been ordered in the past by the Soviet leadership to cooperate with their respective governments and to compromise their revolutionary goals. Such marching orders have caused Third World communist parties unending problems and more often than not have had disastrous consequences for them and done little for Moscow's standing in the eyes of Third World governments. Similarly, arming the Ugandan dictator Idi Amin with Soviet and Czechoslovakian weapons (via Libya) also did not enhance Moscow's image in Africa. Lenin certainly imbued Marxist ideology with a degree of

Table 11-1
Relative Burden of Military Expenditures[a]

Military Expenditures as % of GNP (1980)	GNP per Capita (1980)				
	Less than $200	$200–499	$500–999	$1000–2999	$3000 and over
10% and over		Mauritania			
5–9.99%	Ethiopia Guinea-Bissau Chad (1979)	Somalia Egypt Tanzania	Zimbabwe Morocco		
2–4.99%	Upper Volta Burundi Mali Rwanda	Madagascar Kenya (75) Angola Mozambique (78) Cape Verde Zaire Sudan Senegal Togo Benin	Equatorial Guinea (75) Congo Zambia Botswana Swaziland	South Africa Nigeria Algeria	
1–1.99%		Guinea (75) Central African Republic Malawi Liberia Sierra Leone	Uganda Cameroon Sao Tome and Principe	Tunisia Ivory Coast	Libya
Less than 1%		Lesotho Gambia, The	Ghana Mauritius		Gabon

Source: U.S. Arms Control and Disarmament Agency, *World Military Expenditures and Arms Transfers 1971–1980*, March 1983, Washington, D.C., p. 28.

[a]Countries listed in columns in descending order by level of Military Expenditures/GNP. ME/GNP ratios reflect 1980 data with the exceptions noted by years.

flexibility, but the obvious manipulation of local communist parties, their subordination to the dictates of *Realpolitik,* and support for a bloodthirsty tyrant loathed by virtually every African leader, tends to associate the term *opportunism* with *cynicism.*

A much more important decision taken by the Soviets, however, involved switching their support from Somalia to Ethiopia in 1977–1978 when it became apparent Moscow could no longer maintain the goodwill of both the Siad Barre regime in Mogadiscio and Colonel Mengistu Haile Mariam's revolutionary government in Addis Ababa. This action is usually portrayed as the result of a calculated and rational decision-making process in which Moscow deemed Ethiopia—a country with a larger population and a strategically better location—a more important client state. Such thinking might have actually occurred. But what one must not overlook is that: (1) the decision had to be made as the result of a Soviet failure as mediator to reconcile the two opponents; (2) the decision has undoubtedly raised doubts in the minds of many African leaders as to Moscow's reliability as an ally. While the Soviets tried to justify their switch of support on the ideological grounds that the Mengistu regime had more potential to develop into a truly Marxist-Leninist state, this conveniently overlooks the fact that the Soviets now were forced to turn their backs on the Cuban-trained Marxist Eritrean People's Liberation Front (EPLF) which they had previously supported. Furthermore, Arab leaders on the continent certainly took note that the policy reversal involved dropping a basically Arab-Moslem regime (Somalia) for a black African government. Organization of African Unity (OAU) protestations to the contrary, this north–south split is a fact of African life.

In the United States it is often argued that unless the American government follows a consistent policy of supporting its allies, Washington will develop the reputation of being unreliable. This will eventually have negative consequences for American foreign policy and international standing. Consistency, therefore, is essential. If there is any validity to this line of argument, then the same logic should apply to Soviet foreign policy. Segmented thinking, in which we view each Soviet action in isolation and award Moscow a plus or a minus depending on the relative degree of success or failure in a particular case, is a mistake. To think in this way ignores the cumulative impact of Moscow's decisions on African perceptions of the degree of reliability that can be expected from the Soviet Union. This factor must certainly be taken into consideration by African leaders if they are contemplating inviting a Soviet presence (even if for short-run mutual benefit) into their country: Will today's ally be tomorrow's enemy? Opportunism, in other words, has tactical advantages as well as potential costs.

Presence Does Not Equal Control

There is a tendency—most often found in the popular press but in academic articles as well—to equate a Soviet-Cuban presence in a Third World country with various degrees of Soviet control. If Soviet advisers and technicians or Cuban troops are dispatched to Africa, the worst-case analysis is that they are the real exercisers of power in the country, or at the least the patrons upon whom their proteges must rely in order to stay in power. Friendship treaties with regimes in Angola (1976), Mozambique (1977), Ethiopia (1978), and the Congo (1981) and verbal assurances of support that emphasize fraternal ties, anti-imperialist alliances, and socialist unity simply provide evidence of this dependent relationship.

With regards to this popular conception that Soviet presence means control, several observations are in order. First, actually determining the extent of Soviet control in any country is not an easy task; basic information is difficult to come by. How are the concepts of control to be operationalized? What are the indicators?

Second, it is necessary to differentiate between Soviet control of a regime and Soviet control over an entire country. Moscow's experiences in Eastern Europe and Afghanistan suggest that a large military presence is directly related to a high degree of political influence, if not dependency, of a regime on Moscow. In Africa there also seems to be a relationship between the presence of Eastern bloc advisers and Cuban troops and the local regime's reliance on the Soviet Union. But such a presence could, paradoxically, reflect the tenuousness of Moscow's control over the country as a whole. This certainly seems to be the case in Ethiopia, and, in particular, Angola where insurgent groups continue to pose serious problems for the governments in power.

The strong—as Kenneth Waltz has pointed out with respect to the use of force—are those who rarely have to rely on it.[33] The utilization of force is recognition that the less costly alternatives of political influence and coercive diplomacy have not worked. The same logic could apply to the Soviet and Cuban presence in the Third World: The extent or pervasiveness of it is not necessarily directly translated into a commensurate amount of political and military control if one is examining the country as a whole and not simply the regime.[34]

Finally, available evidence suggests that African states associated with Moscow request the Soviet and allied presence, and the Soviets leave when told to go.[35] In terms of entry, the 1975 South African incursion into Angola and the 1977 Somali invasion of Ethiopia can better explain the presence of large numbers of Cuban troops in Africa than a theory relying on Soviet machinations and strong-arm techniques. In Angola, the MPLA of Agostinho Neto probably would have been defeated but for the Cuban intervention, and Colonel Mengistu also required Castro's military assistance to recapture the Ogaden from Somali troops. The Soviets and Cubans were invited in less because of "socialist brotherhood," but more because of desperation and necessity. Angola and Ethiopia were faced with the same conflicting imperatives that face all Third World regimes: On the one hand, the leadership desires sole control over its country; on the other hand, its very survival might require foreign assistance so that the regime can consolidate its power and defeat domestic and regional enemies.

Despite this reliance on the Soviet Union and its allies, the amount of leverage actually attained by Moscow is itself questionable. As David Albright has argued, "To date, all the existing Marxist-Leninist governments in Africa have devised policies tailored to their own local realities and not geared to Soviet prescriptions. Not even those in Angola or Ethiopia have hesitated to follow their own courses, despite their heavy dependence on the Soviet Union to stay in power."[36] Earlier Soviet experiences in Egypt and Somalia merely reinforce this view.[37]

With regard to the Soviets leaving an African state or reducing its presence when ordered to do so, Moscow has always complied: Ghana (1966), Sudan (1971), Egypt (1972), Somalia (1978), and Guinea (1979).[38] Similarly, it would be very surprising if Cuba did not pull its troops out of Angola or Ethiopia if requested to do so by the governments in Luanda and Addis Ababa. No worse term of opprobrium could be levelled at the Soviets nor do more damage to their Third World reputation than to be branded colonialists, thereby indistinguishable from the Western powers.

In sum, what is being argued is that determining the extent of foreign control over a regime or country is not an easy task and should not be cavalierly assumed to be a function of mere military presence. Influence also works both ways, and Third World states have reasons to request outside assistance which have nothing to do with East-West competition. They are quite willing to take advantage of foreign assistance for their own domestic purposes. This point, however, tends to be overlooked if a bipolar perspective is superimposed upon the complexities of African politics.

Paradoxes of Military Assistance

The Soviet Union's major means of exerting influence in Africa are through military and security assistance. This is principally due to the fact that Moscow is unwilling or unable to provide economic aid to Third World states on the scale or quality of Western countries. (See table 11-2.) Commitments elsewhere (Cuba, Vietnam, Afghanistan, Poland) and economic problems at home help to account for this fact. But while military and

Table 11-2
Value of Economic Aid and Arms Exports to Developing States, Cumulative 1976-1980

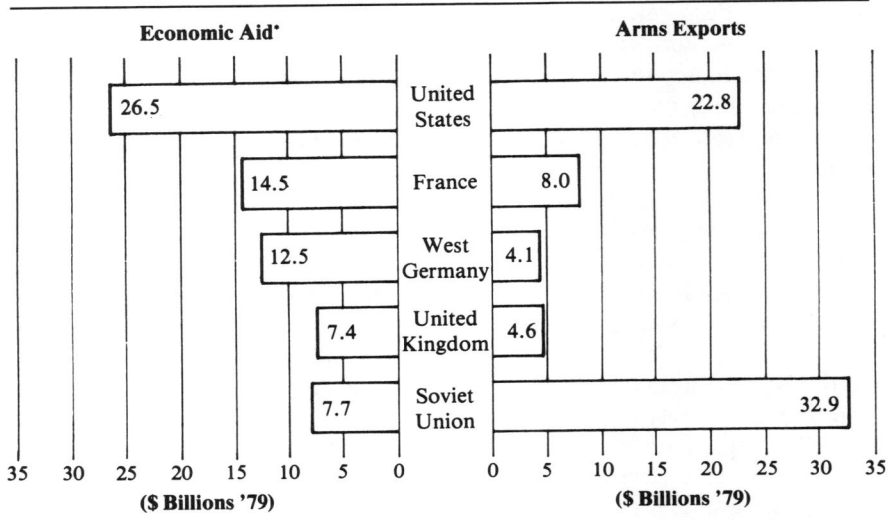

*Source: OECD/DAC. 1981. U.S. Arms Control and Disarmament Agency, *World Military Expenditures and Arms Transfers 1971-1980,* March 1983, Washington, D.C., p. 32.

security assistance can be a source of leverage, they also suffer from inherent limitations. Given the fact that Moscow has provided more arms to Africa in the past ten years than any other outside power, such limitations are particularly worthy of note.[39]

Creating Stability

If there is one task communists are supposedly good at, it is creating strong organizations out of a chaotic social, political, and economic environment. There is a paradox, however, if the Soviets actually succeed in fulfilling this goal of strengthening the party, police, and military in socialist African states: They would create the very stability that makes Soviet protection unnecessary. If the regimes in Angola, Mozambique, and Ethiopia felt secure, the Soviet-Cuban-East German connection might be seen as superfluous.[40]

Arms as Influence

U.S. military assistance programs are justified on the grounds that they aid America's own security by helping to deter acts of aggression against our allies, maintain regional balances, and facilitate the access of American military forces to transit and staging facilities overseas.[41] It is also generally assumed that arms transfers buy political influence over the recipient and allow one to control the ways in which the matériel is utilized. This is a questionable proposition as evidenced by the obvious case of the United States and Israel (e.g., destruction of the Iraqi nuclear plant in 1980, the invasion of Lebanon in 1982). Nor could the Soviets prevent Sadat from using Soviet supplied weaponry as he saw fit against Israel in 1972. More recently, it cannot be confirmed that Moscow has encouraged—let alone planned—Libyan activities against Chad in the summer of 1983.

In fact, it could be argued that, more often than not, the influence relationship works in the opposite direction. This is partly due to a virtually unresolvable problem faced by all states: How does one know "how much is enough" for deterrence and defense? Superpower allies in the Third World tend to have an unquenchable thirst for weaponry and have no trouble in finding reasons to justify more military assistance. The uncertainty, suspicion, and distrust that help to drive the arms race ever upward at the superpower level is mirrored at the regional and local levels in the Third World.

The dilemma for the supplier of weaponry is that to provide too little risks your ally's being deposed by rebellion or invasion; to provide too much risks emboldening your ally to embark upon precipitous military adventures. To threaten to withhold further assistance or spare parts leads to a reputation of being an unreliable supplier; to offer carte blanche threatens to draw one into escalating regional conflicts in which one's client is embroiled. The Soviets, for example, have at the very least been uncomfortable with the way in which the Mengistu regime in Ethiopia has used Soviet aid against rebel groups in Eritrea. Moscow faces even more serious dilemmas in southern Africa. It is usually argued that the Soviets are quite pleased with South African military incursions into Angola and Mozambique as this increases the dependency of the governments in Luanda and Maputo on Moscow. But these actions also hold the potential of direct Soviet–South African military confrontations should the situation deteriorate to the point where there is pressure to increase the number of not only Cuban troops, but perhaps to introduce more Soviet military advisers as well.

The USSR is hence in a position somewhat analogous to that of the United States regarding the use of the Rapid Deployment Force: having declared the Persian Gulf a "vital interest" and promised to defend local regimes militarily, Washington is almost forced to act in the event of external aggression against the region.[42] The Soviet treaties of friendship and cooperation with Angola and Mozambique do not formally require Moscow to defend these regimes, yet inaction—at least in the case of Angola—

would result in Soviet prestige and reputation for reliability being severely damaged. Ideologically, such setbacks would undermine claims that the correlation of forces are continually moving in a favorable direction. The problem is that the conditions under which an increased Soviet commitment might be requested could be much less propitious in the 1980s than in the 1970s. The three Marxist regimes have lost much popular support due to failing economic policies and, in the case of Ethiopia, political repression. Soviet military relief efforts would not necessarily be successful. Furthermore, the Soviets are militarily extended elsewhere, and the quagmire image could eventually come to be applied not only to Vietnam and Afghanistan but also to southern Africa.

Dynamics and Trade-Offs of Involvement

It is often bemoaned that the United States has had poor luck in backing the wrong side in Third World conflicts. In the case of Africa, this is not surprising because, with the exception of Algeria, the United States has felt compelled to mute its criticisms of Western colonial powers in the postwar years in the name of NATO unity and East-West security considerations. As a result, Washington became associated with Portuguese colonialism and had to suffer the consequences in the mid-1970s. The Soviets, however, have experienced more than their share of setbacks in the Third World and face the same trade-offs and dilemmas that accompany the decision by any outside power to become involved in the African political scene.

Choosing Sides

When an outside power backs one faction in a civil war or power struggle, opposition groups almost automatically request aid from other foreign governments, drawing more outsiders into the maelstrom. The situation becomes further polarized and overlaid with an East-West dimension. The obvious danger to the outside power is, what if it backs the wrong side? This is what happened to the Soviets when they placed their bets on Joshua Nkomo's ZAPU instead of Robert Mugabe's ZANU in the struggle for Zimbabwean independence. As a result, the Mugabe government was suspicious of the Soviets and forced Moscow to sign a humiliating statement of noninterference in Zimbabwean internal affairs prior to establishing a Soviet diplomatic presence in Harare.[43]

A common argument is that once Moscow achieves a foothold on the continent, its client regimes will provide a base from which destabilization efforts can be carried out against neighboring states. Libya is often given as an example by those who make the erroneous assumption that Qadhdhafi is controlled by Moscow. Even if this were actually the case, it overlooks the fact that a radical regime or movement, whether or not supported by Moscow, sends nervous tremors through the region and invariably leads neighboring states to move closer to the West:

> Soviet support for Patrice Lumumba in the Congolese civil war helps to explain Zaire's President Mobutu's anticommunist xenophobia, reliance on Washington, and willingness to send troops to defend the government in Chad against Libyan-backed insurgents.
> Guinea's Sékou Touré's earlier reliance on Moscow helped to consolidate French ties with the Ivory Coast, Cameroon, and Senegal.
> Qadhdhafi's activities have strengthened U.S. relations with Egypt, the Sudan, and Tunisia.
> Mozambique's pro-Soviet stance has made neighboring Malawi even more rabidly anti-Soviet and pro-Western in orientation.
> The USSR's support for Algeria and the POLISARIO guerrillas in the Western Sahara strengthened Morocco's ties with Washington.
> The impact of Soviet support for Ethiopia on Somalia's external alignment has already been noted.

The Cuban troops in Angola, initially welcomed by most Black African leaders in 1975, also make these same leaders nervous. If conditions allowed for it, they would much prefer to see the troops sent home. In an oft-quoted statement, one Nigerian leader commented to the OAU in 1978, "To the Soviets and their friends, I should like to say that, having been invited to Africa in order to assist in the liberation struggle and the consolidation of national independence, they should not overstay their welcome. Africa is not about to throw off one colonial yoke for another. Rather, they should hasten the political, economic, and military capability of their African friends to stand on their own . . ."[44] In sum, before accepting the domino or foothold theory of Soviet activity in Africa, one must also be cognizant of these international and regional forces that can potentially counteract further Soviet advances.

Repressive Allies

A danger faced by all Eastern and Western powers in the Third World is that of becoming associated with the crimes of one's client state. This has long been a problem for the United States in Latin America as a result of military assistance and training programs to right-wing authoritarian governments. Similarly, Iran's revolutionary leaders delight in blaming all of their country's problems on the Great Satan who supposedly controlled the shah and his deadly secret police, SAVAK. Moscow now has the opportunity to be similarly blamed for the domestic and foreign policies of its client states by virtue of its successes in the Third World: Ethiopia and Afghanistan are two notable examples in this regard. If Soviet-backed regimes should be overthrown, it is unlikely the new leadership—having been hunted, harrassed, and perhaps tortured by Moscow's supporters—would have much affection for the Soviet Union.

Public Support for Allies

Every state wishes to be known as a faithful ally. After the fall of the Pahlavi dynasty, for example, the United States was particularly concerned with its international reputation and President Reagan pledged that Saudi Arabia would not go the way of the shah. Similarly, Moscow has gone to great lengths to assure the regimes in Ethiopia, Angola, and Mozambique of its undying support in their struggles against internal and external enemies. Although an understandable sentiment, a potential trade-off is involved in such public proclamations: By becoming identified with a particular regime, a superpower can actually undermine its ally if the latter is seen as a mere puppet of foreign powers. On a continent where nonalignment and nationalism are strong forces, this image could prove disastrous. This is particularly true in those countries where individual personalities dominate the political scene. In this regard, the United States has to be careful lest its highly visible support for King Hassan of Morocco, Siad Barre of Somalia, Ja'far al-Numayri of Sudan, and perhaps Hosni Mubarak of Egypt be interpreted as political dominance.[45] Public pronouncements of support conceivably could be the kiss of death.

Furthermore, even if a leader manages to maintain power, the very fact that power is highly personalized always carries with it the possibility of a dramatic foreign policy realignment vis-à-vis East-West ties. Moscow itself has experienced such reversals due to decisions taken by the leadership in Egypt, Guinea, Ghana, and the Sudan. Even the revolutions in southern Africa and Ethiopia might be susceptible to this danger. Although sometimes viewed as being more highly institutionalized and hence internally stable, these regimes have experienced recurrent purges within the ruling elites. Moscow cannot be sure that the outcome of all such struggles will always be to its benefit: In Ethiopia since the revolution started in 1974, one Western diplomat estimates that only 12 of the 126 persons on the original ruling council are still in office, only six wield influence, and only Mengistu retains total power.[46] What would happen to the state of Soviet-Ethiopian relations if the Somali and Eritrean threats faded and Mengistu either reassessed the value of the Moscow connection in light of Ethiopia's economic circumstances, or he was overthrown in a coup d'etat?

In Angola, the most rabid pro-Moscow group has been repressed continually by the Neto and dos Santos leadership. At the beginning of 1983, for example, there were reports that there was a purge of pro-Soviet ideologues in the MPLA in the course of a power struggle.[47] Nor is it likely that the May 1983 visit of President dos Santos to Moscow has allayed completely Soviet fears concerning the Angolan Foreign Minister's visit to London in February 1983 (the first visit by an Angolan minister since independence in 1976) and the Interior Minister's private talks in Washington with U.S. Secretary of State George Shultz in mid-April of the same year.[48]

Even in Mozambique, where Samora Machel continually pledges his support for Moscow, the Soviets must have been piqued at the fact that Machel urged Robert Mugabe to attend the Lancaster House discussions on Zimbabwean independence and then to sign the accord. As a result, a rather strange mutual admiration society apparently has been established between Machel and Prime Minister Margaret Thatcher of Britain.[49]

Although there are dangers for the Soviets as well as their African allies in having Moscow become closely identified with a particular regime, not to give complete support to their allies also risks the USSR's losing influence. The dilemma is that if the Soviets try to hedge their bets by courting various factions in a movement or regime, the leadership may well decide Moscow cannot be trusted and hence dispense with the Soviet connection if domestic, regional, and international conditions allow for it.

Role of Other Outside Powers

Excessive preoccupation with the United States and the USSR results in overlooking the obvious fact that other outside powers have also played important roles in Africa in past years as well as in more recent times. (See table 11-3.) The Chinese were particularly active in the 1960s in courting southern African liberation movements. It is often forgotten that FRELIMO, the current ruling party in Mozambique, was originally sponsored by Beijing and not Moscow. The Chinese—not the Soviets—also had the most influence on the leftist regime in Zanzibar in the early 1960s, in Nyerere's Tanzania, and in Robert Mugabe's ZANU. There is also some evidence that it was Chinese support of Holden Roberto's FNLA that triggered the step-up in Soviet military assistance to the MPLA in March–April 1975.[50] There were, however, no major Chinese diplomatic initiatives in Africa in the second half of the 1970s. But at the end of 1982, Prime Minister Zhao Ziyang began a month-long, ten-nation tour that was meant to signal China's new activist policy toward Africa. One achievement was diplomatic reconciliation with Angola.[51]

Table 11-3
Military Forces and Bases in Africa, 1983

Location of Foreign Forces	Countries of Origin U.S. and Allies[a]		USSR and Allies[a]		Other[b]	
Algeria	—		USSR	1,000	—	
			EG	250		
Angola	—		USSR	2,000[e]	C	25,000[d]
			EG	5,000		
Benin	—		USSR	1,200	—	
Central African Republic	F	1,500	—		—	
Chad	F	na	—		L	3,000
Congo	—		USSR	350	—	
			EG	750		
Djibouti	F	3,700	—		—	
Equatorial Guinea	—		—		M	400
Ethiopia	—		USSR	1,350	C	13,000
			EG	250		
Gabon	F	450	—		—	
Ghana	UK	150	—		—	
Guinea	—		USSR	380	—	
			EG	120		
Guinea-Bissau	—		USSR	600	—	
Ivory Coast	F	450	—		—	
Kenya	US[c]	—	—		—	
	UK	100				
Libya	—		USSR	1,800	—	
			EG	400		
Madagascar	—		EG	300	NK	400
Malawi	—		—		SA	100
Mali	—		USSR	200	—	
Mauritania	—		USSR	200	—	
Morocco	US[c]	—	—		—	
	F	150				
Mozambique	—		USSR	300	C	750
			EG	100		
Namibia	—		—		SA	67,500
Sahara, Western	—		—		M	90,000
Senegal	F	1,170	—		—	
Seychelles	—		—		T	250
Somalia	US[c]	—	—		—	
South Africa	—		—		I	200
Sudan	—		—		E	700
Zaire	F	130	—		—	
	B	350				
Zimbabwe	UK	100	—		Ch	120
					NK	200

Source: Ruth Leger Sivard, *World Military and Social Expenditures 1983* (Washington, D.C.: World Priorities, 1983), p. 9. Reprinted with permission.

[a]NATO countries: F = France, UK = United Kingdom, B = Belgium, Warsaw Pact: EG = East Germany.

[b]C = Cuba, L = Libya, M = Morocco, NK = North Korea, SA = South Africa, T = Tanzania, I = Israel, E = Egypt, Ch = China.

[c]Facilities under construction.

[d]Estimates as of February 1984 (*Christian Science Monitor*, 17 February 1984).

[e]Estimates for USSR and EG as of January 1984 (*New York Times*, 25 January 1984).

Of equal interest has been Portugal's rapprochement with its former colonies. In 1980 Guinea-Bissau began to seek closer ties with Lisbon, in late 1982 Mozambique signed an arms agreement with the Portuguese, and in 1983 Angola strengthened diplomatic relations with its former colonial master. The Soviets must have viewed these events with some suspicion.[52]

France has been the most militarily active former colonial power in Africa. On eight occasions since 1976 Paris has dispatched troops: in 1976 to end rioting in what was to become Djibouti; in 1977-1978 to Mauritania against the POLISARIO Front; in 1977, 1980, and 1983 to Chad; in 1977 and 1978 to Zaire's Shaba province to halt the advances of a separatist movement (the FNLC) based in Angola; and in 1979 to the Central African Republic when Emperor Bokassa was overthrown. France currently has defense agreements with Djibouti, Senegal, the Central African Republic, and Gabon. Troops are stationed in all four countries. Paris also has military assistance agreements with eleven other former colonies. There are over 7000 French troops in all of Africa.[53]

Great Britain deserves much of the credit for the successful completion of the Lancaster House negotiations that created the state of Zimbabwe. This diplomatic achievement was certainly a setback for the Soviet Union, the worst since the expulsion of Soviet personnel from Egypt in 1972.

In sum, the Soviets and their East European and Cuban allies have to be concerned not only with the United States, but also with China and the Western European powers. The latter, due to colonial and postindependence experiences, are tied to Africa in a multiplicity of ways the Soviets have been unable to match: aid, trade, investment, language, values, aspirations, and, in some instances, security concerns.[54]

Moscow and Its Allies

Although the Soviet Union is obviously the senior partner when it comes to making decisions on East bloc policy toward Africa, this does not mean Moscow's allies do not have their own reasons for being involved with the continent. Other chapters in this book make this quite clear. In the case of Cuba, military assistance to Angola in particular has improved Castro's revolutionary and anti-imperialist credentials in the eyes of many African leaders.[55] Nor can it be assumed that the Soviets and their allies always see eye to eye on every issue. Perhaps the best instance, although unconfirmed, is the rumor that the Soviets knew beforehand of the attempted coup against Agostinho Neto of the MPLA by the Alves faction in May 1977 but did not try to stop it or even warn him. Ironically, Cuban troops were used to put down the insurrection.[56]

Conclusions

To date, Soviet involvement in Africa has produced a mixed record. Moscow has experienced disappointments with radical and/or nationalist leaders who earlier seemed so promising: Nkrumah in Ghana, Touré in Guinea, Keita in Mali, Ben Bella in Algeria, Numayri in Sudan, Kaunda in Zambia, Nyerere in Tanzania. In the past ten years, other African countries have been quite willing to accept Soviet aid and profess a dedication to socialism—if not Marxism-Leninism—but prefer to remain officially nonaligned: Benin, Guinea-Bissau, Cape Verde, Equatorial Guinea, Madagascar, Mauritius, Uganda, and the Seychelles. African leaders see no contradiction between nonalignment and seeking military and economic assistance from both East and West.[57]

Moscow would certainly name as successes Angola, Ethiopia, and perhaps Mozambique and the Congo. But in the cases of Ethiopia, Angola, and Mozambique, the Soviets are realizing how difficult it is to aid these regimes in consolidating power. In fact, the problem is that power is not something laying about in the Emperor's palace or Governor General's office, waiting to be seized by revolutionaries; it must be created, mobilized, and expanded.[58] Nevertheless, we can expect the Soviets to back tenaciously their principal African allies—Ethiopia and Angola. Ideology demands at least the appearance that socialism is advancing and not retreating, particularly in countries where Moscow has invested quite a bit in terms of prestige and political support. Perceived national interest, bureaucratic impulse, and past disappointments will reinforce this policy. It remains to be seen if the nonaggression agreements between Angola-Mozambique and South Africa of early 1984 will stand the test of time, and how they will affect the USSR's relations with its clients.

As for the future expansion of Soviet influence on the continent, Moscow will be faced with several problems and dilemmas. First, it is unlikely the Soviet Union will be presented again with such major opportunities similar to Angola, Mozambique, and Ethiopia which led to such optimism in Soviet writings in the 1970s. This is simply because feudal monarchies, colonial regimes, and white-dominated governments are a thing of the past; the obvious important exceptions are South Africa and Namibia. Moscow would also probably gain should the Mobutu regime collapse in Zaire.

Second, the durability of the Soviet relationships with African regimes varies with the intensity of the conflict in which the ally is embroiled: Ethiopia faces problems with Somalia and in Eritrea and hence needs Soviet and Cuban support; South African military strength and guerrilla operations have helped to make Moscow an indispensable ally to Angola and

Mozambique.[59] In fact, it can be argued that the Republic of South Africa, not the Soviet Union, has been the gravest threat to stability in southern Africa given Pretoria's military activities against the Front Line states.[60] The best way to reduce Soviet influence is not to hope that Moscow and Havana become bogged down in Afghanistan-like quagmires in the Horn and southern Africa, but rather to work for solutions to these conflicts (intractable as they may appear) which would make a Soviet-Cuban military presence less of an imperative for certain African regimes.

Third, the Soviets must have some concern over the continuing turn of the continent to the West for economic assistance, trade, and investment. While Moscow sees certain benefits in having the West foot the bill (and was itself quite willing to accept economic aid in the 1920s), it would not want such economic policies translated into increased Western influence.[61] Nevertheless, given the extent of Africa's economic problems, it is very unlikely they will be solved or even significantly mitigated given what can reasonably be expected to be offered by the West.[62] Hence there could be a political backlash that would favor the Soviet Union if African leaders perceived a lack of interest in their problems on the part of OECD states.

Finally, Moscow is faced with a dilemma that can be traced back to the debates between Trotsky and Lenin. On the one hand, the Soviet Union is the self-proclaimed leader of international revolution and progress. On the other hand, Kremlin leaders have to be concerned first of all with their own national interests and role as a superpower which involves commitments and concerns beyond Africa such as the state of East-West relations. Compared to other regions of the world, Africa is simply not a high priority. The history of Soviet involvement in the Third World seems to be one of avoiding the escalation of a regional conflict to the superpower level if at all possible. We can therefore expect future Soviet actions in Africa, as in the past, to be relatively low-risk operations. Naturally, what might be considered a high-risk operation by the West might be perceived as one worth the gamble by Moscow.[63]

Given the chronic instability on the continent and the willingness of rival factions and states to seek outside sources of support, we can hence expect Moscow to take full advantage of opportunities presented to it. This should not be surprising—but not because the Soviets are the "center of an evil empire," communists, or Russians. The fact of the matter is that the Soviet Union is one of the world's two superpowers and as such claims worldwide interests. The West can therefore expect continual challenges as the USSR attempts to extend its political and military influence in a manner consonant with its role as a global power. Future setbacks and successes will result from not only Soviet actions and Western responses, but also from the dynamics of African regional and local politics.

Notes

1. Rowland Evans and Robert Novak, "Moscow's Designs on Africa," *The Washington Post*, 18 September 1981, p. 29; Sol Sanders, "Russia's Mastermind for Southern Africa Strategy," *Business Week*, 17 March 1980; Richard Pipes, "Soviet Global Strategy," *Commentary*, April 1980, pp. 31-39. Master plan approaches are methodologically suspect. They often approach tautologies in that the implicit logic is along the lines of "The Soviets have a global strategy to take over or control key states in the Third World. The Soviets are involved in the Third World, hence such a strategy exists."

2. On these points see Stephen T. Hosmer and Thomas W. Wolfe, *Soviet Policy and Practice toward Third World Conflicts* (Lexington, Mass.: D.C. Heath, Lexington Books, 1983), p. 79; Michael J. Deane, "The Soviet Assessment of the 'Correlation of World Forces': Implications for American Foreign Policy," *Orbis* 20, no. 3 (Fall 1976):625-636; Vernon V. Aspaturian, "Soviet Global Power and the Correlation of Forces," *Problems of Communism*, 29, no. 3 (May-June 1980):1-18; Coit D. Blacker, "Military Power and Prospects," *Washington Quarterly* 6, no. 2 (Spring 1983):55-70; Daniel S. Papp, "National Liberation During Detente: the Soviet Outlook," *International Journal* 32, no. 1 (1977):82-99; W. Scott Thompson, "The African Nexus in Soviet Strategy," in David E. Albright, ed., *Communism in Africa* (Bloomington, Ind. and London: Indiana University Press, 1980), p. 189; Dimitri K. Simes, "Detente, Russian-Style," *Foreign Policy* 32 (Fall 1978):47-62; Donald Zagoria, "Into the Breach: New Soviet Alliances in the Third World," *Foreign Affairs* 57, no. 4 (1979):733-754; Bradford Dismukes and James M. McConnell, eds., *Soviet Naval Diplomacy* (New York: Pergamon Press, 1979). For Soviet viewpoints on the importance of nuclear parity to U.S.-Soviet relations, detente, and the use of proxy forces, see Georgi Arbatov, "Soviet American Relations at a New Stage," *Pravda,* 22 July 1973; Sh. Sanakoyev, "Proletarian Internationalism: A Decisive Factor of Peace and Social Progress," *International Affairs* (Moscow) 6 (1980):81-91.

3. President Reagan has a different view: "Let's not delude ourselves. The Soviet Union underlies all the unrest that is going on. If it weren't engaged in this game of dominoes, there wouldn't be any hot spots in the world." *New York Magazine,* 9 March 1981. On Africa's regional and international problems, see: "Africa: Tensions and Contentions," *Third World Quarterly* 5, no. 2 (April 1983):183-360; Raymond W. Copson, "African International Politics: Underdevelopment and Conflict in the Seventies," *Orbis* 22, no. 1 (July-August 1979):9-13; I. William Zartman, "Coming Political Problems in Black Africa," in Jennifer Seymour Whitaker, ed., *Africa and the United States: Vital Interests* (New York: Univer-

sity Press, 1978), pp. 87–119; David Lamb, *The Africans* (New York: Random House, 1982).

4. On Soviet attitudes to the Third World, see Mark N. Katz, *The Third World in Soviet Military Thought* (Baltimore, Md.: The Johns Hopkins University Press, 1982) and Elizabeth Valkenier, *The Soviet Union and the Third World* (New York: Praeger, 1983). For an article that tries to discern different Soviet schools of thought regarding Africa, see Peter Vanneman and Martin James, "Shaping Soviet African Policy," *Africa Insight* 10, no. 1 (1980):4–10.

5. "Red Stars Over Africa," *Newsweek,* March 13, 1978, p. 37.

6. Colin Legum, "African Outlooks toward the USSR," in Albright, ed., *Communism in Africa,* pp. 14–15.

7. John Marcum, "Lessons of Angola," *Foreign Affairs* 54, no. 3 (April 1976):411.

8. Gerald J. Bender, "Angola: Left, Right, and Wrong," *Foreign Policy* 43 (Summer 1981):56.

9. On the situation in 1981, see Richard Eder, "France Is Sending Arms to Bolster Chad's President Against Libya," *The New York Times,* 28 October 1981, p. 6; Bernard Gwertzman, "U.S. Is Considering Logistical Support for Force in Chad," *The New York Times,* 12 November 1981, p. 1. On the 1983 aid efforts, see Don Oberdorfer, " 'Urgent' Airlift Set of Military Supplies to Forces in Chad," *The Washington Post,* 19 July 1983, p. 10. On the irrelevance of ideologies, see "Back to the Chad Cockpit," *West Africa*, 11 July 1983, p. 1591; Leon Dash, "Foreign Intervention Unlikely to End War in Chad," *The Washington Post,* 30 August 1983, p. 14. For background on the conflict, see C. Bouquet, *Tchad, genèse d'un conflit* (Paris: L'Harmattan, 1982); Virginia Thompson and Richard Adloff, *Conflict in Chad* (Berkeley: University of California Institute of International Studies, 1981); and Alex Rondos, "Why Chad?" *CSIS Africa Notes* no. 18, August 31, 1983. For a Soviet viewpoint, see I. Tarutin, "New Fighting in Chad," *Pravda,* 30 June 1983, p. 5, in *Current Digest of the Soviet Press* 35, no. 26 (July 1983):23; "U.S.–French Strategy in Chad Analyzed," *Izvestiya* in Russian, 13 September 1983, p. 5 as translated in *Foreign Broadcast Information Service Daily Report: Soviet Union*, 15 September 1983, pp. J1–3.

10. For background, see Marina Ottaway and David Ottaway, *Ethiopia: Empire in Revolution* (New York: Africana Publishing, 1978); Marina Ottaway, *Soviet and American Influence in the Horn of Africa* (New York: Praeger Publishers, 1982); and Brian Crozier, *The Soviet Presence in Somalia* (London: The Institute for the Study of Conflict, 1975).

11. "US Decides to Sell Jets to Sudan," *The New York Times,* 6 April 1978, p. B24.

12. Jean-Loup Fievet, "Marxist Congo Turning to West for Trade, Aid," *The Washington Post,* 25 October 1982, p. 18. On Guinea, see Alan

Cowell, "Guinea Is Slowly Breaking Out of Its Tight Cocoon," *The New York Times*, 3 December 1982, p. 2. Other countries that have turned to Moscow because they were spurned by the West would include Algeria, Libya, Somalia, Ethiopia, Uganda, Benin, and Mali. As for liberation movements, examples would include the MPLA in Angola, the South West African People's Organization (SWAPO) and the African National Congress (ANC). Colin Legum "African Outlooks toward the USSR," in Albright, ed., *Communism in Africa*, p. 24.

13. As Yuri Andropov stated in his Central Committee Plenum speech in June 1983 with regard to LDCs that have chosen the path of socialist orientation: "It is one thing to proclaim socialism as one's goal and quite another to build it." "Further Reportage on the 14-15 June CPSU Central Committee Plenum," *Pravda* in Russian 16 June 1983, pp. 1-2, as translated in *FBIS Daily Report: Soviet Union*, June 16, 1983, p. R11. For a realistic assessment of socialism in Africa, see A.P. Butenko, "Some Theoretical Problems in the Transition to Socialism in Countries with an Underdeveloped Economy," *Narody Azii I Afriki* no. 5 (September-October 1982):70-79. On reversals in Egypt and Ghana, see "Socialist Orientation in African Countries Viewed," Moscow Radio in English to Africa, 4 September 1980, in *FBIS Daily Report: Soviet Union*, September 11, 1980, pp. J1-2. See also Anatoly Gromyko, "Socialist Orientation in Africa," *International Affairs* (Moscow) 9 (1979):95-104; O. Orestov, "Independent Africa in the Making," *International Affairs* (Moscow) 11 (1975):14-15; G. Kim and A. Kaufman, "On Sources of Socialist Conceptions in Developing Countries," *World Marxist Review* 14, no. 12 (December 1971):124-128; Prof. R. Ulyanovskiy, "The 'Third World'—Problems of Socialist Orientation," *Mezhdunarodnaia zhizh'* 8 (August 1977):38-42; E.A. Tarabrin, ed., *USSR and Countries of Africa: Friendship, Cooperation, Support for the Anti-Imperialist Struggle*, translated by David Fidlon and Stanislav Ponomarenko (Moscow: Progress Publishers, 1980). For an excellent overview of Soviet attitudes toward the Third World, see Elizabeth Kridl Valkenier, "Development Issues in Recent Soviet Scholarship," *World Politics* 32, no. 4 (July 1980):485-508.

14. On the need to develop a well-organized vanguard party in order to institutionalize the policies of a progressive leadership stratum, even if individual leaders are overthrown, see Yu. G. Sumbatyan, "The Socialist Orientation in the Formation of Vanguard Parties in Africa," *Nauchnyi Kommunizm* no. 3 (1982):87-93; G.B. Starushenko, "The Struggle against Right and Left Opportunism in Africa," in *Leninizm i bor'ba protiv burzhuaznoi ideologii i anti-Kommunizma na sovremennom etape*, ed. by M.B. Mitin (Moscow: 1970), pp. 180-197. On the Ethiopian case that has caused the Soviets some concern, see Aryeh Yodfat, "Ethiopia: Pressure for Political Reorganisation," *Soviet Analyst* 11, no. 21 (October 27, 1982):2-4;

A. Serbin, "Ethiopia: Conquering Time," *Pravda,* 27 February 1982, p. 4 as translated in *FBIS Daily Report: Soviet Union,* 11 March 1982, pp. J1-4. On Soviet attitudes toward Third World military organizations, see Charles C. Petersen, "Third World Military Elites in Soviet Perspective," Professional Paper 262, November 1979, Center for Naval Analyses.

15. Marian Ottaway, "The Theory and Practice of Marxism-Leninism in Mozambique and Ethiopia," in Albright, ed., *Communism in Africa,* p. 144.

16. See Ali Mazrui, Chapter Two, "Africa and International Ideologies," in his *International Relations: The Diplomacy of Dependency and Change* (Boulder, Colo.: Westview Press, 1977); and Alan Cowell, "Marxism and Africa: A Legacy of Humanism and Dictatorship," *The New York Times,* 28 March 1983, p. 11.

17. On the rhetoric versus actions gap of African leaders, see Helen Kitchen, "Eighteen African Guideposts," *Foreign Policy* 37 (Winter 1979-1980), p. 72.

18. "Drought in Africa," *Economist* (London), September 10, 1983, pp. 45-46.

19. David Lamb, "Angola Growing Uneasy with Soviets," *The Washington Post,* 5 June 1980, p. 29. One Western ambassador noted that most Angolan government officials were displeased with Moscow and the latter's amount of economic aid. Instead, the Soviets seemed content to sell weapons and hand out pictures of Marx and Lenin to the local populace. On Angola's political, economic, and military problems, see Alan Cowell, "Angola's Revolution Is Pedaling Along, But Slowly," *The New York Times,* 18 July 1982, p. 16, in which widespread public dissatisfaction with the MPLA-Workers Party is noted. In 1981-1982 an estimated $985 million was earned from exports to the West, but $893 million was required to pay for imports. This did not include about $120 million each year spent on Soviet arms, nor did it include another estimated $50 million spent on the 15,000-20,000 Cuban troops. For articles charting Angola's problems, see Richard Tunsar, "Angola Has Second Thoughts about Help It Gets from East Bloc," *The Christian Science Monitor,* 2 February 1982, p. 6; Alan Cowell, "Angolans Barter as Economy Totters," *The New York Times,* 23 July 1982, p. 2; "Angolan Economy: Wanted—Capitalist Comrades," *Economist* (London), July 24, 1982, pp. 65-67; Xan Smiley, "Inside Angola," *The New York Review of Books,* February 17, 1983, pp. 39-45; Fred Bridgland, "What If the Angolan Rebels Win?" *The Washington Post,* 29 May 1983, p. C2; Edward Girardet, "Angola—Yet to Come to Grips With Independence," *The Christian Science Monitor,* 16 June 1983, p. 12. Pietro Benetazzo, "Angola Paradox: Nation Both Loves, Hates Its East-West Patrons," *The Christian Science Monitor,* 20 January 1984, p. 12.

20. Jonathan Kwitny, " 'Communist' Congo, 'Capitalist' Zaire," *The Wall Street Journal,* 2 July 1980, as cited in Helen Kitchen, "U.S. Interests

In Africa," *The Washington Papers*/98 11 (Praeger and CSIS, 1983):53. See also Fievet, "Marxist Congo Turning to West"; Justine De Lacy, "Western Investors Now Welcome," *The Atlantic,* January 1984, pp. 16–28; "Congo: What Kind of Marxism?" *Africa Confidential,* January 16, 1980, pp. 5–7; Alexandre Mboukou, "Angola-Congo-Zaire: An African Triangle," *Africa Report* 27 (September-October 1982) pp. 39–44; Denis Sassou-Nguesso, "Ten Years of the Congolese Labor Party," *Kommunist* no. 3, (1980); "Congo," *Background Notes,* U.S. Department of State, Bureau of Public Affairs, May 1983, p. 4.

21. Alan Cowell, "Mozambique Keeps to Marxist Route," *The New York Times,* 11 November 1982, p. 18. For background, see Allen Isaacman and Barbara Isaacman, *Sowing the Seeds of Revolution: Mozambique in the Twentieth Century* (Boulder, Colo.: Westview Press, 1983); and Thomas H. Henriksen, *Revolution and Counter Revolution: Mozambique's War of Independence* (Westport, Conn.: Greenwood Press, 1982).

22. "East and West Aid Puts Mozambique on Road to Recovery," *The Times* (London), 8 December 1980, p. 5.

23. "Africa Update," *Africa Report* 28, no. 2 (March–April 1983):34; "Interview: Joaquim Chissano, Foreign Minister of Mozambique," *Africa Report* 28, no. 1 (January–February 1983):44–45. Ken Pottinger, "Mozambique: Preparing to Dump Moscow for Western Aid?" *The Christian Science Monitor,* 7 October 1983, p. 11.

24. Peter Wise, "Mozambican Government Is Reshuffled," *The Washington Post,* 22 May 1983, p. 23. See also "Africa Update," *Africa Report* 28, no. 4 (July–August 1983):35; and also the series of articles in *The New York Times,* 23, 24, 25 May 1983.

25. Jay Ross, "Pretoria-Backed Rebels Bleed Destitute Country," *The Washington Post,* 6 April 1983, p. 1. See also the articles in *The Washington Post* on 7 and 8 April 1983; Alan Cowell, "Leftist Mozambique Sidles Up to West," *The New York Times,* 13 November 1982, p. 2; Paul Van Slambrouck, "Mozambique Tones Down Marxist Rhetoric, Turns 'Practical' on Economy," *The Christian Science Monitor,* 28 April 1983, p. 5; "Corporate Business and Prospects in Mozambique," *Multinational Business* 4 (1982):21–32. For a sharp contrast to the current situation, see Michael T. Kaufman, "Mozambique Is Viewed as Africa's Best Hope for the Flowering of Socialism's 'New Man'," *The New York Times,* 14 November 1977, p. 3.

26. Articles that plot this trend include Bernard Weinraub, "Guinea, in Total Reversal, Asks for More U.S. Investment," *The New York Times,* 2 July 1982, p. 3; Art Pine, "Guinea's Flirtation with Capitalism: African Nation Tries Non-Marxist Methods," *The Wall Street Journal,* 21 September 1982, p. 39; Ahmed Sekou Toure, "Guinea: What Role for U.S. Capital?" *Africa Report* 27 (September-October 1982):18–22; Alan Cowell,

"In Revolutionary Guinea, Some of the Fire Is Gone," *The New York Times,* 9 December 1982, p. 2; Leon Dash, "Guinea's Toure Taking His Revolution Out of the Soviets' Orbit," *The Washington Post,* 23 February 1983, p. 20; Peter Blackburn, "Guinea Slowly Noses Out of Soviet Orbit," *The Christian Science Monitor,* 6 July 1983, p. 8.

27. Bernard Weinraub, "Famine in Africa Is Called Worst in a Decade," *The New York Times,* 7 June 1983, p. 1; Alan Rake, "Ethiopia: Good Housekeeping Provides Investment Opportunities," *African Business* (November 1982):16-18; Helen Winternitz, "Ethiopia Hints at Investment in the Capitalist West," *The Times* (London), 15 September 1981, p. 7.

28. "Africa Update," *Africa Report* 28, no. 1 (January-February 1983):25.

29. David Lamb, "Soviets Lose Base in Equatorial Guinea," *The Los Angeles Times,* 28 January 1980, p. 4. In Guinea-Bissau the fish were processed on board Soviet vessels then sold to the local population in cans labeled "Caught in Russian Waters."

30. "David Rockefeller Says Africans Look to US," *The New York Times,* 10 March 1982, p. 6.

31. See the following articles in Colin Legum, ed., *Africa Contemporary Record, 1980-81* 13 (New York: Africana Publishing, 1982): "Benin: Facing Economic Realities," B463-472; "Cape Verde Islands: End of a Dream for Drought-Stricken Islanders," B473-477; "Mali: A Regime at the Crossroads," B537-547; and "São Tomé and Principe," B441-444. See also Jonathan C. Randal, "Poverty Prods Ghana to Shift West," *The Washington Post,* 29 March 1983, p. 1; Alan Cowell, "In Madagascar, MIG-21's and a Meager Rice Crop," *The New York Times,* 12 June 1983, p. 16; Anne Tyler Norman, "Are the Seychelles Ready for a Change?" *The Washington Times,* 28 June 1983; Jay Ross, "Split in Government in Mauritius Brings Bitter Fight Focusing on Race, Personalities," *The Washington Post,* 20 July 1983, p. 19.

32. June Kronholz, "Whither Africa? Poor Nations Turn Westward for Help, Not Friendship," *The Wall Street Journal,* 21 March 1983, p. 1; "Sub-Sahara Countries Take First Step to End Economic Nightmare," *The Wall Street Journal,* 16 September 1982, p. 1.

33. Kenneth N. Waltz, *Theory of International Politics* (Reading, Mass.: Addison-Wesley, 1979), p. 185.

34. With regard to the United States and Central America: Are more advisers for El Salvador a sign of strength or a sign of a policy failure? It has been argued, however, that the occasional and selective use of force is required to make future threats credible and effective. See Alexander George and Richard Smoke, *Deterrence in American Foreign Policy* (New York: Columbia University Press, 1974).

35. Former Secretary of State Alexander Haig, when asked about Soviet and Cuban forces in Angola, Ethiopia, Afghanistan, and South Yemen, stated: "I hope the Soviet Union would be seeking ways of disengaging from these illegal invasions." *Sunday Times* (London), 8 February 1981, as cited in Fred Halliday, *Soviet Policy in the Arc of Crisis* (Washington, D.C.: Institute for Policy Studies, 1981), p. 128. Aside from the case of Afghanistan, Soviet and Cuban presence was due to the express request of the governments and movements of these countries.

36. David E. Albright, "Conclusion," in Albright, ed., *Communism in Africa*, p. 233.

37. Mohamed Heikal, *The Sphinx and the Commissar: The Rise and Fall of Soviet Influence in the Arab World* (London: Collins, 1978); and David Laitin, "Somalia's Military Government and Scientific Socialism," in Carl G. Rosberg and Thomas M. Callaghy, eds., *Socialism in Sub-Saharan Africa* (Berkeley, Calif.: Institute of International Studies, 1979), pp. 174-206.

38. Kitchen, "Eighteen African Guideposts," p. 73.

39. Bruce E. Arlinghaus, ed., *Arms for Africa* (Lexington, Mass.: D.C. Heath, Lexington Books, 1983).

40. Seth Singleton, "The Natural Ally: Soviet Policy in Southern Africa," in Michael Clough, ed., *Changing Realities in Southern Africa*, Research Series No. 47 (Berkeley: Institute of International Studies, 1982), p. 211.

41. U.S. Department of State, Bureau of Public Affairs, "Arms Transfers and the National Interest," *Current Policy* 279 (May 21, 1981):2.

42. Richard Ned Lebow with Jonathan Cooper, "The Superpowers in the Middle East: The Dynamics of Involvement," in Mark V. Kauppi and R. Craig Nation, eds., *The Soviet Union and the Middle East in the 1980s: Opportunities, Constraints, and Dilemmas* (Lexington, Mass.: D.C. Heath, Lexington Books, 1983), pp. 278-279.

43. Gary Thatcher, "The Russians' Greatest Reverse in Africa in Years," *The Christian Science Monitor*, 22 April 1980, p. 1.

44. Olusegun Obasanjo, "Who Will Determine Africa's Destiny?" *AEI Foreign Policy and Defense Review* 1, no. 1 (1979):72. Reprinted with permission.

45. See Claudia Wright, "Journey to Marrakesh: U.S.-Moroccan Security Relations," *International Security* 7, no. 4 (Spring 1983):163-179; David D. Laitin, "Somalia's A Risk," *The New York Times*, 16 August 1982, p. 15. On the Sudan, see Charles T. Powers, "Dissidents in Impoverished South Sudan Pose Latest Threat to Numeiri Authority," *The Los Angeles Times*, 10 April 1983, p. 1B; David B. Ottaway, "Sweet Dreams, Bitter Realities," *The Washington Post*, 12 March 1983, p. 24; June Kronholz, "Sudan Tries to Recover after Plans to Develop Prove Too Grandiose," *The Wall Street Journal*, 6 May 1983, p. 1.

46. Alan Cowell, "For the New Ethiopia, Old Troubles Grind On," *The New York Times,* 26 June 1983, p. 12. Ethiopia has an arms debt of $2 billion to the Soviet Union, and some three million persons have been displaced by war, drought, and famine. On Ethiopia's leader, see Francois Soudan, "Mengistu Haile Mariam," *Jeune Afrique* 1173 (June 29, 1983): 40–42.

47. "Ruling Party Purged," *Africa Research Bulletin: Political, Social, and Cultural Series*, 20 no. 1 (February 15, 1983):6704–6705 and 6715; "The Departure of Mr. Mudge," *The Times* (London) 24 January 1983, p. 11.

48. "Africa Update," *Africa Report* 28, no. 4 (July-August 1983):35; "Angola-UK," *Africa Research Bulletin: Political, Social, and Cultural Series* 20, no. 2 (March 15, 1983):6748–6749; "A Top Angolan Is Said to Meet Shultz in U.S.," *The New York Times,* 14 April 1983, p. 1. This meeting was the eleventh in two years between Angolan and U.S. officials and the first in Washington, D.C.

49. Jay Ross, "Charismatic Marxist Leader Seeks Broader Ties to West," *The Washington Post,* 8 April 1983, p. 1.

50. David E. Albright, "Moscow's African Policy of the 1970s," in David E. Albright, ed., *Communism in Africa,* pp. 56–57.

51. "Interview: Gong Dafei, Vice-Foreign Minister for African Affairs, the People's Republic of China," *Africa Report* 28 (March-April 1983):20–22. See also *Africa Research Bulletin: Political, Social, and Cultural Series* 19, no. 12 (January 15, 1983):6686; and *ARB* 20, no. 2 (March 15, 1983):6748.

52. Charles Harrison, "Bissau Coup Leaders Want Closer Ties with Lisbon," *The Times* (London), 18 November 1980, p. 7; Shirley Washington, "Mozambique: Portugal's New Initiatives," *Africa Report* 27 (November-December 1982):9–13; Alan Cowell, "Leftist Mozambique Sidles Up to West," *The New York Times,* 13 November 1982, p. 2.

53. Don Cook, "Empire Dead, but French Presence Thrives in Africa," *The Los Angeles Times,* 22 August 1983, p. 1. For background, see Pierre Lellouche and Dominique Moisi, "French Policy in Africa: A Lonely Battle Against Destabilization," *International Security* 3, no. 4 (Spring 1979):108–133.

54. William I. [sic] Zartman, "The USSR in the Third World," *Problems of Communism* 31 (September-October 1982):77.

55. See Thomas H. Henriksen, ed., *Communist Powers and Sub-Saharan Africa* (Stanford, Calif.: Hoover Institution Press, 1981); Brian Crozier, "The Surrogate Forces of the Soviet Union," *Conflict Studies* 92 (London: Institute for the Study of Conflict), February 1978; William J. Durch, "The Cuban Military in Africa and the Middle East: From Algeria to Angola," *Studies in Comparative Communism* (Spring-Summer 1978):34–74; A.M. Kapcia, "Cuba's African Involvement: A New Perspective," *Survey* (Lon-

don) 24 (Spring 1979):142-159; Melvin Croan, "A New Afrika Corps?" *Washington Quarterly*, 3 (Winter 1980):21-37.

56. Not surprisingly, nothing in the Soviet press would prove or disprove this rumor. See "Neto Addresses Nation Following Coup Attempt," Moscow TASS in English, 31 May 1977, in *FBIS Daily Report: Soviet Union*, 1 June 1977, p. H1; and "Neto Cited on Soviet, Cuban Aid, Attempted Coup," in *Pravda* in Russian, 14 June 1977, p. 1 in *FBIS Daily Report: Soviet Union*, 17 June 1977, p. H1. For comments on the Alves-Van Dunen "factional group" and its attempts at "artificially accelerating the revolution," see Rostislav Ulyanovsky, "Agostinho Neto," *Asia and Africa Today* 3 (1982):30-33. See also William H. LeoGrande, "Cuban-Soviet Relations and Cuban Policy in Africa," *Cuban Studies/Estudios Cubanos* 10, no. 1 (January 1980):16-17. A recent financial scandal involved key figures of the MPLA, particularly old-guard ideologues who are mainly mestizo intellectuals and young black nationalists. Lucio Lara, the Secretary-General of the party and considered pro-Moscow, is supposedly in political eclipse and his wife was dismissed from her government post last year. See Richard Hall, "Angola Regime Threatened by Diamond Affair," *The Observer* (London) 24 July 1983.

57. For Soviet works that recognize current obstacles (internal as well as external) to the advance of socialism and Soviet influence, see Anatoly Gromyko, *Afrika: Progress, trudnosti, perspektivy* (Moscow: Politizdat, 1981), reviewed in *International Affairs* (Moscow) 1 (1982):127-129; Anatoly Gromyko and N. Kosukhin, *Present Day Development of Africa* (Moscow: USSR Academy of Sciences, 1980); Y. Tarabin, "Problems of Africa in the 1980s," *International Affairs* (Moscow) 6 (1981):47-57.

58. Samuel P. Huntington, *Political Order in Changing Societies* (New Haven: Yale University Press, 1968), p. 144.

59. Zartman, "The USSR in the Third World," p. 78.

60. Simon Jenkins, "Destabilization in Southern Africa," *Economist* (London), July 16, 1983, pp. 19-28; Allen Isaacman and Barbara Isaacman, "Mozambique: South Africa's Hidden War," *Africa Report* 27 (November-December 1982):4-8; Jennifer S. Whitaker, "Pretoria's Wars," *The New York Times*, 21 January 1983, p. 27.

61. Moscow's bilateral aid commitments have averaged less than $1 billion a year to LDCs ($22.3 b. 1954-1981) and account for less than 3 percent of all international aid flows to noncommunist developing countries. Facts and figures with regards to particular countries and regions of the world can be found in: Central Intelligence Agency, *Communist Aid Activities in Non-Communist Less Developed Countries, 1979 and 1954-1979* (Washington, D.C.: U.S. Government Printing Office, 1980); U.S. Department of State, *Soviet And East European Aid to the Third World, 1981*, February 1983. On changing Soviet attitudes toward Third World

economic development which recognize the role of capitalism, see Elizabeth Kridl Valkenier, "The USSR, the Third World, and the Global Economy," *Problems of Communism* (July-August 1979):17-33; Elizabeth Valkenier, "Soviet Salesman with a New Pitch," *The Christian Science Monitor*, 15 June 1983, p. 23; Anatoly Gromyko, "The Imperialist Threat to Africa," *International Affairs* (Moscow) 7 (1981):47-53. For a Soviet list of recent aid projects see "Official on Nature of Soviet Aid to Africa," TASS (in English) 5 November 1982 in *FBIS Daily Report: Soviet Union*, 9 November 1982, p. J1.

62. It is estimated that the population of Africa will double in the next twenty years, outstripping production. In the decade ending in 1979, per capita agricultural production in sub-Saharan Africa dropped to an annual increase of 1.3 percent while population increased 2.7 percent annually. Alan Cowell, "Africa's Angry Young Men," *The New York Times*, 19 December 1982, section VI, p. 39; "Africa's Trade Prospects Brighten But Finance Runs Dry," *Africa Economic Digest* 4, no. 26 (July 1, 1983):2-3; David Winder, "Africa South of the Sahara: Poverty, Hunger, and Refugees," *The Christian Science Monitor*, 18 February 1983, pp. 12-13; Colin Legum, "Africa's Heavy Debts Leave It on a Precipice," *The Christian Science Monitor*, 3 February 1983, p. 1.

63. As Robert Legvold notes with regard to Soviet intervention in Angola: "(1) the Soviet Union was not intervening against a legitimate government; (2) it was not jeopardizing its relations with any African country whose goodwill it prized; (3) it was not risking a heavy direct involvement that could not be easily terminated were the war to drag on or turn out badly; (4) it was not risking a direct confrontation with the United States, not as matters unfolded; and, most important, (5) it was not acting against the will of most African states." "The Soviet Union's Strategic Stake in Africa," in *Africa and the United States: Vital Interests*, edited by Jennifer Seymour Whitaker (New York: New York University Press, 1978), p. 175.

Suggested Readings

David E. Albright, ed., *Communism in Africa* (Bloomington: Indiana University Press, 1980).

David E. Albright, "The USSR and Sub-Saharan Africa in the 1980s," *The Washington Papers*/101, V.XI (1983).

Bruce Arlinghaus, ed., *Arms for Africa* (Lexington, Mass.: D.C. Heath, Lexington Books, 1983).

Zbigniew Brzezinski, ed., *Africa and the Communist World* (Stanford: Hoover Institution, 1963).

Milene Charles, *The Soviet Union and Africa: The History of the Involvement* (Washington, D.C.: University Press of America, 1980).

Chester Crocker, Roger Fontaine, Dmitri Simes, and Robert E. Henderson, *Implications of Soviet and Cuban Activities in Africa for U.S. Policy* (Washington, D.C.: Georgetown University Center for Strategic and International Studies, 1979).

Karen Dawisha, *Soviet Foreign Policy Towards Egypt* (New York: St. Martin's Press, 1979).

Robert H. Donaldson, ed., *The Soviet Union in the Third World: Successes and Failures* (Boulder, Colo.: Westview Press, 1981).

W. Raymond Duncan, ed., *Soviet Policy in Developing Countries* (Huntington, N.Y.: Robert E. Krieger, 1981).

William J. Durch, *The Cuban Military in Africa and the Middle East: From Algeria to Angola*. Professional Paper No. 201 (Arlington, Va.: Center for Naval Analyses, 1977).

E.J. Feuchtwanger and Peter Nailor, eds., *The Soviet Union and the Third World* (London: Macmillan, 1981).

William H. Friedland and Carl G. Rosberg, eds., *African Socialism* (Stanford: Stanford University Press, 1964).

Anatolii Gromyko, *Afrika: progress, trudnosti, perspektivy* (Moscow: Politizdat, 1981).

Walter F. Hahn and Alvin J. Cottrell, *Soviet Shadow Over Africa* (Coral Gables, Fla.: University of Miami Center for Advanced International Studies, 1976).

Dan C. Heldman, *The USSR and Africa: Foreign Policy Under Khrushchev* (New York: Praeger, 1981).

Thomas H. Henriksen, ed., *Communist Powers and Sub-Saharan Africa* (Stanford: Hoover Institution, 1981).

Stephen T. Hosmer and Thomas W. Wolfe, *Soviet Policy and Practice Towards Third-World Conflicts* (Lexington, Mass.: D.C. Heath, Lexington Books, 1982).

Mark N. Katz, *The Third World in Soviet Military Thought* (Baltimore: Johns Hopkins University Press, 1982).
Arthur Jay Klinghoffer, *The Angolan War: A Study in Soviet Policy in the Third World* (Boulder, Colo.: Westview Press, 1980).
Winrich Kühne, *Die Politik der Sowjetunion in Afrika: Bedingungen und Dynamik ihres ideologischen, ökonomischen und militarischen Engagements* (Baden-Baden: Nomos, 1983).
Walter Laqueur, ed., *The Pattern of Soviet Conduct in the Third World* (New York: Praeger, 1983).
Colin Legum, *After Angola: The War Over Southern Africa* (New York: Africana, 1976).
Colin Legum and Bill Lee, *Conflict in the Horn of Africa* (New York: Africana, 1977).
Colin Legum and Bill Lee, *The Horn of Africa in Continuing Crisis* (New York: Africana, 1979).
Robert Legvold, *Soviet Policy in West Africa* (Cambridge, Mass.: Harvard University Press, 1970).
William LeoGrande, *Cuba's Policy in Africa, 1959-1980* (Berkeley: Institute of International Studies, 1980).
Konrad Melchers, *Sowjetische Afrikapolitik von Chruschtschow bis Breschnew* (Berlin: Oberbaum, 1980).
Robert O'Neill, ed., *The Horn of Africa: Regional Conflict and Superpower Involvement* (Canberra: Australian National University Press, 1979).
David Ottaway and Marina Ottaway, *Afrocommunism* (New York: Africana, 1981).
Marina Ottaway, *Soviet and American Influence in the Horn of Africa* (New York: Praeger, 1982).
Mai Palmberg, ed., *Problems of Socialist Orientation in Africa* (Uppsala: Scandinavian Institute of African Studies, 1978).
Roger Pearson, ed., *Sino-Soviet Intervention in Africa* (Washington, D.C.: Council on American Affairs, 1977).
Michael Radu, ed., *Eastern Europe and the Third World* (New York: Praeger, 1981).
David Rees, *Soviet Strategic Penetration of Africa*. Conflict Studies No. 77 (London: Institute for the Study of Conflict, 1976).
Carl G. Rosberg and Thomas M. Callaghy, eds., *Socialism in Sub-Saharan Africa* (Berkeley: Institute of International Studies, 1979).
Alvin Z. Rubinstein, *Red Star on the Nile: The Soviet-Egyptian Influence Relationship Since the June War* (Princeton: Princeton University Press, 1977).
Christopher Stevens, *The Soviet Union and Black Africa* (New York: Holmes and Meier, 1976).
Jiri Valenta and David E. Albright, eds., *The Communist States and Africa* (Bloomington: Indiana University Press, 1984).

Elizabeth Valkenier, *The Soviet Union and the Third World* (New York: Praeger, 1983).
Warren Weinstein and Thomas H. Henriksen, eds., *Soviet and Chinese Aid to African Nations* (New York: Praeger, 1980).
Joseph G. Whelan, et al., *Soviet Policy and United States Response in the Third World* (Washington, D.C.: Committee on Foreign Affairs, 1981).
Edward T. Wilson, *Russia and Black Africa Before World War II* (New York: Holmes and Meier, 1974).

Index

AAPSO, 43, 196, 197
Accra conference, 196–197
Addis Ababa, 197
Aden, 177, 178
Aeroflot, 10, 19
Afghanistan invasion, 2, 3, 29, 108, 112, 113, 120, 232, 236, 253 n.63; African reaction to, 15, 182, 228, 238; air support facilities, 153; and United States, 181, 250 n.35
African Consciencism, 18
African National Congress. *See* ANC
Afro-Asian Conference, 196–197
Afro-Asian People's Solidarity Organization. *See* AAPSO
Afro-Asian Solidarity Committee, 197
Agriculture, 1, 32, 34, 113, 229, 253 n.62
Air defense systems, 37
Airfields, 10, 19, 149–150, 152–154, 155, 158, 160 n.1, 162 n.18
Airlift capacity, 37, 114, 123 n.19
Air Rhodesia Viscount, downing of, 201
Albright, David, 233
Algeria, 2, 5, 11, 44, 197; military aid from, 138; and Morocco, 13; and United States, 236, 237, 246 n.12
Algiers conference, 61
All African People's Conference, 196–197
Aluminum, 60, 64
Alves, Nito, 112, 241
American Relief Administration, 111
Amin, Idi, 13, 14, 131, 229
ANC, 22, 45, 106, 109, 115, 117–118; bases, 114, 121; and Mozambique, 114; and Peoples Republic of China, 119; raids against, 113; and United States, 246 n.12; and Zimbabwe, 121, 198, 202, 218 n.22
Andropov, Iurii, 2, 112, 113, 114, 246 n.13
Angola, 7 n.3, 15, 26, 48, 108, 109–115, 127, 129, 215, 223, 238, 239, 242; African support, 16; air bases, 154; arms transfers to, 37, 110, 130, 131, 140, 141, 160, 247 n.19; and CMEA, 61–62, 67, 68; and Congo, 20; and Cuba, 2, 4, 20, 21, 35, 37, 46, 48, 77, 78, 106, 109, 112, 113, 114, 118–119, 120, 121, 223, 224, 226–227, 232–233, 235, 237, 241, 250 n.35; and Eastern Europe, 66, 77; and East Germany, 21, 77, 78, 79, 87, 88, 90, 95, 99, 109, 112, 114, 234; economic conditions, 40, 42–43, 142, 226–227; exports, 247 n.19; guerilla bases, 117, 201; ideology, 225; industrial production, 115; mining, 79; and multinationals, 8 n.4, 67; and Namibia, 22; oil exports, 106, 110, 115, 226; and Peoples Republic of China, 119, 239; and Portugal, 2, 67, 223, 241; socialist orientation, 32, 33; and South Africa, 20, 21, 53–54 n.42, 76, 78, 106, 111, 113, 114–115, 117, 120, 141, 235, 242–243; strategic importance, 37; treaty of friendship with, 2, 21, 44, 78, 112–113, 131, 232, 235–236; and United States, 3, 8 n.4, 38, 111, 115, 120, 121, 223, 239; and Zaire, 20, 158, 223; and Zimbabwe, 201
Antimony, 64
Anzou strip, 36
Apartheid, 16, 23, 43, 45, 48, 70
Arab Bank for Economic Development in Africa, 11
Arab Gulf, 11, 12, 190
Arabian Sea, 153
Arab League, 11, 173
Arms transfers, 2, 4, 7, 39–40, 42, 125–145, 229; to Angola, 37, 110, 130, 131, 140, 141, 160, 247 n.19; to Benin, 129, 130, 131, 140, 160; to Cape Verde, 127, 129, 130, 140, 160; to Congo, 126, 128, 130, 131,

259

Arms transfers *(cont.)*
160; from Czechoslovakia, 59, 126, 138; to Egypt, 2, 17, 40, 59; to Equatorial Guinea, 129, 130, 160; to Ethiopia, 23, 109, 130, 131, 140, 141, 159, 160, 176–177, 182, 188, 192 n.22, 251 n.46; from France, 136–137, 138, 142; to Ghana, 126, 128; from Great Britain, 127, 136–137, 138, 142; to Guinea, 59, 126, 128, 160; to liberation movements, 127–128, 140, 141; to Madagascar, 129, 130, 160; to Mali, 126, 128, 130; to Mozambique, 129, 130, 131, 140, 141, 160; and naval access, 159–160; to Nigeria, 128, 129, 136, 140; and political influence, 125, 131–142, 232–233, 234–236; repayment terms, 136, 137–138, 142, 247 n.19; to Somalia, 23, 126, 127, 128–129, 159, 160, 170–171, 172, 173, 177, 188, 191 n.13; to Sudan, 126, 160; to Tanzania, 119, 128, 129, 130, 160; to Uganda, 128, 129, 130–131, 229; from United States, 127, 136–137, 138, 142, 174; to Zambia, 119, 130

Arusha Declaration, 28
AS-3 Kangaroo missile, 152–153
AS-5 Kelt missile, 152–153
AS-6 Kingfish missile, 152–153
Asbestos, 64
Asmara, 177
Asoian, Boris, 206
Assab, 24
Aswan air base, 153
Aswan Dam, 17, 40

Ba'athist, 18
Bab al-Mandab, 36, 157, 165, 167, 175, 177
Backfire bomber, 152, 154
Baikal Amur-Maritime rail, 157
Bale province, Ethiopia, 192 n.21
Baluchistan, 153
Banana, President (Zimbabwe), 208
Bandung conference, 9

Barium, 64
Bartlett, Dewey F., 155
Bauxite, 64
Belgian Congo, 2, 18, 27; *see also* Congo; Zaire
Belgium, 10
Ben Bella, Ahmed, 242
Bendjedid, Chadli, 44
Benetazzo, Pietro, 122 n.2
Benguela railway, 70, 121
Benin, 20, 33, 62, 94, 228, 242; arms transfers to, 129, 130, 131, 140, 160; and United States, 246 n.12
Benti, Teferi, 99
Berbera base, 13, 23, 129, 149, 160 n.1, 173, 177, 182; air combat facilities, 152–153, 155, 173; communications station, 161 n.11; U.S. Congressional delegation visit, 155, 173; and United States, 155, 173, 181
Best line, 72
Biafra, 128, 140
Biko, Steve, 118
Bogomolov, 69
Bokassa, Emperor, 241
Botha, Pieter, 115
Botswana, 109, 115–116, 121, 215
Boumédienne, Houari, 44
Brandt Commission, 33
Brazil, investment in Africa, 55 n.56, 111
Brezhnev, Leonid, 3, 52 n.22, 112; arms policy, 127; and Zimbabwe, 200–201, 205, 208
Brezhnev Doctrine, 96
Brzezinski, Zbigniew, 180
Bulgaria, 62, 200, 209
Burundi, 130

Cabinda enclave, 226
Cabral, Amilcar, 70
Cabral, Luis, 77
Caetano, Marcello, 27
Cairo, 197
Cambodia, 79
Cameroon, 15, 44, 237
Camp David process, 36

Cape of Good Hope route, 11, 37, 71–73; interdiction, 154
Cape Verde, 21, 72–73, 91, 228, 242; arms transfers to, 127, 129, 130, 140, 160
Capital investment in Africa, 29, 55 n.56, 66–67, 74–76, 79, 228; *see also* Multinationals
Capitalist development, evaluation of, 96–97, 220–229
Carrington, Lord, 217 n.1
Carter administration, 2, 180–181
Castro, Fidel, 47–48, 178, 241
Ceaucescu, Nicolae, 63
Central African Republic, 241
Central America, 249 n.34
Chad, 36, 223–224, 235, 237; and France, 241
Chemolimpex, 79
Chernenko, Konstantin, 3
Chikerema, James, 199, 201
Chromite, 64, 109
Chromium, 43, 147
CIA, 18, 55–56 n.61, 64, 122 n.7; and arms sales by Soviets, 136
CMEA, 16, 40, 42–43, 61–62, 80; and Angola, 67, 68; and Cuba, 61, 69; and Ethiopia, 42–43; and Mozambique, 42–43, 61–62, 67, 68–69, 70, 110, 142; and raw material needs, 60, 61, 62–68
Coal, 66
Cobalt, 147, 158
Committee of 77, 11–12, 28
Commonwealth of Nations, 16
Communist International, 9
Comoro Islands, 218 n.22
Conakry, 19, 197, 228
Conference of Islamic States, 11
Conference of Nonaligned States, 11–12, 28
Congo, 44, 106, 224–225; and Angola, 20; arms transfers to, 126, 128, 130, 131, 160; and capitalism, 227; and East Germany, 88; oil, 20, 227; treaty of friendship, 131, 232
Congolese Workers Party, 77

Congress of the Society of Economists, 68
Contact Group, 75, 78, 111, 120, 121
Conventional war and Africa, 7, 35, 72, 147–163
COPWE, 24
COREMO, 199
Cotton, 66
Council for Mutual Economic Assistance. *See* CMEA
Coups: anti-Marxist, 77; Soviet involvement in, 18, 44, 55–56 n.61, 222, 241
Croan, Melvin, 101–102 n.1
Crocker, Chester, 37–38
"Crocodile Commando," 198
Csaba, Laszlo, 65–66
Cuba, 7, 138; African reaction to presence, 237; and Angola, 2, 4, 20, 21, 22, 35, 37, 46, 48, 77, 78, 106, 109, 112, 113, 114, 118–119, 120, 121, 223, 224, 226–227, 232–233, 235, 237, 241, 250 n.35; and CMEA, 61, 69; and Congo, 224–225; and Eritrea, 181–182, 242; and Ethiopia, 4, 24, 36, 46, 48, 77, 130, 159, 180, 181–182, 231, 233, 234, 242, 250 n.35; and Mozambique, 109, 112, 234, 235; payment for troops, 227 n.19; and Somalia, 115; and South Africa, 105, 110, 114; and U.S.S.R., 5, 45, 46, 47, 48, 112, 128, 221, 241; and United States, 151; and Zimbabwe, 116, 200, 202–203
Czechoslovakia, 62, 65, 67, 69; arms transfers by, 59, 126, 138; raw material imports, 67–68; and Zimbabwe, 197, 201, 209, 214, 215

Dabengwa, Dumiso, 205, 213
Dadoo, Yusuf, 118
Dahlak Island, 162 n.18, 182
Damascus, 197
Dar-es-Salaam, 197
Debt burdens, 30

Decolonization, 4, 5, 9, 10–12, 16; Portugal, 4, 10, 16, 19, 20, 45, 70, 77, 127–128, 221, 223; and Soviet policy, 49–50
De Gaulle, Charles, 224
Denmark, 223
Diamonds, 109, 115
Diego Garcia, 155, 162
Djibouti, 23, 166, 167, 170, 241
Dneprovsk iron ore mine, 64
Dos Santos, Eduardo, 114
Dos Santos, Marcelino, 200, 239
Dunlop, 79

East African Shipping Line (EASL), 72
East Asia, Soviet commitment, 83 n.37
Eastern Europe and Africa, 59–85, 138, 197, 198, 200, 208
East Germany, 87–103; and Angola, 21, 77, 78, 79, 87, 88, 90, 95, 99, 109, 112, 114, 234; and Congo, 88; and Ethiopia, 79, 87, 88, 90, 91, 95, 99, 234; and Mozambique, 62, 66, 77, 78, 79, 87, 88, 90, 91, 94, 95, 99, 109, 112, 234; and Namibia, 117; and Peoples Democratic Republic of Yemen, 87, 95, 99; raw material needs, 68, 100–101; shipping, 72; technical advisors, 4, 16, 110; trade, 100; treaties of friendship, 78, 87, 96; and U.S.S.R. policy, 5, 46, 76, 92, 221; and Zimbabwe, 116, 201, 205, 209, 213
Economic aid, 3, 18, 40; frustration of Africans with Soviet, 14, 19, 21, 25–26, 47, 48, 110, 142–143, 226–227, 233–234, 247 n.19
Edgington, Sylvia, 98
Egal government, 170, 176
Egypt, 2, 5, 11, 12, 17–18, 31, 36; air combat facilities, 153; arms transfers to, 17, 40, 59; break with U.S.S.R., 14, 18, 25, 44, 98, 153, 158–159, 233, 238; economic aid to, 18, 40; economic policy, 39; and Israel, 235; and United States, 38, 190, 237, 238; and Zimbabwe, 197

Egypt First movement, 18
El Salvador, 249 n.34
Entumbane conflict, 207
Equatorial Guinea, 13, 228, 242; arms transfers, 129, 130, 160
Eritrea, 166, 167, 168, 171, 176–177; liberation movement, 13, 24, 129–130, 171, 174, 176, 181, 188, 224, 228, 235; and United States, 184, 185–186
Eritrean Liberation Front, 188
Eritrean People's Liberation Forces, 188, 231
Ethiopia, 10, 15, 23–25, 44, 222, 231, 238, 242; access, 159–160; arms transfers to, 23, 109, 130, 131, 140, 141, 159, 160, 176–177, 182, 188, 192 n.22, 251 n.46; bases in, 131; and CMEA, 42–43; and Cuba, 4, 24, 36, 46, 48, 77, 130, 159, 180, 181–182, 231, 233, 234, 242, 250 n.35; Derg, 99, 130, 173–174, 176, 177, 178, 180, 192 n.22, 193 n.23; and East Germany, 79, 87, 88, 90, 91, 95, 99, 234; economic aid to, 142; economy, 228, 236; ideology, 225–226; land reform, 176, 177, 178; and Libya, 12; naval facility, 162 n.18; and Peoples Democratic Republic of Yemen, 12, 178; revolution, 4, 77, 169, 174, 176; socialist orientation, 32, 33; and Somalia, 2, 13, 23–25, 129–130, 140, 159, 165–193, 224, 228; treaty of friendship with 2, 44, 131, 182, 232; and United States, 13, 24, 38, 127, 130, 159, 165, 168–169, 171–172, 173–174, 177, 178–180, 183–190, 224, 228, 246 n.12; and Zimbabwe, 201; see also Horn of Africa
Ethiopian Worker's party, 24
Ethnic groups, 5, 44, 175, 176
European Economic Community, 16, 70, 227; see also Lomé Convention

Falklands war, 15
Ferrochromium, 163 n.26

Fischer, Oskar, 99
Fishing, 54 n.53, 73, 136, 228, 229
Fituni, L.L., 55 n.56
FNLA, 20, 118, 223, 239
FNLC, 158, 241
France: aid, 19, 20; arms transfers, 136–137, 138, 142; and Chad, 241; decolonization, 10; and Djibouti, 241; and Gabon, 16, 241; and Guinea, 19, 224, 228; and Horn of Africa, 165, 166, 167, 181, 191 n.2; and Ivory Coast, 237; and Mali, 19–20; and Mauritania, 241; and Senegal, 16, 19, 237, 241; and Zaire, 241
Francophone Community, 16, 19–20, 21
Freight rates, 72–73
FRELIMO, 21, 22, 70, 111, 112, 113, 119, 200, 215; and Eastern Europe, 70, 87, 90; and Peoples Republic of China, 118, 239; and Zimbabwe, 215
FROLIZI, 201, 202
Front for the Liberation of Mozambique. *See* FRELIMO
Front Line States, 45, 109, 110, 115–116, 202; arms purchases, 109, 140, 141; security guarantees to 4, 37; and South Africa, 38, 196, 243; and United States, 120–121; and Warsaw Pact countries, 76; and Zimbabwe, 214–215

Gabon, 15, 39; and France, 16, 241
Gambia, 73
Garoeb, Moses, 117
Ghana, 2, 4, 18, 31, 44, 197, 228, 233, 238; arms transfers to, 126, 128; overthrow of Nkrumah, 88, 98, 198
Gold, 109
Gorschkov, Admiral, 72, 157
Great Britain, 15, 241; aid, 19; arms transfers, 127, 136–137, 138, 142; and Horn of Africa, 165, 166, 167, 168, 169–171, 181, 190–191 n.1; and Zimbabwe, 121, 211, 241

Green Book (Qadhdhafi), 25
Grenada, 15, 112
Gromyko, Anatolii, 30, 32
Gromyko, Andrei, 112, 113
Group of 77, 11-12, 28, 77
Grupos dinamizadores, 66
Guinea, 2, 19, 94; airfields, 149; and Arab states, 11; arms transfers to, 59, 126, 128, 160; bauxite, 40; break with U.S.S.R., 14, 227–228, 233, 238; fishing pact, 228; and United States, 228
Guinea-Bissau, 19, 21, 73, 77, 91, 127, 242; arms transfers to, 129, 138, 160; economy, 228; oil, 228; and Portugal, 241
Gulf of Aden, 149
Gulf Oil, 226
Gutu, Wako, 192 n.21

Haig, Alexander, 250 n.35
Haile Selassie, 13, 167–169, 171, 182, 183, 184, 190–191 n.1; overthrow, 23, 27, 173, 176, 221
Harare, U.S. embassy, 123 n.21
Hassan, King, 238
Hatfield, Mark, 162 n.17
Haud, 168, 169–170
Honecker, Erich, 75, 87, 88, 91–92, 93, 94
Hoover, Herbert, 111
Horn of Africa, 6, 7, 23–25, 44, 105, 165–193, 224, 243; strategic importance, 12, 36, 53; and United Nations, 168, 169, 171; and United States, 6, 36, 53; *see also* Ethiopia; Somalia
Humbold University, 66
Hungary, 62, 65–66, 68, 69, 79, 209
Husak, Gustav, 69, 83 n.34

Il-38 May ASW planes, 149, 162 n.18
Ilichev, Leonid, 201, 205
India, 120, 223
Indian Ocean, 11, 12, 36–37, 127, 131; naval deployment, 149, 151, 155; and United States, 148

Indian Ocean Squadron, 149, 151
Inter-African News Agency, 208–209
Internal security, 108, 111, 115, 233–234
International Affairs, 61, 122 n.5
International Conference in Support of the Liberation Movements in the Portuguese Colonies and Southern Africa, 199
International Development Agency, 16
International Monetary Fund, 16, 121
International Scientific Conference, 95
International Union of Students, 43
Iran, 37, 113, 153, 181, 237, 238
Iraq, 113, 235
Israel, 12, 17, 45, 235; and Lebanon, 113, 235; and U.S.S.R., 17–18; and United States, 18, 235
Italy: communist party, 188; and Horn of Africa, 165, 166, 167–169, 170, 171, 172, 191 ns.2, 11
Itumbi (Tanzania) training camp, 198, 200
Ivory Coast, 15, 19, 228, 237
Izvestiia, 203, 204

Jeune Africa, 38
Joint ventures, 62, 79

Kagnew Station, 169, 174, 178, 180, 183, 184, 192 n.17
Kampuchea, 15
Kangai, Kumbirai, 205
Kara-class guided missile cruiser, 162 n.20
Katanga province, 126, 158
Kaunda, Kenneth, 214, 215, 242
Keita, Modeiba, 19, 31, 242
Kenya, 16, 44; Northern Frontier District, 23, 168, 170; and Somalia, 23, 126, 180; and United States, 38, 190
Khama, Seretse, 215
Khartoum conference, 199
Khruschev, Nikita, 18, 69, 98, 106, 126–127
Kingiesepp phosphorus, 64
Kirkpatrick, Jeane, 116
Kissinger, Henry, 74

Kommunist, 117
Korean Airlines Flight 007, 116
Korean War, 168
Kosygin, Alexi, 127
Krupp, 79
Kupfuma, Abisha, 209
Kynda-class cruisers, 162 n.20

Lagos Action Plan, 33–34
Lamberz, Werner, 90
Lancaster House settlement, 106, 108, 117, 142, 202, 203–204, 239, 241
Land reform, 32, 34, 77; and Ethiopia, 176, 177, 178
Lara, Lucio, 252 n.56
Larkin, Bruce, 199
Latin America, 237
Lawson, Colin, 62, 63–64, 66, 79–80
Lebanon, 113, 235
Legum, Colin, 201, 215
Legvold, Robert, 77, 253 n.63
Lehfeld, Horst, 94–96
Le Monde, 3
Lenin, 229–231
Liberation movements, 12, 43, 44, 48, 215–216; arms transfers to, 127–128, 140, 141; and Warsaw Pact countries, 75–76, 77
Liberia, 4, 10, 39, 77
Libya, 5, 11, 12, 25, 44, 138, 236–237; arms deals with, 25, 40; and Chad, 36, 223–224, 235, 237; and East Germany, 87; and Ethiopia, 12; and oil exports, 68; and Peoples Democratic Republic of Yemen, 12; and United States, 38, 246 n.12
Lomé Conference, 43, 69, 70, 111, 121, 227
Lowenthal, Richard, 75
Luanda port facilities, 67
Lumumba, Patrice, 18, 27, 106, 126, 237
Lusaka Commonwealth Conference, 203
Lusaka raids, 78

Mabhida, Moses, 124 n.24
Machel, Samora, 69, 112, 113–114, 200, 205, 214, 215, 227, 239

Maçias, Nquema, 13
Madagascar, 91, 228, 242; arms transfers to, 129, 130, 160
Maghrib, 11
Mahan, Admiral, 109
Mahrdel, Christian, 93-94
Malawi, 237
Mali, 2, 11, 19-20, 31, 88, 228; arms transfers to, 126, 128, 130
Malianga, Moton, 198
Manganese, 64, 109, 147
Mangena, Alfred, 213
Mangwende, Witness, 208, 219 n.32
Manica, Mozambique, 62, 77
Mao Zedong, 46, 111, 223
Maputo, 78, 113
Marshal Vasilievski class tanker, 73
Marx, Karl, 69, 77
Marxist-Leninist parties, 20, 21, 30-31, 77, 90, 108, 229-230, 247 n.19; and Ethiopia, 4, 6, 14, 24-25, 32; and Somalia, 175; Soviet failure to control, 229-231; and Zimbabwe, 212-214
Massawa, 24
Matabeleland, 116, 209
Matula, 113
Mauritania, 5, 11, 74
Mauritius, 228, 242
Menelik, Emperor, 166
Mengistu Mariam, Haile, 24, 130, 165, 177, 178, 231, 233, 238
Mexico, 39
Mgagao training camp, 200
Middle East and Africa, 3, 11-12, 35, 36, 114, 143
Mikhailovsk mine, 64
Military advisors, 112; and Congo, 224-225; and control of countries, 232; and Somalia, 127, 173; and Sudan, 224
Military aid. *See* Arms transfers
Minerals, 40, 43, 61; and Eastern Europe, 59-68; interdiction of supplies, 74-75, 109, 147; and U.S. policy, 119; *see also* Oil; Raw materials
Mining, 62, 79, 136

Mirskii, G., 32-33
Missiles, 136, 152, 155, 156
MNR, 21, 113, 121
Moatize coalfields, 66
Mobuto, 237
Mogadiscio, 23
MOLINACO, 218 n.22
Molybdenum, 64
Monrovia Declaration (OAU), 33-34
Morflot, 72-73
Morocco, 5, 11, 15, 59; and Algeria, 13; phosphate industry, 13, 40; and United States, 38, 237, 238
Mortality rate in Africa, 229
Moshkov, Yu., 122 n.7
Movimento Nacional da Resistencia. *See* MNR
Moyo, Jason Z., 213
Mozambique, 21, 26, 37, 108, 109, 110, 127, 215, 237, 238, 239, 242; arms transfers to, 129, 130, 131, 140, 141, 160; and CMEA, 42-43, 61-62, 67, 68-69, 70, 110; and Cuba, 109, 112, 234, 235; and Eastern Europe, 66-67, 79; and East Germany, 62, 66, 77, 78, 79, 87, 88, 90, 91, 94, 95, 99, 109, 112, 234; food aid by United States, 113, 120-121; GNP, 227; ideology, 225-226; minerals, 61, 62, 79; and multinationals, 67; and OAU, 111; and Peoples Republic of China, 15, 27, 113, 119; and Portugal, 111, 113, 241; and socialist orientation, 33, 113; and South Africa, 76, 110, 111, 113, 114, 141, 227, 235, 242; strategic importance, 36-37, 77, 154; treaty of friendship, 2, 21, 44, 78, 112-113, 131, 232, 235-236; and United States, 3, 113, 120-121; and Zimbabwe, 195, 200, 201, 206, 211, 214-215
Mozambique Channel, 37
MPLA, 2, 20, 21, 26, 111, 113, 114, 218 n.22, 223, 232; arms shipments to, 129, 140; division within, 112; and East Germany, 95; financial

MPLA *(cont.)*
  scandal, 252 n.56; pro-Soviet elements, purge of, 239; and United States, 121, 246 n.12
Mubarak, Hosni, 25, 36, 238
Mugabe, Robert, 13, 22, 108, 116, 195–196, 198, 200, 201, 203, 204–206, 207–208, 211, 216–217, 217 n.1, 236, 239
Multinationals, 19, 60, 74–76, 79, 211; and Angola, 8 n.4, 67; and Mozambique, 67
Munangagwa, Emmerson, 198
Muslims, 23, 25, 231
Muzenda, Simon, 201, 207
Muzorewa, Abel, 202–203, 204

Nairobi, 197
Namibia, 16, 17, 22, 110, 116–117, 216, 242; and Angola, 22; and East Germany, 117; elections, 78; liberation movement, 38, 106, 114, 141; negotiations over, 111, 120, 121, 142; and South Africa, 43, 45–46, 115, 117, 141; and United States, 116
Nanking Academy, 198, 199
Nasir, Gamal Abd al-, 2, 13, 25, 31, 126, 224
National Democratic party, 197, 212
National-democratic phase, 30, 31–32, 89, 92, 98
National Front for the Liberation of Angola. *See* FNLA
National Front for the Liberation of the Congo. *See* FNLC
National Movement for Resistance. *See* MNR
National party (South Africa), 114–115
National Security Council, 38
National Union for the Total Independence of Angola. *See* UNITA
Nationalism, 5, 45
Nationalization programs, 32, 62
NATO, 236; and northern Africa, 5; and Portugal, 16, 127; and southern Africa, 72, 73, 74, 78–79; Soviet African strategy and, 147, 150–156

Naval forces, 148; bases, 13, 17, 19, 23, 24, 25, 36–37, 128, 129, 149, 155–156, 160 n.1, 175, 177, 221, 228; expansion of, 10, 35, 71, 72–73, 127; and Sino-Soviet war, 156–157; support facilities, 148–150; visitation rights, 4
Ndangana, William, 198
Neocolonialism, 9, 28–30, 34–35, 49, 60, 70, 74, 97
Neto, Agostinho, 20, 112, 232–233, 239, 241
New Internaal Economic Order, 28, 33
New Times, 72, 206, 207–208
N'Guesso, Sassou, 227
Nhongo, Rex, 201
Nicaragua, 112
Niger, 11
Nigeria, 4, 44, 120, 128, 223, 237; arms transfers to, 128, 129, 136, 140; oil, 57 n.74, 151–152
Nkala, Enos, 207
Nkomo, Joshua, 13, 22, 106, 108, 116, 195, 196, 197, 198, 201, 202, 203, 204, 207, 209, 211, 212–213, 214, 216–217, 236
Nkrumah, Kwame, 2, 18, 31, 88, 126, 242; overthrow, 88, 98, 128
Nobutu, Joseph, 18
Noncapitalist path of development, 30–35, 51 n.18
North Korea, 20, 108, 138; and Zimbabwe, 200, 203, 209
Nuclear weapons, 10–11, 12, 54 n.45
Nujomo, Sam, 22, 117, 119
Numayri, Ja'far al-, 14, 18, 98, 224, 238, 242
Nyerere, Julius, 200, 214, 226, 239, 242
Nziramasanga, Mark, 206–207

Obansanjo, President, 145 n.20
Objects of Soviet policy, 12–15, 27–57
Obote, Milton, 128
Ogaden, 23, 115, 159, 168, 169–170, 171, 175, 176–178, 180, 181–182, 184–188, 224, 228, 233; oil, 168, 183

Index

Oil: and Angola, 106, 110, 115, 226; and Congo, 20, 227; and Guinea-Bissau, 228; and Libya, 68; and multinationals, 60, 228; and Nigeria, 57 n.74, 151–152; and Ogaden, 168, 183; Soviet sales to East Europe, 63, 64; tanker routes, interdiction, 35, 37–38, 71–72, 150–151
OPEC, 61, 63, 136, 231
Operation Protea, 53–54 n.42
Opportunism and Soviet policy, 48, 222, 229–231
Organization of African Unity (OAU), 43–44, 47, 127, 237; African Liberation Committee, 201; and Angola, 111; and Arab League, 11; and economic policy, 33–34; and Israel, 12; and Mozambique, 111; and nonalignment, 15–16; and Somalia, 23–24, 180
Ottaway, David, 34
Ottaway, Marina, 34, 225
Oueddei, Goukouni, 223

PAIGC, 218 n.22
Pakistan, 153
Pan-Africanist Congress of South Africa, 199
Panama, 73
Patriotic Front, 117, 119, 202–203, 204, 205
Peoples Liberation Army of Namibia. See PLAN
Peoples Republic of China, 9, 16; and ANC, 119; and Angola, 20, 26, 119, 223, 239; arms transfers to, 118; and Ethiopia, 182; and FNLA, 118, 223, 239; and FRELIMO, 118, 239; military training, 20–21; and Mozambique, 15, 21, 113, 119; and nonaligned nations, 15; and Somalia, 23, 163 n.24, 172, 191 n.11; and South Africa, 22; and southern Africa, 118–119, 216, 239; strategic importance of Africa in war with Soviets, 156–157; and Tanzania, 118, 119, 128, 157, 239; and U.S.S.R., 3, 11, 12, 16, 20, 46–47, 108, 118–119, 128, 156–157, 199; and United States, 198, 116; and Vietnam, 119; and Zambia, 118, 119; and Zimbabwe, 22, 108
Peoples Republic of Yemen, 24, 32, 130, 131, 138, 250 n.35; access, 159–160; and East Germany, 87, 95, 99; and Ethiopia, 12, 178; and Libya, 12; and Peoples Republic of China, 157, 163 n.24
Perim Island, 157
Persian Gulf, 153
Petya-class frigates, 149
Phosphates, 13, 40, 74
Pirelli, 79
PLAN, 106, 117
Plan for Multilateral Integration, 61
Platinum, 43, 144
PLO, 113
Poland, 3, 61, 62, 68, 79; crisis in, 69, 108, 112; shipping, 72
POLISARIO, 36, 159, 237, 241
Political influence, 125, 131–147, 232–233, 234–236
Pont Noire, 20
Popular Movement for the Liberation of Angola. See MPLA
Population of Africa, 253 n.62
Port facilities, 67, 148–149, 155–156, 158, 160 n.1; see also Naval forces, bases
Port Harcourt, 151
Portugal: and Angola, 2, 67, 223, 241; decolonization, 4, 10, 16, 19, 20, 45, 70, 77, 127–128, 221, 223; and Guinea-Bissau, 241; and militarization of Africa, 143; and Mozambique, 111, 113, 241; and NATO, 66, 127; and United States, 236
Pravda, 202, 203, 204
Primakov, Evgenii, 31
Proletarian elements, 34, 94; and South Africa, 117, 118
Proxy combat forces, 158, 244 n.2
Puja, Frigyes, 75

Qadhdhafi, Mu'ammar al-, 13, 25, 44, 237

Racism, 16
Rapid Deployment Force, 12, 36, 181, 235
Rashidov, Sh. R., 205
Raw materials, 60, 61, 62–67, 73, 100–101; *see also* Minerals; Oil
Reagan administration, 238, 244 n.3; African policy, 38, 120, 122 n.5, 223
Red Sea, 11, 12, 24, 25, 156, 167
Report to the Club of Rome (Tinbergen), 33
Revolutionary-democratic phase, 30, 31–32, 90, 92, 210–211
Rhodesia, 16, 78, 197, 198, 200, 203, 211, 214–215
Roberto, Holden, 20, 239
Rockefeller, David, 228
Romania, 62–63, 66–67, 77; and Zimbabwe, 200, 205, 209

Sachs, Ignacy, 60, 61
Sadat, Anwar, 14, 25, 36, 153, 235
Sadza, Dr., 208–209
Sahel, 36
São Tomé e Principe, 21, 228
Saudi Arabia, 173, 181, 238
SAVAK, 237
Savimbi, Jonas, 20, 122 n.7, 223
Schaufele, Williams, 192 n.17
Sea Power of the State (Gorshkov), 157
Sea routes, interdiction by Soviets, 35, 37–38, 71–73, 74–75, 147, 150–152
Sékou Touré, Ahmed, 14, 19, 98, 126, 224, 227–228, 242
Senegal, 11, 15, 228; and France, 16, 19, 237, 241
Seychelle Islands, 154, 228, 242
Shaba province, Zaire, 158, 241
Shamuyarira, Nathan, 198, 218 n.10
Sharpeville riots, 117
Shiryaev, 69
Shona, 116, 206–207
Shultz, George, 239

Siad Barre, Mohammed, 14, 23, 31, 155, 159, 165, 169, 172, 175, 177, 178, 180, 184, 231, 238
Sierra Leone, 73
Sinclair Oil, 168
Sithole, Ndabaningi, 197, 198, 212, 216–217, 217 n.6
Six Day War, 17–18
Sixth Fleet, 153, 156
Smith, Alan, 64–65
Smith, Ian, 202–203, 204, 206, 213
Socialist orientation, 31–35, 45, 48, 49, 90–91, 109, 225, 246 n.13; and Angola, 32, 33, 115; and Ethiopia, 32, 33; and Mozambique, 33, 113
Socialist Unity party (SED), 87
Somali Socialist Revolutionary party, 175
Somalia, 2, 44; air bases in, 19, 154–155; and Arab states, 11, 192 n.16; arms transfers to, 23, 126, 127, 128–129, 160, 170–171, 172, 173, 177, 188, 191 n.13; bases in, 147, 149, *see also* Berbera base; break with U.S.S.R., 14, 23–24, 25, 44, 98, 129–130, 158–159, 178, 231, 237; and Cuba, 115; and Ethiopia, 2, 13, 23–25, 129–130, 140, 159, 165–193, 224, 228; foreign aid to, 191 n.11; irredentism, 23, 126, 129, 159, 170, 171, 178–180, 185; and Kenya, 23, 126, 180; and OAU, 23–24, 180; regionalism, 184; Supreme Revolutionary Council, 175; treaty of friendship, 159, 173, 180, 182; and United States, 38, 165, 171, 173, 178, 180–181, 182, 184–188, 191 n.11, 238, 246 n.12; *see also* Horn of Africa
Somaliland, 166–167, 168, 170
South Africa, 10, 15, 16, 43, 45–46, 48, 113, 117–118, 215–226, 242; air strikes, 78, 141; and Angola, 20, 21, 53–54 n.42, 76, 78, 106, 111, 113, 114–115, 117, 120, 141, 235, 243–243; confrontation with, risk of, 78–79, 114, 115, 141, 155–156, 235;

and Cuba, 105, 110, 114; defense forces, 21, 38, 54 n.45, 78, 113, 141, 162 n.19; economic policy, 39, 70–71; Front Line States, 38, 196, 243; liberation movement, 17, 22, 38; minerals, 43; and Mozambique, 76, 110, 111, 113, 114, 141, 227, 242; and Namibia, 43, 45–46, 115, 117, 141; raids, 78, 106, 113, 124 n.27, 141; referendum, 114–115; and United States, 3, 38, 45, 78–79, 105, 115, 119, 120; and Zimbabwe, 116
South African Communist Party (SACP), 22, 117, 118
South West Africa Patrol, 151
South West Africa People's Organization. *See* SWAPO
South Yemen. *See* Peoples Republic of Yemen
Southern Africa, 21–23, 26, 45–46, 59–85, 105–124; and CMEA, 67–71; and East Europe, 59–85; economic development, 70–71; and Peoples Republic of China, 118–119, 216, 239; strategic importance of, 12, 36–37, 106; and United States, 6, 74, 119–121; and Warsaw Pact, 74, 75–79, 151
Southern African Development Coordination Conference, 70–71, 111
Southern Rhodesian African National Congress (SR-ANC), 197
South-South relations, 33–34
Southwest Asian war, Africa in event of, 153–154
Soviet Academy of Scientists, 59
Soviet All Union Central Council of Trade Unions, 209
Soweto, 106–108, 117
Spain, 10
Spencer, John, 190–191 n.1
Stalin, Joseph, 11
Stoilensk mine, 64
Strait of Hormuz, 37
Strategic-military planning and Africa, 7, 11, 12, 35–38, 47–48, 71–72, 147–163

Sudan, 14, 18, 19, 25, 98, 224–225, 233; arms transfers to, 126, 160; and United States, 237, 238
Suez Canal, 11, 156–157, 163 n.24
Sukarno, Ahmed, 126
Suppression of Communism Act, 117
Surveillance flights, 149–150
SWAPO, 22, 45, 78, 106, 109, 113, 114, 115, 116–117, 119, 120, 218 n.22, 246 n.12
Sweden, 55 n.56, 223
Syria, 21, 113, 138

T-58-class patrol boats, 149
Takawira, Leopold, 198
Tambo, Oliver, 22, 119
Tanzania, 109, 210; arms transfers to, 119, 128, 129, 130, 160; and Peoples Republic of China, 118, 119, 128, 157, 239; strategic importance, 36–37; and Zimbabwe, 22, 198, 200, 214
Tarabrin, E., 38
Tarabrin, Yuri, 122 n.6.
TASS, 208–209
Taurus, 79
Technical assistance, 14, 25–26, 40, 113
Thatcher, Margaret, 239
Tigre, 24
Tin, 60, 64
Tinbergen, Jan, 33
Titanium, 64
Tito, 111
Tongogara, Josiah, 198
Trade policies, 25, 39–43; Eastern Europe, 59, 62–63; and neocolonialism, 29
Trans World Airlines, 168
Transnational corporations. *See* Multinationals
Trans-Siberian railway, 157
Treaties of friendship, 44; and Angola, 2, 21, 44, 78, 112–113, 131, 232, 235–236; and Congo, 131, 232; and East Germany, 78, 87, 96; and Egypt, 182; and Ethiopia, 2, 44, 131, 182, 232; and Mozambique, 2,

Treaties of friendship *(cont.)*
21, 44, 78, 112–113, 131, 232, 235–236; and Somalia, 159, 173, 180, 182
Tribalism, 5, 223
Tripartite Alliance, 12
Tsushima Straits, 157
Tu-16 Badgers, 152, 153
Tu-95 Bear, 149–150, 152–153
Tungsten, 64
Tunisia, 5, 11, 237
Turkey, 37

Uganda, 4, 13, 242, 246; arms transfers to, 128, 129, 130–131, 229
Ujamaa socialism, 226
Ulyanovsky, R., 84 n.65
Umkhonto we Sizwe, 108, 118
UNIP, 95
UNITA, 20, 21, 77, 114, 118, 121, 122 n.7, 199, 223
Unitechna, 79
United Nations, 1, 44; African policies in, 15, 116, 229; and Horn of Africa, 168, 169, 171; and Zimbabwe, 195, 196, 212
United States, 2, 112, 115, 128, 129; and Afghanistan invasion, 181, 250 n.35; and Angola, 3, 8 n.4, 38, 111, 115, 121, 223, 239; arms transfers, 127, 136–137, 138, 142, 174; and Benin, 246 n.12; and Berbera base, 155, 173, 181; and Central America, 249 n.34; and Egypt, 38, 190, 237, 238; and Eritrea, 184, 185–186; and Ethiopia, 13, 24, 38, 127, 130, 159, 165, 168–169, 171–172, 173–174, 177, 178–180, 183–190, 224, 228, 246 n.12; and Front Line States, 120–121; and Guinea, 228; and Horn of Africa, 6, 36, 53; and Israel, 18, 235; and Kenya, 38, 190; and Latin America, 237; and minerals, 119; and Morocco, 38, 237, 238; and Mozambique, 3, 113, 120–121; and Namibia, 116; naval forces, 149–150, 152–153, 156; and Portugal, 236; and Somalia, 38, 165, 171, 173, 178, 180–181, 182, 184–188, 191 n.11, 238, 246 n.12; and South Africa, 3, 38, 45, 78–79, 109, 115, 119, 120; and southern Africa, 6, 74, 119–121; and Sudan, 224, 237, 238; and Vietnam, 118, 129, 221; and Zaire, 237; and Zambia, 121
U.S. Arms Control and Disarmament Agency, 191 n.13
U.S. Information Service, 178–180
Upper Volta, 11
Urimbo, Mayor, 200
Ussuri river, 119
Ustinov, 113

Vanadium, 64
Vdovin, Valentin, 113
Vietnam, 9, 24, 45, 236; and CMEA, 67, 69, 110; naval facilities, 149; and Peoples Republic of China, 119; and U.S. policy, effects on, 118, 129, 221
Vivo, Raul Valdez, 203
Vladivostok, 149
Volsky, Dmitry, 72

Wall Street Journal, 227
Waltz, Kenneth, 232
Warsaw Pact countries, 6; and coordination of Soviet policy, 43, 46, 47; and NATO war, Africa in, 147, 150–156; and southern Africa, 74, 75–79, 114
Weinland, Robert G., 162 n.20
West Africa, 7 n.2, 44, 72–73
West Germany, 171
Western Somalia Liberation Front, 176, 178, 181, 192 n.21
World Bank, 228
World Federation of Trade Unions, 43
World Marxist Review, 118
World Peace Council, 43
World Trade Conference (Nairobi), 96

Index

Yanbu, 151
Yepishev, A.A., 113
Yugoslavia, 200, 201, 223

Zaire, 44, 237; and Angola, 20, 158, 223; economic policy, 39; and France, 241; and United States, 237
Zambesia, Mozambique, 62, 77
Zambia, 95, 109, 115–116, 210; aid to, 78; arms transfers to, 119, 130; and East Germany, 87; ideology, 226; and Peoples Republic of China, 118, 119; and United States, 121; and Zimbabwe, 202, 207, 214
ZANLA, 198, 200, 201, 203, 214–215
ZANU, 22, 108, 114, 116, 118, 119, 195, 198, 199, 200, 201–207, 209–217, 236, 239
Zanzibar 239
ZAPU, 22, 106, 116, 119, 195, 196, 197, 198, 199, 201–217, 236
Zhao Ziyang, 119, 239
Zimbabwe, 7, 13, 22, 108, 114, 115–116, 117, 119, 236; and ANC, 121, 198, 202, 212, 218 n.22; and Angola, 201; and Cuba, 116, 200, 202–203; and Czechoslovakia, 197, 201, 209, 214, 215; and Eastern European countries, 75, 197, 198, 200, 201, 209; and East Germany, 116, 201, 205, 209, 213; and Egypt, 197; and Ethiopia, 201; and Front Line States, 214–215; and Great Britain, 121, 211, 241; minerals, 109; and Mozambique, 195, 200, 201, 206, 211, 214–215; and North Korea, 200, 203, 209; and Peoples Republic of China, 116, 119, 121, 196, 197, 198, 199–200, 203, 205, 206, 209, 212, 213, 214, 216; and Romania, 200, 205, 209; and South Africa, 116; and Tanzania, 22, 198, 200; and United Nations, 195, 196, 212; and United States, 116, 121, 211; and Zaire, 202, 207, 214
Zimbabwe African National Union. *See* ZANU
Zimbabwe African People's Union. *See* ZAPU
Zimbabwe Congress of Trade Unions, 209
Zimbabwe Mass Media Trust, 208–209
Zimbabwe National Liberation Army. *See* ZANLA
ZIMCORD, 208
ZIPRA, 108

About the Contributors

Christopher Coker is a lecturer in international relations at the London School of Economics. He is author of *US Military Power in the 1980s* (New York: Macmillan, 1984) and many articles on U.S. and Soviet policy in Africa. His forthcoming book *NATO, the Warsaw Pact and Africa 1949–83* will be published shortly. He is also editor of *The Atlantic Quarterly*.

Joachim Krause is senior research fellow at the Stiftung Wissenschaft und Politik, Research Institute for International Affairs, Ebenhausen near Munich. He received his doctorate from the Free University of Berlin in 1982. He has written on arms control, East–West relations, and the international arms trade. His recent book is *Soviet Military Aid Policy towards the Third World* (forthcoming 1984, Baden-Baden).

Colin Legum is a well-known journalist with many years of experience in Africa. He is the author of numerous academic articles and is editor of *Africa Contemporary Record*. His books include *Pan-Africanism: A Short Political Guide* (1965); *The Western Crisis Over Southern Africa* (1979); with Bill Lee, *The Horn of Africa in Continuing Crisis* (1979); and with others, *Africa in the 1980s: A Continent in Crisis* (1979).

Marina Ottaway is author of *Soviet and American Influence in the Horn of Africa* (1982) and (with David Ottaway) *Ethiopia: Empire in Revolution* (1978) and *Afrocommunism* (1981). She is currently associated with the American University in Cairo.

Bernard von Plate is research associate at the Stiftung Wissenschaft und Politik, Research Institute for International Affairs, Ebenhausen. He has published several articles on foreign policy and ideological problems of the German Democratic Republic.

Richard B. Remnek is currently associated with the Russian studies program at the U.S. Army Russian Institute in Garmisch-Partenkirchen, West Germany. He is the author of *Soviet Scholars and Soviet Foreign Policy* (1975) and editor of *Social Scientists and Policy Making in the USSR* (1977). He has also written many articles on Soviet political, strategic, and military affairs.

Seth Singleton is Research Associate at the Russian Research Center, Harvard University. He specializes in Soviet foreign policy toward the Third

World and Africa in particular. His most recently published article appears in the Winter 1983-84 issue of *The Washington Quarterly*.

Keith Somerville has covered African affairs as a journalist, contributing regularly to *Africa Contemporary Record, African Business,* and *New African*. He has also published articles in *West Africa, Third World Quarterly*, and *International Relations*. He is currently associated with the Department of Politics at the University of Southampton, England, where he is conducting research on Soviet involvement in southern Africa.

About the Editors

R. Craig Nation is assistant professor, University of Southern California, School of International Relations, and specializes in Soviet foreign relations.

Mark V. Kauppi is assistant professor of political science, University of Colorado at Colorado Springs. His current research interest involves Soviet activity in the Third World.

DT 38.9 .S65 S68

The Soviet impact in Africa

SS $27.50   J10269

AUG 12 '85 C

CIr 4 6/94

Please Do Not Remove Card From Pocket

YOUR LIBRARY CARD

may be used at all library agencies. You are, of course, responsible for all materials checked out on it. As a courtesy to others please return materials promptly. A service charge is assessed for overdue materials.

The SAINT PAUL PUBLIC LIBRARY